*The Elocutionists*

MUSIC IN AMERICAN LIFE

*A list of books in the series appears
at the end of this book.*

# The Elocutionists

## *Women, Music, and the Spoken Word*

MARIAN WILSON KIMBER

*University of Illinois Press*

URBANA, CHICAGO, AND SPRINGFIELD

Publication of this book was supported by grants from
the H. Earle Johnson Fund of the Society for American
Music, from the AMS 75 PAYS Endowment of the
American Musicological Society, funded in part by
the National Endowment for the Humanities and
the Andrew W. Mellon Foundation, and from the
University of Iowa School of Music and College of
Liberal Arts and Sciences.

Printed and bound in Great Britain by
Marston Book Services Ltd, Oxfordshire

Library of Congress Cataloging-in-Publication Data
Names: Kimber, Marian Wilson, 1960– author.
Title: The elocutionists : women, music, and the spoken
    word / Marian Wilson Kimber.
Description: Urbana : University of Illinois Press,
    2017. | Series: Music in American life | Includes
    bibliographical references and index.
Identifiers: LCCN 2016023977 (print) | LCCN
    2016041884 (ebook) | ISBN 9780252040719 (hardback)
    | ISBN 9780252082221 (paper) | ISBN 9780252099151
    (ebook)
Subjects: LCSH: Oral interpretation. | Elocutionists—
    United States. | Women and literature—United
    States—History—19th century. | Women and
    literature—United States—History—20th century. |
    Women performance artists—United States. | Music
    theater—United States. | Readers' theater. | Choral
    speaking. | Oral reading—United States. | BISAC:
    MUSIC / History & Criticism. | SOCIAL SCIENCE /
    Women's Studies.
Classification: LCC PN4145 .K56 2017 (print) | LCC
    PN4145 (ebook) | DDC 808.5/4—dc23
LC record available at https://lccn.loc.gov/2016023977

# Contents

# Preface

## *Hearing Lost Voices*

"Do you know what I'm going to be when I grow up?
I'm going to be an elo-cu-tion-ist."
"What's that?"
"A woman who recites at concerts."
—L. M. Montgomery, *Emily of New Moon*

Over a decade ago, while researching the reception history of Felix Mendelssohn's *A Midsummer Night's Dream*, I discovered that concerts featuring an actress reading Shakespeare's play were a popular way to program the composer's op. 61 incidental music.[1] The most famous speaker and in many ways the originator of such performances was the actress Fanny Kemble, who had abandoned the stage for a career reading Shakespeare's plays to captivated audiences in England and America. Contemporary descriptions of Kemble marveled at her vocal skills, describing not only her ability to differentiate between characters, but also the way in which listeners were transfixed by the sheer sound of her voice. The critic for Boston's *Daily Evening Transcript* wrote, "Her voice was never so rich, rotund and perfectly under her command. Her enunciation is as clear, distinct and full in the lowest tones as the notes of a musical box."[2] Kemble was not alone in receiving such praise; many other theatrical professionals, whose voices are now lost to the era before recorded sound, were hailed as "musical." Such evocative descriptions led me to search for clues to the sorts of vocal training Kemble and her contemporaries would have received. One afternoon I found myself browsing the nineteenth-century elocution books and recitation anthologies in the library of the university where I was employed. (That this institution, like many others with schools of music, had once been a woman's college only emerged as significant to me later.) Here I encountered one of the numerous books of poetry designed for aural performance published around 1900 by Henry Davenport Northrop.

After glancing at photographs of oddly costumed women posing stiffly as if engaged in amateur theatricals and perusing the sentimental poetry provided with simple piano renditions of "Jesus, Lover of My Soul" or "Comin' thro' the Rye," I reshelved the volume, concluding that such parlor entertainments had little to do with the world of high culture I was trying to explain.

This was the first of numerous incorrect assumptions I found it necessary to discard in my exploration of the intersection of music and speech that began in the mid-nineteenth century. I came to learn that the same performers who aspired to read Shakespeare with Mendelssohn's music might well have also recited "Rock of Ages" to the accompaniment of the well-known hymn. The sound of the spoken word heard with music may be ubiquitous in movies and other media of our time, but earlier incarnations, widespread at the turn of the twentieth century, are now mostly forgotten. Performances of poetic recitation with music—which occurred in America in settings from concert halls to touring Chautauqua tents, from women's clubs to the parlors of amateur performers—have fallen out of collective cultural memory. The reasons for this artistic amnesia are multiple and complex. While the use of musical excerpts evoking a particular *melos* to heighten dramatic effect has a long theatrical history,[3] "accompanied recitation" was more an outgrowth of the elocution movement than a genre that had its roots purely in music or theater. In an earlier age, children were educated through oral repetition, adults entertained one another through reading aloud, touring professionals appeared in platform performances, and a body of written literature defined the discipline of elocution and its theory, practice, and pedagogy. However, *elocutionist* is no longer a recognized profession and is rarely indexed in biographical dictionaries or treated in scholarship except as peripheral to theater history or as the long-ago origins of speech communications or performance studies. *Melodrama*, the most common term for the combination of music and speech, now more frequently refers to a theatrical genre or literary style; when referring to music, it most often evokes practices found on the operatic and theatrical stage. Musicians largely overlook melodrama's history as an independent musical genre and treat compositions combining speech and music as occasional historical oddities, resurrected for patriotic celebrations or to entertain children. That *melodrama* ever quite solidified as a recognizable, independent musical genre can, perhaps, even be called into question by the wide range of terms that were used to refer to works that combined speech and music: not only *melodrama*, but also *accompanied recitation, pianologue, musical reading*, and others.

The history of the intersection of music and elocution in American culture has fallen through the disciplinary cracks between music, theater, dance, speech, and literary history. The numerous historical studies of nineteenth-century concert life concentrate purely on the emergence of specific musical repertoire, not the role of the spoken word in public programs.[4] Joan Shelley Rubin has produced a major history of poetry in American society that describes the frequency of poetic recitation but overlooks its place in concert life.[5] Scholars of literature are less interested in its oral performance than its inner meanings. Rhetoric historians, such as Nan Johnson, have explored the cultural place of recitation anthologies, but the coexistence of musical accompaniments is beyond their consideration.[6] Elocutionists are sometimes mislabeled as "actors" or overlooked by theater historians, who have naturally gravitated toward consideration of staged productions, not solo monologues;[7] in contrast, a recent treatment of individual elocutionists has examined their written legacies entirely apart from their platform appearances.[8] The Delsarte poses that accompanied such performances have been studied by dance historians, but the memory of their history survives only through a fleeting appearance in the 1957 Broadway musical *The Music Man*.[9]

The invisibility of recitation with music is also a product of its historical existence outside the conventions of genre and notation. Although an upsurge in scholarship considering all forms of melodrama will undoubtedly further our historical understanding,[10] musicological approaches to melodrama have concentrated primarily on notated pieces by the best-known composers, as in Jacqueline Waeber's monograph, which covers works by figures from Jean-Jacques Rousseau to Arnold Schoenberg.[11] However, turn-of-the-century publications for reciters, such as Northrop's anthologies, indicate that in America there was a significant body of spoken literature commonly performed with previously composed musical accompaniment. This practice has gone unexamined because it falls outside traditional conceptions of the musical work.

In my first forays into the written record about melodrama, I encountered a profound ambivalence about the practice. The most negative responses appeared in the twentieth century as part of anti-Victorian reactions against its poetic content, its stylized performance style, its seemingly unliterary theatricality, and its undeniable emotional excesses. Yet even contemporary voices had sounded misgivings about the combination of speech and music. Some objections were purely practical—before sound amplification, audibility and balance were a problem in large halls, and many writers dwelled on the difficulties of coordinating speaker and accompaniment. Other objections were primarily aesthetic, motivated by an uneasy sense that speech and music are fundamentally separate entities that do not belong together. Spoken-word performers found music to be an unnecessary novelty, a distraction from literary interpretation. For musicians, speech interrupted instrumental music's striving to be the ultimate expression, pulling it from Romantic heights down to a mundane specificity. When the overwhelming reaction against elocution took place among speech professionals, who had begun to style themselves as "oral interpreters," its more extreme artistic forms, such as musically accompanied recitation, seem to have fallen from favor as well.

I, too, initially found that many of the best-known Romantic melodramas did not translate well in modern performances. I struggled with how this music could have been so popular a century ago and, like previous critics, felt that somehow the genre itself was inherently flawed. On a long drive to a conference, I was considering melodrama's aesthetic failures when a more recent example, Aaron Copland's *Lincoln Portrait*, came on the radio. Even emanating from a tiny car speaker, the words spoken by James Earl Jones— "Fellow citizens, we cannot escape history"—deep, rich, resonant, and made more stirring by Copland's setting, instantly changed my mind.[12] Melodrama combines the two most powerful forms of aural expression, music and the human voice, and at its best, has a profound impact.

What also led me to reconsider the possibilities of melodrama was the discovery of historical recordings, examples of the performance practices of an earlier era. Although the late Romantic style of melodramatic music, such as in Richard Strauss's *Enoch Arden*, is well-known to modern listeners; the stylized, pitched style of actors heard in early twentieth-century recordings is not. Our puzzled reactions to melodramatic repertoire may result from our unfamiliarity with its original performance style. What seems like the artificial juxtaposition of two unrelated sounds in modern recordings is not heard in the surviving performances of early speakers, whose voices, expressing emotional extremes with pitch, rhythm, timbre, and even tremolo, are literally, not just figuratively, "musical."

The historical record of recitation with music can be traced to the voices of performers classified with a multitude of labels (*elocutionist, reciter, reader*), who were publicized and reviewed, and who sometimes wrote about the practice. As my initial list of individuals who recited to music grew, it became apparent to me that two important reasons for the cultural invisibility of accompanied recitation were that these performers were, more often than not, women, and that many of the venues in which they performed were either part of women's spheres—the parlor and the woman's club—or, as in the "mother, home, and heaven" of the Chautauqua circuit, constructed to conform to values traditionally associated with feminine spaces. Undoubtedly, many of the famous performers who combined music and the spoken word were male, but I came to understand these figures as similar to high-profile chefs in a world where most cooking is done by women.[13] In L. M. Montgomery's 1923 novel, *Emily of New Moon*, quoted earlier, young Ilse Burnley's basic definition of an elocutionist is female. As nineteenth-century speakers worked to establish themselves as professionals, beginning the sorts of self-evaluation, grandstanding, and territorial battles that mark the formation of a discipline, women emerged as the students who filled the new elocution schools such as Boston's Emerson School and the Curry School of Expression or the newly established academic programs such as the School of Oratory at Northwestern University. After graduation, they became the era's elocutionists, teachers, and authors of recitation anthologies. When the anti-Victorian reaction against elocution swung into full force around the time of World War I, it was, in part, a reaction against its professionalization of women. The habitually derogatory remarks about elocutionists were complaints about the period's "elocution *ladies.*" In spite of having carefully distinguished their professional practices from those of the morally suspect actress, female "public readers" of great literature, such as might be heard in the respectable domestic sphere, were nonetheless transgressive performing female bodies.

For female reciters, poetry was inseparable from its aural manifestation and thus from their physical being: to interpret literature involved both intellectual and emotional engagement, but it was foremost an act of performance that took place in the sound of their voices. Literature scholars have only recently begun to explore the performance history of a text as part of its meanings in a manner that has a longer tradition in musicology.[14] Elocutionists' oral renderings were in some sense musical interpretations: the poem was like a musical score to be read; on the printed page it had only a partial meaning, which would find its ultimate fulfillment in a woman's voice. To create an oral interpretation of a text not only involved attention to its form and content as well as to vocal accuracy, but it also allowed for the possibility of personal expression, in the way that different singers might bring their personal renditions to the same song.

Thus, writers on elocutionary performance consistently drew on musical ideas, musical analogies, musical terminology, and even varieties of musical notation to describe the oral performance of poetry. I do not wish to anachronistically ascribe to period specialists the belief that speech *was* music; the performers described here, from nineteenth-century elocutionists to 1930s conductors of verse-speaking choirs, might be surprised to find their activities analyzed in a volume methodologically rooted in the discipline of musicology. Nonetheless, in nineteenth-century America, performed speech and music were continually intertwined. Speech was a regular part of events that we would now identify as *concerts*; musical selections were an expected part of settings that might best be subsumed under the term *literary*, such as meetings of the women's literary societies and study clubs common to the Progressive Era. The sheer number of locations in which performed speech and music alternated make them virtually impossible to summarize: parlor entertainments, graduations, patriotic celebrations, oratorical contests, Arbor Day celebrations, and religious events, to name but a few. In the twenty-first century, speech is not typically part of concerts, but as period programs attest, nineteenth-century audiences heard nothing unusual in its appearance between musical compositions. If providing accompaniment for speech could sometimes be a contentious activity, conceptually problematic and/or difficult for performers to accomplish successfully, alternating recitations and music was so common as to generate almost no commentary.

Many settings in which speech and music were heard together were, of course, not limited to women, but the huge influx of women into the field of elocution resulted in their close association with events that combined music and recitation; that the so-called literary and musical entertainment became a feminized event has implications for our understanding of the roles of both poetry and music in America. Perhaps the eventual demise of the mixture of the poetic arts and music that we now find somewhat incongruous was inevitable—a result of both the rise of a modernist aesthetic and the development of radio and movies. However, the female elocutionist, with or without musical accompaniment, had attempted to embody high culture, her voice serving as the mellifluous sound of its transmission. She grasped at a place that was socially acceptable for her gender; she did not aspire to create great literature, but literature could instead reside in her physical being. She could communicate its spiritual and moral values while expressing her own individuality, performing alongside her sister musician at the piano. To speak was an expressive, even musical, act, worthy of a place in the same venue as European art music or a beloved popular song; the combination of the two art forms was central to women's concerts. Female elocutionists' fall from any place of artistic recognition they might once have held and the eventual extinction of the literary entertainment represented women's failure to achieve the cultural prominence to which they aspired; thus, my treatment of the intersection of music and poetic recitation by women is also a feminist critique of American culture's rejection of female artistic endeavors.

In order to explain the intersection of music with speech by American women, it has often been necessary for me to reconstruct the role of women in elocution alone; music, although an essential component of this world, often took a secondary role to recitation. The cultural restrictions that gave way, allowing women with artistic aspirations to enter elocution, and their subsequent careers in the field are discussed in chapter 1. Chapter 2 explains the ways in which the period's stylized speech and music were related art forms, alternating in performance and intersecting in published melodramas for voice and piano and well as in unnotated, informal arrangements. Chapters 3 through 6 examine specific practices and subject matter of female performers' word-music combinations. The unstaged concert performances of Shakespeare's *A Midsummer Night's Dream* with Mendelssohn's music in chapter 3 were in keeping with contemporary antitheatrical criticism and represented the epitome of high art. However, elocutionists' desire to separate themselves from the disreputable theatrical and to embody acceptable feminine attributes had a wider influence on both the texts and the music most often heard in their performances. The "accompanied recitations" described in chapter 4 consisted of sentimental Victorian poems performed with hymns or parlor music that recalled the domestic sphere. When engaged in Delsarte poses, women sometimes abandoned speech for similar musical accompaniments that clarified their expressive gestures; chapter 5 centers on a case study of Iowa Delsarte performances and their relationship to the later satire of them in Meredith Willson's *The Music Man*. Women confirmed their own cultured positions through recitation of African American dialect, particularly the poetry of Paul Laurence Dunbar, or engaged in rebellious humor through "child dialect," which imitated children's voices, both discussed in chapter 6.

Chapters 7 and 8 trace spoken-word performance by women into the period between the two world wars. Domestic imagery continued to surround female dramatic readers in the musical ensembles on the Chautauqua tent circuit described in chapter 7, which explores Chautauqua's goal of transmitting culture to rural audiences. In the 1930s and 1940s, elocutionists' opportunities to express themselves as soloists gave way to the verse-speaking choirs discussed in chapter 8, and women's individual voices were subsumed in spoken choral arrangements of modern poetry.

As women came to lead the elocutionary profession, they also became the primary composers of melodrama; almost half of approximately five hundred published English-language melodramas from the period were composed by women, including some thirty female American composers, who came to dominate the genre after World War I.[15] The two most prolific composers of spoken-word compositions were Chicago composer Phyllis Fergus and Frieda Peycke, a composer-reciter in Los Angeles; their two careers and the larger environment of women's music clubs that made them possible are the focus of chapter 9.

On my first meeting with Phyllis Fergus's family, her daughter produced a large poster advertising one of her mother's performances. Over a glamorous 1920s photograph, in large letters, was "Phyllis Fergus, Composer," and it occurred to me that in all my years researching women in music, I had never seen anything like it. Neither had I seen a photo like the one of a motherly Fergus, labeled "Composer—Concert Artist" on the cover of Chicago's *Music News* in 1932, looking over a book, her two toddler daughters on her lap.[16] Not only did recited poetry with music allow some women to have professional careers; their compositions, like those of Fergus and Peycke, were not imitations of a tradition of masculine music, but genuine expressions of women's worlds. The legacy of accompanied recitation, explored in this book's final chapter, was a musical repertoire by and for American women in the early twentieth century. Thus, melodrama can serve as a case study for the intersection of gender and musical genre, demonstrating the ways in which female composers transformed nineteenth-century practices to create works that would specifically appeal to women.

This repertoire, influenced by the generation of elocutionists who lived before the women who composed it, is largely unknown today. Fergus, Peycke, and their contemporaries postdated the peak of elocution's popularity. By the time their notated musical scores replaced the informal accompaniments heard earlier, women's passion for recitation had largely diminished; the reaction against elocutionary practices had erupted and dissolved before their careers were at their heights. Female graduates of elocution schools found themselves teaching "speech," not "expression," and acting in or directing theatrical performances that would have been previously socially unacceptable. Likewise, in music, women's emergence as professional musicians and fledgling successes as composers of late Romantic music suffered with the rise of modernism.[17] Although American women composers often replaced nineteenth-century sentimentality with a comedic aesthetic, their contributions to melodrama, a doubly feminized art with its roots in Romantic music and elocution, were overshadowed in the modernist backlash.

My exploration of women's role in melodrama and its various cultural contexts inevitably generates fundamental questions about the interrelationships of performance, gender, and history. The historical invisibility of musically accompanied recitation by women can demonstrate how artistic and academic disciplines shape knowledge and how gendered artworks are subject to cultural limitations on their artistic value. Women's spoken-word performances with music allow us to explore the role gender plays in negotiating the conflicts between "high" and "low" art and in defining the very nature of the work itself, as well as to illuminate the role of the performer in shaping the meaning of that work. This book shows how closely recitation and music were related in American culture and how their intersection in female-dominated performance spaces, part of women's quest to be associated with the moral good of high culture, resulted in a feminine art form.

# Acknowledgments

I am grateful to numerous people who have helped make this book possible. Douglass Seaton has been a tremendous source of support for all of my scholarly endeavors throughout my career. Denise Von Glahn's invitation to speak to her seminar at Florida State University first motivated me to explore how gender figured in the history of melodrama. Timothy Watkins, of Texas Christian University, organized the lively conference at which I presented my early work on elocutionary performance practices. Sarah Hibberd offered both intellectual stimulation and generous hospitality at the University of Nottingham's 2008 melodrama conference. In addition to Sarah, I am also indebted to melodrama scholars Elinor Olin, Michael Pisani, and Jacqueline Waeber for their research. Valerie Goertzen suggested that my research warranted a book years before it occurred to me, and Jonathan Bellman sent a haranguing e-mail to provoke me to write it when I most needed it.

The readers of the manuscript, Joan Shelley Rubin and Candace Bailey, provided numerous insightful suggestions. Laurie Matheson and the staff of the University of Illinois Press have been wonderful to work with throughout the publication process. The H. Earle Johnson Publication Subvention from the Society for American Music, the American Musicological Society's AMS 75 PAYS, and additional subventions from the University of Iowa's School of Music and College of Liberal Arts and Sciences assisted with the book's publication. My archival research was supported by two Arts and Humanities Initiative Grants, and the University of Iowa helpfully extended the first in the wake of the disastrous flood of 2008. The Iowa Center for Research by Undergraduates funded a summer fellowship for the resourceful Jennifer Brooke, who analyzed child dialect recitations. The University of Iowa Libraries' Special Collections and the Women's Archives have been invaluable, as has its fast, efficient Interlibrary Loan Office. I am indebted to music librarians extraordinaire Ruthann McTyre and Katie Buehner, and to their colleagues on the Music Library Association Listserv for helpful suggestions. The staff at the State Historical Society of Iowa in Iowa City is a treasure and deserves better funding.

My travels have been blessed by encounters with friendly, helpful archivists: Rosemary Cullen and Timothy Engels at the John Hay Library of Brown University, Janet L. Dotterer at Millersville University, Fritz Eifrig and Heidi Marshall of Columbia College, Ian Graham at Wellesley College, Beth Harris at Hollins University, Rebecca Jewett at Ohio State University, Jacqueline Johnson of the Western College Archives of Miami University of Ohio, Kevin Leonard and Janet Olson at Northwestern University, David Miller at Curry College, and Christina Zamon at Emerson College. I was well treated during the weeks I spent at the Chicago History Museum, the American Jewish Archives, and the Tennessee State Library and Archives. Mary Iber of Cornell College and Becky Wadian of Upper Iowa University helped me identify photographs. Dorothy Kelley and Lorna Truck graciously welcomed me to Hoyt Sherman Place and the Des Moines Women's Club. Emma Roberts-Green of the Los Angeles Public Library provided Frieda Peycke's scrapbook. Dale Cockrell and the staff of the Center for Popular Music identified a tune for me. Frances P. O'Neill of the Maryland Historical Society answered my query about the Bard-Avon School, and Mary Oliver of Dayton History provided information about a performance by Paul Laurence Dunbar. I am especially indebted to Jerry Tarver for the years of collecting that created the remarkable Jerry Tarver Elocution, Rhetoric, and Oratory Collection in the Rare Books and Manuscripts Library of Ohio State University, the contents of which added breadth and depth to my research.

Having the ear of whistling expert Maribeth Clark has been helpful and enjoyable. Brian Moon took the time to talk with me about Kitty Cheatham at the Society for American Music, and Michael Cooper and Tom Riis generously read individual chapters. Lindsay Canting sent me her thesis about Vachel Lindsay, and Susan Pickett shared her extensive knowledge about Marion Bauer. Elaine Main and Nancy Polette answered my e-mail inquiries. My gratitude also goes to the alumni of the Florida State University's musicology program for their support whenever I present a paper, as well as to the friendly Mendelssohnians who continue to invite me to entertaining dinners, despite my preoccupation with elocution. At the University of Iowa, Christine Getz, Trevor Harvey, and Nathan Platte have been supportive colleagues. My historically inclined brother Keith has patiently learned a great deal about elocution.

I was pleased to have been invited to help plan an evening of music and recitations for the 2009 British Women's Writers Association Conference, with the enthusiastic team of Meredith Alexander, Laura Capp, Joanne Klassen, Teresa Mangum, and Connie Winthrop. It was illuminating to hear soprano Katherine Eberle's and pianist Rebeka Wortman's performance of *The Story of the Faithful Soul* on that program. The students of my 2011 American Entertainments seminar bravely took on Delsarte poses.

Reynolds Clifford and Thallis Drake generously welcomed me into their lives and trustingly sent me home with their mother Phyllis Fergus's scrapbooks on very short acquaintance. I am deeply grateful for their patience and their support. The late Fred Crane, professor emeritus of the University of Iowa, surprised me with stacks of his research materials, including rare recordings, collected over his long career. This book would not have been possible without his generous gift, and I hope that my work is worthy of his faith in me.

For their love, their patience, and for all that they have done for me, this book is for Michael and Jonathan. Life with you has been anything but "the usual way."

# 1. The Odyssey of a Nice Girl

## Elocution and Women's Cultural Aspirations

> But under all the twisting and halting of her career . . . she knew
> that there had been one thing after all—the need to satisfy the
> craving for something that was deep and beautiful and beyond
> what people called "everyday things."
> —Ruth Suckow, *The Odyssey of a Nice Girl*

Ruth Suckow's 1925 novel, *The Odyssey of a Nice Girl*, which draws on autobiographical details from her own life, centers on a young girl's search for a meaningful place in the world. Marjorie Schoessel, who both plays the piano and appears as a reciter, leaves her small town to study elocution in Boston. Music, literature, and elocution fulfill Marjorie's longing for something "real" and provide her with the beauty she craves. Yet the fine arts have a complex and contradictory place in her life—within a limited framework they are appropriate activities for her gender and help to define her as a "nice girl," but they do not allow her to have a career. Marjorie's odyssey, notes Karen Neubauer, is limited because of its feminine construction; it is the only "kind of an odyssey a female can have and still maintain the coveted 'nice girl' reputation."[1] Art cannot be successfully integrated into Marjorie's day-to-day life, and throughout the novel her involvement with elocution creates frustrations that she is never able to overcome. On a larger level, Marjorie's situation allows modern readers to understand the complicated and sometimes precarious place of performing arts that became associated with women in the Progressive Era. Like Marjorie Schoessel, female elocutionists were striving to find a place for themselves in American cultural life without abandoning socially acceptable gender roles; they ultimately found their efforts rejected and their chosen art form too feminized to be considered culturally valid.

Marjorie engages with higher cultural forms because of her need for something beyond the world of her small Iowa community. Books give her a "queer dreamy feeling,"[2] and elocution and music both create an audible beauty that transcends common life. Marjorie's first realization of deeper artistic expression comes from struggling with the Chopin nocturne assigned by her piano teacher:

> Little parts, little phrases, began to take on a meaning. It was as if she had stood outside . . . and then a door pushed open, she could see inside, and go in deeper and deeper. . . . When people played softly or loudly, they didn't just do it because of the little marks above the measures. They meant it. . . . When Miss Davison called for her Nocturne, she stumbled over the first bars, then all at once she knew more than she had ever known before, and the playing was easier, a kind of singing.[3]

Elocution also allows Marjorie to approach the fulfillment she feels in music. In practicing her speeches, "there was a deep new excitement in 'letting herself go.' . . . This gave glimpses of satisfaction, too . . . a new possession of herself, a loosening of the tight bonds of self-consciousness and timidity."[4]

Elocution and music are linked in Suckow's novel, as they were in the late nineteenth century, through the musical vocabulary used to describe Marjorie's performances: both playing the piano and reciting allow Marjorie to have a "singing" voice. As she read poetry, "words, phrases here and there, sang in her mind, brought that mingled longing and satisfaction."[5] Marjorie's teachers in music and elocution can both produce the sounds to which she aspires. When Miss Davison plays, the notes stand out, "making a kind of shape in the air above the shining piano . . . precise and visible, on a kind of shimmering background."[6] It is a sound that Marjorie recognizes again in Mrs. Courtwick: "There was something different here, something that she had dimly sensed, and wanted . . . the lines that she read stood out, clear and definite, like the music that Miss Davison had played. . . . That was why she must stay at the Academy . . . to find and grasp that beautiful, secret hidden thing for herself."[7] The sound that Marjorie hopes to be able to replicate is gendered yet powerful. In her own poetic readings, Marjorie likes the "little soprano note, that answered to something which she dimly sensed as her own,"[8] and elocution allows her to experience the "intoxication of power and ease and beauty that she had to know, to reach, again."[9] At the Academy recital, Marjorie achieves success: "But she had satisfied herself. . . . She had spoken it—that little clear soprano note—made it her own."[10] For women, to make art is to make an expressly feminine sound.

However, there is no appropriate place for Marjorie's newfound voice when she returns home, and she discovers that the distance between the higher art forms she has been taught and her small town's culture has become wider. Marjorie is now ashamed of her previous recitations. Her mother wants her to perform locally, but Marjorie doesn't have an entire program prepared because popular lowbrow entertainment is not the literature for personal development she learned at the Academy of Expression; she finds that her professional training is useless.[11] The poetry that thrills her privately—that of Tennyson, Longfellow, Whittier, Phoebe and Alice Cary, Owen Meredith, Jean Ingelow—"were not pieces that would 'do to give'—like things from [James Whitcomb] Riley. They were a kind of indulgence, filling her at the same time with elation and helpless dissatisfaction, not fitting into her life."[12] Great poetry, while personally rewarding, does not work in public performance, just as her earlier absorption in Chopin's nocturne led Marjorie to abandon lesser works, such as the "Pansy Waltz" or "Monastery Chimes," that her family enjoys. When she complains about a local woman reading "cheap things," her mother counters that "no one could expect to give nothing but Shakespeare!"[13]

Marjorie is conflicted not just about the content of her repertoire, but also about the act of performance itself. She is especially embarrassed by the flamboyant performance of a local woman, who melodramatically combines text with musical accompaniment:

> She could not explain to them—not even to herself—why it was that she used to sit rigid with a dreadful shame when Mrs. Shrader walked slowly to the platform with a mystic step, opened the manuscript on her reading-stand, and read verses from *The Rubaiyat* with trills and sudden poundings and soft music from the piano. None of it was real—only a word here and there. And it was the very artificiality, all the palaver, that made the ladies smile at one another with a congratulatory air and think that something impressive was being done.[14]

Marjorie recognizes not a successful female performance in the combination of the two art forms that speak to her most, but a failed attempt by women to achieve high culture, and worse, a self-congratulatory inability to recognize pretension. It is not so much that Marjorie's education has enabled her to transcend this world; it seems that she fears *any* attempt at performance on her part will simply confirm her place in it. Marjorie eventually abandons elocution and takes an office job. Nonetheless, at the novel's close she is still longing for that which art has given to her—"that satisfaction that was warmth in the blood, that gave life a glowing centre"—but which she is somehow denied.[15]

In writing *The Odyssey of a Nice Girl*, Ruth Suckow drew on her own experiences to create a realistic, if critical, portrayal of the role of elocution in women's lives. The small-town Iowa native personally understood the motivations behind "nice girls'" engagement with literature and the arts, and the tensions surrounding their ambitions because of their gender. The grandchild of German immigrants, like her fictional counterpart, and the daughter of a Congregationalist minister, Ruth was surrounded by the suppers and entertainments at which young women like Marjorie might perform poetry; at only age seven, Ruth "delivered a nice recitation" at a social event in Algona.[16] Suckow was exposed to the literature and music appropriate for a respectable girl. Her father read selections by Charles Dickens out loud, and her "play characters" were literary and historical figures: King David, Martha Washington, and Tom Sawyer.[17] Early photos of the author reinforce the image of a cultured young lady: at twelve she holds a book, and as a teenager poses at the piano (figure 1.1); one can easily imagine the romanticizing Marjorie in her place.[18]

The world in which Ruth and other middle-class girls grew up was one in which both music and literature, made audible through elocution, represented the highest form of feminine culture. Suckow later described a parlor through a young girl's eyes; at the center of the domestic sphere were signifiers she "trustingly believed to set a true standard of elegance—a piano with a dumb pedal, a mahogany center table with a Battenburg doily and a mottled-leather copy of *Hiawatha*."[19] Despite the gentility of music and literature, women's cultural aspirations were blocked by societal norms. Thus Suckow could write, in 1926, that although any Iowa town "lets its women folk go in for books and frills in the Woman's Club," this world was nonetheless "suspicious of 'culture'" and the kind of prominent display that elocutionary or musical performance required.[20] Suckow's recollections of churchwomen emphasized the "cautious fixedness" of their activities: "If musical, they might play the pipe organ, sing or lead the choir—in fact, would be urged, more than urged to do so—they could always teach Sunday School classes, make little talks in the Missionary Society, 'lead the Devotion.' But it seemed that I would be better not to go very far intellectually, to keep always within the bounds of churchly convention."[21]

Suckow apparently found her dramatic activities at Grinnell College insufficient, leaving to enroll in elocutionist Silas Curry's School of Expression in Boston in 1913. The character of Marjorie was reportedly based on a fellow Curry student, not Suckow herself; nonetheless, much of what Marjorie encounters, including the specific texts that she performed, closely resembles the author's experiences.[22] Marjorie recites a "child's piece," similar to Eugene Field's "The Doll's Wooing," which Ruth performed in 1913; Ruth performed poetry by John Masefield and Alfred, Lord Tennyson, perhaps the inspiration for Marjorie's lyric gift. Marjorie's triumph is to play Titania in *A Midsummer Night's Dream* before she graduates; Suckow appeared as a rustic in the play in 1915. Marjorie is offered (but does not take) a job at a conservatory in Mississippi; graduates of the School of Expression taught at three Mississippi colleges.[23] A couple runs the fictional Academy of Expression: Mr. Courtwick, a missionary for his particular pedagogical method, and his intimidating, businesswoman wife. While they were presumably based on Silas and Anna Baright Curry, their name in a manuscript of the novel, "Southwick," links

Figure 1.1. Ruth Suckow at the piano. Papers of Ruth Suckow, University of Iowa Libraries, Special Collections.

them to Henry L. Southwick, president of Boston's Emerson College of Expression from 1908 until 1932, and his wife, Jessie Eldridge Southwick, who taught there. Marjorie's parents expect her to open an elocution studio; upon Ruth's return to Iowa, she advertised her availability as a teacher in speech arts, "a Reader, and as a Director of Plays and all forms of Dramatic Art."[24] But not surprisingly, jobs directing plays in 1915 in Manchester, Iowa, with a population of just under three thousand, were not forthcoming, and the studio was abandoned.

Suckow, like Marjorie and countless other female elocution graduates, did not pursue a career as a professional reader or teacher. She instead became one of the regionalist writers of the 1920s and '30s, known for her detailed treatments of life in the Midwest. Her *Odyssey of a Nice Girl* is not a romanticized account of one girl's experience with elocutionary education; its insights into the gendered forces that shaped women's careers stem both from the author's firsthand involvement with elocution and from the widespread disillusionment with its failures after the movement had peaked. Suckow produced a novel that is achingly realistic in its understanding of what Marjorie and her nonfictional peers deeply desired, but, with hindsight, she was also cognizant of how their artistic endeavors might fail. Marjorie's problems are not hers alone, but are representative of those faced by women in elocution at the turn of the twentieth century; they are problems that originated with the limitations surrounding their earliest involvement with the spoken word.

## Finding Their Voices:
## American Women and Elocution

Women's attraction to elocution as a cultural activity and ultimately a profession can be traced to the late eighteenth and nineteenth centuries. Fundamental to women's later emergence as speakers was the pervasiveness of oral repetition as a pedagogical method in the American educational system. Before the late nineteenth century, to learn to read was to learn to read out loud.[25] Textbooks designed to teach children basic literacy were known as *spellers*, *readers*, and *speakers*. Books issued in series, such as McGuffey's Readers, which served more than 116 million children between 1839 and 1920,[26] or the similar books by Charles Saunders, popular in the 1840s and '50s, usually contained a speaker as one of its advanced volumes; yet readers, too, were used for children's oral reading practice.[27] Students were made to demonstrate numerous topics though recitation—multiplication tables, geography, verb forms, and so on. Education literature was full of cautionary warnings that teachers' charges should understand what they were reciting, not merely parrot information without comprehension.[28] Speech, however, remained central to girls' education, and it was in their childhood that they first encountered "the body as a vehicle for public performance,"[29] which was the basis for elocution as a performing art.

In classical rhetoric, *elocutio* referred to the technical means by which a written work would come to be spoken. Because rhetoric instruction was part of formal education, both female and male pupils were exposed to language made audible, even though oratory was "culturally coded as masculine."[30] The study of elocution was considered a moral and intellectual good, particularly for men, as it prepared them to be rhetorically persuasive in careers as lawyers, ministers, and politicians. Women were historically excluded from the masculine world of public speech in professional lives, and their voices were to be put to gender-appropriate uses. Adrienne Herndon, who taught elocution at Atlanta University, recalled that her mother did not believe her childhood achievements in the spoken word would amount to anything, exclaiming, "Why could you not have been born a boy? . . . Then you could make us proud by your oratory."[31]

Because women were expected to remain in the domestic sphere, pedagogues felt compelled to offer justifications for their study of elocution, often supplying reasons similar to those supporting music lessons. The author of an 1839 reader for young ladies wrote, "A fine reader may contribute as much pleasure to the domestic circle, during the course of life, as a skillful performer on the harp or pianoforte. The instrument for reading is ever at hand, and seldom out of tune. . . . When a young lady has acquired this accomplishment, why should she not entertain a circle of friends by reading, as readily as she would sing or play for them?"[32] *The American Lady's Preceptor* found that painting, music, and dancing, though "expensively and tediously taught," were seldom practiced after a few years, and believed that girls' "intellectual powers" should be cultivated through a "fondness for elegant literature" instead.[33] Elocutionary skills would enable women to entertain their families and to contribute to their children's education. In 1846 Anna Russell declared that "the key note of poetry, seems to have been lent to woman. On the ear of infancy and childhood, her voice was meant to fall."[34] Lydia Sigourney emphasized that reading well was a graceful accomplishment, the purpose of which was "to comfort the sick" and "make the evening fireside delightful," rather than for women's personal display.[35] An etiquette book recommended vocal training in order to enhance feminine and thus domestic virtues: "Sweeten your voices, my fair ones, and it will sweeten your life and your homes."[36] Nonetheless, writing on women's education made clear that their speech was to remain within the confines of what was appropriate to womanliness. Russell's description of the ideal female voice suggests that women were not to aspire to the louder extremes of public oratory: "A sweet voice . . . is oftener the gift of the quiet and unobtrusive. Loudness or rapidity of utterance is incompatible with it. . . . The sounds follow each other like drops of water from a fountain. It is like the brooding note of a dove. . . . It is a glorious gift in a woman."[37] Not surprisingly, in mid-century readers for "young ladies," oratorical addresses were often omitted, and while *pronuntiatio* was covered, the physical poses necessary for public performance, *actio*, initially were not.[38] One male elocutionist recalled that even when women did perform in the postbellum period, they were not supposed to make gestures: "They were to stand with gloves on and hands folded and say their piece; but to make any motion was out of all decency!"[39]

Thus, oral performance, like musical performance, was socially acceptable for women within certain confines: in the home or the school, or even in civic ceremonies if they performed as amateurs. Although female political figures, such as suffragists, encountered resistance to their speaking appearances on the public platform because of their gender, schoolgirls' academic appearances were a different matter. Carolyn Eastman has documented speeches by American girls in the late eighteenth century that advocate for women as orators but finds that "an increasingly narrow and private conception of female eloquence" had taken hold by the 1820s.[40] Nonetheless, girls reciting in graduation performances that celebrated their achievements were common throughout the nineteenth century. Lindal Buchanan notes the mixed messages American girls received: they had engaged in academic oratory "all the while being admonished to restrict their eloquence to home and hearth."[41] The degree to which female students were allowed to exhibit their oratorical skills for their families and communities varied by time period and geographical region; in the mid-nineteenth century, some girls who had composed essays for exhibitions or graduation exercises were not permitted to read them and were forced to sit quietly while men read their prose.[42]

Even when girls were allowed to speak, musical performances, readings, and poetic recitations were considered more appropriate for them than speeches.[43] A fictional account of an 1850s class exhibition, "How the Boys Become Good Speakers," recounted how the girls gained "an equal share" through reading their compositions between the boy's speeches and performing "A Floral Play" in poetry.[44] Similar gender divisions existed in the performances of actual children later in the century. Programs from academies and high schools in the 1880s show girls engaged in essays, readings, and recitations, and boys performing oratory and declamations.[45] At the exhibitions of Park College in Missouri, male students typically gave "orations" while female students read "essays," almost without exception, into the 1890s.[46] The discrepancy between what was allowed in an educational context, however public, and the masculine political platform resembles the nineteenth-century expectation that women, especially those of upper-class status, were to be well trained in music but not to perform publicly. Female students in the South may have faced fewer restrictions on their speech;[47] however, the genteel Southern lady did not engage in public display. In her 1912 memoir, Harriott Horry Ravenel of Charleston recalled that antebellum ladies "shunned all public exercise or display of talent or beauty. Their letters were admirable, but they did not write books. They charmed drawing rooms with their voices or music, but never appeared on a stage. They talked delightfully, but did not make speeches."[48] For women, then, elocution became not a natural extension of their education in rhetoric and writing into public oratory, but one of the subjects deemed "ornamental," along with music and the other fine arts.[49] Schools' catalogs typically listed elocution lessons with those for music and drawing, available for an additional fee.

Ultimately, women's speech was found to be more acceptable when the speaker merely served as a vessel for a literary (and hence, often masculine) voice, rather than the audible embodiment of their own, potentially transgressive rhetoric. Women studied music to learn male composers' pieces; they studied elocution to recite literature by others, not their own writings. Women's entrance into elocution was possible because it allowed socially acceptable private activities from the educational and domestic spheres to become public. Taking *Hiawatha* from its lace doily in the parlor and reciting it on the platform before an audience was typical of the expansion of feminine activities into a wider realm by Progressive-Era women.

## The March of Progress: Women's Success in Elocution

Suckow's novel was published after a period of rapid change for American women. During the Progressive Era, middle- and upper-class white women increasingly gained access to higher education; between 1890 and 1920, the number of women attending college rose from 56,000 to almost 283,000.[50] Women took on new roles in public life in unprecedented numbers. Judith Tick has documented the influx of women into music as teachers, performers, and composers.[51] Similarly, women entered elocution, studying at the numerous oratory schools available to them, giving platform performances, and teaching at educational institutions, at music conservatories, and privately in their homes. A 1912 article from the *Atlantic Monthly* noted that women now dominated American culture and were "steadily monopolizing learning, teaching, literature, the fine arts, music, the church, and the theatre . . . taking over the field of liberal culture."[52]

Justified as a logical and morally necessary extension of the feminine sphere, women's new activities were bolstered by the women's club movement. Women's desires for cultural enrichment were first met by literary study clubs created for self-education.[53] Club meetings were also many women's first opportunity to talk before a group. Hanna Robinson, who joined the New England Women's Club in 1869, could not bring herself to speak at a meeting for two years;[54] by 1892, Anna B. McMahan, president of a Quincy, Illinois, club, described how women's readings and presentations had "taught us not to fear the sound of our own voices."[55] Yet even appearances in semipublic spaces could threaten to undermine women's femininity; elocution professional Anna Morgan warned against women's attempts to speak with "pomp and masculine assertiveness" because "the assumption of virile methods" was "in bad taste."[56]

Many societies came to abandon literary study in order to advocate for community improvement: suffrage, temperance, child welfare, the creation of libraries and parks, and access to fine arts. Scholars have concentrated on women's groups engaged in such political activism, overshadowing the artistic clubs that provided women with venues at which they could perform as well as both personal and financial support. Although women's groups supported arts activities in their communities and female patrons had a significant influence on the funding and management of arts organizations,[57] Karen Blair has described the milieu of most women's clubs as "separate and self-defined, an invisible amateur arts subculture whose members were serious and knowledgeable but invisible."[58] That women's performances were regularly reported in newspapers' society pages, rather than in sections devoted to arts and entertainment, suggested that they had an amateur status. The implication that women's artistic activities were inherently inferior to those of men had a significant impact on the reputations of female elocutionists.

The entrance of women into elocution parallels the general increase of women in public life in the Progressive Era. Elocution as a discipline (and elocutionist as a profession) was initially a field for men, who served as speech professors in higher education and produced textbooks and anthologies. However, this male domain changed in the final decades of the nineteenth century. An essay in an etiquette manual first published in 1873 described the "march of progress" and the "results of civilization" as manifested in women's changed status, concluding, "Whether engaged in general lecture, moral teaching, political discussion, or legal argument, she will be found the exponent of truth and co-worker with man in reform."[59] In spite of the author's optimism regarding women's public rhetorical role, an accompanying engraving depicted the new female orator in a parlor-like setting, confirming that her voice would more likely be heard in entertainment—"recitation, reading, tableau and conversation"—than in political speech. Yet the author was correct that the previously male domain of elocution was changing. E. B. Warman's 1889 book on vocal training describes the importance of the voice in various professions, only using the pronoun *she* for the teacher, not the minister, lawyer, or lecturer; nonetheless, the book's illustrations all feature women.[60] Such change was not always welcome. "Facing her first audience," the frontispiece for *The Ideal Speaker and Entertainer* from 1910, shows a well-dressed young suffrage advocate facing a crowded auditorium. Although the subheading asserts that "the woman orator is becoming as popular as the man orator," audience members chat, yawn, or sleep.[61]

By the end of the century, as female reciters found ready performance venues at literary societies or women's clubs, published recitation materials began to reflect women's efforts and tastes.[62] Speakers designed for females had traditionally differed from those for males; the prefaces to early nineteenth-century pedagogical books for girls frequently stressed their appropriateness for their intended readers and, as one editor wrote, assured the "scrupulous regard to delicacy in the pieces inserted," which were more "appropriate to the duties, employments, and the dispositions of the softer sex."[63] Such books could include didactic essays about women's roles, though they sometimes featured more selections by female poets than did similar books for males, which contained classical oratory and political speeches.[64] In the second half of the century, the best-known elocution books were authored by men, but as more women entered the field, they began to produce pedagogical publications as well.[65] The largest number of elocution books by women were parlor anthologies, collections for children, or textbooks designed for use in educational settings.[66] Female authors sometimes condensed the content of typical texts into a reduced form, including their most frequently assigned selections, to be used with their female classes. A number of women's texts reflect individualistic pedagogical approaches not found in the core of the elocutionary literature.[67]

Because of the widespread popularity of elocution beyond academic circles, anthologies from the 1890s and later differ from those of earlier eras. Political oratory and moralistic essays were replaced with poetry designed to appeal to women performing in both domestic and public venues. Not only were female reciters depicted on covers and in illustrations, they were also increasingly represented as the editors of popular collections; for example, Frances Putnam Pogle, who attended Northwestern's School of Oratory in the 1890s, coauthored an anthology that was reprinted several times.[68] While the first half of previous textbooks consisted of scholarly instruction in vocal techniques, concluding with selections to be spoken, newer "parlor books" eliminated the instructional preface or kept it to a minimum, leaving room for large quantities of popular poetry, music, and photographs of performers in dramatic poses, sometimes in costume.[69] Appendices could include popular songs, physical drills, pantomimes, or instructions for how to organize literary clubs or social events at which performances might take place. Thus, one volume could provide enough variety for a range of literary entertainments. Many of these books were designed as gifts, featuring dedication pages to be inscribed with the recipient's name (e.g., "Presented to Leila from Grandmother, Christmas 1895"), reinforcing a presumed domestic use.

When the National Association of Elocutionists had its first meeting in the summer of 1892 at the all-male Columbia College, the *New York Times* reported that about three-quarters of the attendees were women, describing how "their trim costumes and fluttering fans . . . made gay the sober interior of the big lecture room."[70] Men held the bulk of the offices in the association, although this began to change as the female members gradually took on more roles. However, the semiprofessional status of many female elocutionists, who made careers accepting engagements at schools, churches, and clubs, has made them less visible historically; the only woman provided with a biography in *Werner's Directory of Elocutionists*[71] is Emma Dunning Banks, even though female teachers and platform artists dominate the advertisements in the back of the book. Alvina Carolyn Winkler (Paterson) of Troy, New York, who began appearing in public at age nine, gave her first professional engagement at a church at only fourteen; she reported that she "cleared twenty-two dollars, and managed the whole affair alone, besides selling seventy-two tickets in two days."[72] Winkler continued to arrange paid engagements with musicians and other entertainers, appearing before an audience of seven hundred at age seventeen.

Men were most often the founders of oratory departments in American universities, but students in such programs and in elocution schools were overwhelmingly women. In Boston, the Curry School of Expression, Emerson College, and the New England Conservatory's short-lived School of Elocution were all dominated by female pupils, as was the Cincinnati School of Expression, which opened a dormitory for women around 1908. Likewise, the force behind Northwestern University's School of Oratory was Robert McLean Cumnock, but its students were largely women; a 1921 Northwestern songbook contained the number "It's Great to Be an Oratory Girl."[73] Female elocution graduates typically entered the professional ranks as private teachers or at educational institutions or music conservatories; many conservatories had both *music* and *elocution* in their names. Regardless of how successful they were as platform soloists, most women taught.[74] Several prominent pedagogues were associated with schools named for or led with their husbands: Jessie Eldridge Southwick at Emerson, Rachel Shoemaker at the National School of Elocution Oratory in Philadelphia, and Inez King at Bryon King's School of Oratory in Pittsburgh. The school Anna Baright founded was renamed the School of Expression after she married Silas Curry, and eventually become Curry College. Many women founded schools of elocution of varying sizes in their communities. Julia and Annie Gregory Thomas established a Conservatory of Elocution in New York in 1878. The Cumnock School of Oratory in Los Angeles, modeled after Northwestern, was entirely staffed by women in 1899 and 1900. In Chicago, Ida Morey Riley and Mary Ann Blood founded the Columbia School of Oratory in 1890, which survives as Columbia College, and Anna Morgan directed a School of Expression in the Fine Arts Building on Michigan Avenue. The New Orleans College of Oratory and Elocution, founded by Lily Whitaker in 1887, lasted for forty years; around 1900 it had four branch schools as well.[75]

*Lest We Forget* provides a partial overview of the careers of the 383 graduates of Edna Chaffee Noble's Detroit Training School (DTS) between 1879 and 1904.[76] Only twenty-one DTS students were men, and about half of these adopted a profession unrelated to their speech training. Slightly less than half of the women married, and although some abandoned their professional aspirations for domestic life, many continued to teach and to appear in or assist with local entertainments. More than half the graduates taught, in schools, privately in their homes and studios, or both; fifteen women opened their own institutions, although some of these were short-lived. Slightly less than half of Detroit's alumnae described themselves as giving platform appearances, although it is difficult to determine whether they performed in a professional or an amateur capacity. Nonetheless, few graduates admitted having taken the training purely for personal edification with no professional ambitions in mind. Many, like Helen Estelle Mulvey of Seattle, were modest in reporting their efforts. Mulvey had toured the state of Washington and taught privately and in the public schools, but she reported that "I have not continued steadfastly in the good work. . . . My career has been rather uneventful, and yet successful in a quiet way."[77]

As the Detroit Training School alumni demonstrate, female elocutionists' careers varied widely. Ethel Robinson, a 1912 graduate of Northwestern, taught at the Jennie Bliss School of Music in nearby Oak Park, appearing in its recitals and before church and women's groups.[78] Upon wedding her college sweetheart in 1914, she moved to Janesville, Wisconsin, where marriage and motherhood effectively ended her career. Margaret Paul performed in the Midwest while attending Cornell College in 1907 and 1908. After a year studying at the Leland Powers School in Boston (all she could afford), Paul toured the Chautauqua summer circuits in 1914 and 1915. She later turned to teaching speech exclusively, first at Lenox College in Hopkinton, Iowa, and then at Emerson High School in Gary, Indiana, for twenty-five years.[79] Pauline Sherwood Townsend, a graduate of the New England Conservatory, taught at women's colleges across the South: Mississippi's Belhaven College (1895–99), Virginia's Hollins Institute (1899–1903), and then Belmont College in Nashville until 1939.[80] Townsend's career outlasted the elocution movement, and she directed plays and became active in pageantry in later years. In contrast to these women, Cincinnati elocutionist Jennie Mannheimer (later Jane Manner) maintained a performing career for approximately forty years, from around 1891 to 1943. Mannheimer performed poetry as well as plays, appearing before women's clubs and Jewish organizations and at private salons and hotels (such as New York's Waldorf Astoria), yet teaching always served as an income source. She resigned her position at the Cincinnati College of Music in 1907 to return to the Cincinnati School of Expression, which she had founded in 1894 and ran with her sister Edna; the school also offered lessons in piano, organ, voice, and violin. Mannheimer performed in New York City and established a studio after the sisters moved there in 1918.

## Acting versus Elocution, Respectability, and Literature in Performance

A female elocutionist was more socially acceptable than a woman who appeared on the theatrical stage, where the dangers of bodily display and the long association of actresses with prostitution loomed. When women did appear professionally to read or recite, their publicity materials were careful not to call them *actresses*, even if they performed solo versions of plays; for example, in an early publicity brochure, Mannheimer stands decorously behind a podium "reading," not acting, and many performers called themselves *readers* even when they performed memorized selections.[81] Touring elocutionists were frequently hired for church entertainments, and local committees who engaged them were wary of signs of disreputable theatricality. Joint programs given by Rachel and Jacob Shoemaker from around 1869 to 1872 typically opened with scripture, seemingly sanctifying their performance, before the elocutionists moved on to selections by Dickens, Shakespeare, Tennyson, Whittier, and Poe.[82] Decades later, one church committee cut the word *dramatic* off the phrase *dramatic and humorous recitals* from the flyer of Canadian performer Jessie Alexander because it "looked too theatrical for a church."[83]

The performances of many elocutionists would today probably be characterized as acting; however, elocution's rhetorical roots allowed it to maintain a separate identity. *Characterization*, or *impersonation*, was a subset of a larger field, mentioned in only a few elocution texts, and could take place entirely apart from costumed drama. When the *Shaftesbury Magazine of Oratory* introduced impersonation as a career in 1895, it attempted to disassociate it from theater, calling it a "new profession" and offering readers assurances that it was "intellectual, chaste, and ennobling."[84] One could certainly study elocution if aspiring to a theatrical career, and actresses' vocal production was central to their personas and written about in the press. But engaging in elocution did not qualify one for the stage; former actress Olive Logan was quick to point out that "a pretty girl, with large luminous eyes, laboring under strong excitement, and reciting in a hurried tone familiar lines" for "admiring friends" was hardly prepared for a theatrical future.[85] Of course, actresses such as Fanny Kemble or Charlotte Cushman gave readings in which they drew on their acting experience. Nonetheless, successful professional elocutionists could sometimes meet with failure in attempting a transition from elocution to drama, such as George Riddle, whose abortive foray on the Boston stage was short-lived. Some of elocution's stylized vocal techniques were not transferable to more naturalistic acting; in his letters to aspiring actress Katherine Alvord, fellow student Fred Randolph pointed out that the training she had received at Northwestern's School of Oratory around 1880 would have to be unlearned or it would ruin her theatrical chances: "I do not think your elocutionary work counts for much and what it does count is rather against you." Randolph's warnings were not motivated by a lack of confidence in Alvord's abilities, but from his all-too-common belief that "the stage at present is not a fit place for woman."[86]

One notable exception to the acting/elocution divide was Cora Urquhart Potter, who began her career giving recitations for her high-society set, publishing them in 1887.[87] When she left her spouse and child for the stage, a tremendous scandal ensued, even though she had seemingly predicted her future by reciting George Sims's "'Ostler Joe," in which a young woman leaves her country husband for London's dissolute theatrical life.[88] Respectable women could recite socially, maintaining an amateur status and remaining insulated from the moral suspicions that had been confirmed when Mrs. Potter's ambitions led her astray. Her reputation aside, Potter and the extensive press coverage she received when she crossed the lines between elocutionist and actress, amateur and professional, demonstrates how infrequently such a transformation occurred due to the possible damage to a woman's social status. Elocutionist Isabel Garghill Beecher told a manager who urged her to "take up the stage" that she wanted her young son to "have every advantage" and didn't want him to be burdened with an "actress mother."[89] When high school student Florence Peck recited a humorous poem at the Rochester, New York, Lyceum to a bit of acclaim in 1901, she fantasized in her diary, "If the stage was the place for a woman I'd go on most for the excitement and for the pleasure."[90] Nonetheless, an acting career was not something the majority of young women engaging in elocution typically pursued before theater became more socially acceptable in the twentieth century. Approximately 16 percent of the female graduates of the Detroit Training School began stage careers between 1879 and 1904; half of those occurred in the last seven years of this period, suggesting their choice was becoming increasingly tolerated. However, over 40 percent of the actresses reported themselves retired, so many women's theatrical attempts had been brief.[91] Some platform performers appeared in dramatic productions in their communities, but frequently as amateurs; Alvina Winkler Paterson returned from dramatic training in New York City to act in plays in her hometown in the 1910s, but these were not professional productions.[92] Actress Sarah Cowell Le Moyne, who left the stage temporarily to be a dramatic reader, managed to establish her respectability because of her serious literary tastes, which included works by Shakespeare and Browning. While some elocutionists may have been frustrated actresses and elocution school graduates sometimes undertook dramatic or vaudeville careers, large numbers appear to have had no other aspirations than those within elocution itself.

Like actresses, elocutionists did face some of the dangers inherent in public presentation of their bodies while engaging in what was ostensibly only vocal display. In his review of *Odyssey of a Nice Girl*, H. L. Mencken acknowledged, "An elocutionist of course, is not downright obscene, like . . . a fancy dancer, but even an elocutionist is somehow suspect!"[93] Female elocutionists met this difficulty in various ways, finding bodily control in stylized poses and proselytizing, via Delsartism, that a spiritual essence could be expressed with their physical bodies (see chapter 5). But to a certain extent, the female elocutionist, by reading out loud or reciting as she might in her own parlor, signaled that she was not transgressing the boundaries of appropriate behavior for her gender.

The catalogs of elocution schools reflect the gender expectations of the late nineteenth century; their course offerings rarely stress any theatrical end, but most often prepared students for teaching, less frequently for the platform. The School of Expression at the summer Chautauqua assemblies in upstate New York readily admitted that it trained attendees for self-expression, not because "they intend to inflict the public with their readings."[94] The New England Conservatory's Elocution School offered a "Home Reading Course" for the students who had "no idea of becoming professional Elocutionists" yet who desired to recite "in a quiet way, for the pleasure of their immediate friends or at private gatherings"; this description resembles the young woman, book in hand, next to a pianist waiting her turn, reciting for several adults and a small girl who is depicted on the title page of *Readings and Recitations for Winter Evenings* (1895) (figure 1.2).[95] Anna Morgan's Chicago Conservatory, which began as an elocution school but hosted full theatrical productions (including an all-female *Hamlet* in 1903) and produced graduates who became acting professionals, was a notable exception to the institutions female students typically attended.[96] Not surprisingly, at Curry's 1915 graduation exercises, Suckow was the only student who received the diploma for "dramatic artists"—the remaining graduates were awarded degrees for public speaking (two men) and teaching, "general culture," and "philosophic realization" (primarily women).[97] Unlike her author, Marjorie never aspires to a theatrical career, but as a typical "nice girl," remains within the safer feminine world of elocution. In the decades following World War I, as negative attitudes toward theater lessened, more schools of expression added dramatic training to their curricula and produced staged and "acted" plays rather than plays that were merely "read." A mid- to late 1920s catalog from Elizabeth Morse's School

Figure 1.2. Title page, B. J. Fernie, *Readings and Recitations for Winter Evenings* (New York: Christian Herald, 1895).

of Expression in St. Louis admitted, almost apologetically, "The staging of plays is now so universally demanded at churches, schools, and colleges that it is necessary for students to equip themselves in this line of work."[98]

In spite of their entry into the public sphere and their usurping oratorical roles traditionally held by men, women could justify their involvement in elocution in that they were transmitting great literature. Angela Sorby has noted that schoolgirls were first exposed to the idea that poetry was "a script for oral reading, half-done and finished only when read rhetorically."[99] Members of the National Association of Elocutionists continually expressed this idea; Mrs. Arthur Ransom told the 1900 assembly, "There is something in the human voice itself which all the books in all the world can never supply."[100] Thus, women's voices became vessels for the transmission of high culture, serving as completions for their chosen works. Through them, the voice of the poet, invoking timeless truths, could speak. To perform this function was both to give life to the poet's vision and to express oneself, to give one's own interpretation of the text. Nan Johnson has described how readers believed that they benefited "intellectually and morally from both the study and the performance of the work," and that audiences were "similarly improved" by hearing them.[101] Morgan boldly claimed a place for the performer alongside the text's author:

> Q: How much honor is due me when I interpret and read a poem in a great way?
> A: You share the honor almost equally with the author, because you are able to see as much, sometimes more, than he did.[102]

Thus, in their communication of literary truths, the goal of female elocutionists was to be an exalted one. In 1899, Jessie Southwick addressed Emerson students with Progressive-Era sentiments couched in missionary zeal: "O girls, be in earnest! . . . This is a woman's age, an age when women are endeavoring to reach out into larger possibilities. . . . There is a spirit in this age which means that woman is destined to shine upon the world and help reveal the meaning of life. She can do it. *We* can do it."[103]

Like Marjorie, many women experienced the "intoxication of power" when they brought their own vocal interpretation to texts and felt transported to a wider realm through their association with the artistry of the poetry they recited. Elocutionists frequently saw their own talent of orally interpreting text to be the equivalent of a musician's performance; for decades Jane Manner's publicity flyers displayed a quotation prominently on their covers: "What the musician is to music, the reader is to literature—an interpreter, a re-creator, a translator." In many ways, elocution's basis in solo performance made the reciter's career more like that of a musician than an actress, and enabled female speakers to have an unusual degree of control over the content and style of their performances. Women worked to link their public identities with specific texts, adopting individual works and performing them with enough frequency to become associated with them, in the way that a singer becomes known for her rendition of a particular song.

In theory at least, in order for women to make their performances socially acceptable, their chosen repertoire needed to represent the highest form of literary art. Even women who engaged in characterization presented themselves as readers; an 1882 program of Helen Potter, the best known impersonator of her era, is shaped like a book and features Potter demurely holding a volume on its cover (figure 1.3).[104] The height of elocution coincided with the increasing sacralization of culture in America described by Lawrence Levine; in taking on the role of priestesses of great literature, female elocutionists were similar to the arts patrons who endeavored to make museums and concert halls temples for elevating public tastes.[105] Speakers before the Elocutionists' Association frequently urged members to strive "toward the cultivation of the best literary tastes" and to introduce audiences to "the better class of selections."[106] Many elocutionists stressed that spoken texts should exemplify morality and truth. Eleanor O'Grady called for recitations exemplifying "beauty, truth, and vir-

Figure 1.3. Flyer for Helen Potter (1882). Jerry Tarver Elocution, Rhetoric, and Oratory Collection in the Rare Books and Manuscripts Library of the Ohio State University Libraries.

tue,"[107] and instructors emphasized that the bodily control they taught allowed art to be linked "with divinity."[108] Isabel Garghill Beecher's performance at Christ Presbyterian Church in Madison, Wisconsin, in 1912 was hailed as equal to "a sermon," and her program represented the most successful evening "service" the pastor had ever experienced.[109]

Sentiments stressing elocution's strong link to good literature represented more a call for better programming than a description of the wide-ranging poetic, dramatic, and literary works that elocutionists actually performed. Female performers did recite Shakespeare, Tennyson, and Longfellow, but as Marjorie's mother suggested, they were just as likely to imitate the dialects of African Americans, European immigrants, or small children; to give humorous sketches appropriate for vaudeville; or to recite poetry from popular periodicals that hardly qualified as literary masterworks. While works by major poets appear in the anthologies of the 1890s and 1900s, a huge number of less artistic texts, many reprinted without acknowledgment, make up the bulk of the poetry published there; the primary goal of such volumes was entertainment, not the transmission or canonization of poetic masterpieces. The tension Marjorie experiences between high and low repertoire in the novel is remarkably accurate, as surviving programs reveal that audiences were more likely to hear "Aunt Doleful's Visit" than Shakespeare. The texts on either end of the cultural hierarchy that women programmed are still recognizable as representing the highbrow versus lowbrow division that generated period writers' complaints. However, there were countless works in between these extremes to which a cultural status is now far more difficult to assign, texts that predate the potentially appropriate term *middlebrow*, which was coined in the 1920s. These poems, as well as the songs and salon pieces heard on women's programs, might now fail to meet an artistic ideal or critical standard; nonetheless, they may well have represented high culture to the audiences that heard them. In addition, some of the poetry unquestionably considered to be good literature in the late nineteenth century later fell from acclaim in the twentieth, just as many late Romantic compositions that made regular concert appearances were rejected with the rise of newer, modern musical styles. Indeed, most of Marjorie's literary favorites, which she believed too highbrow for her community, no longer hold a significant place in academic literary circles, even Longfellow, whose fall from his position as the most revered poet of his day has been explored by Christoph Irmscher.[110]

Ultimately, elocutionists had to please their listeners, and despite the confidently expressed goals of their profession, they, like Marjorie, undoubtedly found that a variety of selections rather than a steady diet of serious literature was more successful. Turn-of-the-century programs of women's entertainments reveal that performers and audiences embraced a much wider range of both texts and music than the cultural dichotomies that we have inherited from the era might suggest.

## Women's Artistic Endeavors and the Anti-Elocution Reaction

The female elocutionist was ubiquitous in the late nineteenth century, reciting poetry at civic functions or between numbers at concerts, appearing in solo programs, and teaching in educational institutions and private studios. Women's entrance into elocution, made possible by societal changes, also left it in a precarious position. Historically, when women enter a profession,

it becomes devalued by the patriarchal culture at large, and women's dominance of elocution led to questions as to whether it was a fit profession for a
man. By 1901, it was estimated that 90 percent of instructors were female;[111]
so many elocutionists were women that male elocutionists were sometimes
viewed as effeminate. In 1899, prominent elocutionists addressed the issue
"Should a Young Man Take Up Elocution?" following an interview in *Werner's
Magazine* with Harriet Webb, who complained of male elocutionists "curling
their hair" and "truckling to women" at "pink teas."[112] On the discovery that
only two men were enrolled in Northwestern's oratory school, the *New York
Journal* joked about "an almost Adamless Eden" with "two bridegrooms for
150 brides."[113] The 1911 catalog for Columbia College called special attention to the need for "strong young men who can teach Expression" to remind
prospective male students of the institution's openings.[114]

Contemporary satires of elocutionists often ridiculed female performers.
The height of elocution was recalled as a "fearful malady" that had "swept the
nation." In 1917 Eleanor Gates compared "taking elocution" to coming down
with an illness: "at a picnic, or an afternoon tea, or a church 'social,' (anything
for an excuse!) you found yourself caught unawares by one of these afflicted
friends and cornered. . . . Gradually, like a distemper, the thing died out."[115] The
sacralization of culture that had given women an entry point into elocutionary
performance also served as a means of critiquing their efforts. In the backlash
against elocution, women who aspired to high culture were frequent subjects
of ridicule. For example, an 1886 article divided the five thousand female elocutionists in New York into the categories of "readers, reciters, narrators, and
spouters" requiring the endurance of prizefighters to perform book-length texts:

> Young ladies who give readings of "Faust" and "Childe Harold" are ignorant of
> the capacities of the opposite sex. At the first hour, the male brute begins to groan.
> The second hour makes him hate his species. These readers have to undergo the
> most severe training in athletics. They practice with Indian clubs two hours in
> the morning, walk five miles before breakfast, put on the gloves an hour with
> their trainer, eat a raw egg, are sponged off with whiskey, and then kept on the
> parallel till dinner time. They thus acquire staying power.[116]

A 1905 postcard pictures "The Elocutionist" as a pompous-looking woman
below volumes by Shakespeare, Longfellow, Tennyson, Byron, and Milton,
accompanied by a limerick (figure 1.4):

> Some reciters are terrible bores
> And drive all their friends out of doors,
> And the patter of feet
> As the listeners retreat
> They take for the sound of encores!

However, performers who programmed popular texts, engaging in unliterary "parlor recitations," were disdained as inferior representatives of their profession. Lily Hollingshead's opening speech at the Elocution Association's first meeting transmitting the ideas of her grandfather, noted pedagogue James Murdoch, contrasted feminine amateur elocution with masculine professionalism: "Merely a drawing-room accomplishment . . . to be employed in doing pretty little things nicely," as opposed to a tool in "preparing speakers for the platform, the stage, the pulpit, the bar, and for life."[117] In 1900, Henry Gaines Hawn claimed that no one desired to be considered "instructors of an accomplishment . . . used semi-occasionally in church entertainments."[118] Unfortunately, the underlying reason for dismissals of women's efforts at elocution were more frequently their gender than any critical assessment of their contributions; while certainly many untrained, amateurish female elocutionists must have helped create the stereotypes that sprang up about them, given the large numbers of women in the field, there were undoubtedly many accomplished performers as well.

The controversies about what to call the discipline of speech—the countless assurances that *expression* or *interpretation* were in no way like their predecessor, *elocution*, with its dreadful (read "feminine") excesses—initially seem to be the sort of clarification necessary to the solidification of a discipline. Yet these arguments were also attempts to disassociate the field from its continuing feminization, in its endeavor to remain a serious male discourse. The continual assertions that elocution was mere mechanical reproduction of language, rather than representing actual understanding, essentialized women as performing bodies, distinguishing them from masculine intellect. Through their voices women had claimed the highest form of language, literature, as their own; the rejection of elocution and the criticism that it was underdeveloped compared to "interpretation" tried to take back language for men. As late as 1960, Giles Wilkeson Gray's article "What Was Elocution?" opened with a telling analogy: "Few young women appreciate being referred to as *hussies*; nor would many of us be willing to admit that we are teachers of *elocution*."[119] Much of the period prejudice against women elocutionists was transmitted into later scholarship; for example, rather than viewing female performers and pedagogues as enriching the cultural lives of their communities, John Gentile calls the "local 'Elocutionary lady'" a common small-town "malady."[120] In sharp contrast is the central figure of the semiautobiographical novel *Consider Miss Lily*, based on Alyene Porter's experiences at Mrs. A. A. Cocke's School of Expression in Dallas. Pupils of the fictional "Miss Lily" revere her, finding her "indestructible" and a teacher of life as well as vocal technique.[121] Likewise, the recollections of an actual "Miss Lily," the founder of a New Orleans elocution college, Lily Whitaker, even border on the hagiographic; in the 1950s

THE ELOCUTIONIST

Some reciters are terrible bores
And drive all their friends out of doors.
And the patter of feet
As the listeners retreat
They take for the sound of encores!

Figure 1.4. R. Hill, "The Elocutionist," postcard (1905). Author's personal collection.

former pupils recalled being "fascinated by that vital woman."[122] Negative views of elocution are changing, however; acknowledging performance studies' problematic historiography, Paul Edwards critiques elocution's dismissal in the narrative of the evolution of speech, asking, "What is the thing that we tell ourselves we no longer do?"[123] Elizabeth Bell anthropomorphizes elocution, not as a "nice girl," but as the "bag lady" of performance, writing: "Elocution as resistance—as acceptable public display of the unconfined and unconstricted body; as a woman's way of perceiving and expressing emotion in a public setting; as sanctioned space for speech that contraindicated stereotypes of silent woman—flies in the face of historical creations of elocution as 'malpractice.'"[124]

From the standpoint of period purists, any modifications to elocution that emphasized its performative nature were subject to criticism, as they took it farther from its rhetorical, masculine roots; literary interpretation was preferable to anything that resembled lowbrow entertainments. The addition of music to elocutionary selections, which added needed variety in programming, fell into the latter category; Nan Johnson has identified "exercises with musical accompaniments" as one example of the gendered materials designed for female users of parlor books.[125] The fictional Marjorie reacted negatively to the poetry recited to "thumping" piano music enjoyed by local women, in spite of the fact that music, too, was considered an appropriate activity for women. At the 1895 meeting of the Elocutionists' Association, participants spoke on "the relation of statue-posing, musically-accompanied recitations and bird-notes to the art of elocution;"[126] of the three, more speakers defended musical recitation than the other two practices, but questions surrounding its appropriateness had nonetheless arisen. In 1916, Maude May Babcock grouped musical accompaniments with vocal imitations of "bells, bugles, birds, or beasts," as mere entertainment, designed to be "startling and extraordinary" and to cover speakers' inability to transmit "spiritual reality." As in acting, the danger was engaging in personal display rather than transmitting the author's voice.[127] Like Marjorie, Babcock found musical accompaniments to be a component of lower artistic forms, which endangered elocution's work toward achieving an elite cultural status: "So long as leading platform readers entertain their audiences with such elevating chanting impersonation, with a musical accompaniment . . . just so long have we a mission to set ourselves determinedly to the eradication of such performances. What recognition can we find among the cultured and learned when such exhibitions are tolerated?"[128] Today musical recitation rarely figures at all in historical accounts of elocution, because it is all too easily be lumped with the "false gods"—"statue-posing, bird-calls and imitations of children"—that supposedly brought on its degeneration and demise.[129]

## Human Beings of Terrible Veracity: The Story of Nice Girls

*The Odyssey of a Nice Girl* was not one of Suckow's most successful novels, though perhaps some of the resulting criticism was due to its refusal to romanticize women in elocution. There was no easy solution to the problems of a young woman who aspired to high culture—as Mencken wrote, "It is not correct form in Buena Vista to moon and dream"[130]—at least no solution that would not contradict the novel's realistic approach. The story's lackluster ending, Marjorie's marriage and relegation to a fruit orchard in Colorado, has left critics unenthusiastic and Suckow admirers defensive. That Marjorie, with all her dreams, was only an ordinary "nice girl" after all makes her somehow defective. "Ultimately," writes Mary Jean DeMarr, "it seems all to come to not very much."[131] Suckow admitted that "a character should have intrinsic interest as well as reality, and of that my last little heroine—if you care to call her that—has too little."[132] But Marjorie is a victim of her surroundings; as Leedice Kissane asserts, she "needs freedom to fulfill herself as an individual. In the provincial boundaries of her environment, such freedom is impossible."[133] Kissane's further observation, "that true excellence is somehow subversive,"[134] is largely correct, and in this case more so, because of the gender restrictions that Marjorie and her nonfictional counterparts faced. Mencken described Suckow's ability to "discern and evoke the eternal tragedy in the life of man;"[135] he could have more accurately written "the tragedy in the life of woman."

The strongest criticisms of *The Odyssey of a Nice Girl* were misogynistic in tone. The *New York Times* reviewer complained that "girlhood is an utterly negative theme. No woman . . . is of any positive significance apart from her relation to man and motherhood."[136] Young girls who longed for a wider cultural world were easily dismissed, relegated to lives bound by biology and patriarchy. Another reviewer predicted that the story would be a "classic for girls," and one English professor exclaimed, "A man really ought not to be reading it."[137] In contrast, critics who appreciated the novel recognized that the heroine's gender was at the root of her difficulties, difficulties also faced by other women. John Frederick found that Marjorie epitomized "the attempt of American women to find lives of their own,"[138] and acknowledged that "Ruth Suckow's women . . . are not such figures as middle-aged masculine reviewers tend to fall in love with. But they are human beings of terrible veracity. And they are human beings related in their experience to the most critical social contours of our times."[139] Many women readers must have recognized the "terrible veracity" of Marjorie's life. In 1931, Suckow received a heartfelt letter from Mildred Cook, a twenty-five-year-old librarian from Cincinnati:

Dear Miss Suckow,
   There must be a well-beaten track to your door, or at least to your mail box, by nice girls who have shared your odyssey. I am shamefaced about writing because I believe that authors should not be plagued by their fond readers. . . . I simply want to tell you, because I must, what your "Odyssey of a Nice Girl" meant to me.
   My roots are Irish, not German, planted in Ohio, not Iowa, soil. But heritage aside, I am your nice girl. I am not going to say that you have solved any problem for me, or even that you revealed me to myself. I am painfully well acquainted with myself. But no one before ever interpreted for me what I am constantly trying to synthesize into some sort of unity. . . .

> Education, they told us in school, was preparation for complete living. Now
> complete living seems as remote as it did then, and time is slipping away. . . . I
> never have much patience with books which help one to "escape." I don't want
> to escape. I want to find what seems to be escaping from me.[140]

For one reader, and probably for many others, Suckow captured the difficulties of being a woman who aspired to a wider cultural life and the yearning
for more that motivated women to look beyond the domestic sphere and their
basic education, and toward literature and the fine arts.

Cook's reaction to the novel's denouement is unknown. Perhaps she understood Marjorie's compromises as the ones that women such as herself faced.
By the time *The Odyssey of a Nice Girl* appeared, elocution was an activity
that had been popular with a previous generation and had already been, if not
abandoned, renamed as *expression* or *oral interpretation* and transformed. The
National Association of Elocutionists became the National Speech Arts Association in 1906, but had disbanded by 1917.[141] It was replaced by the National
Association of Academic Teachers of Public Speaking, founded by seventeen
men, which stressed "practical," "virile" forms of rhetorical display: persuasive
oratory, formal debate, and speech contests based on athletic models rather than
the performing arts.[142] The prevailing sense was that elocutionary performance
was an antiquated, sentimental activity better left to die unmourned. Thus, the
discipline of speech lost some of its focus on the transmission of literature and
on individual artistic performance as its central activity. All of this suggests a
deliberate break from the elocutionary activities most popular with women.

What happened to Marjorie Schoessel in Suckow's novel is what happened
to the odyssey of women's elocutionary culture. Elocution represented a careful
negotiation that enabled women to adopt performance as a mode of expression.
Female elocutionists worked to assert and maintain their link with traditional
women's roles, appearing as the "nice girl" of performance, even as they broke
the previous boundaries of women's silence. Reciting in safe venues such as
women's clubs and under the umbrellas of "literature" or "self-improvement,"
performers whose careers took them into more public spaces, such as touring
Chautauqua tents, brought the packaging of the private sphere with them (see
chapter 7). The anti-elocution reaction was not only the rejection of women's
professionalism, but also of their attempt to achieve a cultural place performing
"great art." The female elocutionist, ridiculed for her seemingly pretentious
attempt to establish herself in a masculine world, her physicality, her supposed
amateurishness, and her aspiration to represent something more, something
"real," was ultimately dismissed, and, like Marjorie, rendered voiceless. Yet
for a period, women stood alone on platforms across America and uttered that
"clear soprano note," and audiences listened.

# 2. Making Elocution Musical

## *Accompanied Recitation and the Musical Voice*

Reading and speaking become inseparably connected
with music . . . for Music is but an elegant and refined
species of elocution.
—Charles P. Bronson (1842)

I think nothing grander than beautiful, noble thoughts,
accompanied by music that is in sympathy with them.
—Marguerite A. Baker (1897)

An 1849 article in the *Home Journal* titled "New Profession for Ladies"
noted the popularity of concerts combining recitation with music, as led by
actresses Fanny Kemble and Sophie Schröder, and suggested that this might
be the ideal occupation for women for "distinction and profit."[1] Actresses had
long been musically accompanied in the theater and occasionally performed
poetic selections to music; for example, Mrs. Barnes gave William Collins's
"Ode on the Passions" in New York between 1816 and 1837, between acts or
at benefit performances.[2] With the increasing popularity of elocution, musical
accompaniment to speech could take place in a variety of new contexts. In the
1890s, anthologist Henry Davenport Northrop described the combination's
continuing appeal: "The skillful recitationist of either sex, who can express
some part of the sentiment by appropriate strains of music never fails to cap-
tivate the hearers and meet with hearty applause."[3]

Musically accompanied recitation, a largely informal arrangement in which
a previously unrelated musical composition was added to a spoken text, could
enhance the emotional impact of a performance for listeners, as well as adding variety to a solo reciter's program. The widespread availability of reciters
engaged in such unnotated practices influenced the production of melodrama
between approximately 1890 and 1930, although published scores, which
required a speaker to be musically literate, were initially programmed less

frequently.[4] Both based in performance, elocution and music were nonetheless closely linked art forms; even elocutionists who recited without music conceived of their vocal interpretation of text as a fundamentally musical act, albeit more complex and more creatively expressive than song. Elocutionists' musical recitations not only broadened the definition of what constituted melodrama, they were also a means by which female performers could exercise their creativity outside the more masculine confines of literature or musical composition.

Because the period's many "literary and musical entertainments," programs that featured both music and the spoken word, were often given in private settings or for churches, clubs, or civic organizations, printed programs for them do not always survive. Yet it is clear that music was readily available to elocutionists. Pianists were often on hand at concerts featuring reciters, and touring elocutionists appeared alongside local talent performing piano music, vocal solos, part-songs, or other instrumental music. Recitations with musical accompaniment were performed far less frequently than those without music; nonetheless, they were not uncommon. They may have been heard even more than surviving documents reveal, as programs typically did not indicate whether the pianist played *during* the poetry. Publicity flyers and programs often indicated readings with music without noting the specific compositions heard or whether accompanists improvised; in fact, programs sometimes indicate only the speaker's name and a reading or recitation, not its title, particularly for final numbers; performers were thus free to select repertoire to fit an audience's tastes or mood. Even so, it is possible to document the musical practices of the women who performed in period entertainments.

Recitation books designed for home entertainment, schools, or amateur events provided sample programs suitable for holiday celebrations or on certain topics: "love," "temperance," or "patriotism," for example. They indicated where music should occur and sometimes suggested musical numbers to be performed. A "Parlor Entertainment" in Emma Griffith Lumm's *The Twentieth-Century Speaker* (1898) features humorous and pathetic readings, a story with a moral, poetry by Longfellow acted out in charade or in costume, as well as piano, violin, and whistling selections; the program concludes with a well-known song for everyone to sing, to be capped off with refreshments and a "rollicking good time."[5] Professional elocutionists often appeared on programs that were similar in content to domestic entertainments. For example, in 1910, Detroit elocutionist Nellie Peck Saunders performed art music, including the melodramas *Das Hexenlied* by Max von Schillings and Richard Strauss's *Enoch Arden*; she described herself as "a refined artist" and noted her "reputation of giving high class programs."[6] However, the audiences she— and numerous others—entertained while touring the platform circuit were instead treated to a variety program: vocal solos, duets, and readings, some with music, demonstrating the wide range of what Saunders considered "high class."[7] Similar entertainments performed by and for children were detailed in publications specifically intended for elementary schools and churches. In the novel *Anne of Green Gables* (1908) by L. M. Montgomery, the students of Miss Stacey "get up a concert"; its choral works and vocal solo are only facets of a multidimensional event that centers on recitations and dialogues, to the excitement of the dramatically inclined Anne Shirley, who plans to "groan heartrendingly" in her recitation.[8]

The program that contained a mixture of musical selections and spoken-word performances became standard fare for American women in the nineteenth century and lasted well into the twentieth. Musical selections were often heard in an individual elocutionist's program, functioning as prelude, postlude, or interlude between numbers, providing rest for the speaker and time for audiences to reflect on a poem. Late nineteenth-century programs could contain ten or more selections, featuring multiple musicians and one or more speakers; while several texts or musical works might occasionally be given together in a small group, multimovement compositions were rarely programmed. This mixed format was typical of the longer student recitals at the Currys' School of Expression in Boston into the 1920s (and later at schools at which Curry graduates taught), although spoken numbers dominated the programming. Elocutionists sometimes gave special consideration to the overall trajectory of their programs and the relationship between the music and the poetry to be heard. An 1895 article explained how music served to introduce spoken pieces, but when "inserted between recitations, one or the other must suffer unless great care is taken to blend the numbers"; radically contrasting selections should not immediately follow one another, especially in the case of "dramatic" texts.[9] Readers who performed solo renditions of plays sometimes featured music on their programs as well. For more than two decades, the play recitals of Curry students typically opened with piano music, usually a character piece to function as an overture, though sometimes one or more songs were heard instead. When Jane Manner presented plays, her programs featured music before or after her performance or to separate the acts. The pieces played by pianist Adele Westfield, with whom Manner toured between 1905 and 1907, were sometimes considered to be background music; the *Peoria Star* recounted that Westfield "made an excellent impression when she managed to make herself heard, which wasn't often as the audience insisted on talking at the top of its lungs."[10] Elocution school programs sometimes had little or no music in them, yet the entertainments given by the students of literary societies at such institutions typically interspersed spoken word with songs or piano solos. At Northwestern's School of Oratory, music was only heard at the public readings of director Robert Cumnock as part of the festivities surrounding its yearly graduation exercises. However, from 1909 to 1911, Ethel Robinson appeared on several musical programs organized by fellow students; her scrapbook contains homemade programs listing readings and piano, voice, and violin solos.[11] In the 1890s, Emerson College's Southwick Society programs regularly featured almost as much music as speech.

At the meetings of women's clubs, recitations were likewise heard along with musical works, although programs were shorter, often half the length of a more public event. Chicago's Klio Association, founded in 1887 with the goal of self-improvement in music and literature, hosted "musicales" that featured readings as well as music, including selections by the club's chorus; at regular meetings, lectures or papers on various topics by club members alternated with music. For themed programs, music and the spoken word were related. For example, an 1897 lecture on "The Japanese" was preceded by a medley of songs from Gilbert and Sullivan's *The Mikado*; "An Afternoon with Beethoven" contained Harriet Snider's paper on the composer, as well as the "Moonlight" Sonata and "Adelaide," performed by visiting male faculty members of the Hinshaw Conservatory of Music and Dramatic Art.[12] Many clubs that did not have music as their focus frequently featured musical selections at their meetings as a matter of course, and readers were regular members of music clubs. For example, Icey Teel Harling, founder of an expression school in Davenport, Iowa, in 1918, was a member of that city's Chaminade Club for more than fifty years.[13] Thus, music's role in elocutionary events was not prescribed, but the performance of both music and text was generally expected in a variety of contexts and was largely taken for granted.

Given that music and recitation frequently alternated in performance, it was inevitable that they should sometimes be heard simultaneously. Descriptions of the addition of music to recited poetry are found in women's magazines, such as *Harper's Bazaar*, which in 1901 suggested that performances "where someone who is a good elocutionist recited to low music" were "in vogue with New York hostesses."[14] A 1904 article in the same magazine reflected on how to make social gatherings "endurable and even entertaining" by including musical recitation: "We are not all such music-lovers that we would rather listen to music than talk, but we are willing to stop talking long enough to listen at intervals to some one who has a charmingly pitched voice recite to a low, harmonious piano accompaniment a German Lied, a French chanson, or a bit from 'Hiawatha' or Browning."[15] In the 1880s and 1890s, *Werner's Voice Magazine*, the leading periodical for elocutionists, featured articles on performing to music and occasionally provided selections to recite with musical excerpts.[16] Edgar S. Werner's company also issued a book dedicated to "musical effects" in 1911; it does not contain the standard combinations most often heard on the platform or found in parlor anthologies, suggesting that the publisher believed there was a large enough market of performers reciting with music to justify issuing an entire volume of newer material.[17]

Music and elocution were combined outside of the conventions of musical notation in various ways: the texts of songs could be spoken to their accompaniments, and musical improvisation or previously composed music could be used to accompany speech. One writer described how "delicate strains of music—chords and arpeggios played soft[ly] through and between certain lines of the poem" were a pleasing effect.[18] In 1897, when *Werner's Magazine* called for opinions about the combination of recitation and music, several responses mentioned that the practice required an accompanist capable of improvising.[19] The poem "Widow Malone," published in Emma Griffith Lumm's 1898 speaker, is accompanied by the direction: "Have a trained musician improvise an accompaniment."[20] That improvisation had apparently not become entirely uncommon by time of the publication of Jane Manner's anthology, *The Silver Treasury*, in 1934—is suggested by her inclusion of Gustave Becker's essay "Recitation with Music," which describes how he had supplied improvised accompaniment "to the recitations of poems or dramatic readings," as well as by Manner's direction to improvise music for George Croly's "Belshazzar."[21] Little was documented about period improvisation, and whether such accompaniments resembled the music of melodramatic stage productions or silent film cannot be determined; however, music could be treated secondarily as background, setting the general mood, or be tailored to reflect changes in the text's narrative.

The free adaptation of known compositions into spoken performances was popular among reciters, as the simplest combinations were easily accomplished. A respondent to a reader of *Werner's Voice Magazine* searching for a teacher specializing in musical recitation questioned the need for formal instruction, as adaptations of appropriate music "would naturally suggest themselves to any good reader or teacher."[22] Reciters in a series of articles published in *Werner's Magazine* in 1897 mentioned more than sixty selections that they had performed or had heard performed with music (many of which are discussed in chapter 4).[23] Thus, there was a core repertoire of musically accompanied recitations, even though the practice remained largely unnotated. The texts that most invited the addition of music were those that contained specific musical references or included the lyrics of a song, the music of which could then be heard as accompaniment or as an interlude in the appropriate spot(s). Recitation books that included music typically only provided brief excerpts, such as songs in simple piano arrangements, for this purpose. In this way, familiar music could be used to evoke a particular situation or to represent musical events in the text. Quotations of actual songs in poems could be recited with the corresponding music; "Twickenham Ferry," mentioned by many reciters, was frequently published in anthologies with a brief line of music from the song of the same name to accompany its refrain.[24] Some elocutionists mixed song excerpts into their spoken performances and actually sang such refrains rather than reciting them to music. Because entire songs could also be recited to their accompaniments, melodramatic compositions were later issued by publishers with notated pitches in their vocal lines, so that they could be either spoken or sung, or some combination of both techniques, reflecting nineteenth-century practices.

It seems likely that the most common combinations of music and text originated from reciters themselves and that anthologies were actually documenting ongoing practices rather than creating new groupings. In Farningham's "The Drowning Singer" (also known as "The Last Hymn"), a sailor, lost at sea, sings the hymn "Jesus, Lover of My Soul," which was provided in a piano arrangement to accompany the lines in which the drowning man is singing. The poem had appeared in anthologies without music, then in later books such as *The Peerless Reciter* with the hymn, as if performing it with music had become customary.[25] Likewise, many elocutionists noted that they had Benjamin F. Taylor's poem "Money Musk" in their repertoire; however, the addition of the fiddle tune "Money Musk" was first published in Emma Dunning Banks's *Original Recitations with Lesson Talks*.[26] Werner's *Musical Effects* sometimes listed particular combinations as being in the repertoire of a specific female performer.[27]

Published scores provide some evidence for a relationship between unnotated practices and composed melodrama. Some long-standing favorites with reciters, such as Poe's "The Raven" and Longfellow's *Hiawatha*, were chosen by composers to set to music, although many texts seem never to have been previously performed to music not specifically composed for them.[28] However, the multiple arrangements for poems such as "King Robert of Sicily," culminating in the full melodramatic setting by Rossetter G. Cole in 1906, was a reflection of the ongoing popularity of reciting particular texts with music. Anthologies frequently indicated exactly where music to represent the monks' chanting in Longfellow's poem should occur and occasionally provided scores (discussed in chapter 4).[29] Less frequently were publications issued in which new poetic texts were added to well-known compositions; several piano works by Chopin were published with poetry to be spoken included above the staves, perhaps reflecting contemporary practices.[30] In addition, recitations known to have been performed with added music were sometimes published in sheet music arrangements. Owen Meredith's "Aux Italiens" was performed by elocutionists with Giuseppe Verdi's music for two decades before Charles Roberts's 1907 publication of the poem accompanied by the excerpt from *Il*

*Trovatore* mentioned in its text; Roberts had previously performed the poem with a string quartet in 1886, and Gustav Kobbé described his own informal arrangement in *Good Housekeeping*.[31] Composer Edgar Stillman Kelley arranged the "statue scene" from Shakespeare's *A Winter's Tale* to Beethoven's "Moonlight" Sonata; its 1908 publication probably resulted from a commission from Werner.[32] Advertisements mentioned that "Miss Stella King and other prominent reciters" were already performing the scene to Beethoven's music.[33] If unable to locate appropriate music for spoken selections, reciters could again turn to Werner's company, which publicized that it could provide "pieces with music written to order."[34]

## Training the Musical Voice: Pitch in Elocutionary Style

While it is possible to reconstruct the musical settings for recitation, it is more difficult to recapture the performance style of the speakers, which, according to period elocution textbooks, would have had marked elements of pitch as well as rhythm. Authors frequently resorted to musical analogies, musical terminology, and even musical notation in order to explain the contours of speech; indeed, in 1842 Charles Bronson claimed that music was actually a form of elocution.[35] Most elocution texts of the second half of the nineteenth century, drawing on the seminal writings of James Rush, contained substantial treatment of pitch, using the term *modulation*, not in the harmonic sense, but instead to convey characteristics such as "melody (effect on the ear of a succession of vocal notes), pitch (elevation or depression of tone), slides (ascending and descending inflection), cadence (tone with which the sentence terminates), and time (rate of speech and use of pause)."[36]

Numerous writers recommended that instructors use music pedagogically, relying on the piano or another instrument to demonstrate pitch to student reciters.[37] A typical exercise was the repetition of a sentence up the diatonic scale, sometimes found in children's textbooks, including the readers by Charles Sanders and the famous McGuffey.[38] Robert Fulton and Thomas Trueblood provided musical notes colored black to indicate that they were to be sung, followed by the same pitches in white to be spoken for practice.[39] Few authors made references to specific compositions; however, in 1899 William Chamberlain provided passages from Mendelssohn's *Elijah* and Schubert's *Erlkönig* (in English) to demonstrate intervallic content. He advised students to sing the examples and then read their texts with *similar pitch*, disregarding the notated rhythmic patterns, presumably in favor of more natural speech rhythms.

While all speech has fluctuating pitch, the degrees of specificity in elocution books suggest that in practice, reciters employed pitch in a stylized manner.[40]

Many authors found that describing the general ranges of low, middle, and high sufficed, but others wrote pointedly about musical scales and the size and quality of intervals. The influential James Rush asserted that "the rise and fall of the voice in speaking are designated by fixed intervals."[41] Chamberlain indicated the exact central pitch of men's and women's voices and the required high and low "notes" of their speaking voices.[42] Bronson believed that nature had provided "just the thing" for speaking and singing in the diatonic scale, "on which some one of whose notes or tones the pitches of the voice are always found."[43] Henry N. Day required that students be familiar with intervals: major and minor seconds, major and minor thirds, and the tritone, fifth, and octave, and be able to produce them vocally at will.[44]

When elocutionary training emphasized literary interpretation more than the physiological basis for speaking, pitch took on specific emotional content. Bronson described the first three pitches of the scale as appropriate for private conversation or grave and solemn subjects, the middle of the scale useful for imparting information, and the upper three pitches for impassioned words and phrases in which feeling ruled over thought. E. A. Ott provided a level of emotion for each pitch and suggested a corresponding emotional content as follows:[45]

| | | |
|---|---|---|
| 8 | Very high | Excitement |
| 7 | High | Enthusiasm |
| 6 | Slightly raised | Pleasure |
| 5 | Middle | Calmness |
| 4 | Slightly lowered | Approaches seriousness |
| 3 | Low | Seriousness |
| 2 | Very Low | Profundity |
| 1 | Extremely Low | Solemnity |

Authors sometimes distinguished between the use of major and minor scales while speaking. Robert Cumnock called for minor scales and chromatic intervals such as half steps in works of pathos, such as Poe's "The Bells." In his frequently reprinted *Choice Readings*,[46] particular intervals are required for certain kinds of poetic passages: regular reading requires slides of a third, elevated impassioned reading the slide of a fifth or even an octave. Sentences close with the "triad of cadences"—not really a triad, but stepwise movement from the third degree to tonic.[47] Few writers are as specific about pitch, but many make comments about pitch's relationship to text content; for example, Bailey noted that one should glide up on a negative idea and slide down on a positive one.[48] Yet another resemblance to singers' vocal practices is found in pedagogical books' descriptions of *tremolo*, a quavering not unlike vibrato deemed appropriate for passages of sorrow, terror, and distress.[49]

Elocutionists devised various notational systems to indicate pitch.[50] One means was to print the words pointing upward or downward on the page to indicate melodic shape or inflection (figure 2.1).

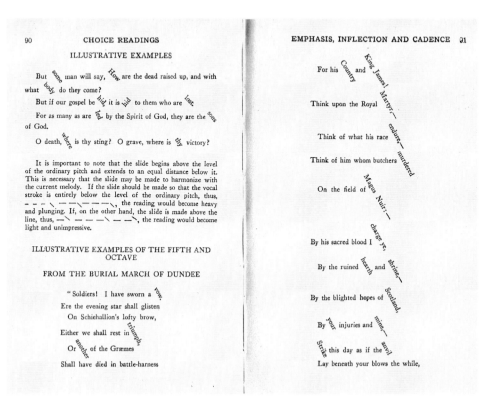

Figure 2.1. Excerpts from Corinthians and William Edmondstoune Aytoun, "The Burial March of Dundee," in Robert McLean Cumnock, *Choice Readings for Public and Private Entertainments and for the Use of Schools, Colleges, and Public Readers, with Elocutionary Advice* (Chicago: A. C. McClurg, 1914), 90–91.

Rush's system, reproduced by numerous authors, employed a combination of musical and graphic symbols. In William Russell's 1882 chart (figure 2.2), noteheads indicate pitch, and tails of varying lengths suggest the intervallic length of the vocal slide. Likewise, Alexander Melville Bell used inflection marks with dots to show the size of spoken intervals.[51]

A staff could hold these symbols or the actual text (figures 2.3 and 2.4).

Figure 2.2. Vocal slides in William Russell, *Orthophony; or, Vocal Culture* (Boston: Houghton Mifflin, 1882), 149.

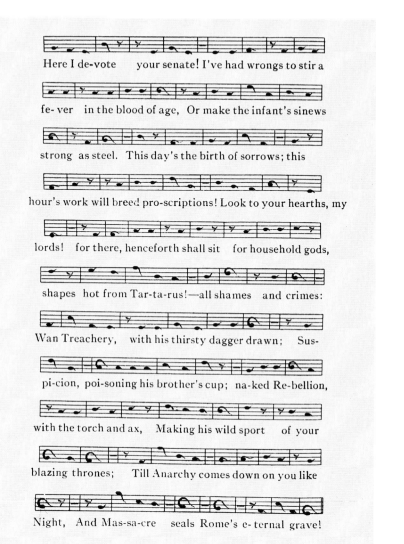

Figure 2.3. George Croly, "Catiline's Defiance," in John R. Scott, *The Technic of the Speaking Voice* (Columbia, MO: E. W. Stephens, 1915), 340.

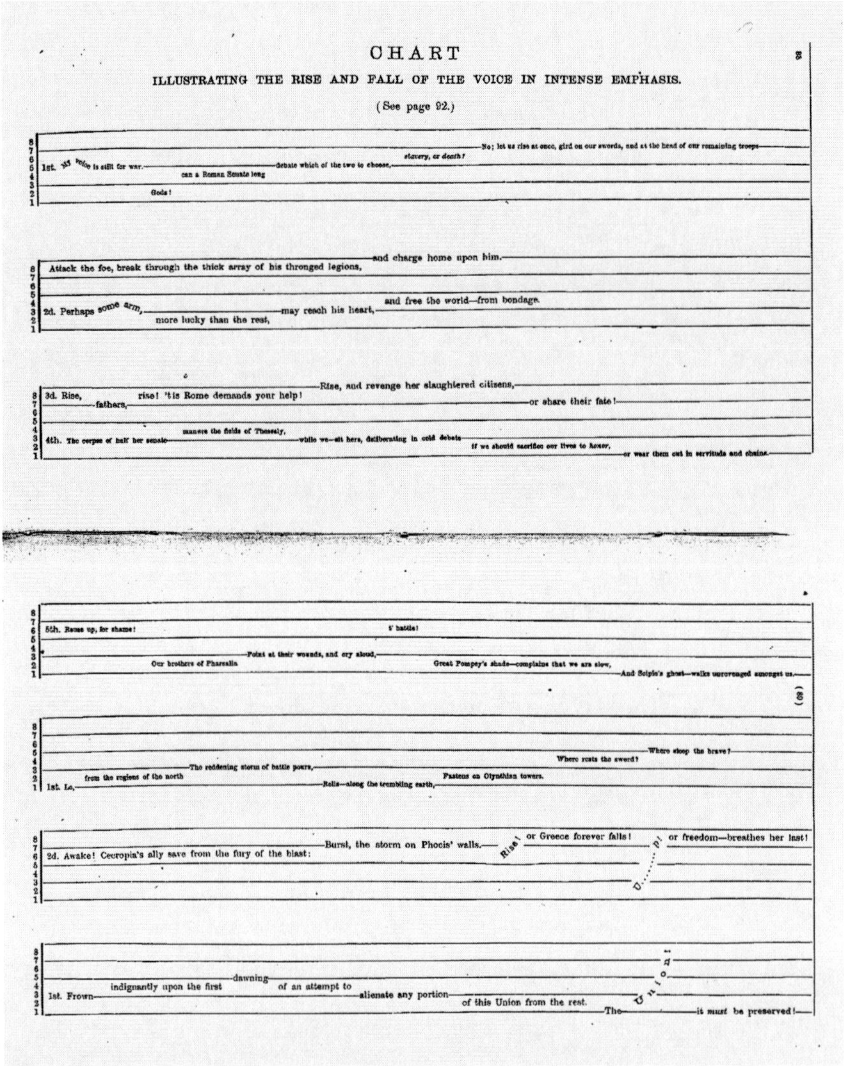

Figure 2.4. Joseph Addison, excerpt from *Cato*, in C. P. Bronson, *Manual of Elocution: Embracing the Philosophy of Vocalization*, ed. Laura M. Bronson (Louisville, KY: John P. Morton, 1873), 88–89.

Even without graphic notation, phrases could be printed with the number of the correct pitch of the scale required, as in figure 2.5, which provides the instruction, "Construct a scale and place the words on it as indicated."[52]

**311.** INTONATIONS and MELODY— These examples are given as general guides, the figures referring to the notes in the Diatonic Scale. 1. (4) But, (5) from the (4) tomb, (5) the (4) voice of (5) nature (6) cries, (6) And, (5) in our (4) ashes, (5) live (4) their won (3) ted (2) fires. 2. But (5) yonder comes (4) rejoicing in the (6) EAST, (5) The (4) powerful (3) King of (2) day. 3. (6) AWAKE! (8) ARISE! (6) or (5) be (3) forever (2) *fallen*. 4. (3) He expired in a (5) *victualling* house, (4) which I hope (5) *I* (3) shall (2) not. 7. (5) Fair (6) *angel*, thy (5) *desire*, which tends to (6) KNOW The *works* of (5) *God*, doth (4) merit (3) *praise*. 8. (5) *Such* (4) honors Ilion to (6) HER (5) *lover* paid, And (5) peaceful slept (4) the mighty (3) Hector's (2) shade. NOTE. Construct a scale and place the words on it as indicated.

Figure 2.5. The *Iliad* (excerpt) from Pope's *Homer*, in [C. P.] Bronson, *Abstract of Elocution and Music, in Accordance with the Principles of Physiology and the Laws of Life, for the Development of Body and Mind* (Auburn, NY: Henry Oliphant, 1842), 43–44.

That some elocution instructors were not trained in music may explain their reluctance to engage in musical notation. Others found the practice less than useful; R. F. Brewer wrote that "drawing up artificial scales of pitch" had "little practical utility" because modulation was "entirely a matter of cultured taste."[53] Regardless, standard notation would not have been able to adequately capture the subtleties of pitches not conveniently located within musical scales, subtleties that many authors acknowledged existed.[54] A few writers, including Fulton and Trueblood, recommended that students transcribe speech using musical notation in order to train their ears and voice;[55] Katherine Jewell Everts suggested marking texts with pitch letters.[56] In 1915, John Rutledge Scott provided a musical transcription of a performance by Helen Potter, which he had heard two evenings in a row (figure 2.6). Scott found that

> the melody conforms to a single definite key, and most of the syllables are upon singing notes. 'Year,' '-way,' and 'field' are sung. 'Down,' '-nie,' second line, and the first '-nie' of the call, are protracted radicals; the vowel being held on its

opening pitch as a singing note, and then, without break, running downward in a smooth, deliberate concrete to a vanish. 'O-o-o-o-o' is after a similar pattern; but the first radical is a pure singing note, smoothly joining the second note, a protracted radical like those mentioned. . . . 'Out' was one time given on the lower note of its alternative notation, and again on the upper.

The very long quantity of the protracted-radical syllables compelled the employment of the four-four measure of music.[57]

Because the poem that Potter recited is strophic, Scott went on to describe the similarities in performance for its subsequent verses, with changes of "force, volume, and fervor"; he suggested the rise of a third for "O-o-o-o-o" in the third verse, and extending the length of the word for an additional measure. He indicated that the phrase "But Nannie did not reply" was "to be half-sung, half-spoken." Potter's interpretation was therefore a model to be imitated by aspiring reciters, though not slavishly. Scott wrote, "As repetition gives familiarity and ease, additional eccentricities of melody will probably suggest themselves."[58]

Authors with musical training, such as William Chamberlain and George Raymond, produced descriptions a bit more decipherable than convoluted graphics. However, many pedagogues seem to have been struggling to put into language what would be more easily teachable through audible demonstration. Reciting speech was described as more complex than singing, which required only the simplest regular motions from pitch to pitch, not spontaneous and continuous vocal movement. Chamberlain wrote, "To create a melody or adapt a rhythm from one's own insight into the significance and requirements of the passage, is higher art than to follow a definitely prescribed form."[59] Ott agreed: "The skillful speaker . . . at once creates and delivers the melody. His art is two-fold, and therefore more difficult than that of the singer."[60] Anna Russell wrote simply, "The art of song is not sweeter than the voice of eloquence."[61]

Despite occasional complaints about a "sing-songy" style or "a kind of singing whine,"[62] more elocutionists warned against monotony of pitch than an excess of it; issues surrounding pitch often arose in discussions of melodrama. Banks described how to "intone the words in time to the music" and warned against singing. Some writers found that pitched speech conflicted with musical accompaniment. Edgar Stillman Kelley disliked recitations with music "when the speaker permits his voice to dwell on a monotone, thus producing most undesirable discords."[63] May Donnally Kelso also protested that, "in reading, the key constantly changes, and this more rapidly than any man-made instrument can follow," resulting in "discordant overtones" or, in her opinion, "noise."[64] In his melodrama article in *Grove's Dictionary*, William Rockstro described the difficulties in "modulating the voice": "The general temptation is to let it glide, insensibly, into some note sounded by the orchestra . . . the effect produced resembles that of a Recitative, sung hideously out of tune."[65]

It was in the fall of the year, and the storm was beating

down on Nan-n i e, away out in the

field. And my son he went to the door, and lifted up his

voice:— 'Nan-n i e! O—o—o—o—o Nannie!'

But Nannie did not re- p l y.

Figure 2.6. John Scott's transcription of Helen Potter reciting "The Sheep's Sermon" in *The Technic of the Speaking Voice* (Columbia, MO: E. W. Stephens, 1915), 380.

In contrast, former singer David Bispham was praised because his speech did not "clash with the music,"[66] and Chicago elocutionist Lydia Bell worked with her accompanist, who performed music specifically based on the "motives" of her speaking voice.[67] Further evidence of the dominance of spoken pitch in melodramatic performances is Cora Worrell-Alford's suggestion that accompanists might have to transpose music to fit the range of the reciter's voice.[68]

What was described in elocution manuals is borne out in early recordings of actors.[69] Perhaps the best available example of contemporary melodramatic vocal practices is a 1913 performance by Percy Hemus of Max Heinrich's setting of Poe's "The Raven."[70] Hemus utilizes a style between speech and singing, adopting something even closer to singing for important phrases, such as the final stanza's "shall be lifted" (with ascending pitch to create word painting) and the work's refrain, "Quoth the Raven, 'Nevermore!'"[71] The speaker's grief over "Lenore" and his increasing hysteria about the ominous raven allow Hemus to engage in elocutionary extremes, with expressive use of pitch and tremolo; the latter occurs in the description of the speaker's lost love, "[whom the] angels name Lenore—/ Nameless here for evermore." That Hemus's performance practices are not merely an isolated example is suggested by Ludwig Wüllner's 1933 recording of Max von Schillings's *Das Hexenlied*. As described by Edward Kravitt, Wüllner bridges "the gap between the spoken and sung word" using portamentos, sustaining vowels, and "speaking upon actual pitches, sometimes to the contour of the melody in the music." The result is, like Hemus's recording, a performance marked by "sheer intensity" and "in a manner that any modern listener would find extravagant."[72]

The reforms advocated by early twentieth-century elocutionists emphasized the expression of literary meaning over the production of musical sounds, though it is difficult to establish when pitched techniques were relinquished for a more natural speaking style.[73] The technical details of mid-nineteenth-century elocution manuals were largely abandoned in the parlor books marketed to amateur performers at the turn of the century. However, elocutionists had been trained in practices that made the speaking voice into a refined and expressive musical instrument, capable of subtleties of pitch, melody, and rhythm. Because spoken passages had an audibly *musical* basis in performance, accompanied recitation was viewed as the successful fusion of two *musical* elements, a "hybrid art."[74]

## Jane Manner's "Readings with Music" and the Creation of Melodramatic Performance

No recordings of Jane Manner, with her "hauntingly lovely voice,"[75] are known to survive, so it is impossible to know if her performances resembled those of nineteenth-century elocutionists or whether they changed over the course of her four decades as a reader (figure 2.7). Manner was only one of more than a hundred female reciters who featured music in their programs; she was by no means the most famous, although the length of her professional life—and that she performed the full range of melodramatic approaches available to reciters—makes her career particularly informative about contemporary practices. At the same time, Manner's repertoire is representative of her personal background and taste, which tended more toward European classical music than that of many of her contemporaries.

Manner's upbringing as the child of highly cultured German-speaking Jewish immigrants prepared her for her lifelong engagement with literature and music. Her rabbi father and schoolteacher mother both wrote poetry; Louise Mannheimer was active in Jewish women's organizations and was the composer of a published song.[76] Her daughter earned degrees at Hebrew Union College and the University of Cincinnati, and it is probable that, like other members of her family, Manner had some musical training; she attended concerts and expressed her opinions about compositions in her diary.[77] Manner's heritage led her to recite German poetry for Cincinnati's German-speaking literary societies and to program works by Jewish authors. *Merely Mary Ann*, which she gave over sixty times, was by the Jewish author Israel Zangwill, but the story of the love life of a struggling composer, lacking references to Jewish culture, could be as easily programmed for the Daughters of the American Revolution (DAR) as for the Temple Sisterhood.[78] Manner changed her name from Jennie Mannheimer to Jane Manner in 1918, presumably because of the

Figure 2.7. Jane Manner (Jennie Mannheimer). Courtesy of the Jacob Rader Marcus Center of the American Jewish Archives, Cincinnati, Ohio, americanjewisharchives.org.

anti-German sentiment surrounding World War I, as she continued to perform for Jewish audiences.

Music was regularly featured on Manner's programs. The 1890s programs on which she or her students performed consisted of alternating musical numbers and spoken-word selections, from ten to twenty or so in all. In addition to presentations of plays with music, including Shakespeare's *A Midsummer Night's Dream* with Mendelssohn's incidental music, she also performed large-scale melodramatic compositions such as Félicien David's *Le Désert*,

Edvard Grieg's *Bergliot*, and *Hiawatha's Wooing* by Rossetter G. Cole, all
before around 1914. One might expect Manner to have programmed Tennyson's popular *Enoch Arden* in the setting by Strauss, but she did not, perhaps
because it was the specialty of a fellow faculty member at the Cincinnati School
of Expression, Mathilda Stuebing. But large-scale musical works made only
a few appearances on her programs, and Manner more often spoke the texts
of songs to music or adopted known compositions as accompaniments for
her recitations. Although she most often appeared with a pianist, Manner
occasionally performed with a mechanical pianola, an instrument used by
other performers as well.[79]

One long-standing part of Manner's repertoire was Goethe's "Erlkönig,"
performed between 1890 and 1929 in either German or English translation,
depending on her audience, sometimes with Franz Schubert's music.[80] On occasion she used Franz Liszt's arrangement, which incorporates Schubert's vocal
melody into the piano part and includes the text above the music, making the
score resemble that of a melodrama.[81] Another of Manner's most frequently
programmed poems was James Whitcomb Riley's "Old Sweetheart of Mine";
in spite of the five melodramatic versions of this text published between 1906
and 1921, Manner preferred reciting it to Robert Schumann's *Träumerei*, doing so for approximately thirty years.[82] The selection of a classical musical
accompaniment for the poem not only set the emotional tone of the reading,
but it also had the potential to raise the status of the performed combination to
"high art." Although some speech professionals believed that the addition of
music to recitations lowered them from literature to entertainment, Manner's
longtime use of music by canonic classical composers with texts of varying
literary merit created distinctive hybrids, the music of which had a significant
role in determining their place on the cultural spectrum.

Two sources—Manner's handwritten book of "Readings with Music" and
her published anthology, *The Silver Treasury*—reflect her own performance
history and provide evidence for the range of word-music combinations available to performers (listed in the appendix). Between 1930 and 1934, Manner
copied out "Readings with Music" into a diary; its first fifty pages contain
thirty handwritten poems, most followed by indications of the corresponding music, typically brief piano pieces that could have easily been adapted as
accompaniments, such as Liszt's *Liebestraum*, Mendelssohn's *Spring Song*, or
Chopin's Berceuse, op. 57.[83] However, almost as many are songs, for which the
text is meant to be spoken, rather than sung, including Carrie Jacobs-Bond's
"Just A-Wearyin' for You" and Liza Lehmann's "There Are Fairies at the
Bottom of Our Garden."[84] The overlap of poems with those in *The Silver
Treasury*, which appeared around the time Manner finished copying texts into
the volume, suggests she was compiling these combinations for publication;

Gustave Becker's essay on melodrama that she also included later became the introduction for *The Silver Treasury*'s readings with music. However only half of the published anthology's eighteen selections come from the handwritten book. Pencil notations in the German version of "Erlkönig" indicating the number of beats rest between verses or at the ends of lines suggest that Manner actually utilized the earlier volume in performance without any need for a musical score.

A large portion of the poems with music in *The Silver Treasury* came from Manner's own performance experience. They included selections from early in her career—"Erlkönig" and her mother's poem "Segen Wirkend,"[85] as well as texts popularly performed with music before World War I—for example, "Aux Italiens," "Sandalphon," and "The Raven"; for the latter two, Manner suggested melodramatic settings published decades earlier.[86] The volume's less commonly heard poetry either shows Manner updating accompanied recitation repertoire or reflects newer changes to her programming. In the early 1930s she advertised her availability to teach "Readings with Music," and 1934 programs show her students performing four of her publication's selections with music.[87] Two poems—Longfellow's "The Bridge" and "The Day Is Done"—were spoken by a soloist and together by multiple students, reflecting the trend of choral speaking (discussed in chapter 8).[88]

Manner's published suggestions for musical accompaniments represent the complete range of melodramatic performance styles in her career and those of other reciters. For five texts she indicated published melodramas: For *Hiawatha's Wooing*, Manner recommended Rossetter G. Cole's setting, which she had performed in the teens. Although Manner had often performed plays with added music, only one scene from Henrik Ibsen's *Peer Gynt* is listed along with Edvard Grieg's incidental music. Four songs are included in the anthology: "Erlkönig," Mendelssohn's "Auf Flügeln des Gesanges," and a German spinning song, all found in the handwritten volume as well; Henry Bishop's "Home, Sweet Home" is a new addition. Seven poems are to be combined with well-known Romantic pieces such as Camille Saint-Saëns's *The Swan* and Antonín Dvořák's *Songs My Mother Taught Me*, and Psalm 23 is accompanied with the Largo ("Ombra mai fù") from *Xerxes* by George Frideric Handel; in these cases instrumental music is to be added in the fashion common at the end of the previous century. The accompaniments' slow tempos prevent them from becoming distractions from the spoken text; according to Manner, they "serve as background to help the mood of the reading." For Longfellow's "The Day Is Done," Manner suggested a setting by Wilhelm Schäffer, which was specifically composed for her.[89] Its musical accompaniment is minimal, so as not to get in the way of the spoken text: the poem is heard over sustained or slowly moving chords; more active arpeggiation only appears between lines

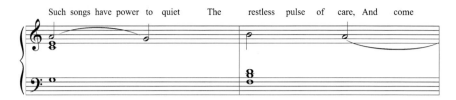

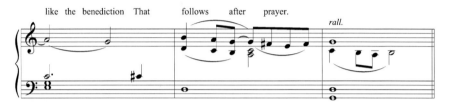

Example 2.1.
THE DAY IS DONE, mm. 42–46
Words by HENRY WADSWORTH LONGFELLOW
Music by WILHELM SCHÄFFER
Copyright ©MCMXXXII (Renewed) M. WITMARK & SONS
All Rights Assigned to and Controlled by ALFRED MUSIC
All Rights Reserved
Used by Permission of ALFRED MUSIC

of text (example 2.1). As this differs from published melodramas with a more substantial musical basis, the piece may be closer to improvisatory practices.

*The Silver Treasury*, in conjunction with Manner's handwritten book, documents one woman's repertoire and illuminates the full range of ways in which music could be added to performances of poetry during her lifetime. Manner's choice of accompaniments reflects the late nineteenth-century practice of using known musical works to enhance the evocative qualities of a spoken text. Manner grouped the different approaches to musical accompaniment together. She, like her contemporaries, clearly considered all of them valid methods of creating melodrama—one could use a published melodramatic setting by a composer, add a well-known composition, recite a song, or have a pianist improvise; these methods all constituted "readings with music," and were part of one continuum, not conceptually different approaches. Although Manner leaned toward classical character pieces as accompaniments, making her offerings more representative of "high art" than many other women's performances, her repertoire nonetheless demonstrates the long-standing flexibility toward text-music combinations, as it also included popular poetry, songs such as "Home, Sweet Home," and amalgamations that might seem unusual to modern sensibilities. As in Longfellow's "The Day Is Done," Manner was willing to "read from some humbler poet" who "heard in his soul the music / Of wonderful melodies."[90]

Manner's long and multifaceted career may have been exceptional, yet many other female elocutionists engaged in the same range of approaches to musical accompaniments. Other performers may not have recited to music frequently enough to require that they copy their selections into a single volume—numerous elocutionists only counted one or two accompanied recitations among their repertoire—but many drew on both notated melodramas and unnotated readings with music. Mrs. Carl Thayer, a reciter from Minneapolis, indicated that she gave "all the well known musical melodramas" (*The Raven, King Robert of Sicily, Enoch Arden*) as well as spoken songs and humorous musical recitations. Detroit performer Franc Adele Burch advertised Strauss's *Enoch Arden* as well as a version of the sentimental favorite "The Volunteer Organist" with four added tunes.[91] In the list of pianologues on Virginia Powell's 1915 flyer, published melodramas are interspersed with songs, presumably spoken to music. Also listed are texts for which no known accompaniments exist; these would require either improvisation or the addition of an unrelated musical work, practices in line with Manner's suggestions. Recordings of two poems by Eugene Field made by Sally Hamlin in 1918 are representative of accompanied recitation practices. They both conclude with Hamlin reciting in rhythm to lullaby accompaniment played by harp: "The Sugarplum Tree" is heard to the opening of Schumann's *Träumerei*, and when "mother sings" at the close of "Wynken, Blynken, and Nod," Hamlin recites to the Welsh song "All through the Night."[92] The diverse approaches to melodrama undertaken by Manner and other women were thus typical of period practices that both transcended notated musical scores and were not shaped by perceived boundaries between highbrow and lowbrow culture.

## Female Reciters, Accompanied Recitation, and the Work Concept

Despite the emergence of a body of repertoire commonly heard with music, female performers who regularly programmed accompanied recitations like Manner appear to have generated many of their creations through their own experimentation. Melodrama's various forms were not regularly taught in elocution schools, which generally found musical accompaniments unnecessary or unwelcome to their literary aspirations. Mrs. Rossleene Hofus-Powell taught "musically-accompanied selections" at the Cleveland School of Elocution and Oratory, but the school was small, graduating fewer than twenty students in 1894.[93] Emerson College's catalogs listed "Music in Selections," but only in a long list of topics in its "Platform Art" course designed to teach students to produce "entertainments of all kinds." The Emerson programs that featured music and recitation—student recitals and graduation exercises, the entertainments of the Southwick Literary Society, and programs by the Alumni Association and College Clubs—show performers reciting between musical selections, but rarely *with* them. Many women began to experiment with music only after they graduated; musically accompanied performances more often appear in alumnæ activities than school programs.[94] Not all musical recitations met with success. Montana elocutionist Ellen Decker Hall recalled her frustrations while touring, as she "practiced for hours with accompanists, being unable to inspire them with sympathy, appearing before my audience utterly worn out, and giving my numbers without music rather than inflict discord on a refined audience."[95]

Period writings indicate an underlying discomfort with the combination of text and music. Some of the difficulties were purely acoustical. Elocutionists complained of thick-textured accompaniments and pianists playing too loudly; one listener acknowledged, "I don't understand what the reader is trying to say on account of the noise the piano makes."[96] Other concerns were related to overall quality—added music was no substitute for effective recitation, and poor performances would "admit neither of good music nor of good reciting."[97] In his 1922 defense of reading to music, John Seaman Garns expressed exasperation with performers' inappropriate addition of music to prose or to texts that were already fundamentally musical and needed no accompaniment instead of to more appropriate genres, such as rhythmic narrative poetry or comedic works. He also believed that some spoken songs were better off in their original, strictly musical renditions.[98] Music could easily get in the way of the transmission of the meaning of the text and create "more sound than sense," or even work against its meaning.[99] L. B. C. Josephs recalled one woman's performance of "The Charge of the Light Brigade" in which she expressionlessly intoned, "Cannon to the right of them," followed by a bass drum struck on the right side of the stage: "This, instead of being a help to the interpretation of the poem, must have set others thinking, as it did me, that the drum would not have time to get around to the other side of the stage to be at the left of them."[100] However, even performers who did not approve of musically accompanied recitation or decreed that the practice was not, in fact, elocution, acknowledged its popularity with audiences, and that it was able to effect emotional reactions in listeners; Worrell-Alford described how "the audience is magnetized and listens with breathless attention."[101]

Garns recognized the sheer complexity involved in "artistic reading to music," which made "tremendous demands upon the artist."[102] Like other speech professionals, he called for a "unified whole" created by "an assisting musician who is part and parcel of the ensemble effect and a reader who senses musical values. . . . The musician must know the literature and appreciate its spirit, as the reader must know the music to the extent of having every progression, interlude and rest in mind."[103] Elocutionists acknowledged that musical recitation required considerable rehearsal to coordinate successfully, although when it worked, it could be both artistic and emotionally powerful. Laura Aldrich found that the combination of voice and music could claim a place as worthy as the masculine realm of oratory: "When, however, the music forms but a background for a rich, harmonious voice, when the accompaniment is subordinated to the thought expressed, and the component parts are so well blended that the listener is conscious only of the beauty of the whole, then, in my estimation, the musically accompanied recitation deserves to be ranked next to oratory, the highest form of the 'greatest of all arts.'"[104] Nonetheless, male elocutionists who performed with music sometimes adopted a defensive tone, as if their professional status and artistic validity was threatened by women's involvement in this activity. Bispham acknowledged that in general, women were more inclined to recite with music, although he condescendingly believed their voices to be "less effective in speech than in song," and he stereotyped women as "carried away by impulse"—as opposed to men, who would "think twice before embarking upon so unusual and so technical a venture"; women supposedly suffered from more enthusiasm than their abilities could support.[105] In 1897 Leonora Oberndorfer recounted a Texas elocutionists' convention at which male "theoretical elocutionists" discounted the musical recitations of young women: "They did not recite, but they were presidents of colleges and knew all about it . . . but never had any experience except that of a platform, with beautiful young ladies whom they instructed,—they came to the conclusion that while it [musical recitation] was a pretty background and might help a struggling artist to obtain an audience, still it should not be classed with elocution."[106] Because music, like elocution, was an art form that had come to be considered feminine, it further feminized elocution through elevating the level of emotion in the performance and its audience. Becker's essay in *The Silver Treasury* distinguishes between the intellectually perceived spoken word and the physical power of music, creating "sympathetic vibrations . . . even without readily definable or concrete significance,"[107] a mind/body dichotomy redolent of a masculine/feminine divide.

In spite of its emotive power, accompanied recitation occupied an uncomfortable place somewhere between music and elocution, disavowed as a worthy representative of either art form. Just as some in the field found that music prevented spoken selections from achieving the true status of elocution, musicians believed that the combination of the spoken word with previously composed music, no matter how effective, could not be considered in the same category with melodramatic compositions by men, which were often cited (sometimes with ancient Greeks' or troubadours' practices) as justification for the use of music at all. British composer Stanley Hawley, whose melodramas were marketed in America by Werner, complained that the practice of stringing together popular tunes to accompany recitation was not the same as these works and could never be considered serious art.[108] Even accompanying text with music by European classical composers as Manner did was insufficient to raise musical recitation to a higher cultural status.

Accompanied recitation might now best be described as having been something between a musical composition and a genre of performed literature. However, in spite of its literary roots, women's practice of reciting with music ultimately challenged the concepts surrounding the idea of the musical work. For instance, Strauss's melodramatic setting of Tennyson's *Enoch Arden* (discussed in chapter 4) is unquestionably considered to be a musical work; however, for musicians the addition of new texts to previously composed pieces by Strauss would not be, even if performed by the same artists in the same venue. Neither would the recitation of *Enoch Arden* to another musical excerpt, no matter how appropriate, typically be considered to be a musical composition, despite its similarity to the genre of melodrama. As period critics attested, music added to spoken poetry might remain uncoordinated, lacking any cohesion with the subtleties of poetic structure and narrative—unlike the complexities of a composition such as *Enoch Arden*, established in and accurately reproduced through a notated score. Historical evidence suggests that at least some accompaniments used by reciters had a level of coordination similar to that of published melodramas, if more than just a few pianists monitored the keys in which they played so as not to clash with reciters' pitched tones or drew on motivic material drawn from the sounds of their voices. Nonetheless, for the elocutionist, the text with music, rather than the music itself, defined the work. Although this combination of literature and music was readily acknowledged to be a performance and even a literary work, it would not, for many, constitute an actual musical work, and did not, during its era. The lack of this designation was, in part, influenced by the gender of the performers involved.

In the late nineteenth century, the definition of the work in Western art music was tied to the idea of the composer as the dominant creative force, producing and controlling a piece of art.[109] But in the case of musically accompanied recitation, the impetus for the work came from the performer(s), most often women such as Manner, who made creative decisions about when and how text and music would interact, resulting in artistic hybrids that she performed throughout her career. Just as women made musical interpretations of language using the pitches and tone qualities of their voices, their addition of musical accompaniments shaped listeners' perceptions of the texts they performed. While not all such combinations were aesthetically successful, they nonetheless allowed female performers to take control over the artwork. By selecting the music themselves, women exerted their artistic power beyond the traditional boundaries of the discipline of elocution established by men and began to usurp the place customarily held by the composer. Belittled by elocutionary purists, musical accompaniments nonetheless assisted female performers in their aim to be the primary force in interpreting the words of the poet and, ultimately, to express themselves.

# 3. Reading the Fairies

## Shakespeare in Concert
## with Mendelssohn's
## A Midsummer Night's Dream

*Seen* the Midsummer Night's Dream can never be,
save by the mind's eye.
—*Athenæum* (1852)

How our hearts glowed and trembled as she read
Interpreting by tones the wondrous pages
Of the great poet who foreruns the ages
—Henry Wadsworth Longfellow

The work that represented the pinnacle of female elocutionists' combination of spoken word and music was Shakespeare's *A Midsummer Night's Dream*, performed as a solo reading and accompanied by Felix Mendelssohn's incidental music, beginning in the early 1850s. Shakespeare was ubiquitous in the world of elocution. Selections from his plays were regularly included in its publications, and elocution schools all taught Shakespeare, offering one or more courses devoted to his works.[1] However, the combination of *A Midsummer Night's Dream* with Mendelssohn's music had theatrical origins, and concert performances represented the spoken word's entrance into musical settings, rather than the reverse. Throughout the nineteenth century, Mendelssohn's music for the play was immensely popular in theaters and concert halls, both his overture, op. 21, composed in 1826, and the incidental music created for the 1843 Berlin production of Ludwig Tieck. Mendelssohn's music became inseparably associated with period theatrical productions; between 1833 and 1957, few British versions of *A Midsummer Night's Dream* took place without Mendelssohn's music,[2] and American performances, modeled after English stagings, followed suit.[3] By 1882, Henry C. Lunn, writing about Shakespeare and Mendelssohn, could claim that "the work of the poet seems now almost incomplete without the addition of the work of the musician."[4]

In the late nineteenth century, spoken-word performances were more frequent in concerts that did not feature professional orchestras, which were capable of programming events consisting entirely of music. Variety concerts made up of multiple short selections were the more common venue for elocutionists, who performed their usual repertoire once or twice between musical numbers; an 1894 Canadian article claimed that a concert without an elocutionist was rare.[5] At a charity concert in Lancaster, Kentucky, in 1898, three women gave readings between ten vocal and piano solos, vocal quartets, and selections by an amateur brass band.[6] A concert offered at Boston's Tremont Temple around 1880 featured an organist, the Swedish Lady Quartette, and a reader, Laura Dainty, who gave three pairs of readings, including "Kentucky Belle," "A Very Naughty Girl's View of Life," and "The Maiden Martyr."[7] In most cases, speakers' selections had no relationship to a concert's music and were simply designed to provide the widest range of entertainment; touring elocutionists often shared platforms with local musical talent, so any coordination of music and texts was unlikely. When elocutionists appeared at civic or patriotic events, they would, of course, recite something appropriate to the occasion.

The less-often-heard incidental music from plays was one of the few instances in which a solo speaker might interact directly with an orchestra, allowing concert audiences to understand the dramatic context for the music heard. Michael Pisani has documented an increase in incidental music by major composers, music that could be performed apart from theatrical productions; speakers enabled conductors to program melodramatic sections of a score for the stage, which would otherwise have been omitted.[8] Shortened texts or summarizations of plays' action were frequently used in place of complete scripts in order to make performances a manageable length. Reviewers sometimes complained about an excess of text in place of music at a concert, but when plays were abridged, they might find the amount of text insufficient to make a plot comprehensible. Nonetheless, the solo performance of an entire play was an act of elocutionary virtuosity, and benefit performances sometimes included actresses reading plays with incidental music, in hopes that the dramatic addition would attract larger audiences. American and British reciters performed a small body of dramatic works with music in concerts, experimenting with readings accompanying Carl Maria von Weber's *Preciosa*, Beethoven's *Egmont*, and Grieg's *Peer Gynt*, as well as programming Goethe's *Faust* and Shakespeare's *Macbeth* with music by various composers.[9] Mendelssohn's scores for chorus and orchestra to accompany *Oedipus at Colonus, Antigone,* and Racine's *Athalie* were all heard with readings between 1847 and 1909, more often in England than in America.[10] Yet none of this music achieved anything like the same popularity as *A Midsummer Night's Dream*, the only work performed in concert with readings on a regular basis for some seventy years.[11]

What ensured the success of *A Midsummer Night's Dream* in this format was the evocative qualities of Mendelssohn's much-loved music, able to generate visual elements in the audience's imaginations that could substitute for the theatrical spectacles that had become standard features of productions of the play. The work was ideal for women, who were capable of taking on the characters associated with Mendelssohn's "fairy" music and replacing the physicality of the scantily clad female fairies in staged productions—both an aesthetic and a moral problem for theatergoers—with a suitably respectable reading of the Bard. Readers were able to transform Shakespeare's work from theater into literature and to reach audiences with antitheatrical prejudices. The *Musical World* acknowledged, "As there are many people . . . who will not visit a theatre to listen to an opera, so there are numbers who, from motives we need not investigate, deny themselves the pleasure of seeing a play acted, and yet have no objection to hearing one read."[12]

Concert readings answered a prevailing strain of nineteenth-century criticism, which declared Shakespeare's dramas to be fundamentally literary and found stage productions of them inherently inferior, distracting audiences from the best qualities of the Bard's language. This problem was particularly associated with *A Midsummer Night's Dream*, stemming from William Hazlitt's much-quoted 1816 critique of Frederick Reynolds's adaptation of the play: "The *ideal* has no place upon the stage which is a picture without perspective. . . . That which is merely an airy shape, a dream, a passing thought, immediately becomes an unmanageable reality."[13] In 1841, a critic for the *New York Herald* described how Shakespeare devotees "pore over its beauties, and revel in the glorious poetry of its author; but on the stage it is quite another affair."[14] Such criticism was repeated throughout the century,[15] against the spirit of the age, however, as spectacle remained an essential component of period productions.[16] Contemporary stagecraft fashioned the necessary illusions for a theatrical "dream": machinery and trapdoors created mysteriously appearing fairies who could become airborne; gas lighting and gauze screens enhanced scenes' otherworldliness. In Laura Keene's panorama in 1859, trees, shrubs, and flowers sprang magically to life, and Augustin Daly's elaborate 1888 production featured fireflies, chirping crickets, and fairies with battery-powered electric lights in their hair and on the tips of their wands.[17]

No matter what visual feasts stage designers managed to contrive, some critics found that these could never match their own imaginations. The *New York Times* declared that the 1906 production by Annie Russell at the Astor Theatre lacked magic despite its fairy spectacles: "A whole troupe of little elves and fairies, very well trained in the antics of fairyland . . . play leap frog, tumble down hill and indulge in a most bewitching coo-cooing. . . . But still no dream feeling."[18] Clearly such exhibitions pleased period audiences, yet the supernatural elements of the play were most often the focus of press criticism. Hazlitt complained that "fairies are not incredible, but fairies six feet high are so";[19] an 1854 staging at New York's Burton's Theater in New York City was praised for its child fairies, preferable to "the heavy heeled, six-footed, broad-shouldered conventionalities" forced on audiences "as fairy gossamer and miniature etherealities."[20] However, it was not just the fairies' size that bothered the critics—they simply seemed too real; the fairy world was simply "too light, changing and ethereal for actors of flesh and blood and the clumsy contrivances of the stage."[21] The solution to these disappointments was to read the play rather than to see it. Desmond MacCarthy spoke for many when he wrote, "I have always enjoyed *A Midsummer Night's Dream* as a poem, not a play."[22] By the mid- to late nineteenth century, professional elocutionists proclaimed that they were the ideal performers to make Shakespeare perfectly palatable on the platform; elocutionist Harriet Webb asserted, "You can't get the pure Shakespeare on the stage"; for true Shakespeare, "there must be the capable reader."[23]

Although male speakers were sometimes featured in concert readings of *A Midsummer Night's Dream*, the play was more often performed by women because the Victorians conceived of fairies as female. Oberon was consistently cast as a woman in England and America from Madame Eliza Vestris's 1840 London production onward, and frequently costumed in attire designed to reveal more of an actress's feminine attributes.[24] Puck, too, was often portrayed by an actress, and numerous female fairies danced in the play's theatrical spectacles. Given the large number of female characters and male characters played by women, *A Midsummer Night's Dream* was an ideal play for female speakers.[25] Male readers became more common only later in the century, although some were criticized for their rendering of the play's fairy portions, suggesting that women's vocal delivery was considered the norm. One exception to the preference for female readers was elocutionist George Riddle (1851–1910), who performed the play with music more times than anyone else. However, the press highlighted Riddle's success with feminine characters; the *New York Times* reported, "Titania, Helena, and Hermia, were so distinctly individualized that to a person who shut his eyes it seemed as if three . . . women were on the stage."[26]

The strong emphasis on the fairy elements associated with women performers was further reinforced by Mendelssohn's music. The composer's "elfin scherzo" style, with its transparent orchestration and fleeting staccato string and woodwind writing, signified the musical depiction of fairies for nineteenth-century listeners, and Mendelssohn came to be considered the quintessential "fairy composer."[27] The fairy style dominates Mendelssohn's overture, and the first piece of incidental music for the play accompanies the entrance of the fairies at the opening of act 2. George Grove, in an oft-quoted statement, declared that *A Midsummer Night's Dream* "brought the fairies into the orchestra and fixed them there."[28] Thus, a reading of the play would offer the audience Shakespeare's poetry stripped of any danger of theatrical excess, while Mendelssohn's music could evoke a fairy world in the listeners' imaginations without weighty reality impinging on the dreamlike state. Percy Fitzgerald wrote that "it is not too much to say that his *Midsummer Night's Dream* music, when played in a concert room, brings up all the images of the beautiful fairy play."[29]

Letting Mendelssohn's musical score substitute for the play's visual elements was not only aesthetically more satisfying but morally safer as well, as fairy costuming emphasized the female body. Period criticism demonstrates an acute awareness of the physicality of the female fairies in stage productions of *A Midsummer Night's Dream*, most often ballet dancers dressed in the flesh-colored tights and shortened gauzy skirts of the newly popular tutu. Throughout the century, when reviewers suggested that Shakespeare's fairy play was better read than seen, they repeatedly focused on the life-size bodies of women depicting fairies. In 1852, one critic praised Fanny Kemble's reading with Mendelssohn's music as superior to a full staging with actresses: "The bodily senses of the most easily captivated recoil from a middle-aged gentlewoman rouged up to perform *Oberon*,—from a material *Puck*, ever so shrill and tricksy,—from a *Pease-blossom*, *Moth*, and *Mustard Seed*, severally more substantial than *Hermia*, *Helena*, and *Hyppolita*."[30] Thirty years later Dutton Cook complained that fairies, "capable of creeping into acorn cups and hanging dewdrops in the ears of cowslips, must be embodied and portrayed by ballet girls more or less muscular and agile, and as little like spiritual creatures as well can be."[31] While clearly part of the problem was that fairies were oversized, the reviews' language—"muscular and agile" and "rouged up"—concentrates on the female body. Tracy Davis has described how diaphanously costumed fairies invited the male gaze: "By associating a skirt's lightness, shortness, and looseness with the desirable qualities of femininity . . . choreography and costuming worked together to please the ubiquitous voyeur."[32] Davis continues, "The defiance of gravity suggested unshod otherworldliness: if, in imagination, the feet were bare, so were the legs, and if the legs were bare the potential revelation of transparent skirts was unlimited."[33] Immediately following his discussion of Mendelssohn in his article "Fairy Music," Henry Lunn turns to stage fairies, writing suggestively, "Fairies live amidst charming surroundings, and evidently in a climate the mildness of which makes the audiences at our metropolitan theatres envious."[34] Thus, although a female reader would have been considered more capable of expressing the poetry of fairyland than a man, she would also be decently garbed in appropriate dress rather than a suggestively revealing costume.

Mendelssohn's evocative score was a successful substitute for elaborate Victorian stagings; his fairy music bridged the space between the serious literary efforts of the woman reading Shakespeare and the treacherous world of the theater, providing the fairies in a safer, musical form. Any imagery the music might produce—merely dreamlike or markedly erotic—remained safely in the listeners' imaginations. In spite of the association of the eroticized female body with Mendelssohn's fairy sounds, the hagiography that surrounded the composer's public image made him an ideal composer for the women who performed with his music. The composer's upper-class status, his success, and his family relations all contributed to his image as the perfect Victorian gentleman.[35] Mendelssohn's supposed moral purity, found in descriptions of him from the 1860s and 1870s, made his music an appropriate choice for women. Many a young woman went down the aisle to the Wedding March from *A Midsummer Night's Dream*, first made popular when one of Queen Victoria's daughters used it for her own wedding. Mendelssohn might have composed fairy music associated with the eroticized female body on the stage, but he could also produce music for respectable married women as well.

## Fanny Kemble's Concert Readings and Performers of the Dream

Readings of Shakespeare's entire plays were first associated with professional actresses. The renowned English actress Fanny Kemble (1809–93) popularized the practice of performing *A Midsummer Night's Dream* with Mendelssohn's music as part of the series of readings of Shakespeare plays that she began in 1847 and continued sporadically until 1869.[36] Although deeply devoted to the texts of Shakespeare, Kemble expressed a strong dissatisfaction with acting and the artificial nature of the stage: "These wretched, tawdry, glittering rags, flung over the breathing forms of ideal loveliness; these miserable, poor, and pitiful substitutes for the glories with which poetry has invested her magnificent and fair creations—the glories with which our imagination reflects them back again . . . how I do loathe my most impotent and unpoetical craft!"[37] Kemble, who regarded Hazlitt's criticism as "excellent,"[38] felt that the theater's visual aspects were inherently a lie that undermined rather than realized Shakespeare's poetic artistry.[39] Faced with legal bills because of her impending divorce from a Georgia plantation owner, Kemble took up solo readings of Shakespeare's plays (figure 3.1).[40] Not only did readings suit her temperament, they were less expensive to produce in an era in which actresses were financially responsible for their own costumes.[41] Kemble performed at a desk, attired in a gown appropriate to the evening's play; for *A Midsummer Night's Dream* she wore "mossy-green velvet or white silk and lace,"[42] which was the only hint of pictorial representation. Kemble's reading tours in Eng-

Figure 3.1. Fanny Kemble reading at the St. James Theatre, *London Illustrated News,* August 10, 1852.

land and America met with popular and financial success. At the Stuyvesant Institute in New York City, she typically read to six or seven hundred persons; Philip Hone described how audience members rushed to claim seats two or three hours before her appearance.[43] After her 1850 reading of *A Midsummer Night's Dream,* Thomas Wentworth Higginson praised "that unequaled voice," declaring, "How shall I describe the immense animal spirits, the utter transformation of voice, face and gesture, with which this extraordinary woman threw herself into the comedy?"[44] Henry Wadsworth Longfellow penned a sonnet in Kemble's honor, and the *Boston Herald* declared, "She is unquestionably *the* Shakespearean reader of the present age."[45]

Kemble had been reading Shakespeare's plays for about three years when she added Mendelssohn's music to her performances; in her personal copy of the plays, she made the necessary cuts for condensed readings and penciled in the locations of the composer's music.[46] Her first American concert reading took place at the Astor Place Opera House on March 21, 1850, as the highlight of her spring run in New York City; it also served as a benefit for the American Musical Fund Society. The concert attracted a large audience and reportedly earned $2,000 for the society. The actress counted herself among the many who "knew and loved Mendelssohn"[47] and had been deeply distressed by his early death.[48] Her first English concert reading seemingly memorialized the composer as it took place on his birthday, February 3, 1852, five years after his death.[49]

The review of Kemble's 1852 performance in London, which complained about the physicality of stage fairies, confirmed that the concert-reading format had remedied the problem: "The play among poems and the poem among plays . . . could not be more deliciously presented than in the form chosen on Tuesday evening,—when the text was read by Mrs. Kemble, and the music of Mendelssohn was performed."[50] Kemble's voice succeeded as a substitute for the play's visual spectacles; Higginson wrote, "I cannot believe [the play] was ever given before—for on the stage the palpable grotesqueness of the asses' ears, nay, of the fairy form even, would spoil it all—'tis too airy for anything but the voice and *her* voice."[51] One magazine article claimed,

> In listening to one of her readings, we have the unexampled pleasure of seeing one of Shakespeare's plays, with each part superbly rendered. Yes, *seeing*, for do we not forget the dais upon which she sits, the dark red screen behind her, the table with its pile of books—do not these simple surroundings dissolve and melt away into arching forests or palace halls at will? and does not each character step before us in the costume of the day, whether it be . . . Titania with her robe of woven moonbeams, or Bottom with his ass's head?[52]

Kemble was hailed as "not merely the versatile actress—there is the sympathy of the refined and fantastic poetess," and Mendelssohn's genius was compared to that of Shakespeare, whom he "intimately understood."[53] Together, the actress and the composer's music represented the ideal rendering of the poetic work.

Fanny Kemble was thus the leading figure of a practice that came to be imitated by other female performers, establishing the regular reading of Shakespeare's play with Mendelssohn's incidental music.[54] Clearly, many readers who followed Kemble, performing the work only once or twice, did not have her ability in reading entire plays. The *Musical World* acknowledged that "the art of reading or reciting a play well does not lie within the capacity of every actor. It requires superior mimetic powers, a varied knowledge of character, and a great command of the voice."[55] As a reviewer of British actress Frances Scott-Siddons's 1869 performance with the New York Philharmonic remarked, "It is no trifling thing for a woman—more particularly one with a comparatively weak voice—to so modulate it and its inflections a[nd] to take, with any degree of success, parts like those of Oberon, Titania, Puck, Flute, Bottom, Quince, &c."[56] Perhaps because of their lack of training in impersonation, elocutionists initially fared less well than theatrical professionals, who brought their stage experience to bear in their performances. Of Kemble, one writer noted that "the stage traditions were evident in her reading," although the reviewer for the *Leeds Mercury* was in the minority when he wrote, "Considering that she has only to *read* the part, does she not throw into it too much of the actress?"[57] Even Scott-Siddons, often regarded as a mediocre actress, was praised for "[throwing] all her soul into the work, instead of the monotonous, dreary style of the majority of dramatic readers."[58]

However, by elocution's height at the end of the century, more readers of *A Midsummer Night's Dream* were elocutionists than actresses. They included Nellie Peck Saunders, who taught at the Detroit Conservatory, and Aletta Waterbury Goss, active in the Chicago Dramatic Society in 1914 and 1915 and whose flyer states she had been trained, in part, by George Riddle. Bertha Kunz Baker's reading at the Assembly in Chautauqua, New York, in August 1909 was particularly memorable, as the lights went out during the Intermezzo. Baker responded to the emergency by joking, "This is program music—lost in the woods!"[59] Although these women would not have wanted to be identified as actresses, many saw themselves in a tradition stemming from Kemble, whose years as a professional reader had made her "the acknowledged standard of excellence in female elocution."[60] Kemble had achieved the goal toward which elocutionists were striving, in that she served as the voice of Shakespeare—the height of great literature—without having to engage in the physicality of staged drama, and was thus able to "normalize female public accomplishment."[61] She had, in the words of Faye Dudden, "broken the narrow confines of both stage and womanhood, and set forth the lineaments of a public life for women that was not defined by male apprehension of the female body."[62] Years after her death, Kemble continued to serve as the model for female performers. Jane Manner considered her own performance of *A Midsummer Night's Dream* with the Cincinnati Symphony Orchestra in 1903 to be one of the highlights of her career and recounted it in her publicity decades later.[63] Manner later published Longfellow's laudatory sonnet about Kemble reading Shakespeare in her poetry anthology; in 1932 it served as her justification for reading aloud in a response to a *New York Times* article complaining that the practice had become old-fashioned, replaced by radio and movies.[64] When Virginia Taylor McCormick penned a poem "To Jane Manner Reading Longfellow," it was an obvious attempt to complete the artistic circle.[65] In McCormick's poem, Manner's voice, like Kemble's, "wakens the dead desire / For beauty, infinite, true," in bringing a message from poet to listener.

Few elocutionists were able to summon an orchestra for all of their performances, thus Mendelssohn's music was heard in various arrangements. Many concert readings took place with piano or organ, and performers were able to draw on Mendelssohn's own arrangement for two pianos, first published in 1844. Reciters also appeared with reduced forces, such as the "12 Symphony men" who accompanied Carolyn Foye Flanders at the New England Conservatory's Jordan Hall.[66] Versions of the play were issued, with or without Mendelssohn's music, bearing titles indicating that they were designed for the performance of the two together.[67] A review of an 1875 edition of the complete play published with a piano-vocal score of Mendelssohn's music notes that "the text of the play which connects the movements is printed *precisely as it should be read*," solving this problem for "schools and private choirs."[68] A 1911 pamphlet subtitled "Fairy Romantic Comedy" condensed the play "for lawn production, for schools of either sex or for girls only"; it ends at Theseus's discovery of the lovers, and all depart to Mendelssohn's Wedding March.[69]

Selections from *A Midsummer Night's Dream* were commonly taught in elocution schools; the 1910 recital of Julia Beach at the Currys' School of Expression included excepts from Frances Hodgson Burnett's novel *A Little Princess* about an orphan at a girls' school, followed by act 2, scene 1, of *A Midsummer Night's Dream*, in which the fairy characters dominate—both appropriate literary repertoire for a young female performer.[70] Beach and her contemporaries continued the tradition of solo performance; elocution students were endeavoring to become the Fanny Kemble of their generation, rather than being prepared for the stage. Even when the talent available in elocution schools made it possible to stage, if not entire plays, one or more scenes with individuals assigned to play characters, performances remained restricted to solo readings. In 1911 the Cincinnati School of Expression put on *A Midsummer Night's Dream* with Mendelssohn's music as a series of monologues with particular students, one after another, taking sections of the play. The line between literature and the more dangerous acting continued to be present, although many schools found ways to push its limitations. At their 1894 commencement recital, nine elocution students at Virginia's Hollins Institute presented a series of ten "Shakespearian Pictures," each based on a single line from a play, concluding with "A Group of Shaksperian [sic] Women"; perhaps these tableaux were in costume, but they appear to have been accompanied by music rather than spoken dialogue.[71] Not until 1902 did Hollins students stage *A Midsummer Night's Dream* with costumed characters, although dramatic productions did not entirely replace elocution; students performed Shakespeare scenes as solos as late as 1908. Given women elocutionists' long-standing involvement with *A Midsummer Night's Dream*, it is not surprising that Ruth Suckow chose it as the site of Marjorie's major success in *The Odyssey of a Nice Girl*.

By the end of the century, concert readings, which had originally represented the pinnacle of poetry and music combined, had become suitable entertainment for children. Two readings with Mendelssohn's music in the 1890s took place in conjunction with the New York Philharmonic's Young People's Concerts; in 1902, Frank Damrosch programmed a reading of the play with Mendelssohn's music at his Symphony Concerts for Young People in New York.[72] The change in the audience for concert readings of *A Midsummer Night's Dream* parallels the evolving status of fairies in the nineteenth century, from frightening, dangerous, supernatural beings that were the subject of major Romantic artworks to diminutive pastel figures appropriate for children's books. In 1915, Walter Damrosch, instead of presenting the Philharmonic Society's Young People's Concert audiences with Shakespeare and Mendelssohn, engaged singer and reciter Kitty Cheatham (discussed in chapter 6), who presented a "group of children's songs relating to fairies and elves and another of nursery rhymes."[73]

Concert readings of *A Midsummer Night's Dream* allowed female performers to associate themselves with the acknowledged genius of both Shakespeare and Mendelssohn, who represented the highest form of culture available to elocutionists. This synthesis of poetry and music, heard in British and American concert halls for more than half a century, was shaped by long-standing reservations about the theatrical realization of Shakespeare's poetry—and lurking behind these reservations was anxiety about the bodies of actresses and dancers garbed as otherworldly, sexual creatures. In reading *A Midsummer Night's Dream*, elocutionists became more voice than body, and the fairy elements were transmitted through Mendelssohn's magical music, mediating the problem of the female body displayed on the stage. Thus, the concert reading made great art safe for women's voices.

# 4. Sentimentality and Gender in Musically Accompanied Recitations

Oh, that the caller might go on calling,
Oh, that the music might go on falling
Like a shower of silver spray,
While we whirled on to the vast Forever,
Where no heart breaks, and no ties sever,
And no one goes away.
—Ella Wheeler Wilcox, "A Waltz-Quadrille"

The most performed musical recitations during the last two decades of the nineteenth century and before World War I were based on sentimental texts that made specific references to music. Most of these poems were standard repertoire for elocutionists, heard countless times on period platforms and continuously reprinted. The elaborately illustrated elocution books marketed to women were prescriptive, recommending such selections for performance, as well as descriptive, a record of the most recited poems. Anthologies were organized by poems' literary content. Pathetic, humorous, dramatic, patriotic, and religious recitations were the most common groupings; temperance, dialect selections, or musical readings were sometimes included as specialized recitation types. Many of the most popular poems were recited by both men and women; however, given the prevalence of accompaniments in women's performances, musical recitations must be viewed with the gender of their performers in mind. Recognizable topics and story types considered appropriate for women reappear in female elocutionists' repertoires, even beyond the designations of *pathetic*, *religious*, or *dramatic*. Recited texts expressed sentimental and religious values and worked to balance female characters' occasional poetic emergence as heroic figures with their appropriate domestic roles.

The poetry recited with music often consisted of narratives that were part of what Joanne Dobson has called the nineteenth century's "sentimental literary tradition."[1] Rather than understanding *sentimental* as reflecting a modern critical stance on texts that, while once popular, now suffer literary scholars' disdain because of their excessive emotionalism and clichéd content, Dobson defines the *sentimental* as an ethos found in a range of written works regardless of their literary merit. Elocutionists performed sentimental literature simply because it was the literary currency of their times. However, it also enabled them to be successful in performance; the "familiar and accessible" sentimental with its "conventional, even stereotypical tropes" would "facilitate communication with a wide and receptive audience."[2] Given the gender boundaries that had to be crossed before women appeared on the platform, it was especially important that their poetic selections be easily accessible to listeners. In a private setting, complex literary texts might be read and reread silently for increased understanding, but elocutionary selections, only communicated through women's voices, needed to be comprehensible in one hearing. The sentimental gave elocutionists the power to evoke strong, empathetic feelings and to move and hold their audiences.

Dobson's definition of literary sentimentalism is an apt description of the content of elocutionists' poetic selections at the end of the nineteenth century: at their core almost all of the texts discussed in this chapter celebrate "human connections, both personal and communal" and acknowledge "the shared devastation of affectional loss."[3] Indeed, the specter of unavoidable loss looms in numerous texts recited by women—loss of a beloved, a parent, or a child. Clichéd images common to sentimental texts serve as "evocative metaphors for a looming existential threat—the potential devastations of deeply experienced human connections."[4] Not all of the poems women typically recited ended in tragedy or mourned an irretrievable past, but the emotions surrounding the continual possibility of the demise of human relationships treated within them was part of their appeal.

Dobson's concept of the "sentimental keepsake" is also apropos to understanding how music functioned in elocutionary performance. Keepsakes are most often physical objects—a lock of hair, a portrait, a child's toy, or any object associated with a lost beloved or an endangered relationship. In many poems, a keepsake becomes "a vivid symbolic embodiment" of "human connection and the inevitability of human loss."[5] In the most common musically accompanied recitations, instead of a physical object or image to serve as the core of a memory, the sound of a specific musical work creates an audible representation of the sentimental bond; for example, a song recalls the speaker's mother, a dance tune evokes the memory of dancing with a lover now gone, or a hymn tune connects a character to the great beyond when facing death. The addition of the actual music described in these texts, with its attendant emotional power, would serve to enhance the listener's sentimental experience. In accompanied recitations it is the music that, in Dobson's words, "embodies the memory of the love, the anguish of separation, and the hope of eventual reunion."[6]

In order for audiences to make an immediate emotional connection with a recitation, the music incorporated into the performance had to be familiar—a well-known song or hymn tune brought its own connotations into the new spoken-word context. The most common musically accompanied recitations can be more easily grouped according to their literary content than by the characteristics of their added music; their texts were more closely related to those of similar poems performed without music than to any musical style or genre. At the same time, the multiple uses of a small group of popular songs and hymns in numerous elocutionary contexts demonstrates the existence of a musical core that could be incorporated into different texts as needed; although performers such as Jane Manner performed musical recitations that drew on classical compositions by European composers, such combinations seem to have been in the minority. The most common reasons for including a musical work in a recitation were to create a more intense dramatic realism and to move listeners by making a sentimental keepsake audible. The poetic selections chosen by female performers celebrate the power of music to bridge past and present, to recall courtship, and to sustain religious faith until death. Not only did songs added to recitations maintain a symbolic value intricately bound up with their sentimental aesthetic approach, but the use of familiar music from the parlor also emphasized the domestic values of women's home lives, making their public performances more socially acceptable.

## Music, Dancing, and Love Lost and Found

Some musical practices were related to women's desire to create sounds beyond that of speaking in order to demonstrate their vocal virtuosity. Performers who had good singing voices could program selections that included lines or verses of actual songs, interspersing the spoken and the sung, and some also incorporated sounds that imitated those of the natural world: wind, bells, birds, or even babies crying.[7] Birdcalls could also be suggested by musical instruments, such as flute or violin.[8] Anna Randall Diehl gave Alfred, Lord Tennyson's "Bugle Song" from *The Princess* with vocally produced bugle sounds,[9] while Mrs. W. F. Sherwin regularly performed it with an actual bugler, as was suggested in Henry Soper's anthology.[10] William Chamberlain believed that Tennyson did not have the actual sound of a bugle in mind and found this sort of realism "a monstrosity," yet audiences felt otherwise.[11] Even though imitative vocal techniques were considered to abandon literary content for mere display, they were typically inspired by performers' interpretations of specific texts. Poems that contained bells were popular, especially Edgar Allan Poe's "The Bells," George W. Bungay's "The Creeds of the Bells," and Edmund Stedman's "Country Sleighing," allowing for performers to specialize in onomatopoeic vocal production.[12] Margaret Walker Price used Schumann's

"Vision" from *Albumblätter*, op. 124; the Bridal Chorus from Wagner's *Lo-hengrin*; a Beethoven Allegro; and Mendelssohn's *Song without Words*, op. 62, no. 3, known as "Funeral March," to reflect the different bells depicted in Poe's poem.[13] Schumann's light, scherzo-like work was appropriate for sleigh bells, and Wagner's bridal music suggested the wedding bells. Presumably, the unidentified Beethoven excerpt was sufficiently vigorous for the third stanza's "shrieking" alarm bells, and the minor-key fanfares of the *Song without Words* made an appropriate finish for the "melancholy menace" and "moaning and groaning" of the final iron bells. Price's use of music was more related to the emotional expression of Poe's poem than to the onomatopoeic imitation of natural sounds and was thus more in keeping with the evocative uses of music typical of accompanied recitations. Although the inclusion of such natural sounds in women's performances was critiqued as representing exaggerated excess, bells and bugles, which mark the passage of time and audibly signal fundamental changes in human relationships, were nonetheless consistent with the sentimental aesthetic of women's accompanied recitations.[14]

Another realistic use of music was the inclusion of dance music for poems with plots that contained dancing. Here music could evoke the physical move-ments of the characters, even if elocutionists performing a text remained sta-tionary. Dance music was typically bound up with poems' nostalgic evocations of past events; it not only simulated motion in a particular locale, but could also conjure up a previous time. Instead of a physical object to serve as the core of a memory, the sound of a specific musical work created the sentimental bond between a character in the recited poem and his or her past, serving to inspire nostalgic feelings in listeners as well.

The most programmed work in this vein was Mary Mapes Dodge's nostal-gic "The Minuet" (also known as "How Grandma Danced"), performed in a variety of ways by both women and girls.[15] The poem describes Grandma dancing the minuet "with stately grace" in her youth, in contrast to the poten-tially shocking "modern jumping, / Hopping, rushing, whirling, bumping." However, the speaker's assurance that "With the minuet in fashion, / Who could fly into a passion?" is clearly intended to be ironic, as a supposed verbal "mistake" reveals both Grandma's and her granddaughter's interest in the opposite sex:

> Modern ways are quite alarming,
> Grandma says; but boys were charming—
> Girls and boys I mean, of course,—
> Long ago.

Most elocution books did not specify any particular music to accompany Dodge's poem; however, the addition of a minuet would have helped create an eighteenth-century atmosphere, rather than the poem's more modern irony. Louise Preece's physical culture book suggests Mozart's minuet from *Don Giovanni*, and Elsie Wilbor's 1890 anthology includes a brief piece by Johann Nepomuk Hummel.[16] Laura Yerkes instructs that a hidden pianist should play softly and that the speaker should keep time to the music.[17] Wilbor insists that only movement, not recitation, should take place during the music, and several anthologies show pictures of costumed children innocently dancing. An opportunity for dancing also occurred in Edith S. Tupper's "Grandmamma's Fan"; here an antique fan prompts a memory in which "time rolls backwards" as "she treads the stately dance."[18] The preponderance of eighteenth-century costumes among reciters was sometimes related to nostalgic and patriotic treatment of America's colonial period; one anthology suggests that "The Minuet" be performed with *Daughters of America*.[19]

A related text performed with dance music was Cora Vandemark's "Grandma at the Masquerade," in which an old woman dances in disguise at a ball and is called "the best on the floor." The text features many verses that might appropriately receive dance accompaniment, such as:

> Now it chanced—and some there were who knew
> That Grandma, in her youth, danced too,
> And all "ye olden steps" she knew;
> So when she heard the music sweet,
> She tried in vain to keep her seat,
> While eagerly her restless feet
> The merry time would mark.[20]

Emma Dunning Banks published the text with a two-strain fiddle tune, writing that it could be "intoned" to *Money Musk* "by improvising and adding one line to each stanza, and eliminating a word where the measure demanded."[21] In Banks's practices, a performer's verbal art could remain as flexible as her musical adoptions. ("Grandmother texts," which came to influence melodramatic compositions by female composers in the twentieth century, are discussed in chapter 10.)

Dancing, music, and romance were intimately connected in recitations that centered on lost loves, including two poems performed with waltzes, Ella Wheeler Wilcox's "A Waltz-Quadrille" and Nora Perry's "That Waltz of Von Weber's." Sections of both Wilcox's and Perry's poems have underlying poetic meters (such as trochaic and dactylic) such that they could readily be paired with a triple-meter waltz accompaniment. Contemporary sources did not specify music for "A Waltz-Quadrille," so performers may have chosen various pieces.[22] In Wilcox's poem, the speaker longs for the dancing never to end, as her lover must depart when it is over:

> I said to my heart: "Let us take our fill
> Of mirth, and music, and love and laughter;
> For it all must end with this waltz-quadrille,
> And life will be never the same life after."

In the poem, music is the symbol of love and romance, and adding dance accompaniment served to depict the ballroom setting and to express the intensity of the speaker's longing. The musical accompaniment to the couple's dancing is at the core of the text's sentimentality, signifying a wished-for world where the inevitable end of love will not occur. One can readily imagine that the cessation of the music in the poem's final stanza and simultaneously in the underlying accompaniment would have created an especially poignant moment in performance, expressing the finality of the loss of the speaker's lover. Music is also central to Perry's similar poem, "That Waltz of Von Weber's," about the memory of an old love affair. When an organ grinder plays the music of the title, an aging bachelor remembers dancing with his first and only love, recalling the youthful enchantment of a time "when our hearts beat in time to our fast-flying feet." Perry's poem was performed to the fifth piece of Carl Reissiger's *Danses brillantes*, op. 26 (1822), popularly if incorrectly known as "Weber's Last Waltz"; John Harris Gutterson of Boston, warning that the music should color, not dominate recitations, stressed that "'wild Weber' is woven *occasionally*."[23]

In numerous recitations, music served to bridge the gap between past and present and to sentimentally evoke what had been lost, as it did in Perry's poem. In "Bundle of Letters," arranged by Blanche Baird Winfield, a woman looks over old photographs and letters, remembering her lost youth and a lover who left her for another.[24] The performer both hums and sings "Long, Long Ago," a song that substitutes for the memorabilia that the audience cannot experience directly.[25] George L. Catlin's "The Street Musicians," which appeared in several anthologies with directions for an "invisible vocal quartet" and/or suggested musical excerpts, features a vagabond band playing the lullaby "Sweet and Low."[26] Upon hearing the music, an old drunkard recalls his mother's singing and repents of his sins. As in other recitations of this sort, the music is a sentimental keepsake of the past that has the power to transform the present. Another recitation commonly performed with music was "The Volunteer Organist," in which a similarly decrepit drunkard appears at a church to accompany the service. His music expresses his personal story, providing spiritual lessons for the congregation:

> Each eye shed tears within that church, the strongest men grew pale;
> The organist in melody had told his own life's tale.
> The sermon of the preacher was no lesson to compare
> With that of life's example who sat in the organ chair;

Elocutionists adopted music diegetically for dramatic effect into the sections of text that refer to the organist's playing; the work may also have been recited to the popular song based on the text.[27]

Several poems arranged by Banks also use music as a sentimental reminder of an earlier romantic relationship. In Banks's stories, a couple dance together at a social event but are then separated for some years, only to reunite at another dance and resume their relationship. Sometimes the story is told in the present, so that its first half is a memory; it thus combines retrospective, sentimental views of the past with the concluding satisfaction of love fulfilled. Banks's publications had wide appeal; a copy of her poem "Soldier's Joy," with penciled markings to indicate the music's locations, can be found in the hand-copied elocution notebook of a young student, Frances Maude Wood, who performed in Alton, Illinois, from approximately 1904 to 1908.[28]

As Banks explained in her instructional "lesson-talks," parts of the recitations are spoken in time to the music, typically fiddle tunes in simple piano arrangements; her musical excerpts were coordinated to fit the meter of the text, not unlike the waltzes informally combined with Perry's and Wilcox's poems. Fiddle tunes might still have been played in the late nineteenth century in New England, yet more likely they were chosen to contribute to the poems' nostalgia for the past.[29] Banks also chose them for their titles' associations; for example, "Soldier's Joy" is used when the woman in the poem of that name agrees to marry a soldier from whom she has been long separated (example 4.1).[30] The moment of their coming together is recited to the first strain of the melody, which also evokes their mutual past.

> Now it's "Swing your partners,"—did Jack hold her closer, closer still?
> Misty tear-drops veiled her bright eyes as she looked up 'gainst her will,
> For she saw determination in the eyes of trusty Jack.
> Felt that he as well as she had set along time's backward track.[31]

That the metrical structure of the poem would have been difficult to align with the 4/4 meter of the fiddle tune suggests that it was chosen more for its evocative title than its musical content.

In Banks's "Two Thanksgiving Dances," music playing in the parlor causes the speaker to recall a Thanksgiving dance ten years earlier, when he danced with his sweetheart, Queenie, and when they fought and parted in the midst of the dance (not unlike "That Waltz of Von Weber's"). Banks's arrangement includes two fiddle tunes; the first is the *Irish Washerwoman*, though it is not identified as such, as its title does not reflect the narrative. The second tune, *Haste to the Wedding*, indicates what the reunited couple is going to do, and its title appears at the end of the poem as well: "When we finished our dance, as she courtseyed [sic] and said: / Let us 'haste to the wedding,' and—haste to be wed."[32] Banks's directions mostly suggest incorporating facial and hand

Example 4.1. First strain of "Soldier's Joy," in Emma Dunning Banks, *Original Recitations with Lesson-Talks* (New York: Edgar S. Werner, 1890), 72.

motions, not actual dancing; she does suggest a few dance steps at the poem's climax, although speakers who played their own accompaniments could not have managed this; music alone would have served to represent the dancing, though its sentimental meaning was even more important than its relationship to physical movement.

Probably the most frequently performed poem about a past love, if not the single work most often heard with music during the period, was the tragic "Aux Italiens" by Owen Meredith (Edward Bulwer-Lytton).[33] At the Paris Opera, the speaker watches Giuseppe Verdi's *Il Trovatore* and recalls his first love, with whom he had quarreled, and has a vision of her returned from the dead. Elocutionists' addition of music was because of the poem's mention of the tenor's singing in the "Miserere" of Verdi's opera, and it closes with lines taken from the libretto, Manrico's request not to be forgotten; in their new context, these lines also speak for the lost beloved:

> And O that music! And O the way
> That voice rang out from the donjon tower
> *Non ti scordar di me,*
> *Non ti scordar di me!*

It is not clear how much of Verdi's music was typically incorporated into performances of "Aux Italiens"; the chorus and blessing for Manrico in death sung by the soprano, Leonora, precede the tenor's music quoted in the poem; though seemingly incompatible with the nostalgic, intimate memories of the deceased young woman, this music nonetheless accompanied them in Charles Roberts's 1907 arrangement, published long after "Aux Italiens" was widely established as a musical recitation.[34] Here Verdi's music functioned merely diegetically, the opera scene continuing in the background of the speaker's recollections. Some of the tenor's lines not quoted in the poem nonetheless make his music appropriate for it, as Manrico longs for death: "Ah! Che la morte ognora / È tarda nel venir / A chi desia morir!" (Alas, why is death ever slow in coming to him who desires to die!). The speaker imagines himself sitting with his dead beloved and decides to marry her rather than his current fiancée, something seemingly only possible if he were to join her in death.

For the many elocutionists who added "Aux Italiens" to their repertoire before Roberts's arrangement was issued, Verdi's music was undoubtedly inserted early in the recitation, as it is the tenor's singing that inspires the speaker's memories. It would have also returned at the very end when the poem quotes "Non ti scordar di me." *The Ideal Orator and Manual of Elocution* (1895) includes only the tenor's section accompanied with piano; it instructs that it be played softly throughout the recitation, even though this would be difficult because the excerpt provided breaks off without a clear cadence. That the music was considered essential in performance is indicated by the fact that the repeated lines of Italian, which appear twice in the poem, are omitted from the printed text; instead they are to be "sung by an invisible assistant in a clear tenor voice."[35] In Roberts's arrangement, the Italian texts are spoken rather than sung to Verdi's melody; the text "She is not dead / and she is not wed" is also accompanied by the refrain (example 4.2).

The specific role that music played in representing personal loss is not always as apparent in other recitations. Although not as widely performed as "Aux Italiens," two other poems heard with music also dealt with separated lovers: Adelaide Proctor's "The Story of the Faithful Soul," discussed in the

Example 4.2. Owen Meredith, *Aux Italiens: Musical Recitation with Lesson Talk*, music by Giuseppe Verdi, arr. Charles Roberts (New York: Edgar S. Werner, 1907), mm. 62–63.

following section, and *Enoch Arden* by Alfred, Lord Tennyson. Many female performers took up Richard Strauss's setting of *Enoch Arden*, which he composed in 1897 for Ernst von Possart and performed with David Bispham on his American tour in 1904. The tale of a sailor who leaves his family and is shipwrecked, only to return years later to find his wife remarried to a childhood friend, was one of Tennyson's most popular poems, in part because of the very sentimental characteristics that caused its later rejection in anti-Victorian criticism. Its topical characteristics link it to other sentimental literature that women adapted for musical recitations: Enoch and Annie are parted lovers, and their third child is sickly and dies. Enoch's sentimental keepsake of his dead son, a lock of hair, reveals his true relationship to his family, and Enoch's sinking ship somewhat recalls "The Last Hymn" (discussed later). Bells are heard both when Philip and Annie wed and when Enoch somehow perceives their ringing in his stranded, hallucinatory state. More important for female performers, *Enoch Arden* celebrates a domestic ideal, expressed in the scene of a comfortable home peopled by the contented family that Enoch witnesses upon his return:

> For cups and silver on the burnish'd board
> Sparkled and shone; so genial was the hearth:
> And on the right hand of the hearth he saw
> Philip, the slighted suitor of old times,
> Stout, rosy, with his babe across his knees;
> And o'er her second father stoopt a girl,
> A later but a loftier Annie Lee,
> Fair-hair'd and tall, and from her lifted hand
> Dangled a length of ribbon and a ring
> To tempt the babe, who rear'd his creasy arms,
> Caught at and ever miss'd it, and they laugh'd;
> And on the left hand of the hearth he saw
> The mother glancing often toward her babe,
> But turning now and then to speak with him,
> Her son, who stood beside her tall and strong,
> And saying that which pleased him, for he smiled.[36]

Philip, who has taken over Enoch's role, is linked to "the fundamental values of conjugal and familial relationships."[37] As Donald Hair has noted, Enoch's devotion to this domestic ideal and his self-sacrificing refusal to identify himself to his wife and children and destroy their harmony causes his tragic end, but it ironically makes him a hero as "the ideal family man."[38]

Although male speakers were also prominently associated with *Enoch Arden*, the domesticity at the core of Tennyson's poem would have naturally made it attractive to women elocutionists. Many women performed it, but few seem to have made it a long-standing part of their repertoire. Because of its length and complexity, and the difficulty of the piano part, the piece was not easily programmed. At almost an hour in length, it would have dominated a recital, eliminating the possibility of a variety-style program. In addition, unlike the published melodramas that have an audible stylistic relationship to informal arrangements with the same text, Strauss's musical approach differs a great deal from the aesthetic of accompanied recitations. Leitmotifs represent the three central characters in the poem—Enoch, Annie, and Philip, each closely identified with a different key; scholars have also identified motifs for the themes of love, Enoch's departure, death, and doom.[39] In the climactic scene in which Enoch vows not to reveal himself to his family, Strauss engaged in Wagnerian treatment of "developing, transforming, and interlinking motives contrapuntally to underscore a story as it unfolds."[40] More generally, the music also depicts landscape, painting the opening waves of the sea with sweeping pictorial scales, and occasionally helps create the sense of physical action: when Philip "crept down" into the wood with a descending melodic line (mm. 77—81); less frequently, it reflects the characters' emotional states, such as the chords that punctuate Philip's outburst, "I hate you Enoch!" (mm. 28–29). While such moments might easily be comprehended by audiences, following the melodrama's structure and motivic development would require far more sophisticated listeners. Furthermore, Strauss did not set all of the passages in Tennyson's poem that might typically have been evoked through music in accompanied recitations. Music helps underscore Enoch's emotional upheaval at seeing his family, and it accompanies his death, but some of the poem's most strongly domestic moments remain unaccompanied. Strauss's music never carries the emotional weight of a sentimental keepsake. Other than the bells, sounded in the piano part, the poem does not refer to music, so there is no motivation for diegetic accompaniment. Although the text of *Enoch Arden* is related to the sentimental accompanied recitations performed by women, Strauss's manner of setting it is largely not.

## Hymns of Women and Angels: Religious Recitations

Female reciters, many of whom made appearances at churches, endeavored to assure audiences of the high moral tone of their selections. Some musically accompanied recitations were appropriately religious in nature, drawing on evocations of Catholic music or Protestant hymns; however, the appearance of music in these works continued to be tied to the idea of loss. "The Story of the Faithful Soul" is in some ways the sacred counterpart to the secular "Aux Italiens." Whereas the latter story is about a man who has lost his love, Proctor's poem centers on a young woman who has died shortly before her wedding and provides her soul's viewpoint from beyond the grave. With its purgatorial setting, the text is closer in tone to the religious poems popular with reciters than it is to the happy reunions in Banks's arrangements. In the story, Archangel Michael allows the woman to return to earth for one minute to console the man who has lost her, with the proviso that she will return to serve a thousand years in purgatory; however, the poem presents a vision back on earth of "A Bridegroom and His Bride," the dead woman's replacement. At the end of the poem, the soul passes into heaven, told by Michael, that "In that one minute's anguish / Your thousand years have passed." The only specific mention of music appears early in the poem, as a "great Te Deum" sounds at the feast of Saint Mary during which the woman's "grieving soul" is introduced. Esther Owen's 1899 instructions for pantomiming while reciting describe the necessary music as beginning "low and mournful" in the second verse, "gradually changing . . . to a more joyful strain" at the appearance of Saint Michael; it "swells" at the "discordant wailing" of the woman and is more subdued as she speaks, becoming stronger as she sees her loved one.[41] Another logical place for music is the end of the poem; a melodramatic setting by Stanley Hawley features a booming, chordal climax as the soul enters heaven.[42]

"King Robert of Sicily" from Henry Wadsworth Longfellow's *Tales of a Wayside Inn,* was another of the most-performed musical recitations, popular with both male and female reciters. The chanting of monks plays an important role in King Robert's fall from and return to grace, naturally suggesting added music. Several women performed "King Robert" with vocal accompaniment in the early 1890s, including Laura Sedgwick Collins, who added chant at an entertainment for the Catholic Benevolent Legion at the Brooklyn Academy, and May Browning, whose benefit for the YWCA featured highly effective chanting "by an invisible chorus of young men."[43] "King Robert" was so widely performed with music that many anthologies, even those without music, indicated that it should occur at the beginning and the end of the poem. Typically, *Mrs. Bosworth's Elocutionary Studies* suggested that music should be heard when priests chant the Magnificat in line 5, and that it should finish following the line "After lulled by the chant monotonous and deep."[44] The music helped both to delineate the opening scene and to define King Robert's character; when he discovers that the chant describes how God "has put down the mighty from their seat, / And has exalted them of low degree," he arrogantly asserts that "no power can push me from my throne." The music signifies the religious truths that Robert rejected; his lack of music is symbolic of his separation from God. For the portion of the poem that takes place after Robert finds himself deposed, forced into the lowly role of court jester, musical accompaniment was abandoned. The musical additions thus shape the poem's overall dramatic narrative and reflect its moral message. Music returns at the poem's close when King Robert acknowledges his own "guilty soul" and his readiness to submit to God's will.

The degree to which music was common in performances of "King Robert of Sicily" is suggested by Chamberlain's objections to it in his 1897 elocution textbook, which rejected the overt dramatization of musical insertions and their potential to overshadow literary meaning: "Should one sing the *Magnificat* in King Robert of Sicily? Decidedly not; to do so is only to call attention to the singer, and to distract the audience from the *theme* of the chant."[45] Nonetheless, anthologies frequently supplied the musical excerpts to be heard, and more than one editor indicated that the poem was appropriate for church performances when given with organ and offstage chorus. In his 1876 book, Toronto elocutionist Richard Lewis included a metered version of the second phrase of the fifth psalm tone for the speaker to sing the text's lines of Latin (example 4.3).

Example 4.3. Chant for Henry Wadsworth
Longfellow, "King Robert of Sicily," in Richard
Lewis, *Lewis's Readings and Recitations: Adapted for
Public and Private Entertainments* (London: Belford,
1876), 57.

Two other books supplied more elaborate vocal settings.[46] *The Ideal Orator and Manual of Elocution* introduced a four-part contrapuntal setting for the monks chanting "Deposuit potentes de sede" in a pseudo-Renaissance contrapuntal style, with directions for singing offstage (example 4.4).[47]

*(Chant.)*

Example 4.4. *Deposuit potentes*, mm. 7–14, for Henry Wadsworth Longfellow, "King Robert of Sicily," in John Wesley Hanson Jr. and Lillian Woodward Gunckel, eds., *The Ideal Orator and Manual of Elocution* (n.p.: Wabash, 1895), 313.

Henry Soper's book provided another four-part setting of the text, this one by Catholic composer L. A. DuMouchel, yet dominated by dotted rhythms and more vigorous in character, suggesting the mighty power of God to which the King must succumb (example 4.5).[48] Soper also included specific instructions that the piece was to be played through by organ before the entrance of the voices, which were to fade out as Robert falls asleep.

In addition to the expected repetition of the vocal music when the monks' chanting returns, some anthologies also indicated particular ways to add music at the close of Longfellow's poem. In Soper's version, at the line, "And through the chant a second melody / Rose like the throbbing of a single string," the organist was to play chords in C major, the key of the Magnificat, "sounding that note continuously." An 1894 recitation book indicated that the subsequent line, "I am an angel, and thou art the king," at which the angel returns the newly humbled Robert to the throne, should be sung "in a clear monotone tenor or soprano—one voice" to enhance the sound of the angel's proclamation.[49] Rossetter G. Cole's substantial melodramatic setting of the entire text, dedicated to David Bispham and published in 1906, retains some stylistic features of the previous musical adaptations: as in Lewis's anthology, the performer is given the option to sing the opening chant (in tone six), as well as the later English-language chant text (example 4.6).

Example 4.5. L. A. DuMouchel, *Deposuit potentes*, mm. 1–6, for Henry Wadsworth Longfellow, "King Robert of Sicily," in Henry M. Soper, *Soper's Select Speaker* ([Chicago]: Soper School of Oratory, 1901), 373.

* The rhythmical notation of this chant (Tone VI) as given here is not to be followed literally, for of course the freedom of the chant does not admit of reduction to exact measure-forms. It is merely approximate – a suggestive guide to those who may not be familiar with the chant in its pure form. Should it be desired to *read* the words of the chant, rather than to sing them, the accompanist will omit the five measures following the chord marked ⌢, holding this chord until the sixth measure.

Example 4.6. Rossetter G. Cole, *King Robert of Sicily* (New York: G. Schirmer, 1906), mm. 66–74 (*ossia* omitted).

Notated pitches also allow the performer to sing the angel's final declaration, similar to informal musical arrangements. Cole also provided instructions for the addition of an organ part to enhance the religious content of sections of the work: its opening scene (mm. 10–95), the first appearance of the angel on his throne (mm. 144–54), and his final reappearance (mm. 329–38).

The mere appearance of angels could suggest the need for music to reciters. Longfellow's poem "Sandalphon" about the angel Sandalphon was sometimes performed with music in order to depict singing angels:

> The Angels of Wind and of Fire
> Chant only one hymn, and expire
> With the song's irresistible stress;
> Expire in their rapture and wonder,
> As harp-strings are broken asunder
> By music they throb to express.

Composer Harvey Worthington Loomis produced a musical setting of the text, published by Werner, featuring harp-like arpeggiation and otherworldly chromaticism.[50] Another example of music used for singing angels occurred in Eugene Field's "The Singing in God's Acre," performed to piano accompaniment by Mrs. Lelle Rhodes Mangang of the Ithaca Conservatory Concert Company in their 1899–1900 season.[51] Two stanzas consist of angels singing a lullaby to God's flowers, creating ideal spots for added music. Mangang may simply have added one of the numerous published song settings of Field's text to her performance.

Familiar hymns, often adopted into recitations, helped guarantee that performances of dramatic narratives had acceptable moral content and were free of the evils of theatrical life. Recitations accompanied by sacred music were especially suitable for entertainments sponsored by women's church groups. Hymn texts could be spoken to their musical settings or heard as recitations without music. Hymns occasionally appeared in elocution books without music: for example, "Nearer, My God, to Thee," by Sarah Flower Adams, in James Murdoch's 1884 *Analytic Elocution*, and, in 1886, Charles Wesley's "Jesus, Lover of My Soul" in Jacob Shoemaker's often reprinted *Practical Elocution*.[52] Shoemaker's widow, Rachel, published eleven hymns in *Advanced Elocution*,[53] and E. B. Warman's *How to Read, Recite and Impersonate* provided instructions for hymn recitation; however, Warman directed his comments to pastors rather than to elocutionists, noting that the practice derived from "lining out" before hymnbooks were common.[54] Because of the Delsarte movement, discussed in chapter 5, many hymns were performed as "illustrated songs" in pantomime.

Although the hymns heard in accompanied recitations were written by both men and women, much evangelical hymnody from between 1870 and

1920 drew on what June Hadden Hobbs has identified as "the language and epistemology of the private sphere"; this helped to create "a feminized Christianity"[55] that was also reflected in religious recitations. The hymns chosen by reciters are characteristic of the work of female hymnodists who "created texts that undermined patriarchal religion by centering power in the home rather than in the church, by locating God within themselves . . . and by emphasizing service rather than conquest."[56] Hymns functioned as religious love songs, reflecting the close relationships at the heart of sentimental nineteenth-century values, and those that were adopted into recitations often stressed the weakness or sin of the singer and the need for sanctuary or purification in Christ, the safe haven. Sentimental hymns explored separation from and unification with the divine, rather than from another human being. In these hymns, the "evocative metaphors for a looming existential threat" common to sentimental literature were typically expressed as the "storms of life." The texts of the three hymns most frequently incorporated into recitations—"Jesus, Lover of My Soul"; "Nearer, My God, to Thee"; and "Rock of Ages"—all share an emphasis on the faithful soul's need to be united with God. In "Jesus, Lover of My Soul" she longs to fly to the bosom of Christ to hide from life's tempests; likewise, in "Rock of Ages," the singer longs to "Let me hide myself in thee" and be cleansed of sin. The public recitations of female performers were thus made more socially acceptable through the addition of hymn tunes that expressed personal weakness and subjugation to God's will.

The appearance of "Jesus, Lover of My Soul" in performances of Marianne Farningham's "The Drowning Singer" (sometimes known as "The Last Hymn") was typically sentimental, in that death and the pain of separation from life was mediated by music stressing how a connection to Christ would substitute for the character's loss. For the shipwrecked man about to drown, the hymn text's literal and metaphorical meanings merged in the final two stanzas of the poem, where the music would have been added.

> Then they listened. He is singing! *"Jesus, lover of my soul!"*
> And the winds brought back the echo, *"While the nearer waters roll;"*
> Strange, indeed, it was to hear him, *"Till the storm of life is past,"*
> Singing bravely from the waters, *"Oh, receive my soul at last!"*
>
> He could have no other refuge! *"Hangs my helpless soul on thee,*
> *Leave, ah, leave me not!"* The singer dropped at last into the sea,
> And the watchers, looking homeward, though their eyes with tears made dim,
> Said, "He passed to be with Jesus in the singing of that hymn."

The hymn text and its music dramatically depict the man's drowning and also express its underlying religious meaning. "The Last Hymn" was widely performed and reprinted in numerous anthologies, including those of Northrop, where it appeared with a simple, textless piano arrangement of the hymn;[57]

Soper noted that it was appropriate for young people's Christian Endeavor programs.[58] Emma Griffith Lumm published a similar text, titled "The Catholic Psalm," in which a woman singing "Ave sanctissima" to her baby during a raging storm inspires the ship's crew to sing as well; the vessel is saved, but the woman dies, passing "safe into harbor." As in "The Last Hymn," the lines of chant to be sung are italicized, but no music is provided.[59]

Both "Nearer, My God, to Thee" and "Rock of Ages" were sung or recited to music in association with new poetic texts based on them. "Nearer, My God, to Thee" was referenced in several poems. The stanzas of "Nearer to Thee" each relayed difficult life situations in which people sang the hymn in order to renew their faith, a further elaboration of its central theme.[60] The second stanza of "Nearer, My God, to Thee" depicts the poet in darkness, weighed down by cares, yet she dreams of the closer connection to God made possible by such a renewal:

> Though, like the wanderer,
> The sun gone down,
> Darkness comes over me,
> My rest a stone;
> Yet in my dreams I'd be
> Nearer, my God, to Thee,
> Nearer, my God, to Thee,—
> Nearer to Thee!

In many cases, music in religious recitations served to transport characters from life unto death. Andrew H. Smith's "Nearer—There," in which soldiers hear their comrade sing the hymn as he lies dying on the battlefield, is also similar to various musical recitations with military topics, described in the following section; its story recalls the hymn's later stanzas, in which the speaker is beckoned by angels to the steps of heaven, "upward to fly."[61] Although there are no signs that either "Nearer to Thee" or "Nearer—There" were as popular as "The Dying Singer," such texts, sprinkled across the elocution literature and provided with directions for singing musical excerpts, indicate the prevalence of freely adapting common hymns.

In addition to "Jesus, Lover of My Soul," the most popular hymn included in recitations was "Rock of Ages."[62] The hymn's music was added to a poem of the same name by Edward H. Rice, which traced a woman's life from girlish innocence through life's troubles, to her death as an old woman; its poetic refrain was taken from the hymn's first two lines, their meaning enriched on each subsequent repetition through new associations with shifting circumstances. Frank Fenno directed that the refrains be sung, first "in a cheerful, sprightly manner," then "sad with much feeling," and finally, "in the weak, broken, trembling voice of age."[63] Although it is not clear whether she sang or recited the hymn, Mrs. Sherwin's "spell-binding" performance of "Rock of Ages," which followed Fenno's trajectory, was praised as more than "a sermon"; it began "with a gay and thoughtless air," transformed until the hymn "became a prayer of intercession."[64] Other hymns served as the basis of recitations in which women grew from youthful innocence through life's sufferings, such as "Abide with Me" by S. H. Thayer, based on the hymn of the same name.[65] In a text similar to "Rock of Ages," "A Woman's Song," published in a children's anthology in 1893, a dying woman sings "Jesus, Lover of My Soul," and at its close, angels bear her song up to paradise, where her soul finds rest.[66] Marie Irish combined the nautical analogies of "The Drowning Singer" with the chronological transformation of young girl to old woman in a tableau complete with an actual boat, all based on "Jesus Savior, Pilot Me."[67] The hymn, which compares Christ to a mother who "stills her child," was in keeping with the feminized religious sentiments of the period that Hobbs has described.

## Women, the Battlefield, and Heroines

Many recitation anthologies contained patriotic poetry about military topics, in which valiant soldiers, immersed in masculine camaraderie, fight dramatic battles. Although male elocutionists would have been the most likely performers of such texts—volumes such as James Brownlee's *Martial Recitations* and George Baker's *Grand Army Speaker* were specifically designed for Civil War veterans[68]—women often performed poetry about soldiers on the battlefield. Female elocutionists appeared at events held for the Fourth of July and Decoration Day, reciting texts that, as Joan Shelley Rubin has noted, served in rituals of memorialization and "civic sacralization."[69] Meetings of Civil War veterans' organizations featured literary and musical entertainments, such as at the so-called campfires at the reunions of the Grand Army of the Republic (GAR). Female members of the ladies' auxiliary or the daughters of aging veterans also appeared in GAR events; Kate Sherwood's campfire anthology contains poems suitable for women to speak at such occasions.[70]

Women's recitations generally did not center on the political contexts for military action or on battle scenes, but frequently dealt with soldiers' connections to the women in their lives; for example, an often-recited poem (rarely performed with music) was the gruesome "Searching for the Slain," in which the mother and wife of a deceased soldier go to retrieve his body amid dying men on the bloody battlefield. In spite of its popularity and its female characters, the poem was a problematic choice for women. In the 1884 satirical poem "The Ballad of Cassandra Brown," the would-be suitor of a lady elocutionist complains of her ready association with its graphic descriptions of the outcome of war:

It's not pleasant for a fellow when the jewel of his soul
Wades through slaughter on the carpet, while her orbs in frenzy roll;
What was I that I should murmur? Yet it gave me grievous pain
That she rose in social gatherings, and Searched among the Slain.

I was forced to look upon her in my desperation dumb,
Knowing well that when her awful opportunity was come
She would give us battle, murder, sudden death at very least,
As a skeleton of warning, and a blight upon the feast.[71]

In contrast, the war-related accompanied recitations most popular with female performers dealt with breaks in fighting during which music comforted soldiers or increased their nostalgia for home. Popular parlor songs mentioned in the text would be played at the appropriate spot, not only in order to depict the narrative, but also to evoke a similar sentiment in the audience as in the fictional soldiers.

The most programmed text of this type was a Civil War poem commonly referred to as "Music on the Rappahannock." It told of a pause in the conflict, during which units of the Union and Confederate armies on either side of the Rappahannock River serenaded one another competitively, each with music that represented their side. At the close, soldiers from both armies fell quiet, as their memories of "Home, Sweet Home" were evoked through hearing the song composed by Henry Bishop—the sound of the well-loved favorite would have created a poignant climax for listeners. Audiences might have known that a historical incident had inspired the poem; although both soldiers' memoirs and Civil War historians are unclear about the date, most assume the event took place near Fredericksburg late in 1862 or early in 1863.[72] Captain George Pingree recalled the bugle's original rendition of the song: "As the sweet sounds rose and fell on the evening air . . . over the Rappahannock, all listened intently, and I don't believe there was a dry eye in all those assembled thousands."[73] So many period sources recount musical interchanges between the armies that the tale achieved a kind of mythic status, which complicates reconstruction of elocutionists' performances. No fewer than five poems about "Music on the Rappahannock" were published in the late nineteenth century, yet no text with that title appeared in books of poetry.[74] The most anthologized poem was John Reuben Thompson's "Music in Camp," which appears in Soper's 1901 anthology with directions for adding "Dixie," "Yankee Doodle," and "Home, Sweet Home."[75] However, elocutionists could also have used C. C. Somerville's poem "Home, Sweet Home"—it was advertised by Werner as early as 1887 as "Music on the Rappahannock" along with music by G. C. Bell, although no copies appear to be extant. Elocutionists could well have adapted familiar songs for their performances without any need for a single published score. Although musical accompaniments and even texts may have varied, some version of the tale of Civil War music was performed in settings from school exhibitions to an 1898 GAR event in Carnegie Hall. At an 1891 Brooklyn benefit for soldier residents of the Home for Consumptives, the reciter Mrs. Nelson was introduced by a former Union general, and her selection had been programmed by request of local GAR members, who were presumably already familiar with the work.[76] Nelson was accompanied by the strings of the orchestra behind the curtain performing "The Star-Spangled Banner," "Hail Columbia," "Rally 'Round the Flag," "Dixie," "Maryland, My Maryland," and "Home, Sweet Home." As the story bypassed any references to the outcomes of particular battles or of the Civil War as a whole, "Music on the Rappahannock" appears to have been as popular with Southern reciters as with those who appeared at GAR events, which stressed national unity.[77] That the performance tradition was long lasting is suggested by Jessie Alexander's 1922 anthology, which contains a variant of Somerville's "Home, Sweet Home" titled "On the Rappahannock"—perhaps she came to modify the text over the long years she performed it.[78] Regardless, Alexander's version specifically indicates where to insert the "Star-Spangled Banner," "Rally 'Round the Flag," "Dixie," and "Home, Sweet Home."

Almost as frequently performed was Bayard Taylor's "Song in Camp," in which Crimean war soldiers sing "Annie Laurie" together before meeting their deaths:

> There was a pause. A guardsman said,
> "We storm the forts to-morrow;
> Sing while we may, another day
> Will bring enough of sorrow."
> . . .
> They sang of love, and not of fame;
> Forgot was Britain's glory:
> Each heart recalled a different name,
> But all sang "Annie Laurie."

The poem ends with images of the young girls mourning the men who had sung of them and the assertion that "The bravest are the tenderest," retaining the soldiers' links to women. Several anthologies suggested that the speaker or a chorus should introduce "Annie Laurie" at the appropriate point in the poem. For the line "But all sang 'Annie Laurie,'" *The Ideal Orator* omitted the title of the song, and simply included three verses of it with piano accompaniment;[79] other anthologies sometimes inserted the first stanza of text (without music) at this point. In 1916, Alexander published directions for aligning the structure of "Annie Laurie" to that of the spoken text, indicating that after the "sorrow" predicted in the third stanza, "a chorus or quartette may hum softly the air of Annie Laurie, faster than usual tempo, keeping in time with the rhythm of the reader through five stanzas, alternating verse—refrain, verse—refrain. Then repeat refrain."[80] Similar instructions are provided for "The Whistling Regiment" by James Clarence Harvey, in which "Annie Laurie" whistled becomes a signal for captured Union soldiers who are rescued by the speaker's sweetheart. Reciters were instructed how to incorporate piano accompaniment and whistling, marked by symbols in the text and "so timed that the last strain of *Annie Laurie* may end with the words, 'would lay me down and die.'" The directions added, "The beat of the drums can be introduced with good effect, but it is better to omit it unless it can be done skilfully."[81]

Although documenting performances of them is difficult, analogous text-music combinations emphasizing the personal connections between women and soldiers sometimes surfaced in period anthologies. Although no copies appear to have survived, Werner advertised sheet music for "Very Dark" by G. M. Rosenberg, in which soldiers gather around a wounded comrade amid the roar of cannons. He dies thinking of home, uttering the words "It's growing very dark, mother," although it is not clear what music accompanied these sentiments. Another example, "Mother's Song," in Mrs. Kinsey's 1893 Sunday school speaker, combines the "singing soldiers" genre with poetic texts that incorporate hymns. In the poem, resting soldiers sing hymns their mothers had taught them, including "Am I a Soldier of the Cross" and "All Hail the Power of Jesus' Name," enabling them to replace fear with "tender thoughts."[82] In almost all of these texts, the music heard is associated, if not directly with women, with home and the feelings it inspires; soldiers' songs are their sentimental keepsakes of their loved ones. In this way, female reciters expressed values associated with women's sphere and domestic life even as they recounted scenes taking place during war.

A few recitations featured women as heroic figures, similar to the men found in poems such as Longfellow's "Paul Revere's Ride" or Thomas Buchanan Read's "Sheridan's Ride." For example, Will Carleton's "The Ride of Jennie McNeal" explicitly compares its title character to both Revere and Sheridan. In John Greenleaf Whittier's "Barbara Frietchie," an old woman defies Stonewall Jackson and flies the Union flag. However, regardless of the gender of their central figures, these texts were not regularly accompanied by music. The most recited poem with a brave heroine was "Curfew Must Not Ring Tonight" by Rose Hartwick Thorpe, in which a woman rescues her imprisoned lover by preventing the bell that will mark his execution from ringing by swinging from its clapper. Widely reprinted—an illustrated version appeared on the cover of *The Elocutionist's Journal* in 1877—the poem's popularity was unrivaled in the late nineteenth century, so much so that it became the text most often cited in criticisms of elocution. Parodied many times and made into silent films in the teens, Thorpe's poem came to represent the artificiality and amateurism associated with female performers. Although its topic groups it with texts that inspired bell tones, "Curfew Must Not Ring Tonight" suggested no music, as its central idea is the *lack* of sound created through young Bessie's heroism. In spite of at least two composed melodramatic settings, Thorpe's poem was typically performed unaccompanied.[83] A popular poem with a similar plot was "How Jane Conquest Rang the Bell" by James Milne, in which a woman leaves her dying child—a common sentimental topos—to ring an alarm, bringing rescuers to a ship burning offshore. In spite of Jane's heroic feat, as suggested by her last name, the poem centers not on her actions that save the ship, but on the reward for her religious faith; having prayed to Christ to watch over her child, she returns to finds him sleeping peacefully. Hallie Quinn Brown's anthology notes that "Jane Conquest" had musical accompaniment, and as she specialized in bell tones, it seems possible that any additions to her performances would have imitated bells.[84]

Brown's book also features a female version of the heroic-ride genre by George Lansing Taylor titled "Fifty Miles an Hour: Mrs. Garfield's Ride to Washington."[85] In the poem, the wife of President Garfield rushes by train to return to her husband's side after an assassin shot him in 1881. Although the topic is patriotic, as the nation cries to God to save its president, the poem's focus is the domestic and personal, demonstrating a woman's religious devotion to her spouse; Mrs. Garfield is "a weak woman," not a heroine:

> O, Wedded Love! Ne'er angel flew
> From Heaven to earth with richer dower!
> Angels waft this true wife through,
> Fifty miles an hour!

Brown added a brief section of prose to close the poem, describing the tragic failure of female love to save Garfield: "Hark! At the midnight hour, borne on the gentle breeze, from an hundred belfries high, listen to the mournful—'toll!' Ring out ye solemn bells, chant your sad farewell! Garfield's gone. A nation's prayers; a mother's love; a wife's tender devotion—stayed not thy hand, O, Death!" Brown's annotations suggest that this text was accompanied by music, which could have assisted in depicting its funeral bells and expression of grief.

Poems such as "The Last Hymn," "Music on the Rappahannock," "Aux Italiens," and "King Robert of Sicily" made regular appearances on female elocutionists' programs. They were performed with music so frequently that their accompaniments, although handled in a flexible manner, nonetheless became a regular, expected part of the performance. The texts that required music fell into recognizable genres based on their thematic content: audiences

were treated to tales of lost love, soldiers longing for home, and sufferers' religious faith in the face of death. Dobson has written that to the "sentimental
mind" the era's common motifs "do not wallow in excessive emotionality;
rather they represent an essential reality and *must* be treated with heightened
feeling;"[86] in elocutionary performance, this heightened feeling was created
with music. At the core of these topics were sentimental values that recalled
women's domestic world and made their performances on the platform acceptable despite their gender. Elocutionists drew on a small group of dances,
hymns, and parlor songs that enabled them to reach into audiences' hearts
and to move them with music that they loved. While spoken-word performers
also gave published melodramatic settings of popular poems with full piano
accompaniments, many of these postdate more informal arrangements. In
any case, they were programmed much less often, not only because of their
complexity and the amount of rehearsal required, but also because, in spite of
their success as musical compositions, they were probably less effective with
audiences than the simple power of a familiar melody. Ultimately, the poems
performed most successfully with musical accompaniments were those in
which the music was already central to their meaning, a sentimental keepsake
expressing love, loss, faith, and the power of human connections.

# 5. Grecian Urns in Iowa Towns
## *Delsarte and* The Music Man

Lovely, ladies, lovely. Now turn. Take the body with
you. Lovely. Now let's have a try at our Grecians Urns.
One Grecian Urn. . . . Two Grecian Urns. . . . . . . and a
fountain. . . . . trickle, trickle, trickle. Splendid, ladies.
—Eulalie, act 2, scene 1, of *The Music Man*

When Meredith's Willson's *The Music Man* became a Broadway hit
in 1957, it was welcomed with unabashed enthusiasm by women's clubs in
the composer's native Iowa. Within the year, club programs from across the
state—from Maquoketa, Mechanicsville, and Mount Pleasant to Redfield,
Red Oak, and Schaller—included the composer or his musical as a study topic.[1]
The appearance of the 1962 movie and its premiere in Willson's hometown of
Mason City generated additional excitement. Underlying much of the early
publicity surrounding *The Music Man* was the assumption that River City
and Mason City were one and the same, and the show's more pointed satire of
early twentieth-century Iowa was brushed over in a rush to declare it an evening of nostalgia and Americana.[2] Whether Iowa's clubwomen were pleased
with Willson's reconstruction of its past was not recorded in the press. Were
older members nostalgic for the era of their youth depicted in the musical?
And did they remember the actual Delsarte exhibitions, popular in Iowa and
across America in the 1890s and 1900s, which were comically portrayed in the
exertions of the mayor's wife, Eulalie Mackecknie Shinn and her less-than-
graceful entourage? For in addition to the "seventy-six trombones" sold to
the gullible residents of River City for their sons, Professor Harold Hill also
inspires attempts at artistic performance by its female residents, inviting the
mayor's wife to chair a "Ladies' Auxiliary for the Classic Dance."[3] Flattered
that her "every move . . . bespeaks Delsarte," Mrs. Shinn valiantly leads a
group of River City women in posing to music. Delsarte was a popular activity for middle- and upper-class women before World War I, but for modern
audiences it is the least recognizable aspect of Willson's re-creation of small-

town cultural life. Not only were Delsarte poses, replicating ancient Greek statuary, intertwined with both elocution and music, they offered a means by which women could validate their bodies in performance by connecting them to the highest art of Western culture. The history of the Delsarte movement reveals that gender is at the core of River City's cultural "trouble," and Willson's satire of women as bodies echoes the reaction against their artistic aspirations in the Progressive Era.

Although the Delsarte system, named for the French singer and teacher François Delsarte (1811–71), is often cited for its influence on modern dance, its American roots were in elocution.[4] Described as training for "physical culture" and "expression," the range of activities that fell under the term *Delsarte* initially drew on elocutionary poses that had been in use for more than a century.[5] In the late nineteenth century, elocutionary stances were extended into physical movements to be presented while reciting or as silent pantomimes (sometimes called *wordless poems*) performed to music. Newly renamed Delsarte anthologies added prefaces about François Delsarte, and while some books' photos of poses were somewhat extraneous to their textual content, directions for and illustrations of pantomiming increased. Editors sometimes provided poems annotated with codes that indicated the appropriate poses.[6] Many women found that Delsarte posing made a suitable finale for their program or was a means of including multiple women in a group performance.

Although he achieved somewhat of a cult status in America decades after his death (inspiring the sales of Delsarte soap and corsets as well as elocution manuals), Delsarte himself wrote little about his teaching method; even during his lifetime, the pedagogue was described as the "magnificent sayer of beautiful nothings."[7] His ideas were transmitted and popularized by Americans, most notably Steele MacKaye (1842–94), who had studied with him in France, and Genevieve Stebbins (b. 1857, retired 1907), who had not. Several of the best-known figures who identified themselves as followers of Delsarte (e.g., Henrietta and Edmund Russell and Henrietta Hovey) appear to have excelled most at self-marketing, exaggeratedly advertising themselves as teachers to the socially prominent and undertaking frequent moves because of employment problems.[8] Practitioners argued vociferously in print about what was and was not true Delsarte, jockeying for the position of authentic Delsarte disciple. However, when Delsarte's daughter Marie visited America in 1892, she expressed surprise that Americans' versions of her father's teachings in no way resembled them.[9]

Just as elocution allowed women to give voice to great literature, Delsarte made women's bodies respectable in performance by associating them with high culture. Although some male performers did teach Delsarte, writing about the method emphasized women's particular claim to the aesthetic realm (a similar claim occurred in music).[10] Stebbins considered her version of Del-sartism to be a combination of science and athletics—gendered male—and aesthetics, which she gendered female.[11] Delsarte was not merely training for performance—it had a strongly mystical tinge and aspired to both a physical dimension, described as having a tripartite division, derived from the similar *mental, motive,* and *vital* classifications of physiognomy, and a spiritual one. Delsarte promised women a new level of physical grace, fitness, beauty, and social success.[12] Posing was to be personally transforming as well as performa-tive; in aiming at expression through physical culture, a Delsarte student would come to feel the specific emotion expressed.[13] Stebbins popularized the practice of posing as Greek statues, gowned in robes, sometimes wearing white makeup to suggest marble; thus Delsarte practitioners came to physically embody an artistic ideal. The 1890 edition of Elsie Wilbor's *Delsarte Recitation Book* featured photos of Greek statues to serve as models for potential posers, and the 1905 publication added photographs of women in tableaux. Stebbins's and others' poses typically centered on female characters from the Bible or myth: Niobe, Miriam, Jephtha, Ester, Isis, Ariadne, Psyche, Ceres, Brunhilde, and Ishtar.[14] Stebbins's pantomimes consisted of both speaking and movement in costume, accompanied by several musical instruments.

Historians have considered Delsartism part of the Progressive-Era move-ment to improve women's health, liberating them from corsets and other dangerously restrictive Victorian attire.[15] Attempts to transform female bod-ies into Greek statues might appear to have been equally restrictive, but as demonstrated by illustrations in Werner's *Voice*, the Venus de Milo was more related to the physical realities of the female body than a corseted waist.[16] The flowing gowns that served as women's costumes allowed them unrestrained breathing and a range of movement, as well as signaling their association with classical rhetoric.[17] In 1892 Emily Bishop claimed that Delsarte could bring a new freedom to women:

> Why do women feel trepidation when they are to read a paper at a literary so-ciety, or to give a five minute talk at the "Club"? Because they are conscious of the instruments of expression—conscious of hands, attitudes, voice, even dress. Fear is born of this self-consciousness, they dare not do what they are capable of doing. When by self-knowledge and self-discipline, women shall gain habitual, easy control of their bodies, they will have achieved an important emancipation.[18]

Practitioners of Delsarte could begin to feel at home in their own bodies, which made them feminine in a masculine world. Perhaps in their stylized bodily control women did experience a new sense of freedom—the photographs in instructional books sometimes reveal them in decidedly unfeminine poses. The text beneath the pose for "Dispersion" in *The Delsarte Speaker* (1895), a woman with outstretched arms, is a line taken from a male-dominated scene in Shakespeare's *Titus Andronicus*: "Scatter and disperse the giddy Goths!"[19] Because the book's poses show both men and women, it could have provided a male figure for this text and its corresponding pose. Taylor Susan Lake has described Delsarte poses as "potent, striking figures" and suggested that women used statue posing to "resist as well as conform to dominant constructions of women as powerless."[20] Some instruction books support this notion: Clara Power Edgerly's tableau "The Death of Virginia" depicts "the faithful nurse, with raised arm and clenched hand" who "calls down vengeance from the gods" for the slaying of a young girl by her father's hand, a powerful image.[21] Such stylized visual manifestations of women involved in dramatic actions were a notable departure from the purely stationary position required for recitation.

The Delsarte movement's influence on both acting and modern dance has been widely noted, and its female adherents have been credited with regendering the "masculine rhetorical body according to feminine qualities of beauty, grace, flexibility, and sensitivity."[22] However, even as they positioned statue posing as drawn from the heritage of Western art, women placed themselves in a position to be essentialized as physical, not intellectual, beings. After increased access to elocutionary education, women had made advances in their right to speak language in ways and in venues previously dominated by men, to stand on platforms and be heard. In some ways, Delsarte represented abandonment of their voices for their bodies because of the belief that physical expression of emotion was superior to language. Steele MacKaye found that the body was more expressive than "music, speech, or the voice," and Stebbins, in particular, rejected language in favor of bodily truth.[23] Delsarte performers might feel a range of emotions not otherwise considered socially acceptable for a woman while performing poses expressing anger or command. Nonetheless, their Greek costuming contained, according to Lake, "contradictory connotations of female eroticism and womanly purity within the controlling gaze of the male spectator."[24] Delsarte performance seemingly represented a sort of feminine *Gesamtkunstwerk*, featuring literature, the visual arts, movement, and accompanying music, yet its original motivating force, the language-based expressions of elocution, faded from prominence. A review of Florence Fowle Adams's pantomime book questioned the existence of any relationship between women's bodies, however pleasing to look at, and literature: "We do not understand exactly why the famine described so vividly by Longfellow should be personified now by a comely, lightly-clad young woman standing on a carpeted floor, and again by the same damsel on a pedestal, but the attitudes are picturesque."[25]

Delsarte performances were criticized by the elocutionary community and subjected to ridicule in *Werner's Voice Magazine*, even as the publisher con-

tinued to be a primary source of Delsarte-related information. Statue posing
and Delsartism were a frequent source of controversy among the National
Association of Elocutionists, as its more traditional members, oriented toward
training the voice to transmit intellectual ideals, naturally resisted the new
emphasis on the body, not to mention the influx of women in pseudo-Grecian
attire.[26] It is often difficult to distinguish criticism of the ideals of Delsartism
with that of the women involved. Elocution pedagogue F. Townsend Southwick
described a Delsartean as someone "of the female sex, whose chief ends and
aims in life are attitudinizing and gushing over the Delsarte philosophy" and
acquiring a "limper," "lackadaisical," and "dreamful" costumed appearance
through "a new aesthetic rig, the like of which was never seen before and will
probably never be seen again."[27] The numerous Delsarte satires were inevitably
gender related. In 1889, the same year that Anna Morgan published *An Hour
with Delsarte* with drawings of various poses,[28] the play *Forty Minutes with a
Crank; or, The Seldarte Craze* parodied Delsarte teachings and featured an
ambitious female student named Minnie Moneybags.[29] In an 1897 satire, a
male suitor retreats after proposing marriage because his sweetheart performs
the wrong Delsarte expression, and he believes she has rejected him.[30] The additional encroachment brought about by the Delsarte movement of women into
elocution, which had traditionally been a male domain, was a major source of
male elocutionists' condescension.[31] In a telling poem, "Cupid vs. Delsarte,"
a professor of elocution at a "well-known eastern college" faces competition
from a beguiling Delsartean, "Eugenia Boaster," whose arts transfix his male
students:

> At the hall the students waited
> For the maiden young and fair,
> Though I knew my business fated,
> With the students I was there.
>
> Dressed in Grecian gown and smiling,
> "We do so," she said, "or so,"
> (Every motion hearts beguiling).
> "Head contrary to torso."
>
> Ah! I thought, such blows to parry
> Would kind Cupid take my part;
> I might then the maiden marry,
> Stay her influence and art.[32]

The threatened professional solves both problems—love and competition—by
marrying Eugenia; her gown is hung in the closet, as Delsarte is laid "on the
shelf," undoubtedly the place that many male elocutionists hoped it would take
within their discipline. The underlying criticism that women were abandoning

their socially condoned place in the domestic sphere was also apparent in an 1893 satirical newspaper article, which promoted the "international system," a series of Delsarte-style exercises based on sweeping, dusting, floor scrubbing, washing, and ironing, as being beneficial both for young women and "an entire household."[33] Another male commentator claimed, "After a woman has crawled over and under all of the down-stairs furniture and skated down a winding staircase, with a dusting cap tilted rakishly over her left eye, she will not feel like paying $4 an hour for a set of Delsarte exercises."[34] Nonetheless, such reactions to Delsarte indicate how popular it actually was.

## Deadly as Nymphs, Naiads, and Graces: Delsarte in Iowa

Historians have examined the Delsarte movement through the careers of its leading advocates and as espoused in its publications; however, average practitioners outside metropolitan areas have received little consideration. Iowa's performances, later fictionalized in *The Music Man*, provide an unusual opportunity for a case study of Delsartean activities. Delsarte was widespread, if the quantity of performances in the state indicates how far the practice had permeated small-town America. Between the late 1880s and 1920, performances took place in approximately fifty different Iowa communities, from major cities like Des Moines and Cedar Rapids to tiny villages such as Ireton and Pomeroy with populations of around five hundred. Given the size of Iowa towns at the turn of the twentieth century, it is not surprising that well over half of the performances occurred in towns of five thousand or less—the multiple "River Cities" of the Iowa landscape.

Only a small portion of Delsarte posing in Iowa was dedicated to the representation of Greek statues. Evenings of Grecian tableaux took place in Des Moines in 1891 and in Cedar Rapids in 1894; another Greek myth display occurred in Des Moines in 1904, organized by the Des Moines Women's Club. Intended to raise money for its art fund, the event reflected the club's artistic interests; it had been displaying paintings in the YMCA building and three years later founded the city's first art gallery. The seventeen scenes to be presented were announced in the newspaper, including four friezes (one from a sarcophagus), "Toilet of the Bride (From a painting found at Herculaneum)" and other scenes popular with Delsarteans, such as the "Niobe Group." The notification allowed viewers to "refurbish" their "rusty" knowledge of Greek art, "which is absolutely necessary to the keen and artistic appreciation and understanding of the entertainment."[35] The *Des Moines Mail and Times* explained that for three-quarters of an hour, the women would "with graceful, rhythmic motion pass from one tableau to another, drawing you as if by a magic spell through the mazes of the old Athenian city disclosing truthful facsimiles of historic treasures inherited from ages long since past."[36] The press hailed the event as "perpetuating and increasing . . . the love of the pure and beautiful." However, the same article revealed that the attraction was not only cultural improvement: "These young ladies, representing the choicest flowers in the coronal of Des Moines' beautiful women, have always been considered admirable in modern dress; but when they add to their own charms the association[s] that cluster around Greek costume and scenes, they will be positively adorable. Dangerous as simple American girls[,] they will be deadly as nymphs, naiads and graces."[37] Even if female performers intended to present an intellectually edifying and artistically refined event, mixed audiences could respond to their physicality as they would to women's bodies in staged events without any aspirations to high culture.

A similar Grecian Art Festival, with many of the same tableaux, was held in Cedar Rapids for the benefit of St. Luke's Hospital in 1904, reported as "not only a charming affair, but an entertainment with an instructive thread running through its woof of drapery and fibre of physical being," which "should revive an interest in the human form divine, not only from an artistic standpoint, but from the further consideration of health and strength."[38] The history and literature section of the Cedar Rapids Woman's Club had hosted tableaux a decade earlier with equally educational motives. A reading of the myth to be depicted preceded the statuary, created by fourteen women and three boys. The figures represented included the nine muses, Juno, Minerva, Athena, Circe, Theia, Flora, Pomona, Themis, Niobe and Child, and the Fates, Graces, and Charites, all for the edification of club members and the public.

More often, Delsarte performances in Iowa were not intended to depict ancient Greek art, and exhibitions were typically one facet of programs that also included music, poetic recitation, oratorical contests, physical education displays, or patriotic tableaux. A Delsarte display was a suitable finale for an evening's entertainment, and its white gown was adopted for any performative posing, whether related to ancient Greece or not. In 1919, when the senior oratory students of Upper Iowa University performed a melodramatic pantomime to Oscar Wilde's fairy-tale-like *The Nightingale and the Rose*, they "wore the old Greek costumes" (figure 5.1).[39] This practice was not limited to Iowa; female students at the New Orleans College of Oratory and Elocution were required to wear white gowns for most performances as late as 1925.[40]

Delsarte in Iowa and elsewhere was primarily a result of women's Progressive-Era community involvement and their desire for social betterment. Performances organized by women's clubs and church groups were staged in opera houses or school auditoriums. Ticket sales typically supported a worthy cause: a library, hospital, or missionary fund. Delsarte's inclusion in private

Figure 5.1. Pose for *The Nightingale and the Rose* by Oscar Wilde, Seniors in Oratory, Upper Iowa University, Fayette, Iowa (1919). State Historical Society of Iowa, Iowa City.

musicales is reported far less frequently. The elaborate celebrations surrounding the 1892 birthday of Carroll's wealthy citizen A. W. Patterson at his mansion was apparently a major community event, as it not only included a Miss Sutherland's poses, but also band music, piano solos, recitation, songs, and refreshment tables on the lawn illuminated by electric lights.[41] Although the majority of Delsarte performers were amateurs, in the pre-World War I period, numerous female elocutionists, some of whom were undoubtedly professionals, incorporated poses into their Iowa performances. When Nellie Peck Saunders's Tableaux d'Art toured the state, Saunders recited and nine young women posed. By the time the professional company appeared in Waterloo and Algona in 1901, Delsarte had already been presented by local schoolgirls, so the ensemble's performance style would not have been completely unfamiliar to the towns' residents.

The ability to teach Delsarte appears to have been a marketable skill for women; newspapers were filled with notices placed by prospective instructors organizing a class for ladies. Sometimes a recital by the would-be teacher introduced the techniques they could teach. After a period of practice, the class presented a public performance, and its instructor moved on to another community. For several weeks, members of the Art Society of Mount Pleasant studied with Anna Morris of Des Moines and then gave a closing exhibition at Saunders' Opera House, which "was attended by a good-sized crowd."[42]

Some arrangements came about through personal acquaintances; between approximately 1891 and 1897, Mary Drew Wilson of Sioux City made numerous
visits to her mother's home in Le Mars, advertising her availability for elocution and Delsarte lessons while she was there. Traveling Delsarteans were also
available to assist women in presenting a local program. For example, Baptist
churchwomen in Anita engaged Evelyn Allen Aitchison, an elocutionist from
Detroit, to direct their 1892 entertainment.[43] Teachers undertaking such a career
must have developed the charm of a Harold Hill to inspire enough enthusiasm
to generate their employment. Anna Morris taught in a number of towns, and
when she visited Cedar Rapids, reciting at and directing its "Grecian Art Festival," community women interested in Delsarte requested that she remain
there afterwards.[44] That Morris had the aptitude to attract would-be posers is
suggested by her third place in the *Des Moines Leader*'s contest for most popular
lady teacher, with over six thousand votes.[45] Elocution instructors also taught
Delsarte in their homes, or, like Florence Dudley Ross of Waterloo, at a music
conservatory; female students of the Ross Conservatory included poses between
the piano and vocal solos on its 1914 and 1915 commencement recitals.[46]

Delsarte training was also offered by the numerous women who taught
spoken-word performance or physical culture at colleges across the state. As
performing artists, they sometimes appeared in concerts with music faculty
members; Dorothy Morton Horning toured the region with Central College's
Concert Company.[47] Student ensembles, most often male glee clubs, often
took the female elocution professor on tour with them; a female reader appeared with Cornell College's orchestra as late as 1927. Many colleges had
schools of oratory offering a two-year program leading to a certificate, and
college catalogs sometimes noted that Delsarte philosophies were behind the
training they offered. Larger programs sometimes had a male professor of
public speaking and a female instructor of expression, maintaining a gendered
divide. Likewise, male students were more likely to fill a school's intercolle-
giate debate team, while oratory recitals with music were the primary venues
for female students' Delsarte exhibitions. Even if posing was not a consistent
feature of the spoken-word recitals at the semester's close, women's literary
societies sponsored entertainments where statue posing took place. In 1908,
Cornell College's Alethean Society gave a public exhibition centered on the
works of Longfellow. Its crowning event was thirteen women standing on
plinths, posing to "The Famine" from *Hiawatha*, spoken by a reciter on one
side of the stage (figure 5.2). The student newspaper called it "one of the best
things ever seen on the auditorium platform," and found the pantomime in a
semidark room with the "soft red glow" of the footlights striking.[48]

Delsarte instructors also appeared at summer Normal Institutes for schoolteachers, training them in poses and marches designed for their elementary

Figure 5.2. "The Famine," from Henry Wadsworth Longfellow's *Hiawatha*,
Alethean Society, Cornell College, Mount Vernon, Iowa (1908). State Historical
Society of Iowa, Iowa City.

and high school students; even kindergarten graduations sometimes had Delsarte drills by "the little misses of the primary department."[49] High school
exhibitions were typically organized by physical education departments, and
moving to express particular emotions or to pose in formation was only one of
various healthy bodily activities, which might also include drills with wands,
hoops, scarves, flags, fans, or brooms. Here, Delsarte, seen in the company
of dumbbell lifting and Indian club swinging, became less about its aesthetic
affect and was largely a demonstration of physical well-being. Such exhibitions
were never without music, heard both to accompany students' exercises and
for its own sake: band selections, piano or chamber works, or songs; recitation
was also regularly featured. In addition to girls' Delsarte and other physical
activities such as fencing, a maypole, and a beanbag toss, the Cedar Rapids
High School's 1896 exhibition included a cornet solo, a trio for two violins and
cello, and four recitations, including Felicia Hemans's popular "Casabianca"
("The Boy Stood on the Burning Deck").[50]

   Because of the physicality of posing and the drills involved in group work,
Delsarte teachers associated with public schools were primarily physical
education instructors rather than elocutionists. Julia Hull, who advertised
in Waterloo in the mid-1890s, was a dance instructor who also taught "deportment" and "modern Delsarte," not oratory.[51] Morris, who worked in the
Des Moines schools, did appear as a reader but also demonstrated Delsarte
and Indian club swinging in her performances. Her book, *Physical Culture in
the Public Schools* (1888), contains exercises and drills to be given at school
exhibitions, as well as Delsarte poses with musical accompaniments. It also
provided suggestions for "Reading and Declamation" with a list of recom-

mended poems for "Concert Declamation," yet unlike recitation anthologies, contained no actual texts.[52]

Local reactions to Delsarte performances were almost always positive. Iowa newspapermen reprinted tongue-in-cheek remarks about statue posing from other papers, but when it came to their own wives and daughters, they were quick to find such displays visually stunning and well worth seeing. The *Cedar Rapids Evening Gazette* described the opening march of two hundred girls dressed in white for a gymnasium exhibition—from which hundreds were reportedly turned away—as "a vision of beauty, youth and purity" and their movements "models of grace and harmony."[53] After a similar event in Des Moines featuring twenty-seven young women, a reviewer hailed the "freshness and spontaneity . . . lacking in the efforts of the most skillful professionals," adding that it was "delightful as a change from the wearisome routine of present day drama."[54] A group of Algona High School girls were so successful in their Delsarte poses at a declamatory contest, performing while the judges made their decision, that they gave two more performances, one at the state oratory contest in Mason City and another at Algona's Spectacular and Industrial Exhibition the following year.[55] There were occasional reports of events not being as well attended as they might have been, but in general, audiences, particularly those in small towns, were grateful for the entertainment; Delsarte was often the centerpiece of a program that inspired civic pride. When Miss Thompson appeared at the social for Tabor College students, the writer for the *Malvern Leader* wrote, "Tabor people seldom have an opportunity to witness an exhibition of this kind and should be duly thankful."[56] Likewise, when two Bancroft teachers planned an entertainment featuring Delsarte tableaux for the benefit of the public schools, the *Algona Republican* noted that the people of Bancroft should be sure to attend to "show that their work is appreciated."[57]

Only rare hints of discomfort with the physicality of Delsarte performance surface in the Iowa press. Perhaps deflecting the thought that Saunders's Tableaux d'Art would present *tableaux vivants* with simulated nudity in the name of art, such as had been controversial in New York City, the group's advertisement assured potential viewers that what they offered was "pure and chaste and elevating in every particular."[58] The *Algona Advance* seemed somewhat surprised that the company's women, who remained in town the day after their performance, were "refined and intelligent."[59] The few photographs of Iowa girls in Delsarte postures, such as the students at Leander Clark College in its 1911 yearbook (figure 5.3), suggest that their gowns provided considerable coverage, more so than the sleeveless attire of Stebbins or other Delsarteans photographed for Werner's publications.

Clearly, if Delsarte was appropriate for schoolgirls, it must have lost the potentially erotic undertones it originally suggested. Only school superin-

Figure 5.3. "Nearer, My God, to Thee," Leander Clark College, Toledo, Iowa
(1911). State Historical Society of Iowa, Iowa City.

tendent Merrill of Waverly, shocked at the dress length of the little girls in
fairy attire doing Delsarte with "beautiful, graceful charm" at the Episcopal
Church, protested that the exhibition was immoral. That Merrill's was a minority opinion is suggested by the reaction of the Waverly newspaper, which
reported on the resulting indignation of the event's female sponsors at length
and warned that Merrill should "go into hiding for a while."[60]

In the 1890s and 1900s in Iowa, pantomimic posing was widespread, and
larger cities such as Waterloo hosted numerous performances by various
groups, but there was no real sense that Delsarte was developing into an ongoing tradition. Most of the performances from the early twentieth century
were by girls, not grown women, and as in the rest of America, Delsarte largely
disappeared after World War I.[61] While it lasted, the practice of Delsarte offered Iowa's women a curious combination of education and spectacle, exercise
and artistry, as part of their search for culture and expression.

## Music for Delsarte

As Delsarte became popular, the use of music in elocutionary performance increased. Although music was an essential aspect of Delsarte exhibitions, commentators typically made only general musical suggestions; when they did specify particular compositions, these were often the same sorts of popular songs or character pieces incorporated into accompanied recitation. Music was especially necessary when poetry was replaced by poses; it functioned to create a mood, filled the time frame created by statue-like stillness, and facilitated Delsarte's physical movements, pacing the transitions between tableaux. Florence Fowle Adams wrote that music for the "slow, mystic transition" from one posing group to another should be "as dreamy and spirituelle as possible," and Eleanor Denig agreed, calling for music of a "dreamy, Romantic character," such as Franz Schubert's *Serenade* or Frederic Chopin's *Berceuse*.[62] Descriptions of Stebbins's classes identified accompanying music by Schubert, Robert Schumann, Franz Liszt, and Anton Rubinstein.[63] Several instruction guides for pantomimes also suggested accompaniments, sometimes music that was readily available; the seemingly exotic "Japanese Fantastics" pantomime given in kimonos with fans was arranged to a medley from Gilbert and Sullivan's *The Mikado*. *Delsartean Pantomimes* by Rachel Shoemaker lists character pieces for piano, including works such as sections of Mendelssohn's *Midsummer Night's Dream* music, Charles Gounod's *Funeral March of a Marionette*, and Louis Moreau Gottschalk's *The Last Hope*. Shoemaker also indicates hymns and songs that could "be used with good effect": "Abide with Me," "The Star-Spangled Banner," "Robin Adair," "I Dreamt I Dwelt in Marble Halls," or "The Last Rose of Summer."[64] These were far more likely to be heard in Delsarte entertainments than classical selections, and Shoemaker seems to be suggesting pieces that were already well known to her readers.

Much of the music provided for Delsarte exercises was dance music; the popular drill "Revel of the Naiads" required only slow waltz music. The compositions in Morris's physical culture textbook consist largely of marches and waltzes, and the *Chansonettes* published for the exercises of Emerson College students were comprised of two extended works in common time. Their multiple repeated strains have regular phrase structures; thick chordal sonorities and a pounding "oom-pah" bass were to be performed maestoso.[65] Music with strongly emphasized metrical patterns and repeated strains, such as marches and waltzes, were in keeping with the more exercise-oriented Delsarte. Stebbins's *Society Gymnastics and Voice-Culture* (1888) provides piano music, largely Romantic character pieces, to accompany the physical movements of Delsarte exercises.[66] Lyrical, slow-tempo melodies over left-hand arpeggiated patterns accompanied "Swaying for Poise" or "Arm Movements," while marches or dance-like music in common time were designed for "Deep Courtesying [*sic*], Sitting, and Rising," and "Walking."

Characteristic music was sometimes used to accompany posing women physically expressing particular attitudes and emotions. The lengthy program at the Humboldt, Iowa, opera house in 1902 featured poses for curiosity, faith, hope, charity, evening prayer, silence, listening, discernment, appeal, vengeance, vanity, anger, protection, and gossip, among others.[67] Several publications supplied appropriate stylized music, in keeping with Delsarte's original rhetorical basis, to depict particular emotions or dramatic moments. Mary Tucker Magill's book, *Pantomimes; or, Wordless Poems*, contains short character pieces by Leopold Fuenkenstein entitled "Expectation," "Affection," "Anger," "Sorrow," "Joy," "Fear," "Religious Devotion," and "Farewell."[68] Magill described how the music suited the sentiment: "Soft and earnest in expectation and affection, stormy in hatred and fear, plaintive in sorrow, brilliant in joy, and soothing in devotion."[69] Each piece is specifically designed to coordinate with actions depicted in the book's text and photographs; the combination of pantomime and music is designed to express specific poems included in the instructions but not actually meant to be spoken in performance. In another example, Emma Griffith Lumm's books feature photographs of one of her students posing, each accompanied by several bars of characteristic music (figure 5.4). The selections include a fanfare-like introduction and music to accompany the expression of ridicule, comedy, prayer, pity, timidity, defiance, impudence, listening, vanity, coquettishness, and accusation. "Defiance" is musically expressed with a crescendo of tremolos and dissonant chords, concluding with a diminished seventh sonority; the two andante bars for timidity conclude with hesitant rests between chords and a shift from major to minor.[70] Only three of Lumm's musical excerpts have texts: "Coquette" uses the song "Comin' thro' the Rye," and "Prayer" consists of eight bars of the hymn "Nearer, My God, to Thee." The final example is the patriotic "The Star-Spangled Banner." The remaining musical excerpts provided are so brief as to last merely seconds; presumably, they are suggestions for the sort of music one might play for posing and/or to reflect the different moods and events of a specific poem. The music might have served as the basis of more extended improvisation; however, as they are in different keys, they could not be easily combined in a single performance.

When poetic texts were entirely abandoned for Delsartean posing, music became essential to a performance's expression of meaning. Audiences who were unfamiliar with Grecian art were sometimes unable to discern the emotive content of women's stylized pantomimes. After the Tableaux d'Art Company's appearance in Elyria, Ohio, in 1903, the press reported, "Had not the story

Figure 5.4. Poses with musical accompaniment from Emma Griffith Lumm, *The New American Speaker, Elocutionist, and Orator* (n.p.: L. H. Walter, 1910), 32.

intended to be illustrated by the performers been printed on the program no one could have guessed what they attempted to portray."[71] In many cases, music solved this problem by providing the sense of an emotion or mood, or more specific meaning through a song's text, either sung or implied though an instrumental version. When Miss Thomas performed a series of poses representing emotions in 1891, the Estherville, Iowa, paper described how "music harmonized every emotion portrayed."[72] In 1890, Margaret Virginia Jenkins's pupils at the Charleston, South Carolina, Female Seminary, posing in a program titled "A Dream of Ancient Greece" (figure 5.5), were accompanied by well-known songs frequently suggested by pedagogues, which assisted onlookers in comprehending their motions. Jenkins desired to "rouse a sense of the signification of words and music," and believed "the pupils succeeded in conveying something of the spirit of the beautiful song."[73] While the audience was "dreaming" of ancient Greece, they were meant to recall the texts of the songs through seeing the performers' physical poses.

Among Werner's numerous publications is sheet music that includes a poem and instructions for and photographs demonstrating the pantomime to be performed; the accompaniment is typically a simple strophic song arranged for piano. For example, "Rock Me to Sleep, Mother," a popular poem by Elizabeth Akers Allen issued with a Virgin Mary–like cover image, is fundamentally a recitation with music, merely dressed up in Delsarte attire, with a Grecian-gowned performer demonstrating the physical motions.[74] A reader or singer behind a screen would only emerge to perform the two verses "not suitable for posing." The simple major-mode song by Anna D. Cooper belies the sentimental poem's deep unhappiness—the adult speaker longs to return to childhood and have her long-gone mother "rock her to sleep," never to wake. The second half of the final stanza is given a choral setting in order to create a climax.

In many cases, women abandoned any pretense of replicating ancient Greek culture entirely, and the popular songs themselves became the basis of their performances, songs that were imbued with considerably fewer cultural pretensions. Although they retained their white gowns (perhaps reconceiving them as biblical costumes or angels' robes), Delsarte performers were far more likely to pantomime to Christian hymnody than pose as the pagan Niobe group. "Nearer, My God, to Thee" (figure 5.3), "Rock of Ages," and "Jesus, Lover of My Soul," heard in accompanied recitations, were also the most frequently performed illustrated songs in Iowa.[75] Published guides provided instructions for women who wanted to pose to popular songs; as many of these publications postdate performances, they sometimes document practices that were already under way. Like "Rock Me to Sleep," the inexpensive pamphlets typically contained a song's lyrics, instructions for posing, and photographs;

| "A Dream of Ancient Greece" | I Dreamt I Dwelt in Marble Halls |
|---|---|
| Exercise in Harmonic Poise | Annie Laurie |
| | Robin Adair |
| | Back to Our Mountains |
| |    from *Il Trovatore* (Verdi) |

"A Dream of Ancient Greece" (continued)

| Nine Attitudes: | |
|---|---|
|   Familiar Repose | Old Rosin the Bow |
|   Ceremony and Respect | No, Sir |
|   Indecision | What are the Wild Waves Saying? |
|   Reflection | Oft in the Stilly Night |
|   Defiance | Marseillaise Hymn |
|   Despair | Ye Banks and Braes o' Bonnie Doon |
|   Animation | Auld Lang Syne |
|   Suspense | Won't you Tell Me Why, Robin? |
|   Vehemence | My Country, 'tis of Thee |
| [Transition] | Last Hope (Gottschalk) |
| Tableaux | Home, Sweet Home |
|   In Sight of Home | |
|   The Birds Singing Gaily | |
|   Heavenly Home | |
|   A Charm from the Skies | |
|   Farewell to Home | |

Figure 5.5. Entertainment given by the pupils of the Charleston, South Carolina, Female Seminary in Margaret Virginia Jenkins, "A Study in Attitude," *Werner's Voice Magazine* 12 (December 1890): 297–300.

musical scores were not included because the songs were familiar: "Comin' thro' the Rye," "The Last Rose of Summer," "My Old Kentucky Home," "Columbia," or "Home, Sweet Home," for example.[76] The abundance of religious pantomimes suggests that women's use of their bodies as vehicles for performance and any potentially sexualized connotations could be mediated through overtly moral, wholesome hymn tunes. Churchgoers were more likely to find "Nearer, My God, to Thee" more socially acceptable for young women than reveling naiads; approximately 30 percent of the Delsarte performances in Iowa took place in churches, explaining the state's popularity of hymn tunes as the basis for posing.

While Delsarte posing may have originated in deliberately highbrow attempts to reproduce Greek art, the musical accompaniments selected by performers demonstrate how it came to be adapted for wider cultural ends. Classical character pieces may have been in line with Delsarte's artistic ideals, but were not as successful as hymn tunes in sacralizing women's movements. In any case, a musical background was crucial to the success of a Delsarte performance without text; a familiar piece of music clarified the intentions of posing performers and could provide more of a sense of meaning for audiences than their physical motions did. In Delsarte performances dominated by music, the spoken word would only occur in the minds of audience members, recalling the lyrics to the songs that accompanied the poses on the platform.

## The Women of River City:
## Gender and Artistic Endeavor in *The Music Man*

Delsarte performances permeated Iowan entertainments during Meredith Willson's early childhood, so the composer certainly experienced Delsarte firsthand. Willson claimed, "I didn't have to make anything up for *The Music Man*. All I had to do was remember."[77] Although we should not take Willson at his word, Mason City was typical in its level of engagement with Delsarte. As early as 1894, a Delsarte ensemble of twenty-four young ladies rehearsed at the Methodist Church, and the town had at least three Delsarte instructors.[78] As a teenager Willson recited at a meeting of his German Club, which also featured girls performing in pantomime.[79] In March 1898, Willson's mother Rosalie, a kindergarten teacher, went to Chicago briefly to study Delsarte at the American Conservatory of Music. The *Cerro Gordo Republican* reported, "We hear that Mrs. Willson will in the future make the Delsarte method of culture a prominent feature of her kindergarten work." The writer added that "our own little Eunice has been greatly benefited by the hours spent with Mrs. Willson."[80] Delsarte for small children typically did not consist of posing as Greek statues, it not being advisable to try to get five-year-olds to stand perfectly still. Instead, little girls were more likely to participate in "doll drills"—moving about holding their dolls—or "broom drills" based on sweeping motions. The year after Rosalie Willson took up Delsarte, Werner published *Poses Plastiques for the Little Ones*, featuring photographs of a small girl posing, accompanied by brief musical excerpts that express various scenes and emotions: pleading, fright, triumph, dancing, meditation, a secret, despair, mirth, defiance, listening, sorrow, and watching.[81] Because Mrs. Willson played the piano—her son said she was his inspiration for the piano teacher and librarian Marian

Paroo—she would have been able to accompany her kindergarteners as they posed or marched about.

By Willson's teen years, Delsarte was disappearing from Iowa. Yet *The Music Man* captures the aspiration to high culture that motivated Delsarte performance and was central to creating civic pride during the Progressive Era. Mason City of 1912 was not the small town that River City seems to be; River City has a population of 2,212, yet Mason City grew to 20,000 residents between 1910 and 1920. Likewise, Mason City was not a place requiring a Professor Hill to organize entertainment. From 1883, it boasted a nine-hundred-seat opera house, and the Bijou movie theater opened in 1906. Regardless, when it comes to the arts in early nineteenth-century America, the musical's specific cultural markers reflect historical reality. Its two "classical" compositions, Norwegian composer Christian Sinding's salon piece "Rustle of Spring" and the work that was to come to fruition through Hill's Think System, Beethoven's Minuet in G, are both found on Iowa women's clubs' programs early in the century. Patriotic entertainments with stereopticon slides or Native American costume tableaux like the one at which Hill first makes his sales pitch also occurred in Iowa. For example, the RARE Club of Walker had an Indian tableau on their Guest Night in 1904, and the Tuesday Club of Griswold had "Indian Huntresses in Headdresses" in pantomime at a 1925 fall festival.[82] Similar costuming to Mrs. Shinn's appearance as Columbia in *The Music Man* can be seen in guides to illustrated song from the 1910s.[83]

Willson's musical accurately depicts the historical gender associations with artistic forms. The newly organized band is for boys, and Marian's piano lessons are for girls, who are more likely to sing of longing for their true love ("Goodnight My Someone") than about their aspiration to play Carnegie Hall. However, Willson's plot, in which Marian is lonely and ostracized, and thus an attractive object of prey for Hill, requires some source of contention between her and the town's women. The ladies of River City, as voiced by Mrs. Shinn, object to Marian's ownership of the books in the library, assuming that her relationship with "Old Miser Madison" who donated them was inappropriate. In the 1962 movie adaptation, Mrs. Shinn is outraged by the contents of those books, finding *The Rubáiyát of Omar Khayyám*, along with the writings of Honoré de Balzac and François Rabelais, to be salacious and inappropriate for children.

Here Willson's fiction gets history wrong, in a manner that deliberately characterizes the women of River City as ignorantly opposed to high culture. Delsarteans or not, Iowa women were more likely to be founding the public library in their town than waging campaigns against it. The Columbian Club of Brooklyn started a library fund in 1898 and helped instigate a tax to pay for its library.[84] Likewise, the Clio Club opened Carroll's library in 1894 with

523 books; six years later, it had 1,200.[85] In addition, although Iowa women's clubs, like similar literary groups across the country, were more likely to be reading American and English authors, a few clubs did take up the French novelists that so scandalize River City's women. The Reading Club of Albia (population ca. 3,000) studied both Rabelais and Balzac in 1899 and 1900; likewise, the N. N. Club of Iowa City read literature by Balzac during 1919 and 1920.[86] Here Willson's plot device—to show River City as provincial and its citizens small-minded and thus unable to see Hill's confidence game for what it is—relies heavily on its women.

Gender is at the core of River City's problems with artistic endeavors, and the musical's Delsarte display is representative of a larger cultural condescension toward women's attempts to perform. As Kimberly Fairbrother Canton has noted, through introducing Mrs. Shinn and the Wa-Tan-Ye girls in a patriotic pageant, Willson has placed its women at the lower end of a cultural divide, apart from the high art associated with the musical's heroine, Marian Paroo, the local librarian.[87] River City is supposed to be a cultural backwater, susceptible to Hill's manipulations, but it already has pianos, pageants, and a well-stocked library when "the Professor" arrives in town. Marian must play the piano relatively well; however, she is quietly running the library, not giving recitals for the community, which often makes do with a player piano.[88] Why is this range of literary and artistic contributions to the town's cultural life insufficient? Because River City's men are not involved.

Hill's accomplishment is not convincing the town to engage in performing—as the Fourth of July celebration demonstrates, its female citizens are already inclined to do so—but, through music, to validate art as an appropriately masculine endeavor: the school board becomes a barbershop quartet, and the boys will form a band. When the males are involved in the creation of River City's cultural life, only then will it be significant, in a way that Marian's piano lessons and Mrs. Shinn's patriotic pageants are not, as they are merely women's efforts. Raymond Knapp has stressed the redemptive power that music, in the form of Hill's supposed band, has to transform lives: those of Marian's depressed, lisping brother, Winthrop; Tommy Djilas, the teenaged delinquent; and the school board members, who cease their squabbling as a barbershop quartet.[89] In contrast to the male characters, the ladies' "classic dance" society, engaging in Delsarte, is merely the musical's comic relief.

The climax of feminine artistic endeavor comes at the ice cream sociable, where instead of embodying powerful Greek goddesses, the ladies pose as Grecian urns—the receptacles on which such characters were painted, suggesting the emptiness of their efforts. Their movements are uncoordinated and ungainly, and decidedly not classic dance or high art. Given that *The Music Man* is set in 1912, just as Delsarte was fading, the introduction of posing into

River City is also too little, too late. Willson's treatment of Delsarte echoes the various satirical criticisms of an earlier era; it also reinscribes the historical tension between women's voices and their bodies in performance. The Grecian urns are as much a failure as the band's rendition of the Minuet in G; however, the women's artistic efforts separate them from the show's mythologizing of music's power. The speech-rhythm based "Pick-a-Little, Talk-a-Little" is the only vocal number for the women as a group, occurring immediately after Hill has convinced them to take up Delsarte; Roberta Freund Schwartz has pointed out that the musical's rhythmic speaking, which Willson called "speak songs," is his means of portraying its "Iowa stubborn" characters.[90] Yet in this number, the female chorus's high-pitched rhythmic repetition is not the turn-of-the-century elocutionary art from which Delsarte developed, but merely the stereotypical sound of women gossiping. The movie adaptation further demeans the women's voices by visually juxtaposing their bobbing heads in feathered hats with a shot of pecking hens. River City's female vocalizations deliberately contrast the lush, intertwining harmonies of the barbershop quartet; by the end of the song, the women's music has become subservient to the men's rendition of "Goodnight Ladies," lyrical and lovely, and completely unlike speech. While the school board members have found their musical voices—having previously slid from speech into song on the words "ice cream"—the women's music suggests they are better off subduing their voices as performing bodies in Delsarte. While rehearsing their poses, they do not sing but merely pantomime to the quartet's "It's You."

Marian is the one person in River City who is familiar with the high culture to which the post-Hill citizenry aspires. However, her understanding of music and literature will not enable her to be accepted as a community member, even though by the end of the drama, music is what has brought River City together.[91] Although omitted in the movie adaptation, the women's dislike of Marian expressed in "Pick-a-Little, Talk-a-Little" is resolved after Hill convinces them to read the "dirty" books Marian suggested and, more importantly, when they see her dance the Shipoopi with Hill. It is her dancing that convinces them to ask Marian to join their group; they are less interested in the offerings of her mind or her assistance in maintaining River City's cultural level than the movements of her body.

Although older, Marian has the same attraction to high art as Marjorie Schoessel in *The Odyssey of a Nice Girl*. As the show's heroine, Marian is never subjected to the indignities of Delsarte poses, River-City style. Yet her cultural engagement is presented as a social impediment for her from her first duet with Mrs. Paroo, who makes clear that having a husband is more important than having read "highfalutin Greeks" or, we might add, posing as "highfalutin Greeks." Marian wants someone in her life who contemplates "what makes

Shakespeare and Beethoven great," not someone who advocates the Think System.[92] But the Romantic conventions of the musical require that Harold and Marian unite as a couple; Marian must abandon her lofty ideals for the reality of Harold Hill, in a sort of Beauty and the Beast plot archetype, loving him both in spite of and because of what he actually is, rather than what he purports to be. Harold's most important attribute is that he is able to convince the citizens of River City that they care about art, something that Marian, as a woman, has been unable to accomplish. Although they have a perfectly good librarian, it takes a man to convince River City's ladies to read Balzac and to put band instruments into the hands of its young men, as well as to sell romance to Marian.

The history of the impact of Iowa's women—its real Marian Paroos—on its artistic life has yet to be written, but many of the cultural institutions they founded for the purposes of high art still exist. Hoyt Sherman Place's 1,252-seat concert hall, built by the Des Moines Women's Club, is still a vibrant artistic center, although the club's posing as naiads and graces is long forgotten. Meredith Willson captured the cultural aspirations that led Progressive-Era women in Iowa and elsewhere to build libraries, patronize music, and engage in Delsarte. The musical's satire of a historical past also reflects the reaction against women's artistic aspirations and Delsarte's failure to emerge as a valued art form. Knapp has written that "in *The Music Man*, music serves as the literal and metaphoric basis of community-building,"[93] but the successful musical community it envisions is largely led by men. By the end of the musical, Mrs. Shinn and the Wa-Tan-Ye girls have been replaced by Hill conducting the boys in the band. Even Marian—smart, determined, and devoted to high culture—must eventually admit that male salesmanship is superior to women's artistic engagement. The women of River City became Grecian urns to be satirized, and like their historical predecessors, they relinquish the music of their voices to become performing bodies. When *The Music Man* ends, River City's citizens have gained a new sense of community, but reflecting the critical backlash against Delsarte and its historical abandonment, the artistic status of the town's women remains unchanged.

# 6. In Another Voice

## Women and Dialect Recitations

Oh, hit's sweetah dan de music
Of an edicated band . . .
—Paul Laurence Dunbar, "When Malindy Sings"

Part of the full range of techniques exhibited by reciters was their ability to perform in dialect. By the time women rose to prominence in elocution, American literature already had a long history of dialect writing, including works by Mark Twain, Joel Chandler Harris, and Irwin Russell.[1] However, in relation to refined elocutionary arts, dialect was technically incorrect speech. Broadly defined by Willis Fletcher Johnson in an 1898 address to the New York School of Expression, dialect was "a form of speech differing from the established language of a race or nation, and peculiar to a certain class of people . . . and marked with either imperfect development, or an admixture of foreign elements, or else with corruption."[2] The catalogs of elocution schools stressed great literature, which would not have included dialect;[3] nonetheless, like musical accompaniment, dialect recitation was widespread. Several dialect types were included in Emerson College's "Platform Art" course, and recitations in dialect appeared on student programs in the 1890s at the New England Conservatory and at Chicago schools in the early 1900s.[4] Dialect selections were not only published in anthologies but can be heard in early Edison sound recordings as well.[5]

Dialect was most often intended to be humorous, and the immigrants or ethnic groups texts mimicked were frequently ridiculed in ways that are now considered offensive; dialect recitations based in the prejudices of an earlier era very often degrade their human subjects in devastating ways. Recitation anthologies included poems in versions of German (or "Dutch"), Irish, Scottish, and African American dialect; occasionally reciters performed in Italian, Scandinavian, Chinese, Yiddish, or French Canadian dialect as well. Poems consisting of speech that suggested rural or lower-class Americans, sometimes

called Yankee dialect or, in the case of the poems of Indiana native James Whitcomb Riley, Hoosier dialect, were extremely common. Dialect-based humor
was considered to be quintessentially American; in imitating the speech of
lower-class citizens, it was simultaneously democratic and anti-intellectual.[6]
Somewhat different in conception, child-dialect recitations, which drew on
the mispronunciations common to small children, were sometimes found in
anthologies intended for children's performances, as well as in those that also
contained texts for adults.

Female performers' engagement with dialect was shaped by complex gender,
racial, and class issues, the nexus of which had some influence on the degree to
which music was utilized in dialect recitations. However, their comedic tone
brought specific opportunities to female elocutionists that were not available
elsewhere, allowing them the freedom to express behavioral norms outside
the confines of conventional femininity. Dialect's association with the popular
stage and elocutionists' need to maintain an antitheatrical respectability resulted in its being more closely associated with male than female performers.
Recitations in dialect were frequently not poems, but monologues with male
speakers meant to be performed in character, and when anthologies identified a
selection "as recited by" a particular performer, that performer was typically a
man; female characters were sometimes treated so satirically that women would
have been less attracted to these portrayals. The humor of dialect recitations
was sometimes based in contemporary issues; performing these monologues
would have brought women closer to engaging in political speech. More important, many women's goal of offering highbrow entertainments could have
caused them to reject selections that had more in common with minstrelsy or
vaudeville than they did with the best literature. Johnson compared language
to the instrument used to perform great classical music: "Would you play
Beethoven's sonatas on an antique harpsichord or an ill-tuned piano, when
you have a concert grand piano in perfect tune at your disposal? Then why try
to express thoughts in some primitive or corrupted dialect when you have the
whole range of pure English speech before you?"[7]

Many recitation books contained few or no dialect selections; these were
published in inexpensive paperbacks devoted solely to the genre. The cartoon-
ish drawings on their covers present male ethnic stereotypes, poorly attired,
sometimes shown within a proscenium or before male audiences, marking their
location in popular theater and in obvious contrast to the women surrounded
by floral borders who grace parlor anthologies. While there was some overlap
between the two types of anthologies, particular selections appeared only in
dialect books, suggesting dialect recitations were somewhat apart from the
mainstream elocutionary literature. These volumes' relationship to literature
was most often in the form of dialect parodies of some of the most popularly

recited poems: "Casabianca," "Sheridan's Ride," "Barbara Frietchie," and "The Charge of the Light Brigade." Yet dialect's fundamental humor stemmed from the supposed inability of non-English speakers or African Americans to speak "correctly," so it relied on the conventions of elocution at its core.

Many women did perform in dialect, advertising their particular ethnic specialties. Dialect recitations may have represented distortions of a linguistic ideal, but a small portion of them featured content that overlapped with female speakers' nondialect texts and thus did not challenge the construction of women's performance space as an extension of the domestic sphere. Thus, women were more likely to perform dialect recitations that expressed sentimental or nostalgic values, or dialect variants of topics regularly taken up in nondialect selections. Not surprisingly, child dialect was the nonstandard speech type most closely associated with women, appearing in numerous parlor anthologies; it was practically nonexistent in the volumes centered on ethnic stereotypes and intended for men.

Women were attracted to dialect recitations in part because of their humor but also because performing them was "excellent vocal practice"[8] and evidence of virtuosic skills. Period descriptions praised performers' accuracy in sounding exactly like African Americans or small children. Reviews stressed the fundamental vocality of women's dialects, emphasizing the sounds that they produced more than any physical immersion in a character, although clearly some performers did full impersonations. In the twentieth century, as the sense that theatrical representation was improper for women lessened, more anthologies began to suggest the use of costumes and dramatic action. "Comedienne Reciter" Evelyne Hilliard listed Irish, Yankee, Hoosier, and Cockney dialects among her abilities, as well as the impersonation of cowboy or child characters.[9] Her chapters in *Amateur and Educational Dramatics* advocated teaching drama for "earning a living" because "clever reciters" and "teachers of literature" were no longer sufficient.[10] Those who had objected to dialect, finding it overly realistic and mere mimicry rather than interpretative art, were eventually overruled by the aesthetic changes reflected in Hilliard's career.

Because dialect represented the inverse of the highbrow, stylized oratory of the educated upper classes, its appearance on female elocutionists' programs made them less of a threat within a masculine oratorical domain. Through speaking dialect, women could downplay their higher elocutionary aspirations, and so, ironically, dialect was yet one more tool to enable women to safely take a position on the platform. Critics of dialect asserted its underdeveloped, uncivilized nature, calling it crude and "as inferior to pure English as a cabin, as a place of abode, is inferior to one of our own houses."[11] The ability to pronounce speech "incorrectly," deliberately deviating from the "standard" English of educated Americans, highlighted that women normally spoke in a "correct" manner, thereby reinforcing their more elevated status; through performing dialect recitations, women established their superiority to the characters they depicted.[12] Contemporary scientific views of most ethnic groups featured in dialect recitations held them to be developmentally inferior to Anglo-Saxon Americans, closer in their cognitive abilities to the level of children than adults. Women, too, fell behind white males in this evolutionary hierarchy, placing the female sex closer to the subjects that they tended to imitate, even as women asserted a kind of supremacy though their spoken-word performances. Paradoxically, women's adoption of a particular dialect form helped to differentiate them from an "Other." The practice was not unique to white performers. *Bits and Odds*, the anthology of African American elocutionist Hallie Quinn Brown, contains selections in African American, German, Irish, and rural dialects. In "An Irish Love Letter," an Irish servant girl's letter is read differently by her mistress than by the illiterate colored girl Gyp. In performing this work, a "cultured" African American like Brown would be positioning herself in a higher social stratum than the two lower-class characters depicted in her performance.[13]

The mixture of performed ethnicity with gender and class status complicated the situation for women on the platform; the issues surrounding which characters speaking in dialect were appropriate for women to portray was one of the reasons that dialect was more prevalent for male performers. Should women engage in too much imitation of their social inferiors, they faced the danger of lowering themselves to the level of the persons whom they vocally embodied. Regardless, many women had one or more dialect recitations in their repertoire, often works related to domestic life. Charles F. Adams's "Leetle Yawcob Strauss," a German-dialect poem about a parent's love for a rambunctious child, was widely anthologized and would have been appropriate for female reciters. Romanticized portrayals of Irish or Scottish characters in rural settings were acceptable (as opposed to urban immigrants in America), and Scottish entertainments or suitably literary Robert Burns evenings were popular.[14] The songs "Annie Laurie" and "Comin' thro' the Rye" were ubiquitous in elocution performance; the latter also frequently accompanied Delsarte-influenced pantomime, as did the Irish song "The Last Rose of Summer."

Just as the contrast between dialect and elocutionary language often created the humor of dialect performances, the tension between the outlook of a "low-class" dialect character and the values of "high culture" was at the center of some of the most popular recitations. These prose monologues featured the voice of an unsophisticated rural or uneducated person who encounters high art, with humorous results. In many texts a character attends a classical music concert for the first time and recounts his or her reaction. The most performed text of this type was George William Bagby's "How Ruby Played," in which "Jud Brownin" hears pianist Anton Rubinstein, and is initially skeptical ("What sort of fool playin' is that?") but then is emotionally swept away, erupts in loud exclamations ("I jumped sprang onto my seat, and jest hollered: '*Go it my Rube!*'"), and is almost hauled out of the concert by policemen for the disturbance.[15] Given the story's satire of both the speaker's ignorance of the world he has entered and the unpleasant stuffiness of its high-toned atmosphere, "How Ruby Played" was the perfect selection for reciters trying to balance the highbrow and the lowbrow. Listeners could feel superior to its naive central character while also identifying with his seeming out of place in a concert hall. The monologue enabled elocutionists to make fun of high culture at the same time they were advocating for it, for at its core, "How Ruby Played" depicts the immense expressive and emotional power of classical music.[16] Likewise, in "Aunt Deborah Hears 'The Messiah,'" the speaker recounts her feelings about Handel's oratorio and provides the wealth of religious imagery that music creates in her mind's eye. Aunt Deborah experiences as extreme an emotional response as Jud Brownin: "My poor soul could hardly bear to stay into the body, an' I held onto the back of the seat in front of me to keep from risin' right up into the air."[17] However, classical music did not fare as well in other texts of this type. In Lucius Perry Hill's "The Opera Encore," the dialect speaker is confused by the plot of the opera featuring "Miss Ma-dam-a-selle," but is completely entranced with the soprano's lowbrow encore, "Home, Sweet Home"; the notebook of elocution student Maude Wood indicates that the song was to be played midway through the poem after the appropriate stanza.[18] Likewise, in "Sense Sally's Been to Europe," by Herbert Laight, the speaker prefers Sally to sing "old-time songs," accompanying herself on the parlor organ, more than the "warbles" and "trills" she makes after foreign operatic training.[19] Occasionally in texts such as "Aunt Sophronia Tabor at the Opera," the lowbrow character is ridiculed. Aunt Sophronia goes to hear the renowned soprano Adelina Patti, in spite of her suspicion that the opera is not a "perfectly proper place"; she declares it an "unchristian scrape" and departs in outrage due to ballet dancers who are "graceless nudities."[20]

Although music was sometimes the topic of dialect recitations, in performance, most took place without accompaniment. Many popular selections were prose monologues, not poetry, and the performance of dialect was enough of a novelty in itself without added music; like reciting with accompaniment, dialect performances were considered a possible specialty for elocutionists. Thus, there does not appear to have been a core repertoire of dialect recitations with music, unlike the sentimental recitations identified in chapter 4. However, Stanley Schell's anthology *Musical Effects*, published in 1911, included numerous accompanied recitations in ethnic and child dialects, suggesting that the informal practice of adopting accompaniments also took place for dialect works. While middle- and upper-class female performers certainly engaged in a range of dialect types, white women's recitations involving music most often represented the speech of persons who were clearly and unquestionably considered their social inferiors: African Americans and children. Texts that evoked African American music-making were the most likely to be accompanied in performance. Child-dialect poetry rarely featured music as a topic, but its prevalence among women performers meant that it eventually came to receive numerous musical settings. The dialect in women's repertoires allowed them to develop new varieties of expressive freedom without compromising their social position, and their recitations came to influence melodramatic compositions by female composers into the twentieth century.

## Banjos and Mammies' Lullabies: African American Dialect Recitations

Women's recitations in African American dialect depicted a stereotypical Old South of dancing, happy slaves playing banjos and fiddles on the plantations of benevolent masters. The characters most associated with blackface minstrelsy—the Uncle Toms, Jim Crows, and Zip Coons of period theatrical and literary representations—were male, and thus did not make regular appearances in women's dialect recitations. Nor were the Ethiopian sermons found in anthologies, monologues in which African American pastors butchered oratorical rhetoric, appropriate for women; instead, sentimental nostalgia prevailed. The end of the nineteenth century, the height of elocution, was a terrible period for African Americans because of mounting legal restrictions dramatically reducing blacks' right to vote and increased lynchings, resulting in their flight to urban regions of the North. A fictionalized construction of the antebellum South, which Jean Wagner has described as "embellished by its remoteness in time,"[21] came to the aid of the repressive politics of the era. The numerous elocution texts that depicted African Americans and/ or included Negro dialect were part of this larger cultural construction of the Old South in literature, minstrel shows, coon songs, and the numerous traveling theatrical adaptations of Harriet Beecher Stowe's *Uncle Tom's Cabin* that toured America throughout the nineteenth century. In addition, between the late 1870s and 1915, Americans could traverse supposed replicas of old plantations at urban exhibitions and in minstrel-influenced extravaganzas such as *Darkest America* (1894) and *Black America* (1895), encountering cotton fields and lands complete with livestock, log cabins, and dancing, singing, and fiddle- and banjo-playing "darkies."[22]

It is difficult to determine how many women performed dialect dressed in costume and blacked their faces with burnt cork, but the practice did take place; the popularity of African American dialect recitations late in the nineteenth century coincided with the increased publication of amateur minstrelsy guides.[23] Illinois reciter Cornelia Neltnor Anthony was photographed wearing blackface in the 1890s when she appeared in a women's minstrel show for the benefit of the West Chicago library, although this was not a regular part of her performances.[24] *Werner's Magazine* published a boy's drill with singing and dancing called "Ten Little Nigger Boys," which required blackface and drew on long-standing racist stereotypes from minstrelsy; it included the instruction "look stupid."[25] But numerous other dialect texts published in the elocution literature do not suggest that performers necessarily turned to costumes or to the physical comedy of minstrelsy. Mary E. Bell, billed as a "Negro impersonator," performed without blackface, relying instead on voice and body: "Every nuance of negro accent, gesture and trick of thought, she reproduces with absolute fidelity," wrote a recommender.[26]

In common scenarios, dancing and the sounds of banjos or fiddles helped create a nostalgic tone surrounding plantation life and provided ready opportunities for accompanied recitations. Schell's *Musical Effects* contains "Black-Ankle Break Down," adapted from white Georgia author Harry Stillwell Edwards. In an extended prose scene, an old man begins to play his fiddle, causing a group of children and a woman to dance; instructions are given for an elaborate plantation staging or tableaux (perhaps requiring blackface) to follow the recitation.[27] The text contains dialect only when African American characters speak, but the syncopations and pentatonic flavor of the simple dialect songs by Minnie Schoeller included help to evoke the scene. Some elocutionists accompanied black writer James Edwin Campbell's "De 'Sprise Pa'ty" with music; the passage in which the prose imitates plucked banjo strings was a suitable spot either to substitute music for banjo sounds or to accompany the speaker with them:

> Now, while I chune dis bawnjer, you 'Rastus, git yo' ha'p!
> Mek music fur de comp'ny; now, niggah, look right sha'p!
> Plunk! plunk! plunk! plunk! plunkety! plunk! plunkety! plunk! plunk!
> Plunk! plunkety! plunk! plunk! plunk! plunk! plunkety! plunk! plunk!

The poem tells how musicians trick Susan Brown into abandoning her religious objections in order to dance, by beginning the music with familiar hymn tunes:

> "Neah-row my Gawd ter Dee" (now dat chune's fur yo' Mu'rr;
> W'en we gits her moll and tim, we gwine to play an urr)
> Now "Rock ob Ages," sof' an' sweet; sing, you niggahs, sing!
> Des hyuh dat tenah an' dat bass! Lawd, how dem raftahs ring!
> Hyuh Susan's cla'r supranah lif' dem tall notes on high!
> She tink'n bout de great white t'rone' an' "Mansions in de sky."[28]

"Nearer, My God, to Thee" and "Rock of Ages," frequently used as accompaniments to texts that referred to them, could also have been added here to humorous effect.

The dialect recitations intended for female speakers featured a Mammy figure as their central figure (that these texts rarely appear in dialect anthologies is additional evidence that such volumes were geared toward men). In visual representations, the Mammy is usually depicted as large and unattractive, her head wrapped in a kerchief, but she is fundamentally maternal and devoted to her charges;[29] these are usually the whites for whom she works, but contrary to stereotype, in many period recitations, Mammy characters mother their own children instead of those of their white overseers. That Mammies might sing to those under their care made it easy to add music to texts about them, and such poems inevitably suggested or included lullabies. "Mammy's Li'l' Boy" by Harry Stillwell Edwards was sometimes performed with music. The female speaker's description of her baby boy, as well as the engraving by Edward Kemble that accompanied publication of the poem in the *Century* in 1888, made clear that he is a white child. The poem features a verse-chorus structure, all or part of which could be sung or recited to music. The chorus's repeated lines (1, 2, and 5) created refrains seemingly designed for singing, not reading:

> Byo baby boy, oh bye,
> By-o li'l' boy!
> Oh, run ter es mammy
> En she tek 'im in 'er arms.
> Mammy's li'l' baby boy.[30]

Elsie Wilbor suggested singing or crooning this stanza "as one would sing it when trying to hush a child to sleep."[31] "A Southern Lullaby" by Virna Sheard was published in the *Standard Canadian Reciter* with the instructions that lines in parentheses be sung or chanted; as almost every other line was so marked, this would represent about half of the poem.[32] Of the accompanied recitations that ran counter to the stereotype in which Mammy is so faithful to her white children that she neglects her own is Lucy C. Jenkins's "Mammy's Pickanin'," which concludes with Mammy singing to her own child; it was published with a short, triple-meter lullaby for the performer to sing and hum.[33] "Cuba's Kindergarten Song" in Lumm's 1898 anthology includes similar stereotypes: the Mammy sings to her "little pickaninny" while the child's father hunts possum. A Stephen Fosteresque song setting of part of the text returns to conclude the recitation; the music makes a fleeting reference to "My Old Kentucky Home" (example 6.1).[34]

Schell's *Musical Effects* contains several recitations for female performers that feature Mammy characters. In the prose monologue "M' Li'l' Black

Big moon sees dat you ain't a-sleep-in' an-y, Bri-er Fox 'll be heah pur-ty soon.

Example 6.1. "Cuba's Kindergarten Song," mm. 5–8, in Emma Griffith Lumm, *The Twentieth-Century Speaker* (Chicago: K. T. Boland, 1899), 393.

Baby," Mrs. Taylor gossips with her neighbor, interrupting herself to reprimand her unruly offspring, but finally cuddling her "pic'aninny" and singing a lullaby; the introduction indicates that Kitty Cheatham, discussed later in this chapter, performed this text.[35]

Although these depictions of African American females draw on racist stereotypes, the maternal values associated with the Mammy character made such selections more acceptable for female elocutionists who wanted to perform in dialect; Edwards's "Mammy's Li'l' Boy" was apparently in Hallie Quinn Brown's repertoire.[36] The voices of Mammies were safer for women on the platform than those of young, sexualized black women or the disruptively wild character of Topsy, featured in productions of *Uncle Tom's Cabin*. As Lisa Anderson has noted, Mammies caring for white children embodied a "pure" maternal function separate from their sexuality,[37] and elocutionists who took on vocal representations of a Mammy would necessarily downplay their own sexuality as well. The strong role that gender and sexuality had in shaping female performers' dialect recitations is suggested by the notable absence in the elocution literature of another racial stereotype, the tragic mulatto woman. An exception is William Dean Howells's text "The Pilot's Story," found in Brown's anthology, *Bits and Odds*.[38] The poem tells how a gambler wins a beautiful slave woman, almost white in skin tone, from her master. But they have a son in St. Louis, and her master had promised to free the distraught woman, who throws herself onto the riverboat wheel and dies. The poem's abolitionist origins might have made it attractive to an African American reciter such as Brown, but in general its implied sexual content is completely at odds with the poetry programmed by women.[39]

Even though Mammies were portrayed as nonsexual and were subject to their white masters, reciters viewed them has having some freedom in their place outside of "civilized" white society; yet this freedom, as Catherine Clinton has asserted, was bound up in the "emasculation of slavery, since she [the Mammy] and she alone projected an image of power wielded by blacks—a power rendered strictly benign and maternal in its influence."[40] In one lesson talk, Henry Gaines Hawn described how black women in the antebellum era "wore only loose garments, were strangers to the corset, and were perfectly free in movement," giving them a physical freedom in line with the vocal freedom of dialect.[41] The Mammy's minimal freedoms, if only in a purely physical manifestation, would have appealed to women who were also abandoning corsets for Delsarte gowns. When Jeanette Robinson Murphy treated the Arche Club of Chicago to a "plantation entertainment" that taught her female audience how to do Mammy imitations, she had them "clap their hands and stamp with one foot in syncopated time," which the press found similar to "a minstrel chorus on a rehearsal or a Georgia camp-meeting in progress."[42] Yet any implied freedoms expressed by Mammy recitations took place well within the confines of race and class, and the sentimentalized ideals of maternal care.

## Paul Laurence Dunbar and Women's Dialect Settings

The remarkable rise to literary prominence of African American poet Paul Laurence Dunbar coincided with the height of elocution, and his poems were quickly taken into women's repertoires and became Chautauqua and lyceum staples; many texts also became the basis of musical settings. Dunbar's relationship to his dialect poems and their place in African American literature have long been contentious issues for literary critics.[43] Henry Louis Gates has described Dunbar's use of dialect as positing both "a certain boldness as well as a certain opportunism," with mixed results;[44] other scholars have pointed out the numerous ways in which the poet's texts deliberately resist racial stereotyping. Yet the role public readings had in Dunbar's professional career and his influence on female performers have received little attention. One of his earliest programs identifies him as a dramatic reader who performed texts by Shakespeare, Tennyson, and Dante Gabriel Rossetti, though not yet his "original recitations,"[45] and *Werner's Magazine* announced his emergence as a new reader for the 1896 season.[46] Although both black and white audiences perceived the poet's performances of dialect poems as authentic African American expression, Dunbar's published output was also shaped by elocutionary practices. Scholars unaware of the popularity of dialect performance during this period have sometimes been confused by Dunbar's production of poems in Hoosier, Irish, and German dialects;[47] of these, he was known to have performed in Irish dialect, to the criticism of the press, which preferred his African American offerings.[48] After the poet's death, his wife, Alice Dunbar-Nelson, became one of the numerous female editors of a recitation book. In 1920, she published *The Dunbar Speaker and Entertainer*, featuring "the best prose and poetic selections by and about the Negro race," but titled like the numerous anthologies issued by and named for elocutionists, not poets.[49] Largely containing serious literature and oratory on African American topics, mainly by black authors, the book's goal was less to entertain than to fill the tremendous gaps in previous anthologies and to educate African American children about their heritage. In addition to portraits of renowned figures such as Frederick Douglass and Booker T. Washington, the volume includes numerous photographs of a young African American girl, wearing a white dress, in Delsarte-style expressive poses, suggesting the expected female audience, yet seemingly incongruous beside poetry about lynchings. Like numerous other recitation books, Dunbar-Nelson's speaker contains sample programs for holidays and other specific occasions, but lists suggested music by African American composers such as Harry T. Burleigh, Samuel Coleridge-Taylor, and Will Marion Cook.

In keeping with musical and literary entertainments, Dunbar's public appearances, often at black churches, consisted of his recitations surrounded by musical numbers: one or two poems given between songs, piano music, or vocal quartets performed by local talent.[50] The poet sometimes appeared with Joseph Douglass, the violinist grandson of Frederick Douglass.[51] Dunbar occasionally engaged in accompanied recitation, reciting his "Corn-Stalk Fiddle" to a string orchestra in 1896[52] and singing lines of "The Party" in 1901.[53] Dunbar's recitation to piano accompaniment in Toledo, Ohio, reportedly had "such a rhythm in it that the onlookers almost imperceptibly swayed their heads, and with beaming faces watched and listened to the poet."[54] While clearly one of Dunbar's goals was to sell his latest book after a recital, his "musical" voice made him successful on the platform. One review called him "an excellent elocutionist, possessing a full, rich and deep voice, which he uses with remarkable discretion."[55] Dunbar obviously understood what appealed to audiences aurally, and many poems he presented to audiences in some way dealt with music, including "Whistlin' Sam," "Itchin' Heels," "Corn-Stalk Fiddle," "Banjo Song," and "The Ol' Tunes." Others, such as "When Malindy Sings" and "Angelina," associate music with a central female figure. Most of these poems became the texts regularly performed by female elocutionists and set by female composers.

Dunbar's emergence as the first widely recognized African American poet made his output desirable repertoire, even for white women who might otherwise have considered dialect not genteel enough for literary entertainments. When Dunbar returned to recite before a largely white, female audience at

Dayton's National Cash Register Company, where he had once been a janitor, he was depicted as personally transformed by his "gift of song," now "faultlessly dressed with an air and mien that bespoke culture and education" (figure 6.1).[56] Dunbar's output could be considered poetry in keeping with high elocutionary ideals, not merely humorous caricatures from vaudeville or minstrelsy; white women could engage in dialect while performing literature, all the while retaining their cultural superiority. "Expressional Power of the Colored Race," a 1901 article in *Werner's Magazine* that endeavored to show blacks' contributions to high culture, hailed Dunbar as the single great African American writer.[57] Yet the article laments Dunbar's European-influenced poetic efforts, finding his dialect poems "most happy, his stories blending quaint negro philosophy, pathetic humor, and gentleness."[58] Another article provides a potential program of his works, similar to those for Longfellow or Tennyson commonly recommended in elocution publications, yet only three of its selections are not in dialect.[59] Literary critics and audiences preferred Dunbar's dialect verse, but ironically, because of the dialect, his works would necessarily remain segregated from the poetic mainstream. Dunbar's status was to be the great African American poet, not a great poet.

Some reciters did treat Dunbar as a major literary figure: Indiana elocutionist May Donnally Kelso recited Dunbar's poetry on a program with that of Rudyard Kipling as part of her "author's sketches," designed to be "dignified" and educational.[60] African American women's literary societies also featured Dunbar's works on their programs—for example at the Phyllis [sic] Wheatley Literary and Social Club of Charleston, South Carolina; the Woman's Improvement Club of Indianapolis; and the Detroit Study Club.[61] Nonetheless, in spite of the high quality and wide-ranging content of Dunbar's verse, performances of it could easily take place in contexts that emphasized the stereotypes associated with African Americans that his writing actually undermined. White performer Emily Farrow Gregory offered a "humorous lecture recital" titled "Cabin Days in Dixie," which included Dunbar's writings amid those of white mythologizer Thomas Nelson Page and mammy imitations.[62] In a 1901 Michigan program directed by Clara MacMonagle-Britten, Dunbar's "When Malindy Sings" and "Li'l Brown Baby" were juxtaposed with Foster's Old South songs "My Old Kentucky Home" and "S'wannee River," the latter performed by thirty small girls in pantomime, as well as with a series of tableaux based on cartoons from Edward Kemble's book *Kemble's Coons.*[63] Although some of the "coon" drawings the girls imitated (somewhat different from Kemble's most racist cartoons) show impoverished though less stereotypical African American children—a baby cradled in a wooden box, a girl holding two dolls, and a grinning boy with a hole-riddled umbrella in the rain—they maintain the image of "happy darkies" in the midst of difficulty.[64] A child tempted by a watermelon represents more common racist imagery.

Figure 6.1. Paul Laurence Dunbar reciting in the women's dining room of the National Cash Register Company, Dayton, Ohio, January 1904. The NCR Archive at Dayton History.

The significance of Dunbar's works and other dialect recitations was obviously different for African American female elocutionists. Although James Weldon Johnson later claimed that Dunbar, hailed as the "poet laureate of the Negro race," was actually dominated by "a section of the white American reading public,"[65] his work nonetheless offered black women a means of further justifying their position as performing artists, a position made even more problematic because of their race. When Mary Mosely Withers became the first African American student to graduate from the Johnson School of Music, Oratory, and Dramatic Art in Minneapolis, she "showed her race pride by choosing a selection from Dunbar" for her part of the graduation program.[66] The available evidence suggests that black elocutionists often gave many of the same texts as white performers; Valetta L. Winslow also specialized in Delsarte posing,[67] and Henrietta Vinton Davis, who aspired to the theater but had to resign herself to elocutionary appearances during portions of her career, was known for giving Shakespeare.[68] However, these performers' repertoires also included works that would specifically appeal to black audiences, such as George Baker's Civil War poem "The Black Regiment" or Mary A. P.

Stansbury's "How He Saved St. Michael's," about a slave who saves a burning church in Charleston, South Carolina. Brown, who programmed "An Evening with Paul Laurence Dunbar" in 1902, already had several dialect recitations in her repertoire before the poet became popular; she was not the only professional African American elocutionist to adopt his poetry.[69] Henrietta Vinton Davis did so as well, reciting "Li'l Brown Baby" and other Dunbar selections.[70] Lillian S. Jeter Davis, a graduate of Silas Neff's College of Oratory in Philadelphia, advertised that she gave an entire Dunbar program, which included many works that were not in dialect.[71] Dunbar's poems also maintained their popularity through an oral performance tradition, even as they fell from literary favor, starting during the Harlem Renaissance. In 1947, Sylvestre Watkins recalled that when he was a boy, "every church social program had a reading from Dunbar. . . . Everyone looked forward to this part of the program."[72] Nancy Tolson and Sandra Seaton have suggested that Dunbar's poetry continued to be recited among black women until much later in the twentieth century; both recall older female relatives reciting Dunbar at home and in the context of black women's clubs, literary societies, and church groups.[73]

Ultimately, Dunbar's use of dialect came to weaken his literary status. Although thirty of Dunbar's poems were published in the influential periodical the *Century*, the dialect in them so desired by white readers meant that they appeared in a section titled "In a Lighter Vein," and the editor of the magazine, Richard Watson, privately intimated that dialect could potentially endanger the cultivated level of the magazine's offerings and negatively influence children's language.[74] Elocution pedagogues were also concerned about the influence of dialect on their pupils; in 1897 the National Association of Elocutionists passed a motion that dialect recitations should not be taught in schools.[75] While Dunbar's poetic abilities may have enabled him to gain entry to the elocution repertoire—his works consistently transcend the stereotypes in the cliché-ridden dialect poems sprinkled throughout recitation publications—it was his use of dialect and the notion that such poems represented lesser fare that allowed him to remain there as insistence that elocutionists provide "good" literature receded. Werner regularly published Dunbar's verse in his collections—but not beside other "great" American or European poets, but rather with occasional poetry by authors now largely forgotten.

Dunbar's influences included poets whose works were particularly popular among elocutionists, such as Longfellow and Riley,[76] and, dialect or no, his subject matter was often in keeping with topics that dominated women's repertoire. In a 1902 interview, he described his dialect works as "negro songs" and acknowledged that they embodied sentimental, feminized values: "The negro song must be sentimental—it must be a love song or a lullaby, or a song of home and longing, or something of that sort."[77] Such values made Dunbar's poems especially appropriate for female reciters. Some poems may have primarily evoked minstrelsy for listeners, but Dunbar was also considered to be a "child" poet; performing in Cleveland in 1901, Bessie Brown Richter recited Dunbar with James Whitcomb Riley and Eugene Field, simulating "childish accents and tones."[78] Manner programmed Dunbar's "Lullaby," in the voice of a Mammy, on a program titled "Love Songs of Childhood," along with Longfellow's "Children," Riley's "The Happy Little Cripple," and Field's "The Limitations of Youth" (in child dialect), a program that opened with the Berceuse from the opera *Jocelyn* by Benjamin Godard, arranged for organ.[79] Dunbar's early death and the portrayal of him as a "boy" by an early biographer, Lida Keck Wiggins, solidified his link to childhood, an association that was certainly exacerbated by a wider condescending attitude toward his race.

Dunbar's poems often depicted music-making and emphasized music's power; many poems were themselves song texts without music. (Dunbar also provided lyrics for Will Marion Cook's musical *In Dahomey.*) "The Ol' Tunes" is not unlike the selections in which uneducated whites encounter high art, in that it compares anthems and arias to "ol'-fashioned" music traditionally sung by African Americans.

> You kin talk about yer anthems
> An' yer arias an' sich,
> An' yer modern choir-singin'
> That you think so awful rich;
> But you orter heerd us youngsters
> In the times now far away,
> A-singin' o' the ol' tunes
> In the ol'-fashioned way.[80]

Texts that contained references to specific songs suggested added accompaniments. Dunbar's poem "Whistling Sam," which he gave in performance and published in *Lyrics of the Hearthside* (1899), features brief melodies interspersed between stanzas, similar to poems with musical excerpts published in recitation books.[81] "Whistling Sam" is related to the singing-soldiers genre, and the mixture of popular and religious tunes is integral to its story. Sam is introduced whistling,[82] and he whistles the spiritual "Git on Board, Little Children."[83] He enlists in the Union army, providing opportunities for excerpts from "The Girl I Left Behind Me" as he leaves his sweetheart and "Battle Cry of Freedom." He cheers his soldier comrades with "Sleep in Jesus" when they are too distraught to sing hymns, though it is only mentioned, not notated with music; he returns from the war quietly whistling "Old One Hundredth." It seems likely that Dunbar either whistled these excerpts in his performances or had them played by a musical instrument.

Dunbar produced a number of poems centered on banjos and fiddles that
were reprinted in the elocution literature and sometimes accompanied with
music. In "Itching Heels," the devout speaker, like Susan Brown in Campbell's
"De 'Sprise Pa'ty," is tempted by the joys of the fiddle; in contrast, "A Banjo
Song" stresses the almost religious consolation that music brings to a weary
slave. One of the few Dunbar poems Werner published that is not in dialect,
"Corn-Stalk Fiddle," presents an evocative depiction of a dance accompanied
by a fiddle, such as is found in Banks's recitations. *Werner's Magazine* suggested adding realism to the poem by performing it with an actual cornstalk
fiddle. One of Werner's anthologies provides the Irish fiddle tune *Garryowen*,
scored for violin and piano, to accompany the dancing sequence, with the
placement of text timed to the meter of the tune; the passage is introduced by
three chords to depict the fiddle's "scrape, scrape, scrape" (example 6.2).[84]

One of the most programmed of Dunbar's texts was "When Malindy Sings,"
which focuses on the power of an individual female voice; it appeared on New
England Conservatory programs as early as 1899. Here, the poet added a racial
dimension to a dialect text that rejects high culture: "When Malindy Sings"
rejects musical training and literacy, here associated with the white "Miss
Lucy," and stresses the natural, spiritual power of the songs from an African
American oral tradition that Malindy renders.

> Easy 'nough fu' folks to hollah,
> Lookin' at de lines an' dots,
> When dey ain't no one kin sence it,
> An' de chune comes in, in spots;
> But fu' real malojous music,
> Dat jes' strikes yo' hea't and clings,
> Jes' you stan' an' listen wif me
> When Malindy sings.
> . . .
>
> Who dat says dat humble praises
> Wif de Master nevah counts?
> Heish yo' mouf, I hyeah dat music,
> Ez hit rises up an' mounts—
> Floatin' by de hills an' valleys,
> Way above dis buryin' sod,
> Ez hit makes its way in glory
> To de very gates of God![85]

The addition of music to "When Malindy Sings" was a regular practice. In a
1909 Victor recording, James A. Myers of the Fisk University Jubilee Quartet
sings rather than speaks the three lines of Malindy's music that are part of the

Example 6.2. Paul Laurence Dunbar, "Corn-Stalk Fiddle,"
accompaniment for last line of stanza 5, in Stanley Schell, ed.,
*Werner's Readings and Recitations, No. 48: Musical Effects* (New
York: Edgar S. Werner, 1911), 163.

text—"Come to Jesus," "Rock of Ages," and "Swing Low, Sweet Chariot."[86] In 1903, when Hallie Quinn Brown recited "Malindy" for the critical evaluation of the National Association of Elocutionists, they had mixed reactions to her singing, but they were even more concerned with whether a woman should perform a poem in a man's voice.[87] Brown countered that relinquishing texts with a masculine persona would eliminate half her repertoire; perhaps Brown's race made her taking on a male voice especially problematic.

Given that many dialect recitations were prose, not poetry, and that "coon songs" were available during this period,[88] it is not surprising that there are far fewer melodramatic settings of dialect recitations than of other types of texts. However, because of its musical topics and songlike structures, Dunbar's poetry was both made into accompanied recitations and taken up by composers. In Brooklyn in 1901, M. M. Smith recited "Angelina" to music by her husband, F. J. Smith, at the Colonia Club reception,[89] and some of Dunbar's poems most popular with women were published with accompaniments for spoken-word performance in the teens and twenties, by both male and female composers.[90]

The stereotypes from recitations are reflected in the published melodramatic settings of dialect texts to varying degrees; while some settings of poems by Dunbar and others contain little that deliberately suggests African American music, many have touches of pentatonicism, chromaticism, or syncopated rhythms meant to flavor the music, albeit in a subtle way. Phyllis Fergus's "When Mistah Sun am Blazin'" (1919) is in the voice of an African American man complaining about being forced to work, drawing on the stereotype of the "lazy Negro."[91] The poem takes place in the South, as evidenced by a singing mockingbird and the watermelon that is the speaker's reward. The hot sun, rather than a white plantation owner, is his master, and the repetition of pseudo-rustic open fifths in the accompaniment, decorated with a chromatic passing tone between the fifth and sixth scale degrees, creates a languid mood. For the second verse, birdcalls are added in the piano's right hand (example 6.3). The rhythm of the final line of each verse, the title of the recitation, is reflected in the accompaniment.

Example 6.3. Phyllis Fergus, "When Mistah Sun am Blazin'" (Chicago: Clayton F. Summy, 1919), mm. 14–18.

The dialect cantillations of Chicago poet-composer Natalie Whitted Price (1864–1923),[92] which could either be recited or sung, include characteristic Mammy stereotypes. In "Mammy's Lullaby," in a lilting six-eight time, a Mammy sings endearments to her child. Price's "Mammy's Little Solder Girl" contrasts a common-time verse in standard English, describing how the speaker's Mammy comforted her, with a 2/4 chorus in dialect in which Mammy gives her advice (example 6.4); this arrangement allows speakers to demonstrate ability in dialect while retaining a white persona. The chorus also exhibits stereotypical African American features: syncopated rhythms and a pentatonic melody in the piano's right hand, all in a Fosteresque march style, evoke the resilient "soldier girl" that the speaker is exhorted to be.

Example 6.4. Natalie Whitted Price, "Mammy's Little Solder Girl" (Chicago: Clayton F. Summy, 1912), chorus, mm. 11–19.

A similar arrangement, in which the verse is followed by a dialect chorus, is heard in Aileen H. Tye's "Mammy's Philosophy"; the dialect is introduced at the end of the verse with the line, "So, listen to Mammy's song," which admonishes the listener that

> Most disappointments an' envy and strife,
> Mos' ub de things what our consciences taint,
> Is because of our wantin' de things that we hain't.[93]

Several published dialect settings emphasize exuberant dancing African American stereotypes: Price's "Sassy Faced Sophia" features a female character who dominates the various social situations introduced in each verse, including a barbecue, corn shucking, and cakewalk. The chorus that describes Sophia is enlivened with dotted rhythms and Scotch snaps. The slightly syncopated accompaniment in Frieda Peycke's setting of Dunbar's popular "Angelina" is intended to imitate the instruments accompanying the dancing: open fifths in the introduction for "the tuning of fiddles," and sustained fifths in the bass line for a "bass viol" (example 6.5).[94]

Example 6.5. Frieda Peycke's setting of Paul Laurence Dunbar's "Angelina" (Chicago: T. S. Denison, 1928), mm. 1–6.

In contrast, there is frequently nothing deliberately African American in the style of some musical accompaniments added to Dunbar's dialect texts, sometimes giving the impression that the poet's expression of black culture has been subsumed by white, Anglo-American elocution. The instructions for Jean Elizabeth Van Dyke's "B'neath the Willers" indicates its depiction of the "old negro" should be given "very tenderly," and her low-registered accompaniment's dotted rhythms are those of a funeral march, not a dance.[95] Although Matt Sandler has suggested that the "boogah man" in Dunbar's "Li'l Brown Baby" is not mere play but a father's preparing his child for the dangers of the white threats and racial oppression he will face, Van Dyke's accompaniment manifests musical innocence through its lullaby-like setting in 6/8 time.[96] Even though the music is transformed by mock-dramatic octaves and tremolos in the bass when the father threatens to let the boogah man devour the child, the change is temporary, and the accompaniment quickly returns to the soothing arpeggiation with which the piece closes. Mary Jordan Lea's setting of Dunbar's "Boogah Man" has a piano introduction featuring supernatural-evoking tritones and accompaniment with occasional low ominous rumbles in the bass (example 6.6).[97] The overall tone is mediated by a predominantly

Example 6.6. Mary Jordan Lea's setting of Paul Laurence Dunbar's "Boogah Man" (Franklin, OH: Eldridge Entertainment House, 1910), mm. 13–17.

diatonic harmonic language and bouncy dotted rhythms, making "Boogah Man" more humorous than threatening. The keyboard technique required to play the work is minimal; thus, the piece might have been composed with child performers in mind.

These settings are far removed from the deliberately syncopated, pentatonic tunes or fiddle melodies meant to evoke plantation life provided by Werner, Price, or Peycke; Dunbar's poems have become part of women composers' musical worlds. At the same time, adapting African American language in musical settings so that they are appropriate for youthful performers infantilizes it and reinforces the stereotype of African Americans as children, the other group most represented in women's dialect recitations.

## Dead Dolls and Little Boys: Women, Comedy, and Child Dialect

Even more than their performance of African American dialect, women's vocal imitations of small children, and especially young boys, were to influence the melodramatic compositions created by women in the twentieth century. Children were considered appropriate topics for female elocutionists because of women's maternal roles; women's higher voices and domestic access to children meant that they would naturally be the best performers of children's language. Although many of the poems that recitation books designated as for juveniles were in standard English, some texts included the modified grammar and spelling that made up child dialect, in which some female performers specialized. Poems in the language of children typically did not appear in anthologies devoted entirely to dialect, in part because these books were intended for male performers, and also because some reciters considered child selections to be impersonations rather than dialect in the strictest sense.

According to Jennifer Brooke, poetic texts could be manipulated to create child dialect in a combination of three ways: first, the text might represent the voice of a child merely through orthographic changes to words that would create misspellings but have no obvious effect on the sound of the words; this has been referred to as "eye dialect."[98] Visual changes would only be obvious to readers, not to listeners, unless performers took the misrepresentations as signals to audibly alter their vocal performances. Texts could also represent children's voices through the dropping of the ends of words and text manipulation such as the running together of sounds; although children and adults speak in a similar fashion in everyday speech, these changes would differentiate the speaker's performance from that of a trained elocutionist, with her refined, accurate diction. Finally, the most obvious way to create child dialect was to incorporate the mispronunciations characteristic of children's speech as it develops. Texts might mix the three approaches or utilize one of them just enough to create a notable difference from standardized English. While some anthologized poems in the first-person voice of a child were written without dialect, elocutionists who specialized in impersonating children might easily have added it. Pitch variants also helped produce the sound of a child; Harriet Saxton's textbook suggested using "rising and falling slides" and that wavelike vocal inflections should go to "as high a pitch as possible."[99] Texts originally intended for children could readily be adapted for adult performances; many of these did not incorporate dialect, as speech pedagogues did not want to reinforce incorrect habits among their students. The publication of "I'se Dood" by Mrs. Frederick Pender, accompanied by photos of a little girl pantomiming, includes both dialect and standard-English versions of the poem, noting that "some people do not care to teach children dialect."[100] Thus, child dialect, like ethnic dialects, was primarily for adults.

Performing as children gave women the opportunity to engage in comedy in a nonthreatening way. Platform performers were faced with the long-standing stereotype that women were incapable of being funny, and taking on another persona helped mediate that conception.[101] In the 1920s, Bessie May Dudley, who performed various dialects and gave costumed child impersonations, had to justify her comedic exaggerations of human nature: "I am only a girl with a talent . . . to make people just a little happier for having heard me. . . . I prove that a woman can have just as great a fund of humor as a man."[102] The supposedly innocent humor surrounding children remained associated with domestic life and separate from adult concerns, in contrast to the more politicized, issue-oriented dialect recitations performed by men. (For example, numerous satirical dialect selections dealt with suffrage and would have represented threateningly political speech in female voices.) Nonetheless, the ability to make audiences laugh is, in itself, a powerful form of control, and women who engaged in comedic performances also transgressed the cultural identification of women with subordination and passivity.[103] By taking on the persona of a mere child, women on the platform helped reduce the sense that they could embody more power than was socially acceptable for their sex; feminist historians have emphasized how a woman in comedy has to construct "rhetorical marginality early in her act."[104] In one example, *Werner's Magazine* praised the carefully unassuming comments of child-dialect specialist Bessie Brown Becker, who self-deprecatingly hoped "someday, to attain a high standard in my simple lines of Riley, Field, and others."[105] Joanne Gilbert has pointed out that comediennes' constructions of themselves as children have traditionally allowed them to remain desexualized and nonthreatening.[106] Female elocutionists' physical suitability to portray a child was thus sometimes an issue; Jessie Alexander insisted that "no grown-up should impersonate childhood or youth, unless physique, voice, and an ingenuous nature combine to create the illusion."[107] Some performers relied on costumes as well as voice; in her advertising flyer, child impersonator Ora Jenkins was depicted in a short dress that hid her woman's physique, one hand pulling on her girlish curls.[108]

Because much of the speech literature was pedagogical in nature, it is difficult to distinguish between texts intended for children's recitation and texts about children intended for adult performers. Most child-dialect selections with music were intended for adults; indeed the most popular recitations about children, such as James Whitcomb Riley's "The Elf Child" ("Little Orphant Annie") or Eugene Field's sentimental "Little Boy Blue," were widely popular with adult speakers (though they were not typically accompanied). There were few child-dialect works performed with informally added accompaniments, but many published compositions. The careful coordination required to create successful accompanied recitations was probably the reason that most children's selections did not have musical accompaniment; nonetheless, the cover of a children's anthology by Maude Jackson, who taught in the Chicago schools, shows two small girls on a church stage, one reciting while the other plays the piano.[109] In reality, children were more likely to recite unaccompanied or to sing, march, or pantomime to musical accompaniment; musically accompanied recitations in child dialect were thus more often intended for adult women.

Regardless, the socialization function of poetry published in anthologies for juveniles and its strict division of gender roles came to influence women's performances and their compositions. Poems were frequently designated as being for boys or for girls, with most obviously gendered selections being those that depicted little girls' joy in engaging in housework and other domestic roles; some texts appear to be in direct response to political challenges from the women's suffrage movement. A "motion song" for both boys and girls, "Women's Rights," provided pantomimed working motions to the tune of "Tramp, Tramp"; its lyrics stressed how each gender thought the other had easier chores and were happy that "women's rights will be soon be here," so that "men shall mind the kitchen" or "pretty girls will do the farming—let them try!"[110] The underlying message was that the two genders should stay in their respective spheres. Many texts pointedly satirized girls and women who neglected their household duties in aspiring to high culture. "A Mother's Advice," published in 1900, stressed that although music and dancing would "please the man," skill in housework rather than the arts would ensure a girl a good marriage.[111] Tom Mason's "We All Know Her," published in an 1899 children's anthology, described how

> She warbled the soprano with dramatic sensibility.
> And dallied with the organ when the organist was sick;
>
> . . .
>
> For real unvarnished culture she betrayed a great propensity;
> Her Tuesday-talks were famous and her Friday-glimmers great

The problem with the young woman's excessive artistic activity was that "she wouldn't wash the dishes" and "her mother darned the socks!"[112]

Girls' doll poetry emphasized their future maternal roles; girls imitated adults in caring for their dolls and fretting over their imaginary illnesses or death. "Doll drills" featured groups of girls holding dolls, singing lullabies, and pantomiming childcare.[113] One of the most performed poems was "The Dead Doll" by Margaret Vandergift, in which a girl's doll dies "of a broken heart, / And a dreadful crack in her head."[114] The somewhat morbid attention to dead dolls may, in part, have been influenced by the nineteenth-century's child mortality rate and its elaborate mourning rituals, or it may simply have been a product of the easily breakable heads of china dolls. However, doll historian Miriam Formanek-Brunell has suggested that the violence against dolls and the resulting funerals in girls' play could have been a means of aggressive resistance against adults' socially prescribed proper maternal play.[115] While in some poems young girls grieve over the "loss" of a doll, a photograph in *The Capitol Speaker* depicts an angry girl suspending a battered doll from a noose, supporting Formanek-Brunell's hypothesis.[116]

The ill or dying doll, found across numerous anthologies, became an important theme in musical settings as well. Dedicated to children's entertainer Kitty Cheatham, discussed in the following section, the most popular doll selection was the song "I've Got a Pain in My Sawdust," which was recited to its accompaniment.[117] In the song the doll succumbs to its internal sufferings rather than breaking its bisque head, as is stereotypical of dead-doll texts. Charles Gounod's *Funeral March of a Marionette* is interjected in the song's final refrain, much in the way that accompanied recitations incorporated known music. Werner responded to the popularity of dead-doll texts by issuing multiple sheet-music settings with varying degrees of accompaniment. In "A Busted Dolly," having been chewed by up by her mistress's dog, a doll ends her recitation by singing about her undeserved injuries and the cruel neglect of children.[118] The owner of "The Broken Doll" is distraught at her doll's demise after a fat woman sits on it.[119] The substantial accompaniment, in two sections, consists of simple chords rhythmically aligned with the words; two verses of the strophic poem are recited to its first section, which cadences midway on the minor mediant to emphasize the situation's pathos ("it is so bad!"). In the second musical section, after dressing her remaining dolls in funereal black, the child imagines her doll in heaven accompanied by a pastoral tonic pedal. The accompaniment introduces a poignant diminished seventh chord at the end of the poem's penultimate line, "I think I'll never laugh no more." Werner also issued, in sheet-music form, "Folks Think We Are Related," containing a poem, accompaniment, and performance instructions; here, the girl's identification with her doll is so intense that she believes they look alike.[120] Nonetheless, the inner verses describe the various potentially fatal illnesses from which the doll has escaped. The verses are recited in rhythm to a common-time accompaniment; the final verses, in which the girl dances with her doll, are provided with waltz music.

Child dialect more often took place in recitations that depicted boys. Women's voices could replicate the pitch level of boys whose voices had not changed, and contemporary psychology, particularly the writings of G. Stanley Hall, found that boys passed through a "feminized" stage in adolescence before reaching a fully developed masculinity;[121] on the evolutionary spectrum, women were sometimes considered unable to reach the full maturity of adult men. Thus, both vocally and developmentally, women would have been the ideal performers to imitate boys and able to portray them with accuracy. "When Mrs. Leland is to take the character of a boy," reported an 1898 article, "she studies a living specimen, and such of her impersonations are in consequence, bright, cunning, piquant, and delightfully realistic."[122] Anna Morgan pointed out that "an excellent test of versatility in the use of the voice is to impersonate the James Whitcomb Riley boys" and listed several poems by the popular poet.[123] Harriet Saxton's textbook, which provided practice excerpts from poems requiring children's voices, many in child dialect, contains an extensive selection of texts depicting boys and young men, and very few with girls' voices.[124]

Women's adaptation of texts in which boys played a central role was also because of the stories found there. The boy was presented as a loveable rascal who broke rules and pushed the boundaries of the acceptable, and yet was typically able to triumph in spite of his breach of societal expectations, or at least could be forgiven. Performing as a young boy allowed women to present themselves in ways that sentimental Victorian texts—full of long-suffering, religious, lovelorn, or grief-stricken women—did not. Typical topics for poems with boys' personas empowered them with a wider range of behavior than that allowed girls: boys regularly refused to attend school or engaged in pranks. Anne Trensky has noted how boys' rough-and-tumble fictional personae make them more endearing to adults, who wish that they, too, were free of the social boundaries that boys ignore.[125] Gilbert, who describes how vaudeville comediennes cultivated child characters, has identified the strategy of ingratiation as central to women's use of children in their humor: "The kid can be naughty and irreverent but, by remaining a kid, assures that she will be perceived as merely a teasing, nonthreatening 'pal.'"[126] This approach, in which the adopted persona engages in unacceptable actions, yet is shielded from criticism because he or she is a child, was especially recognizable in the performances by women who took on boy personas. Any overt transgressions in the fictional boys' behaviors were mediated by their being shown to be decent and bighearted: tales that show a boy as admirable despite his flaws often centered on his relationship with a dog or his assistance to a younger, impoverished, or handicapped boy, themes that appear in the compositions of Frieda Peycke (discussed in chapter 10). By adopting a boy's persona, women were able to experience boys' physical and social freedoms. These freedoms were apparent in boys' speech, which was more likely to be in child dialect than that of girls, who were seemingly less likely to deviate from the expected elocutionary norm; nonetheless, like women's adoption of black dialect, their ability to perform boys' language "incorrectly" reinforced their position as "correct" speakers.

Adopting a boy persona also allowed women to express some decidedly undomestic sentiments on the platform, as boys protested adults' efforts to civilize them. In contrast to stereotypical portrayals of girls as dedicated miniature housewives, boys' texts, sometimes set as musical recitations, complained vociferously about parental enforcement of cleanliness. Retta Jacobs's "Gee Whiz: When Mother Washes Me" (1928) was published by Mary V. McGowan as a song recitation, designed to be either recited or sung.[127] The emphatic opening exclamation—"Soap! Gee Whiz!"—is supported by a grace-note flourish and punctuating chords that reappear after "Hush!," uttered by the speaker's mother (example 6.7). The boy's declaration, "I just wish ev'ry one in the world would throw their soap away," is painted with a descending arpeggio.

Example 6.7. Mary V. McGowan's setting of Retta Jacobs's "Gee Whiz: When Mother Washes Me" (Franklin, OH: Eldridge Entertainment House, 1928), mm. 1–4. Used by permission.

Burges Johnson's similar poem, "Soap, the Oppressor," in which a boy believes that extended washing is making him skinnier, was the basis of Phyllis Fergus's popular strophic setting, dominated by lilting dotted rhythms.[128]

Instead of motherly love of children, boys' disgust and dismay with their household's new baby was a common subject. The plot and child dialect of "Charley's Opinion of the Baby," found in W. R. Vansant's *The Progressive Speaker* (1897), is remarkably similar to that of "Mah Lil Bit Sister," a dialect poem by Elizabeth Gordon set by Frieda Peycke. In both, a small child (in the latter case, a girl) is jealous of a new sibling;[129] Gordon's text opens with, "Doctor say, mah nose done broke," while "Charley's Opinion" has this stanza:

> Doctor told anozzer
> Great big awful lie;
> Nose ain't out of joyent,
> Dat ain't why I cry.

In both poems the humor comes from the implication that child doesn't understand the doctor's expression that his or her "nose is out of joint." Mary Wyman Williams's "The New Brother" is set to a sweet, gently rocking lullaby-like accompaniment that seems incongruous given the older sibling's complaining. His speech is set off by rests between phrases, as if he is silently contemplating the infant and the change in his own situation. He exclaims, "Why he isn't worth a dollar, All he does is cry and holler, more and more,"[130] emphasized by a triplet and chords that fit the text's rhythm (example 6.8). In the final phrase of the recitation, the boy announces, after another thoughtful rest, that he would have rather had a dog.

Example 6.8. Mary Wyman Williams, "The New Brother" (Chicago: Clayton F. Summy; London: Weekes, 1920), mm. 9–11, verse 2.

Their boy personae enabled women to express disdain for the domestic world of housework and motherhood in which they were supposed to be content: dolls are broken, cleanliness is oppressive, and new babies are rejected. Transgressions of gender norms were acceptable in the voices of children, forgiven for their lack of adherence to societal expectations because of their youth. Child-dialect recitations were representative of the kinds of humor that women composers came to incorporate into spoken-word compositions when they began to reject Victorian sentimentality for a more modern view of women's roles. Platform performers who pretended to be children made the power of women's humor less threatening and created the possibility of small acts of resistance to gender norms. Child dialect was far from the high-art goals of elocution, and women whose performances were overtly humorous risked being taken less seriously as purveyors of the moral and literary; for elocutionists who advocated the transmission of great literature, they had become purveyors of fluff entertainment. Nonetheless, for some performers, like Kitty Cheatham, the creation of a child persona was another means for them to express the spiritual, artistic, and educational messages at the heart of elocution.

## Kitty Cheatham and the Career of a Professional Child

Although Kitty Cheatham's career originated in the theater rather than in elocution, in it many of the artistic trends for female spoken-word performers coalesced: African American dialect and child impersonation; a mixture of singing and recitations, sometimes musically accompanied; and the inclusion of spoken word in orchestral concerts. Cheatham abandoned the moniker of *actress* and became known as a *diseuse*—an artist who spoke rather than sang her songs.[131] As a singer she advertised her recitals alongside concerts of classical musicians, and they consisted more of vocal works than poetry. Cheatham presented herself as a proponent and personification of the childlike, and in doing so succeeded in skirting many of the gender issues that faced women on the platform. She was a serious advocate for the music of African Americans, while at the same time she continued to perpetuate the mythology of the Old South and racial stereotypes.

Born in Nashville, Tennessee, in 1864, Katherine Smiley Cheatham began her stage career in the late 1880s, working in the theatrical company of Augustin Daly.[132] In 1894 Cheatham married a Liverpool cotton merchant and left the stage, but she reemerged around 1902 as a salon performer at elite homes in London and then established herself as a performer for children. Cheatham gave biannual recitals in New York immediately following Christmas and near Easter; by 1913 one writer could claim, "The holidays and Miss Cheatham have almost become synonyms."[133] In the teens, Cheatham toured the United States, reportedly traveling as much as fifteen thousand miles per season.[134] During the summers she performed in London, Paris, and various German cities, although World War I slowed her expanding European career. Her performances were fewer in the 1920s; she programmed an Easter concert in 1925 and gave a patriotic recital in 1927. Cheatham made recordings for Victor and Columbia and in the 1920s appeared on radio.

Cheatham readily acknowledged the professional training she had received under Daly, yet she managed to portray her recitals as the public face of a private entertainment for wealthy American socialites and European nobility, in whose drawing rooms she performed during summers abroad. In 1912, the critic of the *Cleveland Plain Dealer* noted that "a report of one of Kitty Cheatham's tours abroad reads more like a royal pilgrimage than the tour of a concert artist."[135] Many of Cheatham's recitals in New York were matinees for audiences dominated by women and children; newspapers noted the social elite who attended these events, including children of the wealthy or artistic.[136] Cheatham's own "distinguished Southern lineage"[137] was prominently featured in her biography: her father had been Nashville's mayor and a member of Tennessee's legislature, and biographical accounts made the usual excuse that a financial downturn had forced her to go on the stage, to her family's dismay.

The packaging of Cheatham's performances as upper-class entertainment seems somewhat incongruous when considering her actual offerings, which combined poems, stories, and songs for and about children with African American dialect recitations and spirituals. In some ways, the association of her concerts with religious holidays made them the ultimate version of the topical programs mounted by women and children in schools and churches across America; Cheatham combined all aspects of the seasonal musical and literary entertainment in one talented individual. Cheatham's voice was small, and she was not considered to be an especially outstanding singer; however, through her occasional fraternization with noted classical musicians and through commissioning new songs by British and American composers, she also managed to associate her children's entertainments with high art.[138] Harpist Carlos Salzedo accompanied her in 1906; composer Engelbert Humperdinck and soprano Geraldine Farrar appeared on one of her concerts in 1910. Cheatham also appeared at benefit events that featured operatic singers David Bispham and Lillian Nordica.[139] Cheatham frequently advertised that she would be performing songs newly composed for her; after a 1908 concert, the *New York Sun* reported that "our newest American composers all sent manuscripts, if not flowers."[140] Although it is difficult to determine which songs Cheatham personally commissioned and which were dedicated to her in hopes of receiving a performance, at least sixty-five works by forty-five composers were associated with her; the composer of a new song occasionally appeared on Cheatham's recital to accompany her in its premiere.[141] As the singer's European career flourished, her repertoire became more international in scope, and she publicized the works she had brought home from her travels, such as Lieder by Max Reger or children's pieces arranged by Béla Bartók.[142] These reports continued to help solidify her association with European classical music. In 1912, *Musical America* found Cheatham's annual recitals as much a part of New York's musical life as the Metropolitan Opera, the New York Philharmonic, or the Kneisel Quartet, claiming that they were "in their way as ennobling and emotionally purifying and elevating as the greatest of poetic tragedies or the sublimest music dramas."[143] Thus, the step from reciting nursery rhymes and singing songs about children to appearing with orchestras in Young People's Concerts, as Cheatham did beginning in the teens, was not as far a leap as might be assumed.

Cheatham's recitals, most often held at the Lyceum Theatre in New York, usually had stage scenery, Christmas trees or Easter flowers, or settings that reflected the lives of children—one in Nashville featured teddy bears, dolls, and hobby horses.[144] In Boston in 1913, Cheatham "did her best" to convince her audience "that it had come not into Jordan Hall but into her own drawing-room."[145] In addition to replicating a domestic setting, Cheatham worked to create a feminine and childlike persona; the singer was almost forty when she began her concerts, but press reports referred to her as a "girl."[146] She wore white ruffled dresses and a large hat, and sometimes dressed as an eighteenth-century shepherdess (figure 6.2). Several newspapers likened her to figures painted by Gainsborough or Watteau, with a "Dresden-China personality";[147] one illustration of her in costume bears a resemblance to *Pinkie*, the 1794 portrait of Sarah Barrett Moulton by Thomas Lawrence.[148] Cheatham's eighteenth-century image was in part because she sometimes sang French

KITTY CHEATHAM

Figure 6.2. Frontispiece for Kitty Cheatham, *A Nursery Garland* (New York: G. Schirmer, 1917).

songs and earlier music to harpsichord accompaniment, but her costumes also served to suggest fictional characters such as Bo Peep or a fairy godmother. Archibald Sullivan's description of the singer as a resident of Babyland, "tripping over fields of daisies . . . while behind her trail miles and miles of dear kiddies following her as they did the 'Pied Piper of Hamelin,'"[149] was the image chosen for her song anthology, *Kitty Cheatham: Her Book*, published in 1915.[150]

Cheatham's youthful nature and the presexual innocence of her recitals was often stressed; Cleveland critic Archie Bell quipped that "maiden aunts would recommend her entertainment to the kiddies."[151] A 1910 article recounted how delighted she was when an elderly Frenchman mistook her for her own daughter.[152] After her divorce, she reverted to "Miss Kitty Cheatham" for the remainder of her career, and her adult marriage was seemingly forgotten.

Cheatham's stylized, childlike vocal performance contributed to her public image. Although few of her texts were in child dialect, a 1906 article claimed that she mimicked a child's voice and manner so perfectly that her young audience felt she seemed "just like one of themselves";[153] the following year another described how her "childish, immature voice . . . sometimes squeaked as if it needed oiling."[154] This voice is heard in Cheatham's recording of "I've Got a Pain in My Sawdust," in which the singer uses her pointed upper registers for the ill doll's voice, making little high-pitched cries of pain and occasionally exhibiting a slightly uncontrolled vibrato and breathy sound as the doll comes closer to expiring. Cheatham's voice and demeanor resulted in performances universally hailed as "quaint" and "charming."[155]

Advertisements for Cheatham's performances indicated that they were aimed at children of all ages and emphasized their educational nature and moral training, claiming that she was not "a mere entertainer," but, in fact, a teacher and "exponent of the very heart of childhood."[156] Cheatham's earlier career as a theatrical ingenue was largely forgotten; in its place was a morally superior figure transmitting childhood's truth, sincerity, and simplicity. Cheatham stated, "I am but a channel for the expression of the message that is given to me."[157] At Cincinnati's Grand Opera House in 1911 she told her audience that "joy, peace and happiness lies in being childlike" and that "I feel I have a message and can do substantial good in the world by spreading the glories, the fascinations of the true child."[158] In part, Cheatham's motivations were religious; a Christian Scientist, she was known to quote Matthew 18:3 on the need to become like children to enter heaven.[159] Cheatham's childlike nature and "soul of the Universal and Immortal Child" were reportedly a result of spiritual transformation.[160] Although Cheatham was a paid actress and entertainer, her role on the platform was acceptable because it resulted from her personal mission to enable others to experience a similar rebirth. Ostensibly children, Cheatham's audiences were as frequently made up of adults as of their offspring. After her 1908 Christmas recital, the *New York Times* reported that her matinees "seem to appeal more especially to those that would like to be children than to those who are."[161] A monologue written for the performer by Graham Robertson promised a return to childhood for adults:

> Children old and overwise,
> O'er whose heads the morrows flew,

To your childhood's Paradise
Wander back with Dream-come-true:
Smile for sigh and gold for grey,
I can give you—Yesterday.[162]

Combined with her childlike persona, the religious trappings of Cheatham's art allowed her to present moral truths that were received as having been appropriately feminized. A 1911 Nashville article described her performances as domestic, internal miniatures in contrast to the great artworks of a gallery, reflecting the wider cultural association of the small and the ornamental with the feminine:

> Miss Cheatham is the seeker, the finder and the teller of the eternal truths that lie at the core of life's trifles. . . . She specializes in the infinitesimal, which after all, is but the other end of the infinite, the quality of size existing only in the eye of man, and not in the eye of God. She is a painter of exquisite miniatures . . . one places her little pictures in an inner gallery of the memory, to be visited oftener than those more spacious halls where hang the larger canvases.[163]

Like other female performers, Cheatham engaged in comedy through the commentary she provided to introduce her numbers. *Musical America* described how "these little monologues, slyly purporting to explain the songs, are masterpieces of playful satire, so delicate as to be robbed of every vestige of the power to hurt, and brimming with delicious humor."[164] Cheatham's subtle comedy never transgressed the boundaries of the feminine; when audiences encountered "a touch of the little polished claw, so daintily sheathed," critics assured readers that "never perhaps is her allure more feminine, more stimulating than when she does that."[165] Cheatham's comedy was tolerated, clothed as it was in the childlike innocence of her stage persona. Unlike elocutionists, Cheatham was not described as speaking child dialect or doing child impersonations, but, according to one reviewer, *"She was a child."*[166] Only rarely was a critic willing to suggest that perhaps "a grown woman singing nursery rhymes for two and a half hours at a stretch to an audience composed largely of adults apparently fully developed mentally strikes me as rather foolish," or that her "sympathy with the ideal child . . . desophisticates her."[167] The latter writer apparently did not recognize that desophisticating herself was a large part of what made Kitty Cheatham successful.

The singer's recitals consisted of songs, recitations, and stories, and could include as many as thirty selections. Reports suggest many of the songs were at least partly spoken (for example, the dialect songs "A Little Negro's Idea as to Why Adam Sinned," by Alex Rogers, and Silvio Hein's "Don't Be What You Ain't").[168] The lengthiest works she programmed—Liza Lehmann's settings of Oscar Wilde's *The Happy Prince* and *The Selfish Giant*—were spoken melodramas. Among the works Cheatham commissioned and programmed were musical recitations, including a setting of François Coppée's "Butterflies," by a British aristocrat, Minnie Cochrane; and an Elizabethan lyric, "Phillida Flouts Me," set by melodrama composer Stanley Hawley.[169] Cheatham denied that she was an elocutionist—she was presented in the press as a one-of-a-kind performer—yet her careful attention to language and its so-called higher meanings was in keeping with elocutionary goals. The critic for the *New Haven Register* described how "Kitty Cheatham knows well the meaning of words. . . . Our language, as she uses it, becomes a thing of youth and beauty."[170]

Like elocutionists, Cheatham's repertoire included "doll" numbers: the songs "'Plaint of the Little Bisque Doll," also known as "I've Got a Pain in My Sawdust," and Jessie L. Gaynor's "My Dear Jerushy," in which a girl continues to love her doll despite its deteriorating physical condition, were standard fare in her concerts for many years.[171] The strophic "Jerushy," with a syllabic, pattery text setting and a concluding lament, "My *poor* Jerushy," set to a dissonant chord, could easily have been recited as well as sung. Cheatham's papers include a score of "Dolly's Holiday" by Ewan Dale with her markings; in the song's second verse, the doll describes children's abuse, similar to the doll texts found in recitation anthologies:

> Next they throw us on our backs,
> In the fire they melt our wax
> Till our delicate complexion is no more,
> And our heads they open wide,
> Just to see the works inside,
> And we're batter'd into bits upon the floor.[172]

The *New York Times* described how Cheatham's boy recitations were "able to show them at their best or at their worst."[173] Cheatham performed brief selections from John Alden Carpenter's *Improving Songs for Anxious Children*, which contained deliberately simple accompaniments and featured boys who objected to taking part in potentially feminizing activities.[174] In "Making Calls," the boy finds visiting old ladies with his mother "a waste of an afternoon." Two boys complain about artistic training: the speaker of "Practicing" believes that his piano practice, reflected in the continual eighth notes of the accompaniment, "never does any good," and in "A Wicked Child," a boy at dancing school describes how "while I'm learning waltzing, / My parents I revile." Another boy objects to his "Red Hair," because his curls make him resemble "silly girls." "The Liar" resembles many child recitations in which boys get into trouble for eating forbidden foods; however, in Carpenter's song the boy's indulgence in a pastry is moralistically punished with stomach pain.

Cheatham began appearing with orchestras in the teens, adding her child and African American selections to their concerts and providing commentary on the ensembles' repertoire. She was a soloist with the New York Philharmonic in Young People's Concerts on various occasions and replicated her matinee performances with Leopold Stokowski and the Philadelphia Orchestra in 1914. She also appeared at Carnegie Hall in 1912 with the Russian Symphony Orchestra, which presented Anton Arensky's Variations on a Theme of Tchaikovsky; Cheatham recited the "Legend" (known in English as "Crown of Thorns"), the text of Tchaikovsky's song, op. 54, no. 4, on which Arensky's piece was based. The poem by Richard Henry Stoddard, which tells of Jesus as a child in a garden, features the religious imagery typical of the singer's recitals. Cheatham, whose own performances frequently referenced fairy tales, described Felix and Fanny Mendelssohn's involvement with music before the elfin Scherzo of *A Midsummer Night's Dream*; she also provided the entertaining stories behind Haydn's "Farewell" or "Surprise" Symphonies. Cheatham's ready association with the Christmas holidays also made her a natural choice to explain the movements of Tchaikovsky's *Nutcracker* Suite, which she programmed on a 1917 concert with Swedish conductor Edla Söller and "her male orchestra."[175] Cheatham's papers show that she wrote a spoken introduction to the "Waltz of the Flowers" and a poem designed to be sung to it, which she may have performed at this and other events.[176] Cheatham's spirituals were less frequently heard on orchestral concerts, although when she performed African American "songs and tales" at Carnegie Hall in 1914, the Philharmonic Society played Henry Gilbert's *Comedy Overture on Negro Themes*, seemingly as a means of integrating her performance with theirs.[177]

It would be a mistake to assume that Cheatham's orchestral appearances were somehow more adult than her recitals. Rather, Cheatham worked to bring classical music into her childlike world. In her book *Nursery Garland*, the second of two published anthologies of songs from her performances, Cheatham included works associated with children by well-known composers: Brahms's Lullaby, Schumann's op. 79 children's songs, and two selections from the "Toy" Symphony, supposedly by Haydn. However a large portion of the volume is made up of piano arrangements of instrumental works by Bach, Mozart, Haydn, Beethoven, Mendelssohn, Brahms, Tchaikovsky, and others, to which have been added singable texts suitable for children. Many of these were by the writers Burges Johnson and Fullerton Waldo, and were perhaps made at Cheatham's request, as apparently were the texts provided by composer Harvey Worthington Loomis, who also composed songs for Cheatham. The singer's goal of demonstrating the childlike qualities of the great composers is apparent in the newly texted dances by Mozart she included, which were reportedly composed when he was four and six years old.[178] In some cases, Cheatham attempted to unite the greats of literature and music, setting a text by Tennyson to the Andante from Beethoven's Fifth Symphony and one by

Milton to the "Ode to Joy."[179] Some texts reflect Cheatham's educational mission: "Papa Haydn's Surprise," sung to the Andante theme of the "Surprise" Symphony, explained its origins:

> Papa Haydn played a joke
> On those proud and sleepy folk
> After notes that sweetly sang
> Came a sudden Bang![180]

Other texts have no obvious association with the music that accompanies them; for example, the Andante from Brahms's Third Symphony became "The Fairy Travellers," in which fairies happily leave the snoring human beings who can't see them to return to their woodland home. In some instances the added texts are religious, even when the well-known musical accompaniment is not: a theme from Wagner's *Siegfried Idyll* becomes "Child Jesus in the Garden," in which the voice of the Christ child summons angels. Thus the European canonic greats, published alongside arrangements of Cheatham's characteristic spirituals, were simultaneously sacralized and made appropriately childlike.

Cheatham's engagement with African American dialect and songs would seem to have been out of place among nursery rhymes and fairy tales, but the notion that African Americans represented childlike, not fully developed adults suggested that their language and music were appropriate for children, although reviewers noted that these selections were more popular with adult listeners. One newspaper reported, "What Miss Cheatham does not know of children and their ways is certainly not worth knowing. Her sympathies also rest with those children of a larger growth whom it is only courtesy to speak of as 'coloured ladies and gentlemen.'"[181] Cheatham's performances—or at least the ways they were described in the press—were in keeping with the prevailing fictionalized depictions of the Old South. Cheatham reportedly specialized in "the Southern negro, who does not hold by emancipation," and because she was a Southerner, her portrayals were believed to be highly authentic, portraying the "ante-bellum colored folk as they really were."[182] Singing spirituals was yet another means for Cheatham to express her Christian religious values. She recounted how "the old-time negroes were a deeply religious people with a childlike faith" and hailed these supposed children as expressing "a great ethical truth."[183]

The stereotypical tale of Cheatham having learned spirituals from her "negro Mammy" was frequently reported.[184] A black Mammy was featured on her publicity card, which featured a fairy-like Cheatham surrounded by cartoon drawings of the nursery characters that appeared in Elizabeth Sprague Coolidge's *Mother Goose Songs*, which she frequently sang (figure 6.3). The story about the origins of Cheatham's children's programs was based on her

Figure 6.3. Flyer for Kitty Cheatham, Kitty Cheatham Papers, 1892–1946. Tennessee State Library and Archives, Nashville, Tennessee.

recollection of her African American nurse and her supposedly spontaneous singing of "Swing Low, Sweet Chariot" to an aristocratic woman at a French chateau:

> Without knowing why, I began to hum some of the old negro hymns, that were naturally a part of my reverie. The music was like a safety valve to my overcharged feelings, and seated there on a low stool, I began to rock and clap my hands as the old Southern "mammys" do. It seemed to me, at that moment, I was literally a child again and could hear the voice singing to me and feel about me the arms of my beloved old nurse, whom I had loved with a devotion impossible to define and never understood except by those who know from personal experience.[185]

Through her embodiment of the childlike, Kitty Cheatham was merely the means by which the songs of African Americans would be conveyed, as sentimental keepsakes of a lost Southern world.

Cheatham often sang spirituals, frequently unaccompanied. She recorded "Swing Low, Sweet Chariot," "Walk in Jerusalem, Just Like John," and "Sinner, Please Don't Let This Harvest Pass" for Victor in 1916, without accompaniment and in a florid, ornamented style; "I Don't Feel No-Ways Tired" was sung with piano.[186] Between 1910 and 1916 in New York she appeared accompanied by African American baritone and composer Harry T. Burleigh, who played the piano and joined her in singing his own arrangements. Although the press reported them singing in parallel thirds like operatic lovers,[187] both the religious content of the songs and Cheatham's child persona perhaps suggested to audiences the well-known pairing of Uncle Tom and Little Eva from *Uncle Tom's Cabin* instead,[188] as they seemed to protect the two singers from the stereotypical notion of a black male's sexual threat to white females. Cheatham's spiritual performances were surrounded by dialect recitations: Joel Chandler Harris's "Tar Baby" from his *Uncle Remus* stories (also in figure 6.3) and Dunbar's popular "Angelina" and "When Malindy Sings." The latter text, which Cheatham recorded in 1910, was a consistent feature of her programs, allowing her to introduce her own singing of "Swing Low, Sweet Chariot," mentioned near the end of the poem.[189] Like Dunbar's recitations, Cheatham's performances seem to have been highly rhythmic: one performance of "Angelina" "set the audience swaying to the rhythm."[190]

Cheatham was widely, if inaccurately, credited with preservation of the spiritual from the oral tradition. She frequently advocated for the spiritual in the press, stating that "this work that I am doing to keep alive the genuine old negro songs has a positive historic value,"[191] and she provided validity for African American music by regularly explaining to audiences that spirituals were the authentic folk song of the Negro. Fisk University professor John Wesley Work praised Cheatham's understanding "right spirit and proper motive," and found her renditions "sympathetic and characteristic." The *Crisis*, the magazine of the National Association for the Advancement of Colored People, commended Cheatham's recording efforts because they would "afford permanent example of proper interpretation of pure Negro songs."[192] Yet the language she used in describing spirituals was steeped in the evolutionary thinking of the day, often undermining the music's worth even as she praised it; her program at Yale University labeled her African American selections as "primitive and undeveloped."[193] Cheatham criticized African Americans for abandoning their own music because they did not want to recall the era of slavery, and praised Burleigh and Dunbar for "their expounding of negro music as it was in the old plantation days."[194] She credited slavery for raising African Americans from "barbarism" and enabling them to develop their capacity for "expressing a high form of music";[195] however, she demeaned African American musicians' creativity by suggesting, according to a Dallas newspaper, that "the negro's *imitative* faculties have in the majority of cases come uppermost, making him follow the music of the white race rather than develop the native music that could become so attractive."[196] After Cheatham performed "When Malindy Sings" with "Swing Low, Sweet Chariot" for the African American students at Fisk University, home of the choir that had also taken spiritual arrangements to an international audience, she reportedly praised the slaves of the antebellum era:

> I do not want to be thought a defender of slavery, for it was an unfortunate condition. But it was the association with the Southern families that brought out the negro's best qualities and evolved his wonderful spirituals. And the negro of that day was a fine type. Do you know that he was never known to betray a trust? During the war the negro slaves remained and protected the wives and children (even sleeping outside their doors) of their masters while they were away fighting against the cause that was to set them free? The negro of to-day must be made to realize the rare qualities which his forefather expressed even in slavery. It was that which evolved these songs.[197]

Thus, Cheatham sought to validate the role of upper-class whites such as herself in the creation of the music she sang and perpetuated the mythology of the happy slave.

Although Cheatham's wide presentation of spirituals, from San Francisco to Berlin, undoubtedly had an impact on their history, she also regularly sang selections that were far more in keeping with a fictionalized Old South: Stephen Foster's "Old Folks at Home" and the minstrel show song "Dixie," which she recorded in 1910.[198] On one occasion a banjo accompanied her from behind the scenes.[199] Some of the stories she told between songs were racist, such as the tale of the converted "pickaninnies," who went to the altar only to encounter a white-robed bishop, and ran fearfully away, yelling "Ku Klux Klan!"[200] A long-lasting song in Cheatham's repertoire was "Don't Be What You Ain't" by Silvio Hein,[201] not unlike "Mammy's Philosophy" by Aileen Tye, but somewhat more threatening in tone. The chorus concludes,

> When a man is what he isn't
> Den he isn't what he is,
> And as sure as I'm a talkin'
> He's a gwine to get his.

It is difficult not to interpret this message in dialect as reassurance that despite her performances of African American culture and her duets with Harry Burleigh, the native Southerner supported separate racial worlds. Regardless of Cheatham's intentions, it seems likely that much of what she offered to audiences reaffirmed the cultural construction of plantation life nostalgia. Nonetheless, her engagement with the spiritual was unusual for the period, and the songs' textual content was far different from the more stereotypical dialect recitations performed by female elocutionists. The London Times recognized that "Americans who understand and love negroes are not quite as common as women who love children," and concluded, "She is doing good work, from a musical as well as a human and sociological point of view, in bringing these out-of-the-way melodies and thoughts of the child-race of the world before the public."[202]

In spite of the numerous ways in which her infantilized persona affected her public reception, Cheatham also saw herself as having a message for and about women. She supported women's suffrage and envisioned a world in which individuals were free to develop according to their needs rather than conform to gendered codes of behavior: "I believe women, to become more complete and balanced, should develop the good qualities ascribed to men, without wearing mannish clothes or smoking cigarettes; and men, likewise, could become more gentle, more painstaking."[203] Cheatham programmed "Robin Red Breast," a Christian legend, by Swedish author Selma Lagerlöf, the first woman to win the Nobel Prize in Literature, hoping that it would be of inspiration to girls, teaching each one that she could "do the work she was meant to do."[204] After her performing career had ended, Kitty Cheatham continued to pursue oratory with a religious and political message. She gave lectures about her travels, historical figures, and patriotic and religious topics; in the 1930s she spoke at the International Women's Week in Hungary and at Millennial Celebrations in Iceland. In 1936, to the utter surprise of the Ben Franklin Society, when introduced as a trustee's guest, she took the podium and proceeded to speak knowledgeably and extensively about Franklin, becoming the first female speaker to address the group.[205] In a 1912 article, Cheatham tried to transmit her personal bravado to her young female audience, assuring them that women were able to succeed, yet simultaneously reinforcing a humble status inspired by religious ideals:

> One last word, dear girls: Don't ever be afraid of expressing yourselves, even in the smallest way. Just let it be the right motive that impels you. Every little courageous trial helps us on to bigger things; and girls, *we women must be capable of doing big things*—not from a false basis of pride and vainglory, but with the humility which gives us a clear understanding of what our Great Teacher meant when He said: "Blessed are the meek, for they shall inherit the earth."[206]

Ultimately, Cheatham did not see that the ways in which she portrayed herself as diminutive in any way impeded her; rather, as in other women's performances evoking children and African Americans, it was the source of her ability to deliver her message.

# 7. Womanly Women and Moral Uplift

## Female Readers and Concert Companies on the Chautauqua Circuit

Mrs. Beecher does not bear about with her the lime-light glare.
Off the stage she is simply a woman—a womanly woman—
that first and always.
—Paul M. Pearson, Chautauqua bureau manager

Her eyes just sparkle with delight, each move is one of grace,
She has a charm of figure, and a winsome girlish face,
And in between the numbers, where the quartet rings and toots
Doth Coyla charm her hearers, as she coyly elocutes.
—Edwin Weeks, *Coyla May Spring*

The faces of women smile out of the talent brochures of the Redpath Chautauqua Bureau. Young, fresh-faced, and attractive, they pose, elegantly gowned, looking as if they never abandoned their parlors for long summer days on the road, appearing in tent performances across small-town America. In his recollections, longtime circuit supervisor Harry P. Harrison described Chautauqua's musicians as "men and women, young and old, but especially women, lighthearted, pretty girls having fun and frolic on the road," a romanticized description that overlooks the sometimes grueling conditions performers faced.[1] But Harrison captures the image of the women on its platforms that Chautauqua portrayed to its audiences. Along with speeches by noted lecturers, musicians and readers supplied rural communities with so-called culture and moral uplift in afternoon and evening events that combined music and spoken-word entertainments. Chautauqua also served as a site of the continuing tensions between the overtly theatrical and the literary basis of women's performances, and between highbrow ideals and popular offerings of both spoken word and music.

Although it has fallen out of cultural memory, the institution of Chautauqua touched the lives of millions of Americans during the three decades that its performers traveled across the country, making summer appearances in tents in rural regions, typically in towns with populations of fewer than 10,000.[2] Estimates vary, but at its height, anywhere from nine million to twenty million Americans attended Chautauqua performances in a year. The name *Chautauqua* was derived from the summer retreat in Chautauqua, New York, founded for the education of Sunday school teachers in 1874, and was subsequently applied to locally run assemblies that sprang up to supply lectures and arts events and to sponsor religious and educational study groups.[3] However, the Chautauqua tent circuit, which lasted from approximately 1904 to 1930, was a commercial venture with talent supplied by regional entertainment bureaus.[4] The Chautauqua system grew out of the lyceum lecture bureaus, created in the mid-nineteenth century to supply speakers and, later, entertainments for the winter season. The bureaus sold "Culture" to their audiences, and Chautauqua's educational roots gave it a respectability that made musical and elocutionary performance by women possible.

The creation of the circuit system is generally credited to Keith Vawter of the Redpath Lyceum Bureau, and it was well established in the Midwest and beyond by 1910. The number of towns hosting a Chautauqua grew from 555 in 1910 to more than 9,000 in 1921.[5] During its peak years, Chautauqua had some twenty-one companies, five of which were divisions of the Redpath Bureau, generating circuits, around a hundred in all.[6] Although Chautauqua was most successful in the Midwest, performances took place across North America. Managers booked five to seven days' worth of lectures and entertainments for each town, supplying a platform and tent, advance advertising, and a "Junior girl" to organize events for children. Well-organized management of the circuit meant that at any one time, numerous tents—the largest of which held 1,600 to 2,000 people—would be set up in consecutive locations, so that performers spent one day performing in a town before moving on to the tent already in the next.[7]

Women played a major role in Chautauqua. Not only were they performers, but many were active in business capacities: managers, superintendents, and ticket takers. One Chautauqua memoir recalled that "sponsors asking to see a representative from the bureau learned not to be surprised when a woman turned up."[8] Chautauqua provided female residents of isolated rural areas a yearly chance to experience literary and musical performances, and women's groups were a major force in getting Chautauqua to come to their region. Contracts were designed so that a committee from the hosting town was responsible for a financial guarantee, and local residents were recruited to sell tickets. Many women's club members were thus part of the process to bring their communities the cultural good that Chautauqua offered.[9] Women put aside money from household budgets to be able to afford tickets, in the belief that Chautauqua gave their children educational opportunities.[10]

The 4,500 brochures collected by the Redpath Lyceum Bureau were designed for agents to sell the "talent" to future prospects when visiting towns on their circuit to book the next year's contracts.[11] Performer Marian Scott recalled, "So much depended on an attractive and interesting circular."[12] The flyers document the huge range of performers, from hopeful spoken-word performers who only appeared for a few years in a limited region, to longtime professionals who regularly toured the largest Chautauqua circuits and were popular draws for lyceum events during the remainder of the year. Although sometimes revealing more about how Chautauqua administrators wanted musicians and readers to be perceived than about what they performed night after summer night, the flyers are nonetheless a remarkable record of women's continuing role in the intersection of speech and music in concerts into the 1920s. Chautauqua audiences were considered to be conservative and less than sophisticated, and the spoken-word performances provided to them were in many ways the continuation of nineteenth-century practices, although sometimes repackaged as nostalgia. Even as performance styles changed, female artists' platform contributions still needed to perpetuate the gender boundaries embodied in Chautauqua's traditional values of "mother, home, and heaven."

Photographs of female performers often suggested that their natural place was the domestic sphere. While musicians, instruments in hand, typically face the camera as if on a stage, the women readers integral to those ensembles are shown in individual portraits. They stand in a dignified pose, positioned next to a window or in a large chair, visual representations of private, interior spaces; they do not perform and almost never gesture like speakers photographed for recitation manuals. When depicted with other performers, they often hold a book, an iconic symbol of their role, while their colleagues pretend to listen, as in the photograph of the Peerless Princess Quartet from Wichita, Kansas (figure 7.1).

Readers who delivered their repertoire countless times would undoubtedly have had selections memorized,[13] yet their publicity suggested that they were merely replicating a domestic activity, not creating a dramatic public event. The circulars' prose attempted to further this notion, as in the description of the Casford Concert Company from around 1925, which portrayed the three-woman ensemble as "natural artists" with "pleasing personalities"; instead of hearing professional performers, audiences would be "made to feel like they are being entertained by old-time friends." When an organizer complained that one women's ensemble did not "look the part," he was instructed to set the stage "with pretty parlor furniture, chairs, and rugs, the usual touches of domestic life," so that they would feel "as much at home as they would have

Figure 7.1. Peerless Princess Quartet. Redpath Chautauqua Collection, University of Iowa Libraries, Special Collections.

in their own parlors."[14] Chautauqua coach Elias Day's vision of a failed female ensemble was one that "did not know how to walk on to the stage as a hostess would walk into her drawing-room to greet her guests."[15] His imagery is reflected in an advertisement for the Pettit Sisters dominated by photos of the women gathered around an upright piano in their own residence.[16] Chautauqua's women were not to appear as professionals, but merely women stepping out from their homes into the imaginary parlors of future audiences.

## The All-Essential Reader:
## Elocutionary Style and Theatricality

From its beginnings, circuit Chautauqua featured women in programs that combined music and the spoken word. In 1904, Keith Vawter's first group of circuit performers included Estelle M. Clark and the Chicago Lady Entertainers, four women who provided interpretative readings and musical numbers. *Reader* was the preferred designation for Chautauqua performers, although a host of other terms suggested various specializations within spoken performance; the term *elocution* was anathema to Chautauqua booking agents. In 1903, Charles L. Wagner of the Slayton Lyceum Bureau complained of the onslaught of elocution school graduates trilling their Rs and making Delsarte poses, yet in no way professionally prepared for the platform.[17] But professionals had largely moved on from physical culture and regularly offered somewhat anxious assurances that Chautauqua readers were not antiquated Delsarteans or elocutionists: Mary Agnes Doyle was "not a reciter of verse or a delsarte [*sic*] model," and Pauline Lucile Mayo was "of the modern school" and did not "resort to the unnatural tricks of the old-fashioned elocutionist." In spite of the ways that performers were presented to the public, managers sometimes had doubts that those who aspired to "vocal interpretation of great literature" would be successful; in 1910 Harrison expressed to Isabel Garghill Beecher the widespread doubt that a reader of her type "could be appreciated by farmers."[18] By 1919, D. W. Meldrum could claim that vast strides had been made "since those days when a strained and tragic rendition of 'Curfew Must Not Ring Tonight' or 'The Face on the Bar Room Floor' were considered the height of elocutionary endeavor."[19] Instead, offerings were presented as representative of a fresh new style, even though Estelle Clark reportedly gave popular favorites such as Bryant's "Thanatopsis," Longfellow's "Excelsior," Riley's "Out to Old Aunt Mary's," and Tennyson's "The Charge of the Light Brigade," as did other readers.[20] Gay MacLaren found that reading remained "very highbrow and extra cultural";[21] elocution, in contrast, was "literature that cures insomnia" and "draws a house of empty chairs."[22]

According to MacLaren, *reader* first indicated performers who gave entire books or plays in monologue form but rapidly came to refer to all performers of poems, stories, comedic monologues, or dramas.[23] Readers' selections were sometimes referred to as *cuttings*; the term indicated their condensation of larger works and selections of limited text passages. Cuttings were not unlike the short arrangements of operatic and orchestral works in the reduced scoring necessary for the smaller musical ensembles that toured the circuits. However, the term also evokes the scrapbooks in which individuals kept poems cut from other sources, and thus reinforces the link between female readers and the domestic sphere. A program of cuttings was like an aural rendition of pages from the poetry compilations intended for private enjoyment; according to Mike Chasar, such scrapbooks were increasingly viewed as the products of "feminine activity on par with housekeeping."[24] Despite such homey imagery, Harrison described fierce competition between professional readers for their material and their deliberate suppression of authors' names and titles to protect their repertoire from rivals, a practice confirmed by extant programs.[25] Readers' concerns were not unfounded; in 1909, author and dialect performer Martha Gielow found her two books passed off as the product of a performer who had preceded her on the circuit.[26]

Some terms placed performers closer to theatrical professionals: a *monologist* might perform solo renditions of plays, and a *character impersonator* could utilize costumes or theatrical makeup. The subtleties of meaning in such terminology, now readily absorbed into the all-encompassing *actress*, were important to Chautauqua audiences, who were strongly suspicious of all things theatrical. Harrison recalled how the expression *stage woman* was "a tidy euphemism for 'harlot'" and described how "the actor or actress who stood on a platform without make-up noticeable to the customers, dressed in respectable every-day clothes and declaimed a 'piece' accompanied by suitable gestures, had every prospect of entering into heaven and mingling happily with the saints."[27] Contemporary audiences apparently could and did distinguish between different performance styles on the Chautauqua circuit. One review of Ethel Batting noted that "she proved herself not only to be a finished reader but also a delightful actress as well";[28] to read and to act were different activities, although many readers wore costumes and undoubtedly "acted."[29] Nonetheless, even the most theatrical of Chautauqua performers went out of their way to avoid calling themselves an actress; Mary Adeline Nelson was an "interpreter of drama, impersonator, descriptive reader, monologist, pianologist"—four of these five terms would now be subsumed into one. Male performers were more likely than women to be labeled with terminology that implied they were a theatrical professional; in mixed-gender companies, women were designated *readers* or *interpreters* while their male colleagues might be called *characterists* or *impersonators* (although women did sometimes use these terms, as well); many flyers show a man theatrically costumed, while his female partner is safely ensconced in her evening gown and reading role. "What haunted these attempts to distinguish among types of readings," writes Charlotte Canning, "was the way in which theatricality"—and, we can add, gender—"colored and shaped notions of performance."[30]

Paige Lush has estimated that some two hundred and fifty musical acts were touring at Chautauqua's height in the early 1920s, including larger groups such as bands, African American jubilee ensembles, opera companies, and

exotic groups such as Hawaiian musicians.[31] While smaller acts could incorporate a range of novelties to attract potential audiences, at the core was an
ensemble of musicians with a reader. Chautauqua circuits regularly featured
these groups, called *concert companies*, as frequently as every day of the circuit;
Charles Horner found that at Chautauqua's height, concert companies were
"still the most reliable, but were far too few to supply the demand."[32] The
concert company was most often made up of a singer, pianist, reader, and one
other instrumentalist: a violinist, or perhaps a harpist, cellist, or cornetist. The
ensemble was sometimes named for the star of the group, who might be either
a reader or singer. Many groups took their family name, a practice that again
emphasized the respectable domestic roots of the entertainment they offered.
In addition to married couples' companies, there were ensembles with sisters
at their core: the Kiser Sisters, the Hearons Sister Concert Company, or the
Mauer Sisters Ladies Orchestra, for example.[33]

   Chautauqua ensembles ranged from chamber music ensembles with a reader
to groups in which the musical elements of the program were secondary and
served largely as a pretense for comedic and dramatic performances. However,
a reader's appearance with a concert company was not considered a "novelty"
act like yodeling, folk dances, Indian club swinging, or bell ringing. The reader
was a common, even expected, part of a musical ensemble's performance.
MacLaren stated, "No Chautauqua programme was complete without at least
one or two readings."[34] Longtime performer Clay Smith acknowledged that
because of the nature of audiences, a reader was a "life-saver" for musicians
"as a reader can fill twenty minutes with a selection, while, if you tried to put
over a musical selection of the same length under a hot tent, they would all 'go
home on you.'"[35] Musical groups with readers also gave shorter programs as
"preludes" to the lecturers who appeared on the circuit, and in such cases, the
music sometimes served as the primary draw; musician Frances Perry-Cowan
recalled, "Many people who could not be enticed to listen to a dry speech
were lured by a musical prelude."[36] Even readers who did not regularly appear
with musicians advertised that their programs worked well with music, such
as Grace Peirce Burr, who indicated that she could supply special readings
for musical programs. Many solo performers advertised that they had been
the reader for musical ensembles. The renowned Katharine Ridgeway began
as the reader with the male Temple Quartette, and then toured with her own
concert company. When she became a solo act, she appeared with an unnamed
"accomplished" pianist, sometimes one acquired for her by the Redpath Bureau.[37] Chautauqua's emphasis on the spoken word, from dramatic readings
to political oratory, shaped how musical events were perceived, so much so
that concerts were even referred to as lectures. MacLaren remembered once

hearing a "baritone soloist introduced as 'Mr. Blank, who will lecture on the "Road to Mandalay.""""[38]

   While it would be incorrect to assume that Chautauqua's political and educational lecturers were all men and the readers of poetry and drama were all women, in general, its programs reflected a cultural division in which public oratory was coded male, and elocution, heard within a musical milieu, was most often coded female. Circuit owner Charles Horner acknowledged this division, describing the oratorical superiority of males, who have been "working at the job for centuries," as contrasting with women's roles in the artistic realm, holding "a rank as high or even higher than their masculine contemporaries on the stage and in opera, or any sort of dramatic readings," and thus the equal of men in "the art of expression."[39] Horner was clearly influenced by what he knew. Of the readers who appeared with musicians in the Redpath Bureau's surviving publicity flyers, women outnumbered men approximately three to one. Female readers most often appeared with groups made up largely or entirely of women; such groups ranged from as few as two performers to a more typical three or four, although the less customary women's orchestras sometimes had eight or more players (figure 7.2).

   Because a common theme of Chautauqua publicity was the wide variety of types of entertainment any one ensemble could offer, members of musical ensembles regularly took more than one role in their performances. Female readers were also singers and pianists, not to mention cornetists, saxophonists, guitarists, mandolinists, banjo or marimba players, and whistlers. Likewise, musicians who were not identified as spoken-word performers were sometimes costumed in photographs and appeared in their ensemble's skit or "musical sketch" at the conclusion of a program. Costumes and sketches became more common in the late teens and twenties, as professional producers began to devise programs with nostalgic or patriotic themes for the groups they managed.[40] The necessity of including readings in a musical program sometimes led to musicians who read unsuccessfully or minimally accompanied spoken-word performances played by speakers untrained in music. Clay Smith contrasted the experienced reader of the Smith-Spring-Holmes Orchestral Quintet, Coyla May Spring, to an "*ordinary reciter*, some one who has taken it up because she is the wife of one of the members of the company."[41] At the Reader's Round Table of the International Lyceum and Chautauqua Association in 1924, Paul Pearson complained of performers who added music merely to cover poor recitation: "She knows she can't read. So she tickles a few keys to accompaniment of some nonsense jingle that is supposed to be foolproof for any amateur. It is generally a sorry performance!" Longtime reader Jeannette Kling agreed that no manager should "allow any member of a company, although he may

Figure 7.2. Metropolitan Ladies' Orchestra with reader and pianologist Ione Leonore Hart (*far right*), Racine, Wisconsin, Chautauqua, July 22, 1912, in *Lyceumite and Talent* (August 1912): 31. Redpath Chautauqua Collection, University of Iowa Libraries, Special Collections.

never have recited before to speak a piece or execute a pianolog in order to fill a gap in a program."[42]

## Womanhood, Performance, and Respectability

Flyers stressed not only readers' talents and professional training, but also the respectability of their programs and, more importantly, their essential womanhood.[43] Women's advertising assured rural Americans that the content they offered would receive "not only the hearty approval of the general amusement-loving public, but of all church-going people of culture as well."[44] The brochures of a less experienced reader with fewer reviews to reprint contained letters from men who presided over the churches, YMCAs, and clubs at which she had performed, establishing that she retained her feminine qualities despite her platform appearances.[45] In 1911 Audrey Spangler Mortland was recommended by a Toledo pastor as "an excellent artist in her profession" and also, like Isabel Garghill Beecher in the description preceding this chapter, "a *womanly woman*" with "modesty and retiring characteristics."[46] Evelyn Lewis was commended by a conservatory president as "a perfect type of womanhood and a magnificent reader."[47] Potential audiences had to be reassured about women's character and social standing, yet at the same time women's participation in Chautauqua was part of what made it morally uplifting. A pair of cartoons comparing the lyceum and Chautauqua to their commercial

Figure 7.3. Ned Woodman, "The Lyceum and Chautauqua" and "Their Imitators," from the *Lyceum Magazine*, April 1917. Redpath Chautauqua Collection, University of Iowa Libraries, Special Collections.

imitators featured gowned allegorical female figures for "religion," "reform," "education," "inspiration," and "art," accompanied by tiny cherubs representing "amusement," "entertainment," and "pecuniary success" (figure 7.3). The contrasting cartoon depicts a male jester, drummer, and juggler to represent "amusement," "sensation," and "cleverness" as well as a bloated "quantity not quality," leaving the women, transformed into waifish, hungry-looking children, behind. "Entertainment" and "pecuniary success" were combined into a sexualized female figure in a shorter skirt and high-heeled shoes holding a bag of money. Thus, what was best about Chautauqua was gendered female, although mere providers of commercial diversions were cast as women of lesser character.

The theme that performance of good literature ennobled female readers, who were able to retain their essential femininity, runs through Chautauqua publicity. Women's biographies occasionally detail the factors that led them to the platform in order to stress their adherence to prevailing gender boundaries; for example, the death of Franc Adele Burch's father made it necessary for her to support herself, suggesting that she would not have otherwise chosen a public career. Sarah Mildred Willmer's flyer emphasizes that she deliberately rejected the stage, "choosing the chautauqua because it affords a clean, consistent opportunity to read to the masses—to exalt their ideals, to elevate their standards, to improve their tastes, and to increase their love for and appreciation of the good and pure in people, and in literature." The success of Beecher, one of the most noteworthy readers during Chautauqua's earlier years, was credited to her teacher, Robert Cumnock, and the "sympathetic criticism" of her husband, not her own skills and ambition.[48] The description of Burch was typical in emphasizing how her "supreme womanliness . . . proves to the critical public that a woman may do public work and still keep her womanly reserve and the exaltation that comes from a close association with the wholesome characters in literature." Many such descriptions skirt the issue of a woman putting herself forward on the public platform by downplaying the more performative aspects of her readings. The *Methodist Advocate Journal* described how Irene Bewley "becomes so completely the person she represents and the sentiments she expresses that the hearer does not think of her at all. In personal appearance, in her general bearing, and in voice and manner she is the dignified, graceful, womanly woman."[49] Thus, by performing, Bewley supposedly managed to avoid the questionable act of subjecting herself to the public's gaze and retained her respectability because her "self" literally disappeared. The publicity for Edith Parker of the Alexis Recital Company is preceded by a quotation from *King Lear*: "Her voice was ever soft, / Gentle and low, an excellent thing in woman," suggesting that she remained within appropriate gender boundaries; ironically, if the quotation accurately described Parker's abilities, tent audiences would have been unable to hear her. Not merely Chautauqua bureaus, but women themselves were concerned about their professional reputations. In 1910 Nellie Peck Saunders expressed her concern that an upcoming performance during fair week in a Michigan town would endanger her "reputation of giving high class programs" and "as a refined artist," and her subsequent report details the event's success in spite of the "rough element of drunken rowdies" in the crowd.[50]

In many cases, an ensemble's gender was central to its marketing. The Lady Entertainers' brochure from around 1910 is characteristic: "Fresh and hopeful and smiling as the springtime of life, the Lady Entertainers flash their glorious light upon you and are gone like a dream of enchantment. They are just four girls, refined, talented and clever, but each with an individuality and a charm entirely her own." Manager Louis O. Runner regularly assembled these enchanting "ladies orchestras"—in reality a chamber ensemble—including the Mendelssohn, Schubert, Berkeley, and Columbia Sextettes; the Metropolitan Musical Club; the Chicago Ladies Orchestra; and the Play-Singers, all of which advertised readings in their concerts.[51] Other ensembles came out of the training institutes set up in major cities where Chautauqua managements were based.[52] Descriptions of larger women's groups were less likely to stress their members' conservatory training or professional experience and instead advertised performers primarily on the basis of their appearance, as in the Corine Jessop Company's publicity: "A glance at the pictures . . . will show that it is a company that is not hard to look at." Managers found the Smith-Spring-Holmes Orchestral Quintet to be an easy sell because of the evocative names of its reader and soprano: Coyla May Spring and her sister, cellist Lotus Flower. Harrison wrote, "Neither the girls' looks nor Lotus Flower's smile was disappointing. Nor their music." He added, "Looks never mattered with the male singers."[53] Horner recalled bluntly, "As Vawter would have said, girls were good merchandise then, as now."[54] For Chautauqua managers, attractive women who helped them with the bottom line won out over any advertised larger educational and cultural goals, and performers took note of appearances when forming their ensembles. Soprano and reader Beulah Buck complained of "freakish-looking" singers who "do not look the part," though "if pretty and refined," lacking in musical essentials.[55] Musicians sometimes objected to these practices; in a 1920 article, "Are You Booking Pictures or People?," Clay Smith (ironically the husband of the lovely Coyla May) complained that agents were selling ensembles of attractive young women who had never actually practiced together.[56]

Publicity and performances had to balance a feminine respectability in keeping with a "clean" moral tone with the deliberate use of sex appeal. Costuming was carefully monitored for standards of taste that would not offend small-town America. Marian Scott described her theatrical company's dresses as "simple and very moral," "pretty and quite proper," though insufficiently "flamboyant."[57] Horner noted that although "young performers had much sport in giggling that 'We must be refined,'" women had to meet dress standards off as well as on the platform, avoiding a "plunging neckline or even too much make-up."[58] Within certain less sexualized limits, female costuming was nonetheless considered an important feature of a performance. Coyla May Spring recalled that beautifully gowned readers were "the glamour girls of the Talent,"[59] such as Katharine Ridgeway, known for audiences' reactions to her stunning appearance: "When she walked out into the lights, a long expressive 'ah-h-h' was wont to escape involuntarily from the women in her audience. . . . Miss Ridgeway's tall, statuesque figure, draped often in billowing yards of chiffon or lace, usually white with a long train, her arm-length kid gloves, the elegant feather boa around her shoulder, the enormous ostrich plumes on her hat, when she wore a hat, caused envy in every feminine heart."[60] Beecher was described as maintaining an attractive appearance within acceptable guidelines: "She is never conspicuous in her dress. Your really well-gowned woman never is. She never wears costumes that rise up and smite you as you gaze."[61] Clever costuming increasingly reflected the musical selections being performed, such as Scottish costumes for performances of "Annie Laurie" and "Comin' thro' the Rye," or hoop-skirted antebellum dresses for Stephen Foster songs romanticizing the Old South. Violinist Enola Calvin Handley's group, the Philharmonic Ensemble, wore imitation Chinese outfits for a segment of musical exoticism that included Rimsky-Korsakov's "Song of India" from *Sadko* and "Hymn to the Sun" from *Le Coq d'Or, In a Persian Garden* by Liza Lehmann, and Cyril Scott's *Caprice Chinois*.[62]

The number of all-female companies increased during World War I, as some male performers left Chautauqua for the armed forces. Scott recalled that many of these "Girl companies" were more attractive than talented: "Girls out of high school a year or two, trained to 'read' indifferently, sing a little in wheezy soprano, jangle on guitars or ukes. But they were usually pretty girls. They were fresh and vital."[63] In the flyer for the Military Girls, the drum faced the wrong direction because none of the young women had yet to learn to play it.[64] Fay Petitt of the Anitas, a singing orchestra, had little elocutionary training, and her flute-playing ability extended no further than the few numbers on the program.[65] Scott nonetheless found the "girl orchestras" after the war to be "pretty good ones."[66]

## Accompanied Recitation under the Tent

In keeping with Chautauqua's emphasis on education and self-improvement, women readers advertised a range of poetic and dramatic repertoire, but at its core were the works heard in numerous other contexts: texts by Shakespeare, Longfellow, Tennyson, and Browning, alongside child and African American dialect works by Riley, Field, and Dunbar. Chautauqua publicity stressed readers' desire to present interpretations of great literature, yet like previous elocutionists, their selections ranged across the implied cultural hierarchy; many professionals claimed equal ability in Shakespeare and "darkey dialect," and others performed little that would now be considered literary. Hazel Neen Johnson's brochures list works by major poets; however, her sample program includes only the two least known authors—Edmund Vance Cooke, a poet who also toured the circuits, and Pauline Phelps, whose writings were marketed to spoken-word performers. Smith suggested that readers who were "clever in child dialect and humorous selections" were especially popular; advertisements for child impersonators frequently show them in costume, sometimes clutching dolls.[67] Emily Waterman, who could "lisp like a four-year-old," became known for her performances of "I've Got a Pain in My Sawdust" (from Kitty Cheatham's repertoire) that "brought down the house."[68]

Almost any spoken text typically heard on the Chautauqua platform could be performed to music, most often with piano, though occasionally with harp or even in "guitarologues." Tennyson's *Enoch Arden* was advertised as a particular favorite of both female and male readers, and many performers noted that they utilized Strauss's melodramatic setting; after hearing Beecher's performance, one critic hailed it as the pièce de résistance, claiming "no better art was ever viewed from the platform."[69] Various works of Longfellow were heard with music, most often the popular "King Robert of Sicily" (discussed in chapter 4), which offered a characteristically Chautauquan moral. Harrison found that it "filled the old rule that people often like best the things with which they are most familiar. . . . It was a musical program, but some people, at least, went home thinking, 'I, too, like King Robert of Sicily, shall strive to be a better man.'"[70] Riley's "An Old Sweetheart of Mine" was often heard with music, most often in the setting by Chautauqua composer Walter Howe Jones.[71] Selected poems by Field, Wilcox, Browning, Kipling, and Dunbar were commonly accompanied. Beyond the works of these poets, there was a wide range of both readily recognizable and little-known texts, including dialect selections, performed with music, over a hundred in all (including recitations discussed in chapter 4). Many additional poems may have been accompanied because performers' circulars often indicated musical readings without specifying particular texts. Ridgeway's brochures do not list accompanied works, although one of her most requested selections was the moralizing poem "Not Understood" by Thomas Bracken, which she read to music composed by her husband, Percy G. Hunt.[72] Sample programs of Pearl D. Miller exemplify the variety of performers' offerings; they include unnamed texts with or without music ("spring poems," "Kipling poems," "pianologues") interspersed between selections by O. Henry, Booth Tarkington, Edgar Guest, and Alfred Noyes, as well as child sketches, dramatic and humorous stories, cuttings from plays, and monologues such as *Minnie at the Movies*.

While a few reciters on the Chautauqua circuit advertised that they performed Strauss's *Enoch Arden*, Schillings's *Das Hexenlied*, Cole's *King Robert of Sicily*, or various settings of *Hiawatha*, the term *melodrama* does not appear frequently in publicity materials, perhaps because potential audiences would not have understood its meaning. When Beecher, one of the most serious readers, took up performing to music, her manager, Charles Wagner, applied to copyright *cantillation* so that it would remain associated with her, although the term remained rare.[73] For a time, Beecher's repertoire included the standard melodramas as well as Oliver Hunckel's poetic retelling of Richard Wagner's *Parsifal* with the music arranged for organ, harp, trumpet, and chimes by her accompanist, Tillie Mae Haines, in a performance that fell outside the conventional boundaries of published compositions. Many Chautauqua and lyceum performers listed *Parsifal* in their repertoire, some with music, presumably in arrangements differing from Haines's, which remained unpublished. Operatic vocal selections were performed by many companies, and readers also gave

John Luther Long's short story *Madame Butterfly*, sometimes with added music from Giacomo Puccini's opera.

Like Beecher's manager, some performers tried to coin their own terms (such as Edward Berhing Hitchcock's *dramalogs* for "dramatic readings with incidental music"), usually without success.[74] Chautauqua performers most often described the combination of music and speech using modifications of the terms for their spoken numbers: *musical reading*, a modification of *reading*, or *pianologue*, a transformation of *monologue*. The musical sketch, or brief play that closed many programs, was in some sense a natural expansion of the costume song from one company member to the entire ensemble. These sketches typically incorporated well-known musical works. For example, Myretta Chatham devised a finale for her concert company titled "The Wooing of Penelope," which featured four characters and "fragments of popular operatic and standard numbers," such as "Some Day He'll Come" ("Un bel di vedremo") from *Madama Butterfly*, a barcarole (perhaps by Offenbach), and a Chautauqua favorite, "The Rosary," by Ethelbert Nevin. It is not clear how much plot versus how much music a musical sketch might contain; however, it was possible to include a great deal of music. The Riner Sisters, Imogene and Marguerite, appearing with a baritone, performed "The Man without a Country," singing thirty-five "national airs" in approximately twenty-five minutes.

Although *pianologue* was the most frequently used term, it did not find as wide a usage outside of Chautauqua as *musical reading* (with the possible exception of its use in vaudeville). The terms were largely interchangeable with the exception that, according to Coyla May Spring, "It was a pianologue if the reader played the instrument but was a musical reading if someone else played the musical accompaniment."[75] *Pianologue* seems to have referred to selections in which speech and music were combined somewhat loosely or were simpler so that they might be performed by the same individual; given that few published works labeled *pianologue* exist (and some that do cannot be specifically linked to Chautauqua), the music would have had to be improvised or to consist of selections from previously composed works. Both musical readings and pianologues could be humorous in tone. Marian Scott did a musical reading called "Irish Names" while wearing a green costume, with her husband providing piano accompaniment. The Irish names were spoken very rapidly in brogue to dance tunes—"Irish Jig," "Turkey in the Straw," "Irish Washerwoman"—at least until Scott lost her concentration midway and vocally stumbled, forcing her husband to resort to a loud accelerando to cover her error.[76] Individual performers' arrangements of text and music seem to have varied widely in complexity. The performances of longtime Chautauquan Charles T. Grilley, who spoke to harp accompaniments by Van Veachton Rogers, was compared favorably by one critic to the accompanied recitations described in chapter 4:

> I had certainly heard the possibilities of musical accompaniment to a reading,
> had heard scores of ambitious elocutionists in claw and shimmer go thru the
> mincemeat and tatter passion while the lady at the piano fumbled around the
> edges. I had about decided that the two shows were run at once to catch the en-
> tire crowd, some of which wouldn't like either. I never could see the connection
> between "Nearer, My God, to Thee" and "When the Frost is on the Punkin"
> with the bronchitis stop put on. . . . Which shows what a wooden head I have.
> . . . Grilley began to recite. . . . Rogers works part of the time and rests part. . . .
> But most of the time he was playing a harp accompaniment to the piece. It was
> just like two people telling it—one in English and the other in French, so that
> all the audience could get it. Every outburst of Charley's brot [*sic*] another from
> the harp, just the same shade of feeling. Grilley was the book and Rogers the
> pictures, or vice versa. When Grilley was solemn the harp wept right along the
> edges of the words. When he was gay Rogers thumped roars of laughter and
> handfuls of fun from the strings.
>
> It was a sympathetic duet—rather a trio, for the audience kept breaking in
> with roars and joyspills. I had never imagined that two men and a harp could go
> so completely amalgamate.[77]

The careful coordination required in a performance such as this seems to
have been unusual, a result of the two men having worked together for seventeen years.

Pianologues were occasionally published as piano pieces with text indicated above the staff; thus, the genre also included fully notated works. The
generic flexibility of the term is seen in the flyer of Virginia Powell, who listed
twenty-nine pianologues among her repertoire, some of which were originally published as musical recitations and others of which were indicated with
the authors of their texts (Eugene Field, Ella Wheeler Wilcox, Fred Emerson
Brooks), suggesting their accompaniments were variable. Powell indicated she
made an adaptation of "The Washerwoman's Friend," herself; the text features
a refrain based on the song of the washerwoman, which could be sung in performance.[78] Other works, listed with their composers, are primarily songs that
Powell must have spoken rather than sung; Smith referred to the possibility of
spoken songs when he found the new pieces he reviewed for *Lyceum* magazine
suitable to be adapted for speech. In 1917, when Georgia teacher Mary Alice
Ross wrote to the Redpath Bureau hoping for a summer position and listing
fourteen pianologues in her repertoire, most of them were songs.[79]

The striking photos of Mary Louise Cassidy-Woelber posing at the piano
in her "musical impressions of poems" may give some indication of what took
place when a single woman recited, accompanying herself on the piano (figure
7.4). The photographs in Woelber's 1911 brochure are accompanied by a few
lines or a stanza of poetry, making clear that her slightly contortionist poses

"*Lucky thing I aint a girl,*
*Or I'd be skeered to death,*
*Bein' I'm a boy I duck my head*
*and hold my breath.*"

Figure 7.4. Mary Louise Cassidy-Woelber in Eugene Field's "Seein'
Things" (1911). Redpath Chautauqua Collection, University of Iowa
Libraries, Special Collections.

are depicting the dramatic action of individual texts. Woelber informed Harrison that some works were spoken and others were sung, yet her selections are in many ways typical of the range of materials spoken to music.[80] Three of the five are by Eugene Field, including the sentimental "Little Boy Blue" and "Seein' Things" in the child dialect of a small boy. The banjo of Dunbar's dialect poem "A Virginia Reel" naturally suggests adding music. Rudyard Kipling's "Gunga Din" is perhaps a less typical accompanied selection, but Kipling was very popular on Chautauqua programs. Woelber's posing, looking wide-eyed and tucking her face behind her arm for the frightened boy in

"Seein' Things" or dramatically burying her head in her hand for the distraught "China Plate" in Field's "The Duel" shows close attention to individual lines of poetry; however, if she made such exaggerated poses during her recitals, the amount of music that could accompany them would have been minimal, only what she could perform with one hand.

In the mid-1920s, Clay Smith began to publish the pianologues he composed for his wife Coyla May Spring to perform, providing a glimpse of the circuit's more formal musical practices.[81] His compositions all have vocal lines fully notated with pitches and rhythms; Smith believed that pianologues' accompaniments should "carry a definite melody throughout as a thread or guide for the words." He indicated that the piano parts should differ from those for songs:

> The harmonies of the accompaniment should furnish suitable background and lend atmosphere to the word picture, giving occasional emphasis to the lines without in any way detracting from them. Since most artists supply their own accompaniments, the piano part should be so written that the hands may be kept rather close together, in order that the performer while turning to the face the audience may still be able to play the accompaniment without any special inconvenience. To [*sic*] much attention to the key-board might spoil the whole thing.[82]

In their simple chordal textures and technically unchallenging piano parts, Smith's compositions are similar to many works by women composers of the same period (discussed in chapter 10), works that he sometimes reviewed for *Lyceum* magazine. They featured lyrics geared toward Chautauqua audiences: sentimental treatments of home and neighborhood, in keeping with the Chautauquan emphasis on the importance of small-town life, and texts in African American or child dialect. Smith's chosen texts sometimes advocated traditional gender roles in a way that female composers' works do not, but would have been in keeping with the values of home and community in the marketing of Chautauqua to rural audiences. "The Old Fashioned Woman" extols the virtues of the "sane, normal," "housekeeping women, / The motherly women who knew how to cook," who are no longer found in cities, but are, like Chautauqua audiences, "out in the country." It is not known if Smith's own wife, ironically a traveling professional, featured this work in her performances.[83]

## Chautauqua and Cultural Tastes

The presence of readers on Chautauqua programs declined during the mid-1910s, then dropped off steeply after about 1923; none of the musical groups billed for Redpath-Vawter's 1924 season appear to have had readers.[84] As early as 1918, Adrian Newens, writing in *Lyceum*, identified the concert hall as the source of Chautauqua's music and theater as the model for its dramatic ensembles—he apparently no longer considered spoken-word performance of literature a primary source of its offerings.[85] Subsequent publications about Chautauqua have stressed how readers and impersonators gave way to full plays, breaking down America's antitheatrical prejudices.[86] In the course of this narrative of the triumph of dramatic art, many writers express a characteristic disdain for elocution. Harrison called elocution a plague from which no community was immune, and dismissed the "early elocutionist, memory of whose stylized presentations makes a modern critic shudder."[87] The penultimate chapter of Nydia Reynolds's dissertation endeavors to establish that Chautauqua readers were "oral interpreters" who did not engage in an elocutionary style.[88] However, the preponderance of professional women readers traveling in concert companies across America belies the notion that elocutionary performances were considered inferior by Chautauqua audiences.

Commentators are less clear about the influence of Chautauqua's music on American tastes. Scholars of oratory lament the increase in "specialty entertainment, crowded with zither players and yodelers and bell ringers" at the expense of public exploration of serious political issues.[89] However, Harrison believed that Chautauqua was able to bring audiences to a higher musical understanding; yodelers and pianists who juggled gave way to symphonic ensembles and prima donnas: "Thousands of middle-class audiences, in the meantime, had learned to ask for Beethoven, Bach and Brahms. Cities all over the nation, once just small towns, whose music-hungry people filled the big brown tents on hot summer afternoons, today enjoy their own symphony orchestras."[90] Likewise, Hugh Orchard, writing during the era of Chautauqua's popularity and in keeping with its political message about the importance of rural communities, asserted that it had democratized music: "Musical appreciation was no longer confined to a few aristocrats, with means and time for special study, but was extended in liberal measure to all who gather under the canvas tops."[91] Victoria and Robert Ormond Case, more critical of the Chautauqua phenomenon, later painted a picture of its decline being closely linked to the artistic level of the musical programs:

> It was when the music failed that Main Street began to doubt Chautauqua. Along toward the end there were too many saxophone solos, too many shrill girlish trios recruited from the next county, too much of the bird whistler and bell ringer and piano monologues in costume, and singers who drew cartoons and modeled in clay. Everybody laughed of course, at the novelty musical instruments—saws, bottle, sleigh bells, and the weird patented hybrids—and even applauded the pianist who doubled as a hayseed and built his medley around the Missouri mule, but they didn't really like it. They could do that sort of thing themselves. They wanted that troupe that played the best in the world and gave them theme

and theory so the young people could understand more of music than they knew before. They wanted the cellist and the violinist and the harps and the ensembles and all too often got a clown, with the audience asked to join in the chorus of "Put on Your Old Gray Bonnet."[92]

This range of opinions merely continued the conflicts over musical taste that simmered during Chautauqua's height. Music, like literature, was considered to be a moral good, able to lift audiences from despondency, build their characters, and provide harmony, order, and beauty in their lives.[93] Thus, high musical standards were as important as literary ones; writers on Chautauqua insisted that "the best literature, the highest thought, the finest music will be appreciated by anybody anywhere."[94] In response to the frequent call for musicians to provide more popular selections, Charles Dixon insisted that Chautauqua performers had the responsibility to "give an audience what it needs, rather than what it wants."[95] Audiences' failure to respond to classical music was sometimes blamed on the musicians themselves, accused both of levels of ability unequal to great music and a kind of self-aggrandizement in deigning to associate themselves with renowned composers whose offerings they did not adequately understand. Musicians needed to rise to level of orators who transmitted literary ideals: a 1914 article claimed that "Wagner, Mozart, Schubert, Mendelssohn, Beethoven, Bach and Verdi wrote the same messages Shakespeare, Emerson, Beecher and every great man writes out of his life to the people—messages of cheer, inspiration and leadership. . . . But the messages of the musician haven't been heard because the fiddler or singer was not great enough, strong enough, loving enough, reverent enough, to bear them, and when they failed they reported 'the people don't like classical music.'"[96] Bureau managers asserted that leading performers who appeared on the circuits, such as renowned soprano Ernestine Schumann-Heink, could transcend any difficulties, and that "people would respond to artistic music when artists presented it."[97]

Not everyone was convinced. B. C. Boer complained that audiences were in "classical agony" and insisted that "a great percentage of the classical music has no place on the chautauqua or lyceum platform at all."[98] In his role as a journalist for *Lyceum* magazine, Smith published numerous articles praising groups with repertoire based in European art music, and he regularly complained about poor musical quality, calling for the programming of good music. However, he did not necessarily mean canonic composers. Smith's reviews introduced songs in a popular style that were designed to bring some freshness to programs plagued by the circuits' vocal standards: "The Rosary," "The Trail of the Lonesome Pine," or "Silver Threads among the Gold."[99] The music publisher Witmark developed a Department C for Chautauqua music, and other publishers regularly attended the yearly International Lyceum Association convention conventions to market their newest popular offerings to circuit musicians. Other writers on musical taste insisted that older popular songs had, in fact, become classics worthy of their place on programs. Ernest Gamble wrote, "Classic music does not mean music that no one can understand, but music that lives, that will stand the test of years. . . . Who can hear such classics as 'I Know That My Redeemer Liveth,' 'Annie Laurie' and the like without being elevated, refined and bettered?"[100] The Smith-Spring-Holmes Orchestral Quintet's programming reflects this full range: an audience who sat through a brief classical composition was rewarded with one or more popular encores, frequently songs. For example, after Lotus Flower Spring performed David Popper's *Polonaise de Concert* on cello, audiences heard Thurlow Lieurance's Indianist "Waters of Minnetonka" and James Bland's minstrel song "Carry Me Back to Old Virginny." Smith's compositions for saxophone and brass instruments included variations and fantasies on ubiquitous songs such as "Annie Laurie," "My Old Kentucky Home," Comin' thro' the Rye," and "Old Folks at Home."[101]

Later historical reports of Chautauqua's musical life, tales that emphasize either the triumph of classical music or the decline into vapid popular genres, seem oversimplified. Their conceptions of what constituted the highbrow and lowbrow ends of Chautauqua's musical spectrum are both exaggerated. The novelty acts were not perhaps so omnipresent; neither were Bach, Beethoven, and Brahms the usual staples of Chautauqua repertoire. The names of ensembles identified with classical elites such as Schubert or Mendelssohn signified Chautauqua's stated aims, yet Lush has found that such groups did not actually play those composers' works.[102] Musical professionals who traveled the circuits recognized the commercial need of pleasing the crowd, not "the select artistic few."[103] However, they also felt that with careful programming, audiences could be educated. For example, Carl Lampert, from Theodore Thomas's orchestra, the leader of the costumed Schumann Quintet, assisted listeners through spoken commentary. Chautauqua publications noted that the spread of the phonograph had also raised audience's tastes, enabling them to program more European art music. Nonetheless, the music of Chautauqua frequently remained in a realm best characterized as middlebrow. Smith described the usual repertoire as "good music, not severely classical, but not cheap music and very little of the so-called popular, and no Jazz at all," more like smaller arrangements of urban symphony "pops" concerts.[104] Smith was well aware that his audiences were uninterested in works longer than seven or eight minutes or vocal music in languages other than English. He advised, "Don't try to use a long, heavy concert or symphony which runs from fifteen to twenty-five minutes. This is appropriate for a recital where you are playing to a strictly music audience, but out of place and hard to put over in our field."[105] The numerous songs and short character pieces, not multimovement works, that were programmed by Chautauqua's concert companies were also found on many other programs of the period, including earlier musical and literary entertainments. Thus, Chautauqua's music, like its literary selections, most often fell somewhere in between the later recounted extremes of canonic art and popular, expendable music. Producer H. O. Rounds wrote, "There is a middle ground where art, tact, common sense and experience meet, where the music is selected for the enjoyment and edification of the audiences before whom it is to be performed."[106]

Gay MacLaren emphasized that "since culture was the aim of every Chautauqua performance, classical music was considered essential for balance whether it was appreciated or not."[107] But it did not go entirely unappreciated. One of the most regularly heard works was the operatic sextet from act 1 of Gaetano Donizetti's *Lucia di Lammermoor*. At Chautauqua's height, one musical group kept a record of the most requested music. Four popular songs made the list: Carrie Jacobs-Bond's "A Perfect Day"; James Lyman Molloy's "Irish" song, "Love's Old Sweet Song"; the British song "I Hear You Calling Me" by Charles Marshall; and the Hawaiian "Aloha Oe" by Queen Lili'uokalani. The remainder included brief classical favorites, such as Beethoven's Minuet in G, Rubinstein's Melody in F, Mendelssohn's *Spring Song*, the Largo from Handel's *Xerxes*, the *Meditation* from Massenet's *Thaïs*, and opera arias, such as "One Fine Day" from Puccini's *Madama Butterfly*.[108] Such short, fundamentally melodious works, sometimes also used for accompanied recitations, differed from the "hymns and folk songs sung by their neighbors."[109]

In her study of Chautauqua music, Lush concludes that in its final years, "economic pragmatism outweighed philosophical rhetoric" and the programming of popular music increased on the circuits.[110] Although during Chautauqua's lifetime both musical and literary selections existed in what we might now find to be a peculiar mixture of high and low culture, the music of Chautauqua undoubtedly had an impact on its rural audiences, perhaps even more than the readers, who sometimes performed texts with which audiences were already familiar. After several decades of Chautauqua, listeners had more exposure to a wider range of musical repertoire. Keith Vawter found that "an old town demands and appreciates a higher grade of program than a new town," and that programs had to be both "sufficiently high-brow, or cultured . . . to suit our old towns, yet carrying sufficient of the best in popular numbers to attract the ever present and much deserving beginner."[111] A standard feature of Chautauqua memoirs is the recounting of the tremendous emotional impact of a mere week's worth of culture on remote rural residents. For example, one Saskatchewan woman thanked a Chautauqua supervisor with tears in her eyes, saying, "You can never know what this has meant to me! Just to hear good music again!" and introducing her eighteen-year-old son, who had never before heard a violin.[112] While some might now fault Chautauqua's mission to spread culture as naive, or criticize its offerings as too commercial or catering "to the lowest common denominator,"[113] that it had an impact is undeniable. Smith's pianologue, "The Listener's Faces," is a musician's view of audience members listening "rapt and mute" to music in "the brown Chautauqua tents," music that provides them with "soul-transfiguring beauty."[114] As Horner put it, "They walked out of a Chautauqua tent with a new light in their eyes."[115]

Large numbers of women performers took this range of musical and literary diversions to rural communities. In turn, Chautauqua provided a venue for the increased professionalization of female artists, from readers to cornet players to May Valentine, the conductor of her own opera company.[116] But the influx of women was achieved, in part, by taking forms of entertainment that represented the domestic sphere and putting them on the platform.[117] The combination of "read" literature and music created culture for audiences, yet culture in which the performing female body was made less threatening by ensuring that it came in the form of delightful young women with charming personalities. The reader with music on the Chautauqua circuit was possible only as a "a Refined, Artistic, Womanly Woman" devoted to "Lifting Her Hearers to the Higher Things in Life."[118]

# 8.  Multiplying Voices

## *American Women and the Music of Choral Speaking*

If the new art of verse-speaking has taught us anything,
it is that poetry is music and must be rendered as such.
—Marjorie Gullan

In 1935, Rose Walsh reminisced about the group recitations by elocution classes at the commencement exercises of ladies' seminaries four decades earlier: "In flowing white dresses, drilled perfect pose, graceful bodily movement and good speech unison, they recited *The Legend of the Organ Builder* or *Aux Italiens* now high, now low, now louder, now softer, now slower, now faster, and awed admiring relatives and friends."[1] But Walsh went on to describe an unfortunate fictional graduate who returns home to polite but unenthusiastic responses to her recitations—"Very nice, my dear"—tolerant smiles from male listeners, and outright rejection from her male escort, a military academy graduate: "Oh, we always laughed at the girls who went in for that sort of thing." Walsh's explanation of the lack of enthusiasm for elocution, which had been found to be artificial and affected, was not based on her tale's obvious gender division, but in the lack of a formalized plan for developing the speaking chorus to the level of the singing chorus. To her thinking, the problem was not group recitation itself, but poor performance that "resulted in derision."[2] And thus, the art form was ripe for revival.

For Walsh and the other women who led the movement to create "verse-speaking" choirs in the 1930s and '40s, numerous reciters speaking together could "amplify" a poem's interpretation, "just as an orchestra amplifies the solo rendition of a musical composition."[3] Choric performance was similar to solo recitation, in that the sound produced was intended to communicate a poem's meaning to an audience. Many of the seemingly musical techniques involved in elocution training were transferred to choirs under a conductor's direction. Speaking choirs expressively recited poetry in unison or in arrangements that utilized pitched voices and alternated individuals' speech with that of larger groups. Although some twentieth-century compositions for choir contain sections that are spoken instead of sung, choral recitation falls outside most musicians' conception of what constitutes a musical work.[4] However, period writers consistently relied more on musical terminology and concepts to describe their activities than on the technical specifications established in nineteenth-century elocution books. The tension between sensuous sound for sound's sake and poetic meaning, which was both a motivating force *and* a cause of concern for these women, suggests that the power of choral speaking was, in fact, a musical power that could transcend its linguistic roots. Choral speaking represented yet another means by which women worked toward the position in America's high culture to which they aspired.

Choral speaking first became popular in England, led by several British playwrights who adopted unison speaking in imitation of Greek choruses.[5] American speech instructors found their inspiration in Marjorie Gullan, the founder of verse-speaking choirs in Glasgow and London in the 1920s, who visited the United States to teach choric speaking classes. Speaking in groups was not new in America; the phrase *concert recitation* appeared on programs and in anthologies from the late nineteenth century onward. In 1873, female students at the Lake Erie Seminary in Painesville, Ohio, opened their Elocutionary Entertainment with the entire class's concert exercise of John Greenleaf Whittier's "Barbara Frietchie."[6] Choral speaking became more widespread in the 1930s and 1940s, as Joan Shelley Rubin has noted, as part of "efforts that linked an interest in the art of the 'people' to the renewal of American life."[7] A practical reason may have also influenced the scoring practice's development: elocution school graduates found employment in schools and colleges, where they faced the challenge of teaching, not one-on-one lessons, but entire classes of potential reciters. A San Jose State Teachers College instructor wrote that choral speech "spells salvation" for teachers "confronted with the problem of directing large numbers of students."[8] English teachers were encouraged to incorporate choral speaking into their classrooms as well, and soon literature became available to assist in the creation of choirs of adults and children, from the primary grades through high school.

Although males did participate in choral speaking, women wrote almost all of the field's pedagogical literature, and the practice was particularly popular in women's colleges, occurring at Vassar, Wellesley, Mount Holyoke, Marygrove, Russell Sage, Skidmore, and Maryville Colleges. Discussions of the attributes necessary for ensemble directors regularly referred to the conductor as *she*, pronoun usage that is striking in an era when most music conductors were men. In spite of Walsh's aspiration to establish choral speaking as a legitimate art form, it was hindered by its ongoing association with women, serving more frequently as a pedagogical tool for teaching children than accepted as an avenue for artistic expression. The fifteen-member Milwaukee Verse-Speaking Choir directed by Agnes Curren Hamm was treated with amusement and condescension when the women performed a program with Carl Sandburg in 1942. The *Milwaukee Journal* described how his "Jazz Fantasia" was being heard in local kitchens and noted that some poets "might object to having their verses rendered to the accompaniment of the egg beater."[9]

Pedagogical manuals pointed to historical precedents to justify choral speaking's validity, claiming the authority of Greek drama and tracing the practice to Christian liturgical chanting of biblical psalms. They sometimes located the practice's primitive roots in Africa or in American Indian rituals, or, if maintaining a Eurocentric approach, referred to troubadour poems or British ballads with choral refrains (conveniently overlooking any extant melodies for singing this poetry). Choral speaking was positioned, not so much as a new development or the continuation of elocutionary practices, but as "revival of an ancient art." Some writers referred to recent European developments, particularly choral speaking's appearance at British music festivals and the work of Marjorie Gullan, with whom many American women felt honored to have studied. Cecilia Gordon was effusive: "To hear her render poetry was to hear music."[10]

Nonetheless, choral-speaking advocates frequently adopted a defensive tone about their chosen art form, attempting to deflect expected objections by emphasizing that their written descriptions could in no way substitute for the experience of a live performance; many explained how hearing a choral-speaking recital led to their love of the style. Writers reiterated that rote recitation by school classes for pedagogical reasons was not the same thing as choral speaking. Choric performances were justified as a method of teaching proper speech techniques, enhancing performers' appreciation of poetry, and improving their individual recitation skills; the reluctant student, fearful of solo performance, could flourish in a choral setting. Justifications also reflected the aesthetic beliefs of the Depression era, stressing social usefulness and character development in the context of larger civic values; choric speech could prevent antisocial tendencies by "gathering people together for the object of group enjoyment."[11] It could also contribute to increased nationalistic feeling; choral anthologies often featured regional texts by American poets. Gullan, after teaching at Columbia University's Teachers College, felt compelled to publish an anthology heavily laden with American texts for American choirs.[12] The poems of Carl Sandburg, Stephen Vincent Benét, and Vachel Lindsay (known for his oral performances[13]), were added to long-standing works by Kipling, Tennyson, and Longfellow recited in previous decades to provide indigenous American expression through rhythms that had "grown out of the American scene."[14]

Descriptions of how to select works appropriate for choirs stressed that the poems should not be personal, seemingly abandoning previously popular nineteenth-century works (although unmetered modernist verse was also sometimes rejected as inappropriate or too difficult). Poems that would work in a choral format were more philosophical or communal than self-indulgently expressive. Many pedagogues recommended that interpretations be democratically worked out in discussions in which all choir members participated (while allowing for directors' guidance in steering groups away from unworkable suggestions). Students would thus learn not only proper enunciation, but would be imbued with the "spirit of cooperation" as well;[15] choral speech was thus seen as a moral good that represented "revitalized community activity."[16]

Although men and boys participated in choral speaking, the literature about its scoring practices often divulges the underlying assumption that speaking poetry is a feminine activity. Carrie Rassmussen believed that a lullaby-like, soft sound, presumably in women's voices, was the ideal starting point for the choral sound.[17] Choral speaking's standard voice types—*light*, *medium*, and *dark*—were most often compared to the soprano, mezzo-soprano, and alto labels for female singers, suggesting the overwhelming prevalence of female (or preadolescent boy) voices.[18] Dark voices were occasionally considered to be male; Harriet Lucas described how "your most typical dark voice is that of the boy whose voice has changed. The most typical light voice is of the little, dainty girl."[19] When choir members included men, it was recommended that women outnumber them two to one because of men's supposedly more robust voices.[20]

Numerous writers suggested programming gender-stereotyped repertoire specifically to engage boys; Emma Meader believed "the male group should have stirring, virile verse such as we find in sea chanties or war verse. Girls are interested in delicate pictures, lovely sounds, in spinning songs and lullabies."[21] Anthologies compiled by Marion Robinson and Rozetta Thurston reflect this gender division: *Poetry for Men to Speak Chorally* includes texts about native Americans, the American West, war, and social revolt, whereas *Poetry for Women to Speak Chorally* includes lullabies and selections about the natural world and fairies.[22] The editors believed their men's anthology met a previously unmet need and that "the most red-blooded men will find here much with a virile hearty appeal."[23] Schoolteachers were particularly sensitive to the supposedly gendered nature of poetry. A high school textbook described how football players who needed English credits accidentally discovered poetry's masculine vitality: "This group heard the story of men driven crazy by the tramp of boots as they soldiered across Africa. . . . . They felt the exultation of a band of Indians at a pow wow. They shared the basic savagery of Negroes in the Congo." The boys inevitably concluded, "I like this kind of thing."[24]

Certain texts, such as Mildred Plew Merryman's "Moon Song," were definitely to be avoided ("Heaven forbid [it] should ever be assigned to boys!"[25]) because instructors wanted to ensure that "boys were not asked to do anything 'lady-like.'"[26] Pedagogues were clearly fighting the lingering assumption that poetic recitation was a woman's art, and they hoped that with the proper selections, boys would discover that poetry "can be a regular 'he-man' affair, in no way related to pink teas and ladies' embroidery clubs."[27] No such special efforts were apparently considered necessary for girls.

## "Food of the Spirit": Cécile de Banke and the Wellesley College Verse-Speaking Choir

One of the most successful verse-speaking choirs was established by Cécile de Banke (1889–1964) at Wellesley College in 1933 (figure 8.1); it gave twenty-seven public performances and lasted until 1948. De Banke's professional background, which included both music and elocution training in her native England as well as melodrama performances, is evidence of the link between choral speaking and previous practices. An aspiring singer eventually hindered by respiratory illness, de Banke made her theatrical debut at age seven as Puck in *A Midsummer Night's Dream* (a play she was later to direct using Mendelssohn's music) and appeared in British theater and pantomime.[28] Her brief, failed attempt in music hall brought her into contact with Clifford Harrison, who was known in London for reciting poetry to music.[29] In 1916 de Banke left England for South Africa, where she founded a School of Elocution and Dramatic Art in Johannesburg. Her 130 students appeared in entertainments described by the press as featuring music to "afford the relief that recitation might do in connection with a vocal recital."[30] In the late teens and twenties, de Banke appeared as an elocutionist in Johannesburg and Cape Town, frequently speaking with piano accompaniment. Her repertoire included *Enoch Arden* with a condensed version of Tennyson's poem to allow for more emphasis on Strauss's music and melodramas by British women: Liza Lehmann's setting of Oscar Wilde's *The Selfish Giant* (also in Cheatham's repertoire) and Amy Elsie Horrocks's *The Lady of Shalott*.[31] Her concert appearances sometimes also featured "musical monologues," or songs spoken to music.

Around 1921 de Banke moved to Cape Town, where she became an instructor at several institutions, including the South African College of Music. Three years later, inspired by English verse speaking, de Banke founded a choir with fifteen of her best female students. In 1929 they made a highly publicized appearance at a concert of the City of Cape Town Municipal Orchestra, performing John Masefield's "Sea Fever," Walter de la Mare's "The Listeners," and Tennyson's "Sweet and Low." In the second half of the concert

Figure 8.1. Cécile de Banke. Sue Page Studio, courtesy of Wellesley College Archives.

they recited Edgar Allan Poe's "The Bells" and a choral ode, "Trojan Women" by Euripides; the choir's red and yellow gowns were designed to suggest a Greek chorus. The audience was captivated by the performance; reviewers stressed the ensemble's complete unanimity, perfect diction, controlled tone, and changes of pitch, as well as its overall power and dignity, producing an art form "rich in expressive possibility."[32] One writer found the choir to be an almost machine-like musical instrument that expressed human emotion:

Miss De Banke appeared, wand in hand. With a flourish she set her machine in action. "Sea Fever," said a great neutral voice. It did not shout but the volume took one aback. Then as an organist might pull out a "stop" marked "Vox Angelica" or "Diapason," so Miss De Banke coaxed "Longing" out of her instrument, using Masefield's verses:

> I must go down to the sea again,
> To the lonely sea and the sky

And I heard all the longing and all the pining of twenty women's voices come from the great composite throat. . . . Miss De Banke was playing a perfect machine, more human and so more compelling than a grand organ.

While one reviewer claimed that the applause was merely personal support for de Banke and her choir, rather "than for what they did," another described how the "mellow resonance of that great voice" performing "Sweet and Low" caused "a stifled sob, a gulp, and . . . handkerchiefs taken out among the audience."[33]

When de Banke joined Wellesley College's faculty in 1932 as a visiting instructor, she found her new colleagues hostile to her professional abilities. While their disdain stemmed in part from her lack of academic training— Wellesley was a pioneering women's institution, and de Banke held no degrees whatsoever—their reaction was also because of their perception of elocution as mere drawing-room exhibitionism of the "speaking of pieces," the sort of feminine "accomplishment" that educated women endeavored to transcend.[34] This atmosphere had predated de Banke's arrival; the previous elocution instructor, Malvina Bennett (1857–1934), was reportedly "extremely sensitive to the indifferent attitude of the academic circle to the subject of speech."[35]

The verse-speaking choir at Wellesley (figure 8.2) was founded as an extracurricular activity but was voted into the curriculum in 1936. First organized to accompany a modern-dance troupe, the choir often gave concerts organized around literary genres and styles, in keeping with its pedagogical purpose. For example, the works on a 1937 program were divided into "Prose Rhythms," "American Rhythms," and "Choral Speaking in Drama." The final portion, openly acknowledged as "Entertainment Values," was nonetheless subdivided into poems about "Men of Character" and "Types of Poetry," retaining its moral and educational functions. The Americana portion included translations of Native American works, poetry of African Americans (including Harlem Renaissance and folk poetry), and poems of the "white man," in this case Sandburg and Lindsay, both popular with verse-speaking choirs. A 1941 event combined Native American and African American works with foreign-language selections from Wellesley's departments of French, Spanish, German, Italian, and Greek, as well as translations of Chinese poetry. Although the choir performed selections by ancient Greeks, Shakespeare, and other earlier poets, twentieth-century American poetry appeared the most frequently on their programs. De Banke's tastes were decidedly modernist: the new or the very old

Figure 8.2. Wellesley Verse-Speaking Choir, 1937–38. Courtesy of Wellesley College Archives.

were favored over anything Victorian. The 1938 program, in which "Children's Verse" was heard before "Negro Rhythms," was not the choral continuation of recitations in child or "negro" dialect. Although T. H. Shackelford's "The Big Bell of Zion" does employ dialect, both this poem and Vachel Lindsay's "The Potatoes' Dance" seem to have been selected for their repetitive texts, which would have provided varied possibilities for choral scorings.[36]

De Banke endeavored to integrate the choir into Wellesley's cultural life. A 1940 program concluded with poetry by seven students written especially for the choir, and the 1947 poetry festival featured texts by current and former Wellesley faculty, including Katharine Lee Bates, known for authoring the lyrics of "America the Beautiful." The choir's Christmas programs, presented annually in the college's chapel between 1936 and 1942, served a quasi-religious function. Organized according to the liturgical year, several programs consisted of poems for Advent, Nativity, and Epiphany; later programs also featured organ preludes and interludes. The poetry consisted of Old English ballads and carols, but modern poems, including those of Eleanor Farjeon, were heard as well. In 1943, the Christmas program was replaced by a late November event titled "Thanksgiving in Time of War." After an organ prelude and fugue by Dieterich Buxtehude, the choir presented a variety of seasonally and patriotically appropriate selections, ranging from a section of Ecclesiastes and poetic arrangements by verse-speaking pioneer Mona Swann to James Whitcomb Riley's "When the Frost Is on the Punkin'" and T. S. Eliot's chorus from "The Rock." Individual choristers read prose excerpts from Thanksgiving proclamations made by George Washington, Abraham Lincoln, Woodrow Wilson, and, only three weeks earlier, Franklin Delano Roosevelt.[37] Particularly appropriate during wartime, Lincoln's Civil War proclamation implored "the Almighty hand to heal the wounds of the nation" and to restore "peace, harmony, tranquility, and union"; Wilson, amid World War I, described Thanksgiving "even in the midst of the tragedy of a world shaken by war and immeasurable disaster, in the midst of sorrow and great peril." FDR's proclamation, the program's penultimate text, stressed national victory. Thus, not only did de Banke see poetry as serving a seasonal and ritualistic purpose, but she valued it as an integral part of contemporary life as well. The choir sometimes performed in local churches or, as in the 1940 and 1942 Christmas programs, with schoolchildren, which de Banke found to be some of its most memorable presentations: "The little ones spoke of the sorrow of 'no room at the inn,' of the joy of Nativity and of the grandeur of Epiphany. The tiny bell-like chimings of the children's voices, supported by the sonorous chords of the girls' voices, took on a tender beauty that has never been forgotten by those who heard it."[38]

In spite of the Verse-Speaking Choir's success, some Wellesley faculty obviously found it insufficiently academic. A curricular change brought about its demise; when a faculty committee revoked the academic credit granted to choristers, its director found that she was no longer able to sustain students' interest.[39] However, during its tenure the Verse-Speaking Choir achieved fame beyond Wellesley because of its radio broadcasts. In May 1935, unable to afford to attend the English Verse-Speaking Association's meeting in Oxford, the choir was instead broadcast worldwide on shortwave radio, and de Banke received responses from as far away as India and Australia.[40] The workshops de Banke gave across North America and the 1937 publication of her textbook *The Art of Choral Speaking* spawned numerous new choral speaking groups; in 1955 she recalled that she had trained some seventeen hundred elementary and high school teachers in choral speaking.[41]

De Banke recognized the nationalistic impulses behind the movement she helped to lead, describing choral speaking's rise as "absolutely American in the mass reaction."[42] She saw speech education as a means of alleviating class distinctions and, like other directors, of furthering democratic ideals: a citizen of any economic or social standing could communicate with "self-assurance" and become an "integrated member of his community."[43] Given that more women than men engaged in choral speaking, its underlying goals could also serve to establish women more strongly within American society. De Banke's sense of choral speaking's mission resonated with her belief that instructors were responsible for giving both men and women the means "to speak with dignity, authority, and truth."[44] One press clipping speculated that perhaps de Banke and others would "restore poetry to its natural place in our national life."[45] However, that the countless women in the verse-speaking groups across the country were seemingly poised for a major role in a cultural revival was overly optimistic.

Nonetheless, de Banke's sense of the necessity for collective activity in order to further America's cultural life inspired the annual poetry festivals she organized between 1943 and 1948.[46] Similar to the English events overseen by John Masefield, the festivals resulted in fourteen poets visiting Wellesley's campus, several of whom took part in choral interpretations of their works as well as reading individually.[47] Florence Converse (a Wellesley graduate), Virginia Huntington, and May Sarton wrote new poems for the choir to speak at the first festival, which was attended by fourteen hundred people.[48] De Banke found an enthusiastic collaborator in poet John Holmes, who encouraged her to "be bold" and invite as many good poets to the second festival as possible.[49] Both de Banke and Holmes believed that the festivals transmitted spiritual values. De Banke wrote to her friend, "Even in these days of concentrated war effort, we have got to keep our grasp on the lovely and lasting values," to which Holmes replied, "You are doing not only poetry, but the endangered life of the spirit a very great good."[50] In the draft of a letter written during World War II to Archibald MacLeish, who appeared at the 1948 festival, de Banke wrote, "If you ask me why I am doing this particular thing at this particular time I will say that it is as a reaction to the fear that in the war emergency our youngsters may lose their hold on the things of fundamental value, and are likely to starve for lack of food of the spirit, as they did in the last war."[51]

Most of the visiting poets expressed delight in hearing the choir recite their works, finding themselves, like William Rose Benét, unexpectedly moved, although their reactions were not uniformly positive.[52] In her correspondence with festival participants, de Banke explored which poems would work best in choral arrangements, but bad choices sometimes resulted. Some poets appeared not to like the performance practices of choral speaking, and, like Winfield Townley Scott, found the choir's renditions of certain poems more successful than others.[53] Leonard Bacon seemed to apologize for an earlier inadvertent slip of the tongue: "I beg you to believe that I did not think that they *bleated* at all."[54] De Banke had intended to have the visiting poets "offer help and suggestions in regard to the interpretation,"[55] but reworking their texts into choral renditions could be problematic, and her letters of thanks to visitors sometimes include defensive remarks regarding their experience of her arrangements. She reported being most pleased with MacLeish's reaction to the performance of his "Way-Station":

> He suddenly rose from his seat in the audience and said with naïve wonder, "I never knew I had written anything as good as that."
> Regardless of the delighted audience who were waiting to applaud, I called, "Would you like to hear it again?"
> "Yes, please," he said, with such fervour that there was a general laugh.[56]

However, in writing to MacLeish afterward, de Banke apologized for being "an insensitive block-head" about his "Landscape as a Nude," and called the problem a result of "the damned and dominating ego." Apparently the poet had found some aspect of the performance excessive, and de Banke took personal responsibility for the interpretation, assuring MacLeish that it was not the choir's fault. She instead credited it to her personal attraction to the "up-soaring swelling of vitality of the voice and speech in this new young country of America. . . . What you heard was my exhultation [*sic*] in a medium that was so appropriate that it broke the bonds of artistry and escaped in a shout."[57] MacLeish graciously acknowledged that "often the interpreter understands more than the creator," and that they simply had differences of interpretation: "It was the one place where my reading would have gone one way where yours went another." In spite of "Landscape as a Nude," he found his Wellesley experience to be extremely rewarding: "I shall not forget that evening. Not even you, with all your sensitiveness and understanding, could you possibly guess what it means to hear your own work presented so beautifully. I came home . . . feeling like the bed of a stream after a spring freshlet."[58] Nonetheless, the episode suggests that regardless of their rhetoric, it was not always easy for verse speakers to reconcile their desire to transmit individual poets' voices with the democratic impulses that opened those poets' works to choral arrangements, thus allowing others to interpret them in a highly public manner. MacLeish objected to the Wellesley choir's performance in the same way that other writers have found composers' musical settings of their texts in some way inappropriate; the music of choral speaking was capable of supplying new and perhaps contradictory meanings for a poetic work.

## Musical Sounds and the Performance of Choral Speaking

Almost nothing in the language of Cécile de Banke's books or those of other choral speaking pedagogues represented a holdover from late nineteenth-century practices.[59] Most writers were adamant in distancing their activities from anything resembling elocution. Florence Pidge warned against reverting "inevitably to the monotonous sing-song type called *concert recitation*" of "the old school,"[60] and the term *recitation*, which had dominated publications at the turn of the twentieth century, was used sparingly; Walsh's horrified vision of problematic verse speaking—degraded by "stopping at insipid or sensational *recitations*"—suggests that the term had acquired the same negative connotations that *elocution* had.[61]

Nonetheless, numerous similarities between elocutionary performances and the newer choral speaking remained. The arrangements of choral anthologies by topic were not unlike those of children's recitation books. Some performers adopted Delsarte-style Grecian attire, but because it could seem inappropriate, choirs instead wore robes or academic gowns. Helen Hicks described seeing "forty girls . . . costumed in the delicate, diaphanous costumes of Greek maidens," reciting, in African American dialect, "Mammy's little baby loves shortenin' bread." The resulting incongruity "was so great the audience had a hard time concentrating on the text."[62] Abandoning poses, choral speakers only occasionally relied on subtler theatrical trappings, such as gauze screens or colored lighting. Some writers nonetheless recommended pantomime in performance. It is difficult to imagine that the gestures prescribed by Agnes Curren Hamm in her choric arrangement of *Hiawatha* did not have something in common with reciters' poses in earlier Delsartean versions.[63] Likewise, the patriotic performance of Grafton, West Virginia, high school students waving red, white, and blue scarves while speaking John Daly's "A Toast to the Flag" was similar to children's flag drills found in turn-of-the-century anthologies.[64]

Choral speakers retained some of the fundamentally musical concepts from elocution manuals: notions of time, meter, rhythm, pause, pitch, and inflection were regularly discussed, meter and rhythm in the most detail. However, writers also developed new terminology to delineate types of arrangements based on changes in vocal scoring; some of the terms were adapted from music: *unison, refrain,* and *antiphonal* speaking (or *two-part work*). To this core they added the expressions *line-a-child*, for poems passed off between all members of a choir, and *sequential*, for various soloists and groups following one another in sequence; in *cumulative* speaking, voices would be added line by line until the entire group was speaking in unison. Children's authors presented arrangements of nursery rhymes or graded lists of poems by both standardized performance types and difficulty levels. Pedagogues were also advised to break up their choirs into smaller groups of three or four persons for performances likened to chamber music, in contrast to the entire group's "orchestral" sound.

Choral speaking's relationship with music was made clear by many authors, who assumed that musicians would naturally recognize its worth.[65] Descriptions of choral speaking sometimes used vaguely metaphorical musical language: a speaker's "instrument [the voice] must be tuned and re-tuned" to meet the poet's "varied demands,"[66] and groups had to "learn to 'orchestrate' their voices, blend them together, to make a symphonic whole."[67] Choral speaking was often touted as a means to develop children's musical abilities, particularly in rhythm. L. M. Simpkins believed that children whose singing had been labeled as monotone were actually afraid to sing, declaring that when they became familiar with rhythm and timing, children would naturally take part in music activities, "just as the slow talkers and readers have done in the reading and recitations."[68] Younger pupils were to respond "to the leader's voice as to a musical instrument"; Elizabeth Keppie suggested that children "move about the room to the music and rhythm of the reading," just as one might dance to music.[69]

Like earlier elocution textbooks, which found that speech's subtleties made it more complex than singing, the choral-speaking literature also attempted to justify the spoken medium as the superior of the two. De Banke stressed that the speaking voice had a wider range than the singing voice, almost three octaves, and because it did not destroy poetic meter as did musical settings, the verse-speaking choir was "the perfect medium for aural poetry."[70] Keppie reminded choirs that although speech lacked musical notation, poetry was nonetheless dead if it remained on the page without oral interpretation: "There are no guideposts for interpreting verse as you find in printed song. No bars or numbers show the rhythm; no signs indicate the tempo; no location of notes gives the variation of the tune. These patterns exist within the meaning of the poem."[71] Most writers considered choral speech to be superior to music in its ability to transmit the meaning as well as the sound of the text. Gordon Bottomley claimed that "expressiveness is enhanced, carrying powers and intelligibility are ever magnified, and the native rhythms of the poem make their effect in a way that they cannot do when underlined—and often masked—by musical composition."[72] Reading a poem silently resembled reading a musical score, enabling one to "*hear* all the tones and overtones of poetic composition, just as Beethoven could read the score of a symphony and hear in his mind every instrument."[73]

The voices of a speaking choir, considered to be musical instruments, were sometimes compared to solo violins within an orchestra or, since adequate breathing was required, wind instruments. Some guides provided seating charts showing directors where to place the sections of light, medium, and dark voices. Louise Abney compared individual voices to instrumental soloists, and linked gender to instrumental groupings: "The deeper voices of the boys come in like the drums, while the high sopranos suggest the violins."[74] Directors worked to develop these instruments into transmitters of "melody." While *melody* was obviously not a term that was used completely literally in this context, as in elocutionary training, pitch contours were crucial, so much so that directors were leery of finding themselves with "tone-deaf" members who would ruin the efforts of the choir.[75] De Banke's writings retained the earlier notion that individuals speak in the major and minor modes depending on a text's emotional content, even specifying major, minor, and harmonic minor scales as available options.[76]

Verse-speaking pedagogues did not invent notational systems to indicate changing pitch levels such as were found in elocution texts; nonetheless, brief examples of text raised and lowered according to pitch appear in several publications. Vertical lines varying in height can be seen in de Banke's *The Art of Choral Speaking* to teach performers how to mark inflection above their texts.[77] Choral speakers' lesser degree of concern about specific pitches may suggest that their performances were less stylized than elocutionists' or may be because rhythm and tempo necessarily became of primary importance in keeping choirs speaking together. A lack of pitch notation was not a handicap, however, because a conductor could lead a choir in "melody" as well as in rhythm, raising or lowering her arm to indicate pitch level.[78] Musical training was often considered to be a necessity for a successful director, who, according to Hicks, needed to "easily detect pitch levels of voices" and "hear and follow lines of melody."[79] Emma Meader suggested that aspiring choral speech directors study the techniques of great orchestral and choral music conductors.[80]

Although varied pitch was considered essential for choral speaking, directors did not come to any consensus about its role. Gullan wrote that pitch unity was not desirable in unison speaking,[81] but she deplored the use of "harmony,"

finding that choirs divided into "sections speaking simultaneously in prear-
ranged pitches" only obscured a poem's meaning.[82] Swann also objected to the
use of a descant line—portions of the choirs speaking different material—not
primarily on the basis of its unintelligibility, but because of the discordance
produced by multiple pitches.[83] But leaders of American choral speaking were
less rigid, and many found pitched effects to be both inevitable and advanta-
geous. Alice Mills described a Greek chorus at Mount Holyoke that "attained
a close harmony on three different pitches in a manner very similar to that
used in singing" as strikingly compelling.[84] Marguerite DeWitt felt the "tone-
patterns" she devised for speech did not interfere with the interpretation of
a poetic text any more than musical accompaniment would; she hoped those
familiar with the "forms hovering between song and speech" in modern music
would be especially interested in choral speaking.[85] De Banke's description of
cumulative speaking acknowledged that one of its purposes was to achieve a
"harmonic effect" in which four groups joined in a "common chord."[86] She
also noticed that a choir's light and dark voices tended to fall a third or a fifth
apart and predicated a future of "illuminative experimental work" in harmony,
despite its difficulties.[87]

It is not possible to generalize about choral-speaking practices on the basis
of the Wellesley choir's two recordings of the hymn "I Saw Three Ships Come
Sailing In," which it performed regularly on Christmas programs,[88] yet the
recordings do provide insights into the degree of pitch the group used. The
structure of the stanzas, individual lines of the verse alternating with two refrain lines, allowed for the first five strophes to be performed with alternation
between solo speakers and the entire choir:

> Solo: I saw three ships come sailing in
> Choir: On Christmas day, on Christmas day
> Solo: I saw three ships come sailing in
> Choir: On Christmas day in the morning.

The first five stanzas each introduced a different solo speaking voice, with
noticeable variations in voice types between them; the individual voices might
easily be classified as light, medium, or dark.[89] The choir gave the final four
strophes in unison, with substantial dynamic variation between the verse and
refrain lines. Individual verse lines were spoken at different dynamic levels
in accordance with their meaning; for example, the joyful "And all the bells
on earth shall ring" was spoken loudly with a crescendo and a slight ascent in
pitch, which created a sense of ringing in the sound of the spoken text.

The pitch content of the choir's performance is the most noticeable in the four
final unison stanzas. The highest-pitched top voice is the most prominent and
has a recognizable melodic shape, which the lower voices follow—this shape is
*not* that of the tune to which this text is commonly sung. The overall range of

the block of moving voices is at least an octave. In contrast, the refrain is spoken almost in unison, much more softly and at a lower pitch level than the lines of verse. The effect is as if an ostinato has been constantly repeating underneath the verse lines, and it then quietly surfaces when the verse rests; of course, this is not the actual case. The regular rhythmic patterns of the strophes (more evident in the slightly faster recording), combined with the pitched speech, creates a chant-like effect. On subsequent repetitions, the refrains, in particular, come to be heard as purely musical, rather than as sounds that evoke linguistic meanings. In the final stanza, the previous rhythmic patterns are modified to create a closing gesture for the work: the last two lines are performed with a ritardando, and there is a slight pause between the final verse line and refrain: "Then let us all rejoice a main / [pause] on Christmas day in the morning."

The Wellesley choir's recording typifies the clearly differentiated and controlled pitch levels widely recognized by writers on choral speech. When pedagogues warned against "sing-song," the perceived danger was not that speech would be entirely abandoned for singing or an excess of pitch, but would suffer from expressive monotony because of lack of variety in both pitch and rhythm. Keppie made clear that musical speaking required responding "to the rhythm and meter of a poem without letting them dominate the meaning."[90] In the second half of "I Saw Three Ships," the repeated refrain comes to be heard as sounds in which music overtakes meaning; nonetheless, the two performances as a whole do not lack in variety or in pitch contours. Because the text itself is repetitious, the musical qualities of de Banke's arrangement are what make the performances aurally interesting.

Many choral poetry anthologies did not specify the changes of vocal scoring that were crucial to the Wellesley recording's success, leaving those decisions to directors or to ensembles' collaborative decision-making processes. Often, directors answered Virginia Sanderson's question "how do you know who shall say the lines?" merely by expressing deference to the ultimate authority: the poet.[91] On the other end of the spectrum were detailed arrangements, such as in *Choric Interludes* (1942), which provided eighteen abbreviations in the text to indicate various vocal groupings.[92] De Banke's notated arrangements also relied on abbreviations for changes of scoring and drew on music in their dynamic markings, crescendos and decrescendos, and terminology such as *rubato* or *rallentando*.[93] Helen Hicks's *The Reading Chorus* (1939) gave marginal expressive indications and performance directions not unlike those published in some of Vachel Lindsay's poems: "light, brisk," "slowly and impressively," "in a romantic manner," "thoughtfully," and numerous others.

More experimental directors, such as Marguerite DeWitt, justified the modifications to poetry made in choral speaking by comparing it to composing: "A composer may repeat certain words, phrases or lines of a poem; he may create refrains, may include a round within the composition, he may[,] in short, add his creation that of the poet. The same things may occur legitimately in group recitation, for there too we deal with a creative art."[94] Others objected to arrangements that became too musical. Mona Swann complained that when poetic texts suffered violent transformation for the sake of choral virtuosity, "too often a poem is torn and twisted, its phrasing distorted and its rhythm shattered, in the effort to gain choric 'effects.'"[95] The literary intelligibility of the poem was never to be obscured, although musical arrangements that somehow sprang from the text and thus represented a legitimate interpretation of the poet's offering were considered acceptable. For example, choirs could enhance poems' use of "onomatopoeia, alliteration and assonance" or emphasize their "staccato lines and sharp consonants or by rolling vowels and liquid sounds."[96] So within certain aesthetic boundaries, many so-called effects were, in fact, possible. Despite her objections to some arrangements, Swann described a soloist or small group of voices speaking over a quiet or muffled background, or the contrast of "inflected speech against a massed monotone," as viable.[97] De Banke devised symbols—an $L$ (light) over a $D$ (dark), or an $S$ (solo) over a $U$ (unison)—to indicate that the speakers associated with the upper letter were to predominate.[98] In the end, the music of the speaking choir had to be compatible with the poetic meaning expressed.[99]

## Women and the Art of Choral Speaking

Because the poem was to be the ultimate focus of the speaking choir, it was supposed to overshadow the women performing it. Whereas elocution had allowed women to become soloists, expressing their personal interpretations of literary works without engaging in the dangers of theater, the speech choir, with its patriotic overtones of civic good, was an even safer venue for feminine expression; the individual woman among the many would be enhancing social welfare, not threatening the prevailing cultural order. However, the result was that a woman's personality would be absorbed into the whole. Gullan advocated communicating "the emotional, imaginative, and intellectual values of the poem . . . without the interposition of the speakers' own personality between the poem and the hearers."[100] To be a choral speaker was, in many ways, to abandon the self,[101] for it was not possible to reach the audience with the poem's meaning without the speakers' "sacrifice of all display tendencies."[102] Gullan was even pleased when one of her choir members was completely unconcerned that her name was left off a program because "the poetry was the thing that mattered and the speakers were there to serve it."[103] Much American literature touted the good that choral speaking would do for the inhibited, the unmusical, and the poor speaker, but in the end, choral speaking's very premise rested on the power of multiple voices in which the individual woman's voice would become subsumed.

Although the female conductor, baton in hand, powerfully leading the group in her interpretation of the poetic text, would seem to have been a step forward for women's leadership in the arts, her role was frequently downplayed. The interpretations at which choirs arrived through discussion among themselves were to be favored over a conductor's singular rendition. Guides to choral speaking stressed that the conductor was not to be a distraction, and that, if possible, she should only start the poem, and an experienced choir would then have no additional need of her. Even when the director did conduct an entire poem, she could be positioned offstage or below the platform so that the audience did not see her.[104] The female conductor was not to be permitted any artistic egocentrism, "the damned and dominating ego," for which even de Banke found a need to apologize.

In 1960, Agnes Curren Hamm, after a long career directing verse-speaking choirs, wrote to the *Quarterly Journal of Speech* lamenting the decline of choral speaking. Citing a study in which almost half of ninety-nine instructors noted that they had previously led speaking choirs and all but fifteen had abandoned them, Hamm defended the practice against charges that it was insufficiently academic and that it was pedagogically useful but was not an "art form."[105] Hamm's query about the demise of choral speaking received a response from Clive Samson, a former colleague of the now-deceased Gullan. Samson reported that the founding light of choral speaking had believed it had failed in America because it had abandoned its original goal of teaching poetry and had become "merely an excuse for self-display" in which "poetry was . . . butchered to make a conductor's holiday."[106] Perhaps, in spite of admonitions to remain subservient to the poetic text, American women had continued to abandon themselves to the joys of performing musical speech.

The list of sacrilegious transgressions on the part of American choirs included visual effects such as "flamboyant costumes . . . like glorified marching girls" and overdone stagings with backdrops and lighting.[107] However, what Samson most objected to was the degree to which the music of choral speaking had overcome the text: "The arbitrary breaking-up of lines irrespective of the poem's form or meaning; 'harmonizing' for the sake of vocal effect, so that the audience was more conscious of sound than sense; the use of artificial speech tunes; in fact, all the old elocutionary tricks that public opinion had forced teachers to abandon in the individual speaking of verse."[108]

In defending the art of choral speech as Walsh had twenty-five years earlier, Samson emphasized that "it was the misuse of choral speaking that was discredited, not choral speaking itself."[109] But as his list makes clear, in their performances, American women had made choral speech into an art form, but as much a musical art form as a poetic one.

# 9. Words and Music Ladies

*The Careers of Phyllis Fergus*
*and Frieda Peycke*

Miss Fergus is one of the rare persons who possess a
naturally lovely voice, and the wistful, lilting softness of
beautifully rounded words rising over the light, rippling
accompaniments of her own composing, could scarcely fail
to gain for her the enthusiastic applause of her hearers.
—*Kenosha (WI) Evening Herald*, 1919

We MUST have Miss Peycke come back . . . it took me
half the night to get into her peculiar swing, and now that
we understand her we MUST have her back.
—*Lakewood Log*, Tacoma, Washington, 1946

On January 30, 1923, Chicago publisher Clayton F. Summy sponsored a concert by two composers whose music he published: Frieda Peycke (1884–1964), visiting from Los Angeles, and Chicagoan Phyllis Fergus
(1887–1964). Described as "the reunion of a happy family"[1] in the considerable
press coverage that followed, the event featured works by the two composers, along with a piece by Adolf Weidig (1867–1931), who had taught both
women composition at the American Conservatory of Music and who was in
attendance. In honor of the occasion, Fergus rewrote the text of her popular
composition "The Usual Way," celebrating the women's studies with Weidig, their interactions with Summy, and their mutual delight in performing
"the work we love to do."[2] Chautauqua baritone Edward Clarke introduced
the event by describing "the ideals and possibilities of the musical reading
as a serious form of entertainment," remarks that may have been the source
of articles in at least seven music magazines advocating for the genre—brief
poems spoken to piano accompaniments—in which Fergus and Peycke composed.[3] Their spoken-word compositions were advertised in magazines for
Chautauqua and lyceum performers, and titles such as "Musical Readings No
Passing Fad, New Art Form Asserts Publisher" suggest that Summy hoped

the publicity would boost sales. Instead of relating the musical readings heard at the concert to accompanied recitation, published descriptions deliberately positioned them closer to high-art melodrama.

All of the articles treated Fergus's and Peycke's spoken-word compositions as serious music. The *Music News* cited large-scale compositions such as Strauss's *Enoch Arden* and Schumann's *Manfred* as predecessors to the women's "less pretentious" pieces. Nonetheless, Summy claimed that in the two women's hands, these works constituted a "new art form." Their compositions were not simplified versions of melodrama, but were instead the "art development" of the pianologue and "a great deal more than elocution with music."[4] Even though the composers' intention was to entertain, they had "a serious musical purpose,"[5] and the articles likened their musical accompaniments to those of far more substantial genres, even suggesting levels of complexity that Peycke's and Fergus's compositions did not contain:

> It is not intended to be a piano patter, but its function is to weave in and out of the story, now supporting, now bearing the full import of the message itself (as in the orchestral parts of a Wagner opera), sometimes identifying itself by themes with a certain character or a special mood, often two themes combining contrapuntally to better illustrate the story carried to the audience. Practically there is no limit to what the composer may do in his endeavor to bring out the thought and emotion back of the poem, which he is illustrating musically.[6]

While this report of both women's styles was basically correct—the music was certainly essential to their pieces' overall mood and meaning—the texts nonetheless predominated, and neither composer produced accompaniments with the thematic specificity of leitmotifs (with the exception of Fergus's "The Highwayman," which was not on the program). Summy more accurately stressed the role of the speaker in the genre he was promoting, rather than its accompaniment: "This new art form offers an opportunity to express the pathos or humor of a poem with all the emotional powers of the speaking voice. The musical reader can point his inflections, can vary his tones according to the moods of the texts, can turn from child readings to tragedy and delicate humor, and have the accompaniment of music that expresses the same ideas."[7] Nonetheless, writers felt it was important to justify the genre in which Fergus and Peycke composed as a higher form of musical culture and were pleased to find that both women aspired to "the same high general principles."[8] Like earlier elocutionists, composers of musical readings had the goal of expressing important truths, although this time doing so through the music rather than the text: "In fact, the position of the composer is precisely that of the artist who illustrates a story or a poem; his mission is to convey, by means of his art, some intangible meaning, some spiritual value which cannot be expressed by the limited use of words."[9]

In hailing the usefulness of musical readings for pedagogical purposes, press reports resembled earlier defenses of elocutionary study, claiming that the genre cultivated poise, developed personality, and taught "the control and assurance" of correct speaking. In addition to increasing students' pianistic technique, the accompaniments' close association with speech could "stimulate intelligent hearing of music," particularly among high school students: "When the reader links a definite theme with a certain character or mood, it cultivates thematic hearing and makes an easy approach to music appreciation."[10] Peycke's and Fergus's musical readings thus transcended earlier accompanied recitation, in that their music was not peripheral to the text; as these were actual compositions, the text allowed listeners to comprehend the musical content instead.

Both Fergus and Peycke had successful careers as composer-reciters, in part because they chose to publicize their musical offerings as something unique. Initially their publicity worked to distinguish their art from its negative association with elocution's past, relabeling their compositions and, as at Summy's concert, positioning them as new manifestations. Peycke called her compositions *musically illustrated readings*, and Fergus adopted the phrase *story poems in musical settings*. Yet their pieces shared similar topics and humorous approaches, as well as a new degree of musical sophistication. There was seemingly a market for the genre in which both composers excelled. In 1924 after the *Farmer's Wife* magazine publicized Fergus's "Soap (the Oppressor)," it reported, "Apparently there are thousands of readers . . . who were looking for good musical readings or pianologues, judging from the large number of calls we received."[11]

Neither Peycke nor Fergus conceived of herself as emerging from a tradition of female reciters because both women's educations had centered on musical training. Fergus was a 1913 graduate of Smith College before she entered the American Conservatory, from which she received her master's degree in 1918. Peycke began her career as a pianist but received training from spoken-word professionals, melodrama revivalist David Bispham and reader Bertha Kunz Baker.[12] Early in her career Peycke toured in a Chautauqua-style concert company, but Fergus's association with Chautauqua was only secondhand, through her acquaintance with Clarke and his violinist wife, Rachel.

The production and circulation of the music of both composers were intimately bound up with their performances. Reviews stressed the women's personal charm, vitality, and individuality—the act of speaking, rather than singing, made their compositions seem to be expressions of their personalities. Peycke's publicity listed the poets responsible for the texts she had set, but reviews stressed her skills as both speaker and pianist and almost never mentioned these authors. Fergus's works were taken up by other performers and appeared on professional and amateur speakers' programs; Peycke published a somewhat larger body of compositions and flirted with making commercial recordings of her performances. However, both artists' careful use of terminology that differentiated their compositions from previous practices also enabled them to establish professional identities as composers, not merely reciters who dabbled in accompaniments. By the end of their careers, however, the two women sometimes found it necessary to explain the genre against concertgoers' collective memory loss. Audiences who had never heard of musical readings might have initially been bewildered, but as the long, flourishing careers of both composers attest, listeners delighted in their performances nonetheless.

Both Fergus and Peycke relied on a wide network of musical and social connections centered in women's clubs and were active in organizations for professional women: Peycke joined the Southern California Press Club, the Ebell Club, and the Dominant Club; Fergus held leadership roles in the National League of American Pen Women. Motivated to be promoters for others as well as for themselves, Peycke served as one of the music directors for the Hollywood Bowl and in leadership roles for the Hollywood Community Sing, and Fergus organized concerts for women composers in cities across the United States. The composers sometimes appeared before mixed audiences; however, because women's clubs were the primary venues for their performances, their concerts were more likely to be reported in newspapers' society pages than amid arts reporting. Fergus and Peycke considered themselves to be professional musicians, but their preferred genre remained associated with women's entertainments, outside of the male cultural mainstream. That the audiences for their compositions were often women influenced the nature of the works that Fergus, Peycke, and other female composers of the early twentieth century produced.

## Phyllis Fergus's Story Poems in the World of Chicago Women's Clubs

Phyllis Fergus (figure 9.1) came from an established Chicago family and was exposed to the wide variety of cultural experiences that the city had to offer. She recalled, "When I was a child . . . I went to first nights with my mother and father and to concerts with my brother."[13] Like many in the second generation of American women to go to college, Fergus was not able to afford to enroll in Smith College until she was in her twenties.[14] At Smith, she studied composition with Henry D. Sleeper and was a member of the Clef Club, which included other student composers. In 1914, the year after she graduated, Fergus returned as the club's guest to hear her works performed in informal concerts in faculty homes. After one program had concluded and refreshments had been served, Phyllis returned to the piano to entertain club members with some-

Figure 9.1. Phyllis Fergus. Author's personal collection.

thing new—"pianologues" or "monologs," the first sign of the compositions that would play such a major role in her career. Back in Chicago, she quickly established what would become a long-running relationship with Summy, who became the publisher of most of her works.[15]

In 1921 Fergus married Thatcher Hoyt, a steel and iron broker, who was supportive of his wife's musical activities. Fergus and her husband resided in the Hoyt family home on North State Parkway, which had been built in 1877,[16] and after the birth of their two daughters, spent part of their time at their restored colonial-era home in New Haven, Vermont, returning to Chicago for the winter season.[17] The family's wealth undoubtedly assisted Fergus in her career; they employed domestic help for household chores and child care. Sometimes identified as "Mrs. Thatcher Hoyt," the composer continued to use "Phyllis Fergus" professionally, and in the 1930s her status as a mother of two children was occasionally highlighted in the press. Fergus's appearances at women's clubs did not mean that she was an amateur. She was paid for her performances, although she sometimes returned her fee as a donation if she felt that the club or charitable organization that had engaged her could not afford her services; royalties from her publications served as financial support for her aging mother.

Fergus's two performances for the College Club in 1915 were the beginning of her lifelong association with numerous arts organizations for women,
clubs typical of the Progressive Era in their emphasis on education, self-improvement, and the acquisition of artistic culture. Chicago's women's clubs
held regular meetings in country clubs, churches, or hotels; wealthier clubs,
such as the Rogers Park Women's Club or the Cordon Club, maintained their
own facilities. The city supported so many women's organizations that individual clubs could specialize in music, art, or literature; the biggest clubs
were frequently made up of smaller divisions that ran study groups, organized
outreach to schools and settlement houses, or engaged in philanthropic work,
funding scholarships or sponsoring performances by aspiring musicians, such
as through a Young Artist's Auxiliary. Cultural clubs provided a peer group
for creative women and access to the arts when women's "place" was still considered to be in the home. A 1921 concert program for the Women's League
justified the advantages of membership for "home women" as enabling them to
share a current artistic and political world with friends and family, maintaining
that club activities would not interfere with but would enhance motherhood
and domestic life: "The League . . . enables me to keep up with my progressive family as well as my friends who can devote much more time than I to
literature, art, drama, music, civic, welfare, and business accomplishments.
It gives me a well-rounded outlook on life. It makes me a real companion to
my children."[18]

The network of Chicago women's arts groups not only provided musical
activities for amateurs, but also served as venues for women who aspired to
musical careers. Karen Blair has described how women's artistic networks
from 1890 to 1930 "shaped the context in which professionals marketed their
artistic wares,"[19] which was certainly the case for Fergus, Peycke, and others.
Musical organizations' monthly meetings were frequently concerts, either by
members or by visiting artists. Membership consisted primarily of pianists
and singers, and sometimes organists, string players, or composers. Clubs
also welcomed associate members who did not perform but could still attend
concerts. Founded in 1895, the Lake View Musical Society, where Fergus frequently performed, was typical in its goal of "the development of the musical
talent of its members and stimulation of musical interest in Chicago."[20] It
sponsored five concerts between November and March; April was its annual
business meeting and May its yearly luncheon, which also featured musical entertainment. The society met at hotels and other different locations,
including churches for December meetings that featured organ music and
Christmas selections. At their peak, Chicago's clubs had large memberships;
the Musicians Club of Women had 634 members during the 1927–28 season.
Like many other clubs, membership declined in the 1930s as a result of the

Depression; however, there were still 374 active members and 179 associate members in 1930.[21]

The Cordon Club, another of the women's organizations in which Fergus was active—she served as president from 1939 to 1941—was founded in 1915 and lasted until 1977; its focus was journalism, literature, and music, and its original bylaws stated that it endeavored to "guard and protect self expression beyond domestic bounds."[22] For some years the Cordon had a music study club that regularly featured performances by its members and others. The club's facilities on the eighth floor of the Fine Arts Building on Michigan Avenue included meeting space, a music room for performances, an art gallery, and a library. During the period that Fergus was president, Cordon members could dine at the club every evening except Saturday. They were treated to a wide variety of events, one almost every day of the week: dinners, teas with visiting celebrities, lectures, travel talks, concerts, art exhibits, brief dramas, movies, and fashion shows. Although Fergus was not in charge of programming, there were more than one hundred events during the two years she was Cordon president, including appearances by journalists and political figures, who spoke on current events and foreign affairs, and such well-known figures as Frederick Stock, conductor of the Chicago Symphony; actors John Barrymore, Edward Everett Horton, Sophie Tucker, and Lillian Gish; and philosopher Mortimer Adler. In other years, composers Sergei Prokofiev, Vincent d'Indy, Percy Grainger, and Charles Wakefield Cadman; conductor Walter Damrosch; and pianist Myra Hess were Cordon guests.

The spoken word did not frequently appear on Chicago women's club concerts, but it was by no means unusual. Music clubs regularly contained readers as a small but continuing constituency, even as late as the 1930s and early 1940s. The Chicago Woman's Musical Club averaged three readers per year between 1929 and 1942; although there was sometimes only one reader, in the final two seasons that readers continued to be listed in program booklets, there were five and six, respectively.[23] Poets such as Natalie Whitted Price, who published musical readings, recited; composers such as Lulu Jones Downing sometimes presented "readings with music" on club programs. Rossetter G. Cole, the composer of several melodramas, sometimes recited on programs accompanied by his pianist wife, an active clubwoman.[24]

Thus, Phyllis Fergus's Chicago was filled with women organizing meetings and cultural events at which she could perform, either as a club member or as a visiting artist. Several clubs sponsored annual member composers' concerts; the Lake View Musical Society and the Woman's Musical Club hosted Chicago composers' concerts that featured music by both women and men. In the late teens, Fergus launched herself headlong into the music-club scene, frequently appearing as a "composer-pianist" at the Birchwood Morning Musicals and the

Rogers Park Women's Club. She often performed for the Lake View Musical Society, the Woman's Musical Club, and the Musicians Club of Women. In the teens and twenties, Fergus often gave recitals with a singer; her concerts featured piano works, songs (her own or those of others), and poems that she spoke to music. When appearing alone, Fergus was more likely to present a program entirely of her story poems. Several of Fergus's compositions required a larger ensemble, including one or more violins, and there were a number of performers who regularly appeared with her during the 1920s. Beatrice Ives Welles (mother of Orson Welles, to whom Fergus taught piano lessons), poet Faith van Valkenburgh Vilas, or Edward Clarke often recited Fergus's melodramatic setting of Alfred Noyes's "The Highwayman," which had a difficult piano accompaniment and thus could not be performed by its composer alone.[25] Fergus also traveled to give concerts in Iowa, Wisconsin, and elsewhere in Illinois; in March 1921 she performed her own compositions at the Milwaukee Art Institute, with five other female musicians. In smaller towns, women's events were held at a local church or civic club; Fergus's engagement for the Women's Club in Galesburg, Illinois, at the Elks Club was publicized in newspapers for several days beforehand, attended by several hundred women, and positively reviewed in the press afterward.

The name Fergus used for her compositions—*story poems*—did not emerge immediately. Early publicity refers to her spoken-word pieces with various terms: *pianologues, monologs, cantillations, musical readings,* or *recitations at the piano.* However, Fergus came to prefer *story poem* and used the expression consistently from 1917 on. Prose fragments on a page inserted into one of the composer's scrapbooks, perhaps part of a draft of a letter to publisher Theodore Presser, requested "to have, please, Story Poems with musical settings by P.F. on the cover." Fergus insisted that "I am trying to make this title phrase my own. I do not want to interfere with others who have used musical illustration or pianologues as their classification."[26] Fergus's attempt to disassociate herself from *pianologues*—she reportedly hated the term—was probably because of its reputation as a piece with minimal musical significance, merely improvised or requiring little pianistic ability.[27]

Fergus was listed on programs, not as someone who "read to music," but as a "Composer" or a "Composer-Pianist." Although story poems might be light in character, they were heard in recitals alongside a wide range of classical pieces, including a Beethoven piano trio, songs by Schumann, the "Habanera" from Bizet's *Carmen*, as well as numerous art songs. Fergus clearly wanted her story poems to be considered worthy musical compositions, not mere entertainment; she stressed that although some of her compositions were humorous, all had "a tendency toward something better in music than an accompanied monologue."[28] By publicizing her spoken-word compositions with an unusual generic label, the *story poem*, Fergus also distinguished herself from other women who were composing melodramatic works.

After 1918, Fergus's programming of story poems increased, perhaps because she discovered that they were the most popular pieces on the mixed recitals of her compositions. Although Fergus had been receiving regular press publicity, that year saw the publication of the most substantial notice of her efforts. Surprisingly, it was not a review of one of her concerts but rather an article about a vaudeville performance at the Majestic Theater that included "crieuse" Janet Adair performing pianologues accompanied by a Miss Adelphi. The reviewer, Amy Leslie, found the vaudevillian's material poor, and suggested a remedy in the form of Fergus's story poems, despite their high-art status:

> If Miss Adair would look up[,] say, the delicious balladry of Phyllis Fergus, a modest but most unusual young person whose creative genius has attracted the observation of the salon and symphony providers, the Adair repertoire would be deepened and widened and no loss of vogue could be threatened. Miss Fergus writes almost sensationally original and choice etudes and flowering songs with delicious accompaniments especially designed for the art of parlando singing. And whilst most of her songs are too exalted in poesy and musicianly endowment to be at all appropriate for regular vaudeville exploitation, still the clever people who put over conversation rhythmically set to music could find among the Fergus songs much exquisite and humorous as well as unique material. . . . Many of them are finding applause in concert and special, restricted performances, principally because of their beautiful music rather than the recitations belonging to the inspiration of the score.[29]

Fergus obviously valued Leslie's praise, for she reprinted the review several times on her publicity flyers, albeit somewhat edited, tellingly omitting any reference to the vaudeville performers who inspired the original publication.

Fergus developed a core repertoire of twenty-five story poems that she programmed consistently yet flexibly; with her regular appearances in and around Chicago, she clearly came to know what worked with audiences. She typically performed four to six story poems together, occasionally as many as eight or ten. Sometimes pieces were grouped according to subject matter, labeled "Grandmother Group," "Child (or Boy) Group," "Grownup Group," or "Darkey Group" (Fergus's settings of texts with African American dialect). Fergus often closed her concerts with more serious works, including her setting of Edmund Vance Cooke's sentimental "The Old Chest Upstairs" and pieces with additional instrumentation: "Thoughts" (by Robert Browning) and "Radiance," both of which had violin obbligato, and "Day Dreams" for speaker, contralto, two violins, and piano, considered an "interesting novelty" by reviewers when the composer introduced it in the early 1920s. "The Highwayman," "Thoughts," and "The Old Chest Upstairs" were sometimes listed as "dramatic readings," not story poems, as they partook of more of a nineteenth-century aesthetic than the texts that the composer usually chose to set.[30]

Most of Fergus's story poems were published in the teens and twenties, including some that rarely appeared on her programs, and she furthered the distribution of her compositions through Lyon and Healy piano rolls.[31] In the same year that Fergus appeared with Peycke, she began performing in afternoon recitals in the company's Chicago hall. At least nine story poems were transferred to piano rolls, as was *The Highwayman*, which was still in manuscript. One program advertised the availability of Fergus's compositions in Lyon and Healey's sheet-music department and provided her testimonial praising Duo-Art rolls: "It seemed quite as though I were at the piano, except that I could now read my Story Poems with greater freedom and ease than ever before."[32] Fergus's association with Lyon and Healy apparently lasted for some years; she appeared in a Cleveland recital sponsored by the company in 1932.[33]

Reviews of Fergus's performances commented positively on her story poems and described both the pieces and the experience of hearing the composer perform them as "delightful" and "charming." Many reviews stressed her "marvelously vital stage personality";[34] thus, her compositional abilities were sometimes overshadowed by her "magnetic" performer's persona. The *Kenosha Evening Herald* considered Fergus's "lovely voice" to be a natural gift[35] with no relationship to elocutionary study, and its beauty was instead favorably compared to that of singers.[36] The act of speaking, rather than singing, made Fergus's performances seem more of a direct outpouring of her "clever personality," which made her "a charming entertainer,"[37] and her individualized "manner of rendition . . . peculiar to herself"[38] was a frequent theme in the press. A description of Fergus's performance at a salon concert hosted by the Clarkes stressed her physical appearance over her creative powers, suggesting that her body was the artwork: "As she sat there, with her face tipped toward her audience, she was indeed herself a story poem, and that a very lovely one."[39]

Although Fergus's successful performance of story poems was directly linked to her abilities as a composer, reviewers found it necessary to couch descriptions of her music in terms that highlighted her feminine gender, incorporating analogies to women's clothing or accessories. One reviewer described how, "as she fitted each musical background about the poem she was illustrating, it was like putting a jewel in a filigreed setting."[40] The *Evening Mail* described her "dainty, elusive accompaniments,"[41] and the *Hollywood News* likened them to lace, "characterized by an airy delicacy and fascinating lacelike charm."[42] Fergus herself drew on a gendered analogy when she compared the process leading from initial inspiration to composing to dressmaking in an interview in the *Chicago Daily News*: "Writing music is like making a dress. It seems easy enough to pin the dress together, but unless you take small stitches, unless you put it together so it will stay, unless you complete your job your first pinning process is futile. So it is with composing music. I hear the same phrase over and over and over again. It beats and beats until I am forced to write it down. That is the inspiration, but after that the work begins. The stitching, the sewing, the putting together."[43]

Some reviews stressed the breadth of emotion in Fergus's repertoire—"Accompaniments ran the gamut of humor, tenderness and pathos and all had a deep human appeal"[44]—and described enthusiastic audience responses. Articles underscored the human insights of her chosen texts, and, as for Chautauqua readers, the uplifting nature of her selections. The Galesburg clubwoman who introduced Fergus told the waiting audience that she "presents the joyous side of life, emphasizing the happiness and pretty part of all her works."[45] Wesley La Violette described how Fergus's "storiettes" each had a point or a moral to it, created through her "keen sympathetic insight," and found her pieces "filled with the sheer joy of living" that provided "refreshing philosophy after a day of toil and burdens."[46] The satirical humor of Fergus's compositions was recognized but infrequently; the *Musical Leader*'s comment that her works "invariably have a punch to them" was atypical.[47] The report that Fergus "invariably has her audiences laughing, crying, chuckling, and delighted by turns through the period of her program when they beg and call for more"[48] might seem exaggerated, but given the number of return engagements she received and the four decades she performed her own compositions, Fergus clearly knew how to develop a rapport with her audiences.[49]

Beginning in the late 1920s, Fergus began to assume leadership roles in the clubs in which she was involved. The bulk of her compositions date from before this period, and it seems that her increased level of club activity resulted in a reduced compositional output. However, Fergus's activism benefited American women musicians and composers; she served on the board of the Women's Symphony Orchestra in Chicago and as music director and then the first musician president of the National League of American Pen Women.[50] In the 1930s she organized a series of high-profile events for women composers, including a concert at Chicago's Century of Progress Exposition and several more in Washington, DC, including one at the White House for First Lady Eleanor Roosevelt, as well as similar events in Miami, San Diego, and elsewhere. Although Fergus generally did not program her own compositions on these concerts, her Pen Women experiences did provide venues outside of Chicago for her to perform story poems; for example, she shared a concert with Amy Beach for the Mozart Club of Jamestown, New York, in 1934. Although Fergus was less active on the national front in her later years, she maintained a regular presence in Chicago's cultural life, continuing to perform into the 1950s for the various clubs at which she had appeared in previous decades.

## Frieda Peycke and "Music That Speaks, Words That Sing"

Frieda Peycke (figure 9.2) worked even harder than Phyllis Fergus to separate herself from any traces of an elocutionary past. As late as 1944 Peycke assured readers of the *Seattle Post-Intelligencer* that her art was "in no way the old fashioned idea of elocution." Her longtime friend Frederick Gamble recalled, "She *was* a diseuse, but as she saw it *never* an 'elocutionist' nor one who recited 'monologues.'"[51] From her youth, the composer was familiar with spoken-word performance. As a piano student at the Chicago Conservatory in 1907, she played interludes between the solo performances of two plays on a "Dramatic Recital" by female students of the School of Expression, and the following year she participated in a concert at her brother's Los Angeles home at which a woman recited Poe's "The Raven."[52] Like Fergus, Peycke did not rely on the terminology used by previous reciters, instead marketing her performances with the phrase *Music that speaks—Poems that sing*. Press reports sometimes called her a *pianologist*, but it was not a term she used; in her letters, Peycke referred to her compositions as *numbers* (or more informally, *my things*).

That writers felt they had to present an explanation of Peycke's "most unusual career" and the differing versions of how she came to pursue her musically illustrated readings suggest that by the middle of the twentieth century, accompanied recitation had fallen from collective memory.[53] Gamble, who penned Peycke's obituary, explained that she had abandoned her career as a pianist to perform her own compositions: "She wanted to present her own works in person. . . . Thus, she developed the musical reading into such a successful art form that it literally took her around the world giving performances."[54] A 1948 article attributed Peycke's career to her lack of facility as a singer: "Miss Frieda Peycke . . . wanted to sing but instead of a singing voice she possessed, instead, a beautiful speaking voice. . . . She asked herself: Why not accompany my talking as I would have accompanied my singing?"[55] Potential agents did not always know what to make of Peycke, sidestepping the issue by referring to her as an "artist." She once instructed Gamble to tell publisher Harold Flammer that "when you hear me, you too may say she's neither fish, fruit, nor fowl."[56] Gamble wrote publicity for his friend that avoided any explanation altogether, stressing her "amazing, magnetic personality" and her "singular capacity to entertain."[57]

Because Peycke produced some of the most substantial accompaniments for spoken-word performances, press descriptions often emphasized the musical

Figure 9.2. Frieda Peycke. John Hay Library, Brown University.

aspects of her style. One newspaper described how "she chooses contemporary poetry or prose, composes music which fits the mood of her selection, and then in a voice called 'hauntingly lovely,' tells—not sings—the story as she plays her own accompaniment. While the melody and the words complement each other, the music is complete in itself and is used by other pianists simply as solo material."[58] Peycke's manuscripts reveal that she sometimes added new texts to a freestanding accompaniment or to one she had composed for another poem; however, there is no evidence that her pieces were ever performed as solo piano works. Clearly, music was to be considered central to her art; Peycke's own flyers billed her first as a composer and second as an *interpreter*, the term that had come to replace *elocutionist, reader,* or *reciter*. Peycke sometimes used "Composer-Entertainer," perhaps because it was unclear to prospective listeners what "interpretation" was. In spite of denying her relationship to elocution, Peycke conceived of her performances as her personal interpretation of the texts she was presenting. When she introduced her 1948 recording of "Foes," she credited the poem to Maurine Hathaway, then added, "the musical setting and interpretation of Frieda Peycke." The musical setting was her composition, the interpretation, her spoken performance. In this she followed in an elocutionary tradition, long after such practices had fallen from favor.

Peycke's first compositions, songs and character pieces, were heard on her programs as early as 1906, although she may have written songs for vaudeville as a teenager.[59] She moved to Southern California around 1910 and became active in the musical life of Los Angeles, sometimes appearing on concerts that featured female readers. Peycke was a member of several concert companies, although none seemed to last for more than one season. In 1912 she appeared with the Golden State Concert Company, which included a male violinist and a female reader who gave serious selections.[60] The group gave ten concerts around the country at the "reading rooms" for employees of the Santa Fe Railway.[61] Peycke also briefly managed the Elite Concert Company: a soprano, tenor, pianist, cornetist, and Helen Field, a nine-year-old who gave musical readings.[62] Peycke's first solo programs as a composer fashioned her as a performer for children similar to Kitty Cheatham; the press described her performances as having "warm human appeal that reaches straight to the heart in the body of a child; and the child heart in the grown up body."[63] As early as 1910, reviewers hailed Peycke as "a true artist, in a literary and musical way" and found her new pianologues or recitations with music to be "clever things."[64] Peycke had found her niche, and for the rest of her career she focused on spoken-word compositions. Although in later years she sometimes shared programs with other musicians, providing a single group of four or five of her pieces, Peycke most often gave concerts performing alone. Like Fergus's pieces, Peycke's offerings were considered to be not only "unfailingly delightful," but appropriately "wholesome, cultured, and refined."[65]

In 1936 Peycke married George Holman, who worked in the district attorney's office, and the couple lived in Beverly Hills. Shortly after her marriage she assured Gamble that she was not abandoning her career, and, like Fergus, she used her maiden name professionally.[66] Holman died in 1942, a year after he had lost his job, and it took some time for Peycke to regain her financial stability. During this period she could not afford to print new flyers to advertise her performances, and she was particularly grateful for new students in her private studio, which helped allay some of her monetary woes. Peycke taught music throughout her career, and the home her father bought her in Los Angeles, in which she lived with her mother, had a small stage appropriate for salon-style concerts. In a 1944 letter, Peycke described a recital there as a "houseful," with "some 58 folks for the liveliest, laughingest, jolliest student-party [I] have had yet."[67] Her pupils included piano students, as well as women and children who learned to perform recitations in Peycke's style. The composer did not publish the short, simple recitations with easy piano parts, such as "The Polliwog" and "Pussy Wants a Corner," that she penned as beginning musical readings to be performed by her pupils, many of them girls, accompanying themselves.

Even though Peycke performed for mixed-gender audiences, her primary audiences were, like Fergus's, women; she appeared before women's clubs or sometimes as part of concerts sponsored by women's organizations. An early flyer lists twenty-six clubs, as well as schools and hotels, at which she had performed.[68] Much of Peycke's touring was to perform for women's groups across the country; by attending the National Federation of Music Clubs, she was able to arrange for concert opportunities in the upcoming year. After the federation's 1936 meeting in Chicago, she wrote that "the program conference opened up dates for the fall October trip."[69] In the fall of 1925 through early 1926, Peycke traveled around the world on the RMS *Carinthia*; her trip took her to China, Japan, Australia, New Zealand, India, and Egypt. She performed in Honolulu and at private events in Auckland and Hong Kong, where she was interviewed by the *South China Morning Post*.[70]

Los Angeles's civic and cultural organizations served as venues for Peycke's performances over the years, in the same way that similar Chicago organizations made Fergus's career possible. Peycke made numerous appearances at the Fine Arts Club of Pasadena and the Dominant Club, consisting of professional female musicians, as well as before church groups.[71] A 1950 letter describes her plans for a home concert for thirty church women, and she recounted doing a "stint" for forty Adventists, all female, after waiting more than an hour until their buffet was finished.[72] Although many such performances were for private groups, these could nonetheless constitute large audiences; in the mid-1940s Peycke appeared at the Ebell Club for an audience of five hundred.[73] In a 1943 letter, she recounted, "I had a nice date with the 300 businessmen of the So. Pas[adena] group Nov. 8th, and next night for the Pas[adena] Fine Arts. Have a D.A.R. Dec 1st—and so it goes."[74]

Peycke regularly performed in individuals' homes. In July 1944 a phone call summoned her to the Heydenreichs, "where I have been several times this past year to do something in the program line,—well they needed me for Sunday night next day! That meant wash and curl hair, get a dress ready, practice and drive there."[75] Peycke was typically invited by the woman of the household for an unpublicized, private event for a female audiences. In May 1945, she described how she "did [a] group which went over BEAUTIFULLY" at the home of a Mrs. Carey and twenty-four of her friends.[76] In October 1947 Peycke was engaged by a Mrs. Fay of Lake Charles, Louisiana, to appear at her home for an elaborate dinner party.[77] Peycke's first group of pieces lasted forty-five minutes, and then she returned for eight more numbers. Her Lake Charles engagement also involved several other performances: an afternoon concert for a church group, during which Peycke found that she needed to change her program to fit her audience's subdued mood, and a morning coffee for "younger married friends" who "just ate up the fun," which she found "most gratifying." All in all, the "composer-interpreter" gave seventy numbers in three programs as well as two small groups after dinner hours. Nonetheless, in spite of what was obviously a series of musical events for the Lake Charles community, the affair remained a private offering without publicity. Peycke described how "Mrs. Fay, although she had plenty of cash is a very simple person & would allow no newspaper to cover or even *mention* the parties, however, I was paid for each one & have a yearly invitation to come back."[78] While the series of recitals Fay sponsored may not have been typical, it is indicative of a continuing women's salon culture that supported the combination of spoken word and music.

Like Fergus, Peycke considered herself a professional musician, not an amateur member of the music groups before which she performed. In 1944, she wrote that she had previously been a member of the Dominant Club, as it was "the only musical professional group," and that she was planning to rejoin.[79] The women's settings at which she appeared and their long history of amateur performance occasionally caused difficulties for Peycke, who expected to be paid for her work. She wrote to Gamble, who was struggling with his own singing career, "Yes we all love to be doing, interpreting, singing, playing individually, yet one can't keep on doing it just to be hearing oneself, a little of the 'where with all' has to come with it, to pay the Bus fares, to tip & up keep on clothes."[80] At one social event, Peycke became offended when a hostess expected her to perform on the spot, and it was not clear whether she had been invited to the occasion socially or professionally. Peycke described how Mrs. Humes asked her to entertain "the whole crowd of 50+ & I told her quietly I was a *Professional* & this was no time for it as all were *standing* & talking." The intervention of a friend did little to alleviate the awkward situation: "Then Mary came & said that was what she wanted (professionally) by my being there *but* as she had made no business arrangement, I said 'When most are gone I'll do a few for the family' & I did it—when only 10 of us were left."[81]

Frieda Peycke composed approximately 340 musical readings. At least seventy-six were published, issued by nine different publishers; approximately 264 remained in manuscript.[82] Peycke's first dated recitation was "America for Me" from 1915, a setting of a poem by Henry Van Dyke that she programmed in her appearances as late as 1948. In concerts, Peycke typically performed her compositions in topical groups of four or more, as many as eight or nine pieces at a time. Like Fergus, she sometimes grouped pieces under appropriate headings as a sort of recited cycle; the connection of a few added chords or a brief phrase on Peycke's recordings suggest in performance she may have connected separate works with improvised piano music. At the Women's Century Club Theater in Seattle in 1948, Peycke gave four sets: three groupings of five to seven pieces each, titled "Life Symbols," "Husbands—Before and After Taking," and "As Others Have Seen You," and a single extended composition.[83]

The bulk of Peycke's pieces drew on texts by living poets, some two-thirds of whom were women, such as Elizabeth Gordon, Maurine Hathaway, and Dorothy D. Miles (Collins); Peycke was personally acquainted with the latter two writers. The composer rarely selected poetry by major literary figures, drawing instead from newspapers and popular magazines, such as the *Christian Science Monitor*, *Good Housekeeping*, or *Better Homes and Gardens*. The poems would have appealed to her female audiences because they frequently dealt with courtship and love, gender differences, motherhood, marriage, children, and domestic tasks. Like Fergus's settings, many feature humorous satire of contemporary life (discussed in chapter 10). Peycke was extremely prolific during the 1920s and 1930s, and by the early 1950s she had created some 270 works from which to choose for her performances.[84] The composer was selective about which works she sent to publishers, providing them only with scores she thought were likely to find acceptance; in 1947 she wrote that she had "four new 'things' done," but only expected three of them to be published.[85] Many of the compositions that remained in manuscript nonetheless made frequent appearances on her programs.

The late 1940s were a particularly active period for Peycke. In the fall of 1946 she traveled to the East Coast to visit the publishing houses that had been issuing her music since the 1920s. The trip resulted in an interview in the *Etude*, for which Peycke later wrote an article, and the publicity generated additional interest in her music.[86] Peycke received letters originating from Texas to Washington, DC, relaying performances of her compositions; teachers requested them in music stores, and one club wanted to use her music for study.[87] The experience gave Peycke a renewed sense of confidence: "That what I have to offer is still 'tops' in anyone's basket. So there!"[88] An employee of the Flammer publishing company suggested that she engage professional management, but the Austin Wilder firm turned her down.[89]

Between around 1946 and 1948, Peycke also made recordings of eighteen of her pieces, but none was commercially released.[90] She had several recordings in hand to give to the staff of Theodore Presser when she visited the firm in October 1946; she seems to have intended her recordings more as calling cards for publishers than as a commercial venture, but found that Presser only wanted two records: "Wanted me at piano instead!"[91] Gamble explained that "masters were made, and plans were made to put them in distribution, but she never arranged for the masters to be sent to her. . . . She was interested only in composing music and performing it in public."[92] In spite of this flurry of activity, Peycke published only a few more works in the late 1940s and early '50s. Her student Marguerite Thompson Schmidt believed that musical recitation was an art form that died with Peycke, not due to a lack of potential performers, but to the commercialism of publishers who lost interest in the genre. Schmidt's comments hint that recitation to music continued to flourish among female performers in women's circles.

Peycke's earliest known appearances performing spoken-word composi-tions date from 1909, and her last documented performance was fifty years later in 1959, when she was seventy-five years old.[93] After almost five decades performing her own music, Peycke was a seasoned entertainer who knew how to please an audience. Gamble described how her performances could "light up a theatre," and Schmidt testified to her teacher's ability to hold an audience "spell-bound," writing, "Her voice, her interpretations, her compositions, along with her musicianship were something one must experience to appreci-ate."[94] Yet Peycke faced numerous audiences who had never encountered the combination of speech and music that had originated in an earlier era, and the bulk of her career took place in an environment with many alternative entertainments. She recounted receiving seven encores after her 1946 concert at the theater near Tacoma, Washington, that Gamble managed,[95] and even though the *Lakewood Log* reported that the enthusiastic listeners felt her pieces allowed them to escape from the trials of the modern world, that world was Peycke's competition. As a result, the size of the audience was very small:

> Those scattered few who listened to Frieda Peycke at the Lakewood Theater the other evening came away feeling that, instead of listening to a mere Words & Music lady, they were carried off into a dreamy, delightful world of fact & fantasy, that is good for this over-specialized, neurotic and over-mechanized world we try to live in. Next day, they all greeted Fred Gamble. "Freddie we MUST have Miss Peycke come back." . . . Poor night for Peycke. Terrace closed. Republican convention downtown. Monday hangover. Rainy day. Hot stuff on the Radio.[96]

Peycke's and Fergus's decision to specialize in spoken-word composition and performance was central to their professional success. The women's organiza-tions before which they appeared influenced the composers' choice of texts, and the topics of some poems had their roots in previous reciters' repertoire. Although their publications list the names of the poets they selected to set to music, audiences who came to hear the two women were there to experience their entertaining personalities and music. Musical accompaniments were no longer a secondary addition to spoken literature by great authors, but were the product of professional musicians, to be heard within a concert setting. Fergus and Peycke did not present themselves as the voice of the poet, but were first and foremost composers of a musical art form.

# 10. Women's Work, Women's Humor

## Musical Recitations by Female Composers

All smokeless stands brooding the large pompous man
And a lady in triumph waves softly her fan.
—Grace Ada Brown, "The Red Fan"

The Red Fan Recital took place on April 21, 1896, in the chamber music room of New York's Carnegie Hall. Organized by composer Nettie Arthur Brown, the event featured California elocutionist Marion Short performing to Brown's piano accompaniments. The *New York Times* recounted that the audience was made up of "artists, readers, and musicians, with a sprinkling of society people," and attendees were listed in the society pages, suggesting that the concert was considered a women's event.[1] Instead of Brown's compositions, the *Musical Courier* emphasized the "red fans of various sizes" and "beautiful palms and rare plants" that decorated the stage, setting off the performers' white attire. The writer described the entertainment as pretty, adding, almost as an afterthought, that it was an "artistic success."[2] Nonetheless, Nettie Arthur Brown considered the premiere of her composition *The Red Fan* at Carnegie Hall that day to be the climax of her brief career.[3] The composer seems not to have been well known in musical circles, although she had served as an accompanist to readers and was a member of various women's literary clubs as well as suffrage societies. Her accompanied recitations represented collaboration with a relative, poet Grace Ada Brown. *The Red Fan*, and two other melodramatic compositions, *The Idyl of an Orchard* and *The Sea*, were advertised in *Werner's Magazine* and taken up by other reciters. *The Red Fan* was the most prominent of the three; one commentator noted in poetry: "And where is the woman, child or man, / Unknown to the tricks of the pert red fan?"[4] Nettie subsequently married a man involved in piano manufacturing and died at age

fifty; most of her compositions remained unpublished, including a suggestively
titled work, *Miss Independence*, "an ideal sketch of a modern woman."[5]

Although reports of Brown's concert downplayed its musical and literary
content, the text of *The Red Fan* celebrates feminine power, and the red fans
decorating Carnegie's recital hall were not mere decoration, but a symbol of
women's increasing influence in the public sphere. Based on an actual incident
at a theatrical carnival, the poem tells how the irritating smoke produced by
a pompous cigar-toting man, accompanied by his meek wife, is sent back to
him by a silent yet powerful woman wielding a red fan:

> I can still see her dark eyes indignant and bright,
> And his victims—their faces aglow with delight!—
> The music is throwing off billows of sound,
> As a smoke-puff goes curling now up now around;
> But before it can reach to the tip of the nose
> Of the bright little lady straight backward it goes,

Brown's triple-meter music jauntily supports the rhythmic recitation of the
comedic text.[6] The accompaniment temporarily moves into the minor mode
and becomes subdued as the speaker's attention turns to the elegant ladies
dancing on the carnival stage: "So soft seems the music so far so complete /
The stars might be singing their way to our feet." The change in mood for this
deliberately romantic poeticism contrasts the subsequent outburst of music
accompanying the harsh return of the wafting smoke, making the passage even
more humorous. The conflict then escalates as the woman

> unfurls that great fan like a red flag of war,
> And wavering and trembling the smoke flies before;
> It wreaths in his hair and encircles his head,—
> His shocked wife leans near him and something is said!
> At last he has learned,—that wonderful man!
> The tricks of the lady who bears the red fan.
> He glares at her wildly,—"Can such things be true?
> Is this not a free country?—what can a man do!
> Is not the air free to pollute if one can?
> What means the small lady who holds the red fan?"

Swirling piano figuration paints the puffing smoke, and the regular musical
phrase structure breaks down briefly for the insertion of fanfare-like motives
after the unfurling of the "red flag." The end of the poem celebrates the power
of the nameless, silent woman, who has won the battle simply by using the ac-
cessory that represents her femininity. The final verse of text is unaccompanied,
except for a cadential phrase beneath its last line, quoted in the epigraph above,

underscoring the woman's success. The text's emphasis on a single woman's power could be further magnified in performance, as advertisements suggested speaking the work chorally or having multiple girls with red fans pantomime to a single reciter; such group performances would imply that *all* women had the potential to wield the power of the lady with the fan.[7]

*The Red Fan* was a forerunner to the compositions created by women in the following decades, both in its humor and in the way it emphasized women's agency without indulging in previous sentimentality. Given the widespread use of accompaniments for recitations by elocutionists late in the nineteenth century, it is not surprising that women composers began to produce fully notated melodramatic pieces. Performers such as Emma Dunning Banks had published poems with suggested accompaniments, and female musicians were naturally attracted to combining music with popularly recited works, such as those of Longfellow or Dunbar. Women who had musical training began to compose their own musical settings. Laura Sedgwick Collins (1859–1927), a reciter as well as a dancer and singer, studied composition with Antonín Dvořák during his New York residency.[8] Her advertisements reported that she "composes and arranges Music for, and gives instruction in Readings, Recitations, Pantomime, Voice."[9] Collins composed a setting for the poem "A Foolish Little Maiden" by Harriette Hammond, found in period recitation books;[10] although its vocal line was notated as a melody to be sung, some women performed this work as accompanied recitation. Like the collaboration of Grace and Nettie Brown, female musicians who worked with reciters sometimes produced melodramatic compositions: Jane Manner's diary records that in 1909 she performed spoken songs by Mary Ehrman with the composer playing her accompaniment, and Evanston, Illinois, composer Sadie Knowland Coe (1864–1906) published a setting of Longfellow's *Hiawatha* that she tried out with and dedicated to Isabel Garghill Beecher.[11]

More than half of the approximately five hundred published English-language melodramas that can be documented from 1890 to 1935 were composed by women. Although by far the most compositions in the genre originated from the pens of Phyllis Fergus and Frieda Peycke, in America more than thirty female composers contributed to the genre after World War I. Clayton Summy's brochure for "Readings with Music and Melodramas" listed compositions by seventeen women and nine men and featured photos of four female composers on the cover: Fergus, Peycke, Natalie Whitted Price, and Mary Wyman Williams.[12] While most women composers published pieces in the teens and twenties, a few continued to create spoken-word pieces into the middle of the twentieth century.

Texts set by women composers, quite often penned by women poets, were clearly intended to be shared with female audiences. Rather than serious poetry by male writers—the great literature for which the culturally ambitious elocutionists of the previous century had advocated—twentieth-century female composers more often selected lighter, topical poetry, and their compositions were referred to by terminology that lacked any suggestion of the emotional excesses of melodrama: *musical readings, recitations with music, song-recitations,* or occasionally *musical monologues* or *cantillations.* These pieces tended to be brief, relaying anecdotes rather than the more complex stories found in elocutionary literature. Some of the texts that women set markedly resemble the popular poetry of the parlor anthologies of the 1890s, while others are products of the times during which they were written. The accompanied recitations in Werner's 1911 *Musical Effects* are evidence of the transition in literary content as Victorian values waned, with many texts expressing nostalgia for "an idealized homeplace . . . in which a wise and loving mother was on guard,"[13] as described by Nan Johnson, as a result of the recognition of modern, urban industrialization, also a common Chautauqua theme. Some of the later compositions published by women were settings of poems that were popular on the Chautauqua circuit.[14] Many texts originally appeared in magazines and newspapers, and they treat women's lives with modern humor. While the pieces' accompaniments establish a mood, their comedic tone is more often in their words than in their music; a frequent exception occurs at their close where the musical accompaniment is varied to punctuate a climactic punch line.

Most of the women who published spoken-word compositions were not well known. Many, like Fergus and Peycke, were involved with women's clubs. Others were teachers whose output consisted largely of pedagogical materials for children. Some prolific European composers, such as Guy d'Hardelot or Liza Lehmann, produced a small number of spoken-word compositions that were performed in the United States.[15] American composer Mana-Zucca (1885–1981), a concert pianist who sang light opera, also fell into this category; her prolific activity included five pieces published as "songs or recitations."[16] Given that many women who authored musical recitations composed only a small handful of such works, it seems probable that some spoken-word compositions remained unpublished. For example, Iowa composer Tina B. Cornic copyrighted a "song or musical reading" titled "Jilted," but it was never commercially issued.[17] Even the prolific Peycke published only a small portion of her musically illustrated readings. Although one might speculate that their unusual scoring made such works less publishable, according to Christopher Reynolds, many female composers of conventional songs created many more works than actually went to press during this era.[18] In addition, some of the spoken-word compositions from the early twentieth century by men had highly gendered content, suggesting that they were intended for female performers and/or audiences.

Surprisingly, unpublished compositions with spoken words appear in the early output of two major modernist composers: Marion Bauer and Ruth Crawford Seeger. Bauer set six texts melodramatically, including brief poems by Robert Browning, Robert Hillyer, Florence Coates, and Charles Kingsley. Most of these works are from around 1912, but at least one dates from as late as 1953. Though several were dedicated to the actors Paul Leyssac and Claude Rains, all remained unpublished.[19] Bauer's approach to two longer texts, Matthew Arnold's *The Forsaken Merman* and Robert Lowell's *The Relief of Lucknow* was similar to that of turn-of-the-century melodramas, and her labeling of her contributions had a relationship to elocutionary genres: the manuscript of *The Relief of Lucknow* (1912), a setting of a frequently anthologized recitation, reveals Bauer wavering about its genre, as its cover lists three designations: "Lyric Readings," "Declamations," and "Recitations."[20] The piece shows evidence of the practice of incorporating known works into accompanied recitation in its inclusion of the songs "The Campbells Are Coming" and "Auld Lang Syne," which are played in the poem by Scottish Highlanders coming to rescue colonists during the Indian Rebellion of 1857.

In contrast, Ruth Crawford Seeger's one melodramatic piece demonstrates a more modernist approach. While a student in Chicago studying composition with Adolf Weidig (who also taught Fergus and Peycke), Crawford Seeger composed *The Adventures of Tom Thumb* (1925), an extended piano work with its fairy-tale text for narrator notated above the staves.[21] Crawford Seeger's composition resembles a suite of character pieces interspersed with narration more than a melodrama. While her music does reflect the story's dramatic character, many movements are only preceded by text, thus large parts of the tale of the tiny boy are unaccompanied by music. *Tom Thumb*'s dissonant harmonic language, as well as its greater length, separate it from the shorter, conventionally tonal works of the composer's female contemporaries, although its child-appropriate topic was similar to those of some women's pieces. Despite the differences between their individual approaches, both Bauer's and Crawford Seeger's works should nonetheless be understood within their wider context: in America, melodramatic performance and composition had become primarily a woman's art form.

More typically, the works marketed as musical readings were circulated as sheet music and were sometimes created by women who primarily produced songs. As Reynolds has noted, the four decades that began with the 1890s saw a tremendous outpouring of songs by female composers;[22] the appearance of melodramatic compositions by women during this period is clearly related to the increased societal acceptance of them as creative artists, albeit in small genres. Indeed, many of the compositions scored for speaker and piano are simple settings with technically easy accompaniments to facilitate performance of both text and music by one person, not unlike popular songs. Women's compositions were frequently in strophic, sectional, or AABA song forms. Many were easy enough for amateurs; as the *Farmer's Wife* noted in 1925, "Musical readings are very popular with our readers because nearly everyone, with practice, can learn to give them creditably."[23] Although elocutionists such as Jane Manner and others left records of speaking particular songs to their accompaniments, it is impossible to determine how many other compositions seemingly intended to be sung were performed as musical recitations instead. In his attempts to promote the genre, Summy advertised many songs by Jessie L. Gaynor (1863–1921) and others as being suited to adaptation for recitation. Other publishers, hoping for a wider market than elocutionists, labeled compositions as *encore songs* and provided a melodic line for a singer, thus guaranteeing flexibility of performance format; some of Peycke's works were given singable vocal lines above the piano part retroactively, even though they were originally intended to be spoken. What separated encore songs from conventional songs was a narrative text and/or a comedic tone that made them more appropriate for speaking than singing.[24]

Women composers abandoned the previous melodramatic aesthetic for comedic visions of the modern age, yet their compositions do sometimes retain a sentimental tone; however, the extremes of emotion associated with death and loss were tempered into nostalgia, largely for childhood or youth. There are numerous sentimental texts about grandmothers, largely relayed from the perspective of grandchildren. The emphasis on morality and spirituality in women's post–World War I compositions might seem to be a continuation of nineteenth-century ideals, functioning to serve as prescriptive guidelines for feminine behavior, but the works female composers produced also advocate determination and persistence, encouraging women's personal strengths. The frequent tragedy of nineteenth-century recitations is replaced by day-to-day experiences specific to women's lives, often treated humorously. The texts composers selected are sometimes portrayals of women that draw on gender stereotypes, but they usually feature ironic twists, which provide, if not a feminist perspective, one that is clearly a woman's view of the contemporary world and its situations.

Courtship, marriage, and children, often at the center of texts selected by female composers, are treated from women's perspectives; some works have underlying messages emphasizing the power women have in relationships with men. Domesticity and marriage are rarely romanticized—rather, they are frequently presented satirically. An early example of the typical critique of men's mistreatment of women is found in the only recitation in *Musical Effects* with a full piano accompaniment, "Only a Man" from the play *Jumping Jupiter,* and the topic reappears in later women's compositions.[25] Draw-

ing on the child dialect of earlier texts, other pieces emphasize the freedoms
of boyhood, sometimes with the underlying critical implication that societal
conditions for girls are unnecessarily restrained. Numerous pieces by women
contain texts that would make them appropriate for children, in part because
children whom women taught performed and/or heard these works. However,
the sophistication of some of the compositions, such as those of Fergus and
Peycke, indicates that their seemingly child-appropriate topics were actually
aimed at adult performers and audiences.

Phyllis Fergus's compositional output demonstrates the stylistic changes
that occurred in melodramatic compositions in the hands of women composers.
Her setting of Alfred Noyes's *The Highwayman* for voice and orchestra was
her only extended work in a previous vein.[26] Programmed in Fergus's concerts
as early as 1917, the piece was labeled a *melodrama* when it was published
in a piano reduction in 1926, and it resembles the settings of Longfellow or
Poe by her male contemporaries Rossetter G. Cole and Arthur Bergh. *The
Highwayman*'s virtuous heroine chooses the moral goodness of a redeeming
death, shooting herself to warn her highwayman lover of the soldiers who await
him, and thus providing the tale's decidedly melodramatic flavor. In Fergus's
setting, specific musical gestures are used to depict events in the poem: the
highwayman's whip tapping on the window is created with staccato sixteenth
notes (m. 82), the landlord's daughter's falling hair is heard in tumbling arpeggiation (m. 147), repeated chords sound the clock striking midnight (m. 223),
and ostinato figures represent distant horses' hooves (mm. 235–36). Longer
thematic material in a vigorous 6/8 meter is heard for the riding highwayman,
and an evocative passage returns with the refrain that mentions moonlight,
articulating a large-scale form that is directly related to the dramatic action.

In contrast, Fergus's approximately sixty story poems have music that creates moods and can be closely related to the rhythms of the spoken texts, but is
primarily accompanimental, not depictive. These pieces range in their level of
complexity from works set strophically with technically unchallenging piano
accompaniments to lyrical character pieces that might almost be heard on their
own, without spoken text. Fergus's compositions are more pianistic, more
wide-ranging harmonically, and more chromatic than those of many other
women. Her melodic gifts are apparent in her accompaniments, though her
melodies seldom amount to tunes that could be sung in place of the recitation,
as was intended in some of her contemporaries' compositions. The left-hand
music of the piano is frequently chordal; the right is tuneful or chordal as
well and can meander through arpeggios or other figuration with a sometimes
speech-like rhythmic flexibility, even if the rhythm does not reflect that of the
specific text being heard. Nonetheless, Fergus's accompaniments are carefully
matched to the moods of her chosen poems, and she often paid close attention

to subtleties of textual content, reinforcing the poem's meaning through small harmonic, rhythmic, or textural changes.

Along with Frieda Peycke, Fergus produced some of the most highly developed examples of the newly transformed genre. Many other composers' accompaniments were fairly rudimentary, and their works were clearly intended for speakers who would be accompanying themselves and needed not to be encumbered by challenging piano parts; not surprisingly, one of Fergus's most popular compositions, "The Usual Way," was also one of the easiest to perform. Peycke's letters reveal that she deliberately simplified her works for an amateur audience because her more complex pieces did not always sell particularly well; she recalled telling a friend about "the many rejections I've had—the many delicious full-fisted chords . . . I deleted,—making the reading sound *most* ordinary to me . . . *But*—led to having new things asked for & *more confidence* of the publishers that my things would see to at least getting their money back."[27] Nonetheless, as Peycke was a fine pianist, her works have some of the most technically advanced accompaniments of the period's musical recitations.

Peycke's settings were remarkably consistent in style throughout the decades she was composing. Textures are consistently homophonic, based in four-part writing, sometimes varied with multi-octave arpeggios that contrast the predominantly chordal framework. Peycke's harmonic language is rich, with many chromatic turns, and sevenths and ninths, recalling the harmonies of popular songs of the period. Like Fergus's story poems, Peycke's musical recitations open with short introductions.[28] If the text to be spoken is brief, then the piece's overall form is typically through-composed, although it may have returning accompanimental figures or textures. These pieces less often rely on the strophic forms used by other composers, and many are in a ternary structure, generally with some modification to the return of the opening material. In fact, the relation of text to music is often not formally exact, such that the repetition of a subsequent verse may or may not coincide with the repetition of the music that previously accompanied it. Peycke's recordings also reveal that she sometimes also performed her pieces this way, as her text placement in recordings often does not coincide with the suggested performance of it in her notated scores.[29] Her performance practices demonstrate that her accompaniments were based in an improvisatory style, adaptable to specific performance situations; in this, they differ from the typical formal constructions of the pieces of her contemporaries.

Peycke's music is nonetheless typical of the entire genre of women's compositions in that while the piano accompaniments set the mood for the poetry to be spoken, they are designed to function more in the background of the performance, secondary to the text. In an *Etude* article, the composer described how "the first consideration is the poem itself, the music making at all times an appropriate but inconspicuous background of beauty, humor, or charm."[30] Although she claimed that "it is astonishing how greatly music can bring effects,"[31] Peycke was evidently referring to the way in which the music's character creates an overall context for the poem, as there are few overtly expressive moments within her pieces other than occasional word painting; far more occur in Fergus's music. In both women's works, modulations and distinctive harmonic changes sometimes take place because of textual content, such as turns to the minor mode for a somber mood. In Peycke's music, the accompaniment often flows quietly under the text; gestures such as arpeggiated flourishes occur mainly during introductions and in the works' final cadences. In both Fergus's and Peycke's compositions, brief chords can help emphasize individual words or lines of the text, or are heard between phrases, somewhat in the style of recitative; this most often occurs in the final line of text, where there is a joke or ironic twist, punctuated with sharply attacked chords. On occasion, short melodic motives reflect the rhythmic and pitch contours of a repeated textual phrase; however, the practice of constructing the primary melody so as to closely coincide with the syllabic construction of the spoken poetry, as occurs in some women's compositions, appears far less often in Fergus's and Peycke's pieces. Many other women's compositions are thus more tied to the style of popular song than are the freewheeling accompaniments of Peycke's compositions or the close readings of Fergus.

The bulk of women's compositions date from the 1910s and 1920s, and they occasionally demonstrate strongly anti-Victorian reactions that satirize earlier styles and practices. Fergus's "Leanore" (1919) parodies morbid, Romantic poetry (in spite of the spelling, its title may refer to Edgar Allan Poe).[32] The plaintive A minor accompaniment opens with a sweeping arpeggiation on an augmented sixth chord with passing tones, descending down the keyboard. The text, a series of darkly suggestive metaphors, is introduced over eighth notes in the pianist's right hand and a lamenting, chromatically descending bass line:

> By the road that has no ending
> To the tower without a door,
> With a hurt that has no mending,
> Will we wander, Leanore?
> Thus in words that have no meaning
> And a song without a tune,
> Will I chant, a desert's gleaning
> Sorrows of a stricken June.
> Barren fields! Gray sheaves of curses
> Bitter bread a soul's complaint.

Example 10.1. Phyllis Fergus, "Leanore" (Chicago: Clayton F. Summy, 1919), mm. 16–18.

Yet it is all tongue in cheek, for at the composition's close, the descending arpeggiation returns as the speaker asks, "Think there's no sense to these verses?," after which the accompaniment's chords quickly cadence on brighter A major as she readily admits, "Well, (Hell,) there ain't" (example 10.1).

While this work rejects overly Romanticized poetic imagery, "The Old Family Album" (1926) by Zoe Hartman and set by Harry L. Aleford openly makes fun of the previous generation of elocutionists who performed such texts.[33] Its instructions suggest that the reader wear an old-fashioned costume and peruse the family album as she describes her relatives. The text resembles those (described in chapter 6) that ridiculed cultural aspirations while imitating lower-class dialect with mispronunciations. In the final verse of the poem, set strophically with a singable vocal part, the speaker discovers a female relation in a Delsarte pose:

> There's Cousin Jane Minervy.
> Don't her eyes look wild and scary?
> She allus was play-actin'
> like a elocutionary,
> And allus dressin' up.
> We all considered her reel flighty,
> Be-cuz she liked to have her picter
> taken in her nightie
> Or in the winder curtains,
> like some female in a story
> Sometimes 'twas Cleopatrary,
> or perhaps 'twas Queen Vic-*tor*-y.

Elocution and the pretensions of high art were now to be rejected. The comedic texts that women composers selected generated works far removed from the literary aspirations of nineteenth-century elocutionists.

## Gender Troubles and Women's Humor

The most significant change between the accompanied recitations of the nineteenth century and the spoken-word pieces created by women in the twentieth is the manner in which the sentimental aesthetic was replaced by humor as the dominant means of expression. Ann Douglas has described sentimentality as being the result of powerlessness: centering on loss, it asserts wider cultural values through the very denial of what is most cherished.[34] In contrast to sentimentality's emotional devastation, humor is an expression of power.[35] "Making your own jokes is equivalent to taking control over your life," writes Gina Barecca.[36] This taking control is in contrast to nineteenth-century female characters who suffer emotionally yet remain fundamentally passive in the face of loss; by actively adopting humor as their aesthetic mode, women composers and performers challenged prevailing cultural norms. "Wit," according to Nancy Walker, "with its associative values of intelligence, perception, and irreverence," requires that prevailing societal values be overturned.[37] While the previous strategy of female elocutionists was to align themselves with established literary works, aspiring to achieve a place for women within a fundamentally masculine high culture, the humor in works by twentieth-century female composers was also related to their gender; it, too, was a means of validating their performances. Joanne Gilbert explains the paradox of humor: "Because it functions as an 'anti-rhetoric,' always disavowing its own subversive potential, humor provides the performer with a unique guarantee—the opportunity to critique with impunity." This "ensures the 'safety' of the status quo—humor, even if subversive, won't be 'taken seriously.'"[38] Musically accompanied recitations could contain underlying social critiques to varying degrees; however, any text that made audiences uncomfortable could be excused as "only" an unpretentious joke. Thus, while women escaped from a masculine literary canon in creating works that reflected their own worlds, their continuing subordinate social position required their strategic reliance on humor in order to make female voices possible.

Historically for women, as for other oppressed groups, the creation of humor represents, as Walker has written, "what it is like to try to meet standards for behavior that are based on stereotypes rather than human beings."[39] Female comics have frequently adopted what would seemingly be demeaning stereotypes in order to subvert them and reveal their oppressive nature;[40] likewise, age-old stereotypes occasionally appear in women's musical recitations: the nagging wife, inept housekeeper, lovelorn woman, or dumb-blonde types.[41] Umberto Eco writes that comic characters break through frames of expectation, here the wider cultural expectations with which women are not necessarily able to comply. The process can transform the understanding of gender roles: "But we are no longer sure that it is the character who is at fault. Maybe the frame is wrong."[42] In spoken-word pieces, as in women's comedy in general, female characters are often survivors of a "world . . . not of their making."[43] Emily Toth summarizes "the target of most humorous writing by women," also found in some musical recitations: "the social roles which imprison us all."[44]

Whereas particular works by women composers would have been appropriate for mixed-gender audiences, others seem to have been created for the female audiences of the clubs and civic organizations before which Fergus, Peycke, and others performed. Walker's description of women's humor as defining a "dialectic in which men are, in many ways, external to women's experiences"[45] is apt for many of these works. Texts that female composers chose to set often reflect an environment that is female-dominated, sometimes because of the deliberate omission of men, and also because of their focus on women's domestic position. Toth delineates the strain of women's humor based in "children, family, chores, and homemaking" that regularly appears in their compositions.[46] Having escaped her home for the women's social groups at which she might hear musical recitations performed, a woman could identify with the "frustrated, imperfect housewife" who sometimes appeared in them and gain a sense that household chores were not "crucial to determining her worth."[47]

Fergus's "It Takes," set in a modified strophic form, subverts the dumb-female stereotype. Its text is seemingly misogynistic, as each verse documents examples of a woman's childish, impractical behavior—shopping without intending to make purchases, returning Christmas presents, dressing in chiffon during winter, traveling without enough money for food—and concludes with the condescending phrase, "Well, it takes a girl to do it every time!" It is not clear who wrote the first verse of text, but Fergus herself penned the remainder, including a closing stanza that undermines the poem's initial outlook on women. In the end, men are criticized for imposing domestic chores on women, who are finally vindicated as the speaker concludes with pride that it takes a girl to calm a crying baby:

> When a man goes to housekeeping his planning is unique
> His finding work for others is sublime
> But to stop the baby crying, and send it off to sleep? Sh!
> Well, it takes a girl to do it every time!

The regular four-measure phrase structure of the accompaniment is broken up by an extra measure to accommodate piano figuration that rises and falls two octaves; this allows for text to be drawn out an additional four beats in verses 1 and 3, and in two instances it provides a dramatic pause before the refrain, "Well, it takes a girl to do it every time!" In the final verse, the descending arpeggio accompanies the "Sh!" as the girl comes into the power of her maternal role.

Peycke's "Telephone Order of a Young Bride" (1932) is also typical of the domestic humor in which women are portrayed as stereotypically incompetent.[48] In the text, the distracted young woman mooning over her new husband incompetently phones to order groceries: "I just can't plan a dinner when I'm thinking of his eyes." The accompanying music is dominated by staccato syncopations, Scotch snaps, and grace-note figures, creating a humorous tone. When the woman requests thirty cans of pancakes and asks if they come "already fried," she causes the shocked grocer to fall dead, a surprise underscored with the tonic chord made dissonant by an added flat sixth scale degree.[49] Although in "Telephone Order" any critique of the overwhelming domestic situation in which the poor young woman has found herself is only implied, in Peycke's "Red Slippers" (1932), the conflict between women's wishes and their restrictions are more overt.[50] The speaker longs for the freedom of gypsy travel, yet cannot escape her chores, confiding, "But I keep my house as slick as a pin, and you'd never guess the turmoil within." The accompaniment, with habanera rhythms and imitation of castanets through disjunct intervals decorated by grace notes, has the flavor of the exotic world for which the speaker longs. However, the tonal stasis of the accompaniment—it is a full fourteen bars into the piece before the harmony changes—suggests the unrelenting tasks of the woman's life. The flat sixth in the accompanimental pattern provides a dissonance that is as painful as it is exotic, a call that the woman is unable to answer. The music suggests that, at least in spirit, the woman manages to transcend the limitations of her life: the refrain that describes her lone rebellious act—"But I wear red slippers while I work"—is heard to a full cadence both times it is spoken at the piece's close and is marked "half singing, mischievously"; the final postlude is to be performed "with gay abandon."

Peycke's setting of "Dame Fashion" (1924) likewise satirizes conventional expectations for women through questioning the power that fashion has over them. The answer to "Who Is Dame Fashion?" is "nobody knows," even though women follow "her" directions explicitly in their dress. Just as women are regularly forced to transform their appearance, the accompaniment's textures change at breaks in the poetic verses, every four or eight bars, in a varied series of musical ideas that repeats midway through the work. The accompaniment's melodic gestures rhythmically coincide with the five syllables in the question about fashion central to the text, and chordal interjections emphasize particular moments in a manner not unlike recitative, such as the interjection "Fashion has spoken: 'go, alter your clothes!'" (example 10.2).

The private and public worlds of women meet in Henry S. Sawyer's setting of Lytton Cox's "The Ladies' Aid" (1923).[51] Its text praises women's roles in

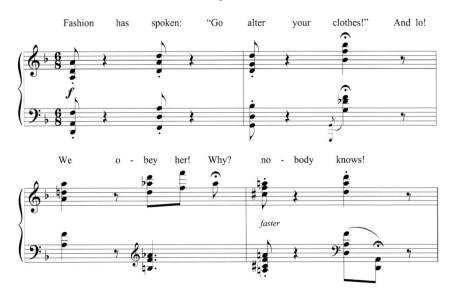

Example 10.2:
DAME FASHION, mm. 48–51
Words and Music by JAMES FOLEY and FRIEDA PEYCKE
©1927 (Renewed) CLAYTON F. SUMMY CO.
All Rights Administered by WB MUSIC CORP.
All Rights Reserved
Used by Permission of ALFRED MUSIC

social organizations, recounting the ways in which their domestic skills can
be brought to bear for the problems facing a church congregation, while lam-
pooning men's inabilities. Set to a lively, tuneful, dotted-rhythm allegretto,
the strophic, three-verse musical reading humorously describes the multiple
activities of the church ladies' aid society. The score's commentary reveals
that the piece is not satirizing the women it presents, noting: "Every audience
enjoys a joke on the *men*."[52] The text stresses that women's stereotypical roles
enable them to achieve what the men cannot:

> There's a refuge never failing for the ills of all the ailing,
> For the burdens that the men folk cannot budge;
> It will make the kettle bubble, pay the debts that vex and trouble
> With a dinner for five hundred or a nickel's worth of fudge.
> When the church bell gets to cracking or the carpet needs some tacking,
> When the sidewalk suddenly begins to sag,
> If the organ wants some tuning or the steeple vines lack pruning,
> If the workers in the vineyard start to linger and to lag.
> When the parson's coat gets shiny, or his missus needs new chiny,

And the int'rest on the mortgage must be paid,
All the brethren in a hurry pass up any further worry
And present the matter to the Ladies' Aid.

Men are all too happy to transfer the church's work to women, who "always bag the bacon" but "never rock the boat." The final verse concludes, "The men just putter round a bit, then on the shelf are laid" in poor comparison to the Ladies' Aid. The piece's instructions suggest that it can be spoken as a musical monologue, or given as a song or a costumed sketch involving several women, with the verse taken by the "ladies' aid president" and the chorus by the society's members.

## The Usual Way: Courtship and Marriage

Romance and marriage are recurring topics in compositions by women, presented as situations in which women necessarily find themselves, despite the problems and limitations of their relationships with men. The texts that Phyllis Fergus chose to set frequently show women as having a higher degree of agency than the more typical scenario in which they merely wait passively to be wooed. Fergus produced several humorous story poems consisting of depictions of courtship that take place outside of the domestic sphere in the natural world and utilizing popular conceptions of lovers in idyllic, pastoral settings. In "Two Fishers" (1915), a couple goes fishing to the dainty accompaniment of sixteenth-note triplets in the upper register of the piano, evoking imagery of ripples of water. Although the fish don't bite, the "baiter is baited" when "Miss Betsy" is placed in the masculine fisherman's role and "catches a 150-pounder," marked by triplet arpeggiation descending to the bass of the piano. "The Canoe" (1916) depicts lovers floating romantically to chains of parallel thirds ascending in the right hand of the piano. As the meter changes from 3/4 to 2/4, the speaker lists the possible outcomes for boating couples; each phrase is rhythmically separated through fermatas in the accompaniment: "Some get lost, and some get wet, and some get drowned, and some get married," insinuating that the latter is not necessarily a desirable alternative. In Fergus's "A Summer Idyll" (1925), lovers "spoon" at a seaside summer resort in seeming romantic bliss, over arpeggiated thirty-second-note pentatonic waves. Although they part in "hysteric despair," the tale does not end in matrimony; the man and woman do not return to the resort the following year, each "for the fear that the other is there."

One of the most popular women's compositions, taken up by many other reciters, was Fergus's satirical "The Usual Way" (1914), based on a text that had been performed as early as the 1890s.[53] Again beginning with a prospective couple fishing together, the piece documents the progress of their understated courtship, emphasizing with the repeated refrain that it all occurred "in the usual way." In the next-to-last stanza, musical humor reveals that the couple have wed, through a quotation of the Wedding March from Mendelssohn's *A Midsummer Night's Dream* (example 10.3), a holdover from the practice of including well-known music in accompanied recitation. The final verse asks pointed questions about the couples' marriage:

> And now that they are married, do they always bill and coo?
> Do they never fret and quarrel, like the other couples do?
> Does he cherish her and love her? Does she honor and obey?

The piano interrupts the refrain, "Well they do," with pounded tone clusters humorously suggesting that marital strife is, indeed, "the usual way" (example 10.4).

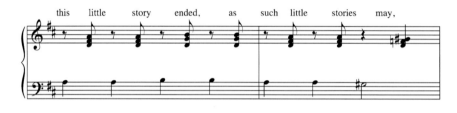

Example 10.3. Phyllis Fergus, "The Usual Way" (Chicago: Clayton F. Summy, 1914), mm. 29–33.

Example 10.4. Phyllis Fergus, "The Usual Way" (Chicago: Clayton F. Summy, 1914), mm. 39–41.

Milwaukee composer Lalla Ryckoff (b. 1891) published two contrasting pieces about the period before married life. In "To Marry—or Not to Marry" (1916), a woman is advised to remain single:

> Mother says, "Be in no hurry!
> Married Life means care and worry!"
> Auntie says, in accents grave,
> "Wife is synonym for slave!"
> Father says, in tones commanding,
> "How does Bradstreet rate his standing!"
> Sister crooning to her twins
> says with marriage woe begins.[54]

Auntie's warning is accompanied by ominous descending octaves in C minor, and the overburdened Sister serenades her twins over a fragment of Brahms's Lullaby. Despite her relations' warnings, the female speaker's eventual decision to wed is set off from the otherwise strophic setting with a slightly more elaborate accompaniment, and, as in "The Usual Way," the piece quotes Mendelssohn's Wedding March at its close.

Ryckoff's "'I Doubt It!'" is characteristic of women's compositions in that it depicts men's commitment to them as problematic.[55] Its speaker pointedly questions a man's inability to resist a woman's charms in three verses, each centering on one of her physical attributes: her lips to be kissed, her hand to be squeezed, her waist to wrap his arm around. The penultimate line of each verse is a question, followed by an answer that serves as the predictable refrain:

> When a pair of red lips are held up to your own,
> With no one to gossip about it!
> Do you pray for endurance to leave them alone?
> Well, maybe you do! But I doubt it.

Each verse's questioning is followed by two measures of untexted piano interlude, in which the speaker (and presumably her audience) consider the possibilities of the man's behavior before the punch lines; all of the verses punctuate "But I doubt it" with widely registered chords that emerge from the simple 6/8 running figures in the piano. In the fourth and final verse, when the man's "tricks" have "captured a heart," the speaker asks, "Will you guard it and keep it and act the good part?" The answer is, of course, "Well maybe you will . . . But I doubt it!" (example 10.5).

Example 10.5. Lalla Ryckoff, "I Doubt It!" (Chicago: Clayton F. Summy, 1923), mm. 29–35.

While Ryckoff merely suggests men's lack of faithfulness, in the narrative of Tina B. Cornic's "Jilted" (1932), the male lover's infidelity is explicit. In each of the two verses the man is rejected by one of his two girlfriends, who recognize his behavior and pointedly declares to the chorus's off-beat chordal accompaniment: "I want someone who'll be true / And that someone is not you."

Men are also depicted as weak and easily manipulated, victims of their own sexual desires. Women are shown to be in charge of the negotiations of courtship, able to control the men who pursue them. In Fergus's "Curls" (1923), men will do anything under the influence of the "saucy word or glance" of a young woman; the accompaniment's arpeggiated seventh chords flirtatiously change between triplets and other rhythmic subdivisions. "Retribution" (1923), an encore song by male composer DeLoss Smith, is told from the man's point of view, yet the young woman in the story retains the upper hand, making it appealing to female audiences.[56] To a lilting 6/8 accompaniment, a shop clerk selling silk asks a young lady for a kiss as payment. The music modulates to the relative minor as the woman boldly orders ten yards of material, and the "young man's heart" stands still on a dominant seventh chord. The return to tonic coincides with the woman's surprising announcement that her grandmother will pay the bill, accompanied by fortissimo cadential chords. In Peycke's A major "How Time Flies" (1919), the clock strikes repeatedly on the dominant scale degree in the piano introduction, setting up the entrance of the text, in which the male speaker tells Kate that he plans to "steal a kiss" at quarter after eight. She "whispers low" to quiet, descending thirty-second-note arpeggiation, then announces, "That clock is fifteen minutes slow"; her final word coincides with a surprising minor subdominant chord, before the final cadence.

Another example of women asserting their control of male suitors was Guy d'Hardelot's song "A Lesson with a Fan" (1898).[57] Fergus frequently gave a dramatic rendition of her arrangement of the song as an encore, playing a sparse accompaniment with one hand while suggestively wielding a fan in the other.[58] To the sprightly grace notes in d'Hardelot's original or Fergus's simpler chords, the speaker describes how a fan enables women to transcend the social restrictions that prevent them from expressing their desires to men. It may be "unladylike to call," but the small wave of a fan across a ballroom "in that fascinating manner" can gain a man's attention. D'Hardelot's instructions suggest that the fan is to be opened and shut on specially marked grace-note figures; Fergus's unpublished arrangement gives more detailed descriptions of the fan's motions. As in many other musical readings by women, the textual refrain, "it's a delicate suggestion, nothing more," gains in irony across several strophes, concluding with the accomplishment of the woman's goal:

> And when he tells the old tale o'er and o'er,
> And vows that he will love you evermore,
> Gather up your little fan,
> And secure him while you can,
> It's a delicate suggestion,
> Nothing more!

Women's compositions do not all illustrate the pursuit of a suitable mate as occurring with ease. Peycke's unpublished "Wishful Waiting" (1947), which she recorded but never released, lists the sorts of men who have interested a young woman, beginning at the age of sixteen and proceeding year by year, from someone "strong and tall" and "blond and lean," to someone "sophisticated," "with a mind."[59] The piece's close, with its typical musically emphasized punch line, reveals the speaker's frustration with not having found the man she desires: "But now, Lord, that I'm Twenty-Five, Oh! Just send me *someone* who's alive!" Peycke emphasizes the transformation in the young woman's psychological state through an unusual harmonic shift from a dominant seventh chord in E-flat major, to a D major triad (bars 48–49), the first of a series of unexpected progressions, first hinting at a brighter tonality, but, like the speaker's inability to change her predicament, eventually leading back to the F major tonic (example 10.6).

Women composers often chose texts that treated the outcomes of romantic coupling and married life as less than ideal. The less typical voice of a

Example 10.6: Frieda Peycke, "Wishful Waiting" (ca. 1947), John Hay Library, Brown University Library, mm. 47–54.

dim-witted man, showing photographs to his new wife, is heard in Peycke's "The Family Album" (1931).[60] While he imagines she will be interested in his baby pictures (and, by association, babies and domestic life in general), on seeing him on his father's knee she merely quips, "Who's the ventriloquist?" Her query and her husband's final refrain, "gee, are'nt [*sic*] women queer?" are highlighted by being spoken without underlying music. In Helen Wing's 1929 setting of Mildred Plew Merryman's "Sunday Afternoon," another portrait of a less-than-ideal marriage, a child explains that when "pop" abandons his wife to play golf, "she can't help but feel / That papa's love ain't quite so real."[61] The child is confused, since when it rains and the father stays home (accompanied by a dreary modulation from D major to F-sharp minor), the couple is at a loss and succumbs to napping. The speech-rhythm-based accompaniment provides opportunities for child impersonation as well as the differing vocal inflections of both parents.

In contrast, some women's compositions present less humorous and more critical commentary on the relationship between the sexes. Aileen Howell Tye wrote both text and music for "Mismated Pairs" (1930), two verses set strophically.[62] The first verse lists mismatched couples who are temperamentally complete opposites. The second verse blames wise, sly Mother Nature for these problematic pairings, concluding that while such couples previously stayed together for better or worse, she can now "mate them in springtime and part them in fall." The most forceful example of the indignities that women face in marriage is heard in Mary Wyman Williams's 1922 setting of Helen Rowland's parody of Rudyard Kipling's ode to masculinity, "If."[63] Rather than being mildly satirical, the text is a devastating portrait of the complete repression of women in marriage. Wives are forced to "keep quiet" and not lose their "gentle little touch" in the face of obvious mistreatment:

> If you can win a husband without trying
> And make him think that he's the prize—not you;
> If you can trust him when you know he's lying,
> And never even let him know you knew;
> If you can wait, and wait, and keep on waiting,
> And greet him, when he comes, with smiling eyes,
> And listen to the old equivocating,
> And never say too much, or look too wise—
> . . .
> If you can hear the earnest words you've spoken
> Twisted to make them sound inane, absurd,
> Or see your dearest hopes and idols broken,
> And never, never say a single word;
> If you can make one heap of your illusions,
> And risk them on One Man to stand or fall,
> And finding all the fairest dreams delusion,
> Can still declare that he was worth it all,
> If you can force your heart and nerves and sinew
> To keep a smiling face until the end,
> And never show what tho'ts are seething in you
> And seem to feel the joy that you pretend. . . .

The F major setting, which repeats midway through the poem, features a winding eighth-note melody, the notes of which match the number of syllables in each phrase of poetry. Increased chromaticism and modulation to A-flat and E minor help intensify the speaker's sentiments, and the closing phrase, "you'll be a wonder" is emphasized with large fortissimo chords. It seems highly unlikely that Williams's composition would have been performed before an audience that contained men. However, when he reviewed the work in 1922, Clay Smith found it a comic parody, and it is the strongest example of a setting of a poem in which women's serious commentary was considered to be humor.[64]

Peycke was also drawn to texts that depicted married life humorously. Her correspondence reveals her interest in "How to Cook a Husband," consisting of a recipe for making sure one's husband is "tender." The composer wrote,

"It's deft, clever and has several laugh spots in it, 'am crazy to get at it,'" and she had set the text by 1949 but never published it.[65] Nonetheless, its droll analogy makes it representative of the sort of poems that attracted the composer throughout her career. In "Is Marriage a Failure?" (1924), her setting of text by Mary Tilden Marshall, a couple offers to immediately pay three dollars to the preacher who has just married them or to give him one hundred dollars later when they are happy, so he chooses to take their three dollars, convinced of the inevitable sorrows in their future. The piano introduction that precedes the story is the typical quotation from Mendelssohn's Wedding March. Peycke's programming of her compositions highlighted the change in women's expectations from blissful romance to more realistic domestic life; in her performances she sometimes grouped her works on courtship and marriage into a set that she called "Husbands—Before and After Taking," which included both humorous and sentimental works. Several of the compositions ("Wishful Waiting," "By What Subtle Means?," and "First Date") are tales of the courtship of young people, while "The Rose in the Dinner Pail" (unpublished) recounts the love of an older wife for her gray-haired, wrinkled husband.[66]

In Peycke's setting of Edgar Guest's less sentimental "Husbands," composed in 1937, a husband is cast as his wife's possession, put on display at concerts and balls "just to prove she has a man"; the description of his condition is set to a sprightly allegretto accompaniment marked by dotted rhythms, in a bluesy harmonic language.

> He's the chap you see at operas with that vacant, patient stare
> That announces very plainly that his wife has hauled him there!
> You can see the music bores him, and you know the "dear old grouch"
> Would much rather she had left him to lie snoring on the couch!
> . . .
> She must take him out to lectures, socials, literary teas,
> And display him to the people, tho' he's plainly ill at ease!
> He's the meek and patient mortal with thinning grayish dome
> Who sits idly in some corner 'til it's "time to take him home"!

The song "Home, Sweet Home," heard in the accompaniment to the final phrase (mm. 39–41), represents the husband's, rather than the woman's, longing for the domestic sphere (example 10.7). Tellingly, the women's world of musical, literary, and social events from which the husband longs to escape is the very world in which Fergus, Peycke, and other women regularly appeared and for which their musical recitations were composed. Peycke's piece reinforces women's aspirations to the world of high art that inspired their entrance into elocution in the late nineteenth century and satirizes men's discomfort with their activities.

*(look about eagerly)*

Who sits    idly   in some corner 'til it's    "time    to take  him     home"!

*reminiscent melody*

Example 10.7:
HUSBANDS, mm. 38–41
Words by EDGAR GUEST
Music by FRIEDA PEYCKE
©1942 (Renewed) CLAYTON F. SUMMY CO.
All Rights Administered by WB MUSIC CORP.
All Rights Reserved
Used by Permission of ALFRED MUSIC

## Grandmothers and Little Boys

In comparison to the accompanied recitations of the nineteenth century, compositions by women were more likely to present women as mature figures. The emergence of stories about older women, most often couched as grandmother recitations, may have been a result of the audience demographic of women's clubs; women who listened to elocutionists in the 1890s could well have become grandmothers by the teens and twenties when most of these compositions were published. Such works are somewhat related to the sentimental dancing grandmothers of "The Minuet" or "Grandma at the Masquerade" (in chapter 4). Other compositions stress the relationship between grandmother and grandchild, and their texts are sometimes in child dialect. The concentration on older women, children, or both was yet another means of avoiding any eroticism or sexuality; in this way, these works do not challenge previous notions of the material appropriate for women's performances. Furthermore, interchanges between a mother or grandmother and a child managed to simultaneously express the sorts of rebellion possible in child-dialect selections while maintaining the status quo, as embodied in the adult female who powerfully curtails any inappropriate childish behavior.

In some texts mothers reflect on the increasing maturity of their children, expressing their underlying grief over the end of their roles as mothers and sentimentally recalling their offsprings' lost childhoods. Peycke's "The Little Gate Bed" (1927) treats a crib as a symbol of loss for the mother whose children have grown up. The "gently rocking" largo music in 6/8 is distinctly lullaby-like, and the poetic verses are set strophically, modulating from C major to D-flat minor for the woman's memories of her children's past life transitions. The minor mode also accompanies the final text, when the woman expresses how "bereft" she feels without toddlers; instead she faces an attic of "broken toys" and "ghosts of joys." In Fergus's similar work, "The Old Chest Upstairs" (1921), with an even more poignant musical setting, the nostalgic speaker examines a chest's contents, which include sentimental keepsakes: pressed flowers, old dance cards, her bridal veil, a baby's shoe, and a doll, all "ghosts" of previous days. After the poem's first eight lines, set to a delicately ornamented melody, fermatas mark two chords to be sustained at the moment that the woman unlocks the chest, and dance rhythms emerge to dominate the piece's center as she recalls long-ago balls and romance. The opening music returns in the minor mode at the text's emotional low point: "O my world is reduced to tears and prayers, / Yet I turn away from the chest upstairs." However, the following six measures in 3/8 time have the flavor of the previous dance music, in support of the text's more positive ending: "Knowing somehow, somewhere, that someone cares!" A somewhat related story is told from a child's perspective in Fergus's "I Wonder" (1923). The boy describes how his father tells him to be a man, and he wonders why his mother has a tear in her eye about his growing up. The father's pronouncements are articulated with a crescendoing dissonant outburst, while the mother's quiet grief is accompanied by a pianissimo legato passage. The sentimental mood is suggested by a brief motive heard in the major mode that immediately repeats in minor; it opens the introduction and reappears between the lines "If I can grow up be a man" and "Why should she shed a tear?," allowing the boy to "wonder."

Grandmother pieces often serve to reestablish relationships between women and children that have seemingly been lost in works such as "The Little Gate Bed" or "The Old Chest Upstairs." Their sentimental texts also present women engaging with memories of an earlier time and sometimes stress the life wisdom that grandmothers have acquired over the years. Having fallen victim to living only for her past in Mary Wyman Williams's "An Old-Fashioned Garden" (1920), Grandmother views her garden's flowers, remembers her earlier love (Grandpa), and "lives in the vanished past."[67] The setting is *siciliano*-like, in 6/8 with dotted rhythms, frequently over an appropriately pastoral pedal tone in F major; Grandmother's vision of her past is set to modulatory passages that include the sadder minor mode. The grandmother in Natalie Whitted Price's "The Patchwork Quilt" (1913) also reconsiders her past through examining quilt swatches that recall previous moments in her life, some of which caused her grief.[68] The strophic setting's steadily moving eighth-note accompaniment doubles the notated vocal line; the four-part form of each verse, ABCA, modulates to the minor mode during the C section. This change is particularly appropriate for the final verse, which contains the moral for the child speaker examining the quilt with Grandmother: life is like a patchwork quilt with its best moments revealed beside its difficulties, or "red is redder when it's by a piece of brown." In Fergus's often performed "'One, Two, Three'" (1923), the grandmother is old and frail, but this does not impede her relationship with a small boy, who is similarly immobilized by a twisted knee. The song's title appears in the chorus, as they play a hide-and-seek guessing game together without leaving their place under a maple tree. The accompaniment provides a poignant mood for the story, in part because of its alternation between major and minor modes.

Even without focusing on grandparenthood, women composers' works sometimes dealt with the issues women face as they grow older. Aging was sometimes a theme treated by Peycke, who remained professionally active into her senior years. In the 1940s she recorded two unpublished works about growing older, the humorous "If Only We Could" (1943) and "Age" (1938).[69] The text of "If Only We Could" compares the human body to the modern automobile and expresses the wish for body parts that are just as easily re-placeable as the repairable mechanical apparatuses of cars. Swinging dotted rhythms and grace-note figures provide the comedic musical lilt; chords sup-port the first four syllables of the punch line, expressing the speaker's desire to "get a stream-lined body." The text of "Age" emphasizes that age is only "a quality of mind," if one does not abandon hope and continues to seek life and love. Arpeggios in both hands characteristic of Peycke's style continually sweep across the keyboard. However, the motivic shape of the accompaniment briefly matches that of a pair of spoken phrases: "no matter how the years go by, no matter how the birthdays fly." In Peycke's manuscript, the accompa-niment for the textual refrain, "You are not old" (mm. 24–26) appears to be similarly constructed, with chordal support directly under the text; however, in her recording, the composer laughs in measure 24, such that the entrance of the text occurs one measure later, and thus the accompanimental chords do not drown out the spoken performance.[70] Although the rhythmic contours of Peycke's accompaniments may have been derived from poetic meters and stresses, she expected a great deal more rhythmic flexibility in performance than is immediately apparent in her scores.

Several deliberately unsentimental grandmother compositions feature the humorous tone characteristic of women composers' creations. In 1918 Fergus published two pieces with texts about grandmothers by Natalie Whitted Price. "My Gran'Ma" features simple, pentatonically inflected music to suggest the young speaker's innocence. The girl describes the various affectionate names her grandmother, for whom she is named, uses for her. When her grandmother has "indijestion," she merely says "Oh!—Annabelle!," the syllables of which are echoed by the melodic motive at the final cadence. "My Mother's Ma (A Modern Grandmother)" (1918) presents a grandmother who is not "obsolete" as her grandson might think, as she is attractively dressed in high heels and a party dress. Although sentimental encounters between grandmothers and grandchildren predominate in female composer's settings, this text deliberately contrasts grandmothers who recall their pasts or dance antiquated minuets with a modern woman, energetic in spite of her perceived age, and it would have undoubtedly appealed to the civically active participants of women's clubs.

The child-dialect recitations of the nineteenth century had far more of an impact on the works of female composers than those in ethnic-dialect types. Women regularly set texts about children or in child dialect, including poems that compare the two genders; these are similar to poetry found in earlier anthologies for children, although many more pieces feature boy speakers than girls. The gender of a child miscreant is not immediately clear in some texts; however, the portrayals of misbehavior in them nonetheless strongly suggest the stereotypical boy: a rule-breaking, rebellious, adventurous, but good-hearted rascal. In contrast, the few compositions that feature girls vary considerably, making it difficult to characterize them. Many pieces that contrast the two genders center on boys, and only on rare occasions are girls depicted positively in the comparison. In 1927 Fergus published settings of a pair of texts by Lillian W. Simpson and Richard Denny, both titled "The Dark," which deliberately highlight the differences between a girl's and a boy's nighttime fears; the latter text particularly resembles Eugene Field's popular "Seein' Things at Night," in which the boy declares, "Lucky thing I ain't a girl or I'd be skeered to death!" The characteristic legato, lullaby-like accompaniment in 6/8 for the girl introduces a descending chromatic scale when she acknowledges that she doesn't like "The Big Dark." She clutches her doll and thinks of her mother, whose fading footsteps down the hall resound quietly in the piano accompaniment, and assures herself that God is everywhere. The boy, who speaks to staccato chords with dotted rhythms in D minor, initially seems braver, and his accompaniment's harmonies are not so obviously chromatic. However, he runs down the hall in terror, first to ascending diminished seventh chord triplets and ultimately to a dramatic two-and-a-half octave glissando that closes the work.

Boys' commentaries on the limitations of girls served as women's recognition of the larger social conditions that shaped their lives. While some of these texts may well have been assigned to the young male pupils of female instructors, adult women also performed them. Peycke particularly specialized in depicting boys, and she composed a large number of boy compositions, even though many remained unpublished. Her stylized timbres and pronunciations when voicing small boys can be heard in her surviving recordings. That her vocal renditions resembled those of previous women who performed boy versions of child dialect is suggested by their similarity to the 1917 recording by Sally Hamlin of Field's "Seein' Things at Night," the deliberate boyishness of which is created through lower-pitched tones and markedly different inflections.[71] When women imitated boys asserting their superiority to girls, the irony would not have been lost on female audiences—they would have been critiquing situations from their own childhoods. In Peycke's "Us Twins" (1922), identical twins are both horrified when considering that their sibling might have been born female, concluding with one brother's final evening prayer, "Thank God that we're both boys," heard over a sustained, hymnlike accompaniment. Boy characters revel in their physical activities, as in Peycke's setting of "What the Boy Said" (1921), a poem by Inez Townsend Tribit in which a boy contrasts his freedoms to the restrictions in girls' lives:[72]

> It must be *fierce* to be a girl,
> They have no fun at all!
> An' if they're hurt a little bit
> They've always got to bawl!
> Girls mostly stick around the house,
> They're trained not to make a noise
> Because they say, it ain't polite
> to act the same as boys.
> Just think, how awful it must be
> to stay at home and sew!

Peycke's regular eighth-note accompaniment increases in activity for the boy's description of his vigorous activities: sweeping arpeggios for swimming, sharply articulated pairs of chords for playing ball and fighting, tumbling figures to accompany his exclamation of "Whoopee!," and the imitation of his physical jump through a leap down the keyboard (example 10.8). The poetry's humor is emphasized through use of the minor mode for the mock-tragic accompaniment, yet the boy's message, "there's lots of times that girls must wish that they wuz boys like *me*!," would have resonated with female audiences. The stereotypical punch-line ending is that the boy is glad he isn't a girl, as he would "just as leave be dead."

A substantial number of compositions center on the adventures of misbehaving children, who come up against the negative reaction of an adult who tries to discipline them. Depictions of boys in rural settings, suggesting their sense of freedom in the natural world, drew on nineteenth-century stereotypes of the boy as a "noble savage" who has not been restrained or corrupted by "civilization."[73] Fergus's output contains numerous works of this type. In her "Spring's

Example 10.8: Frieda Peycke, "What the Boy Said" (New York: Harold Flammer, 1921), mm. 33–38.

A-Comin'" (1926), in child dialect, the change in the seasons prompts a boy to reach for his fishing pole, until his father reminds him of the work that needs to be done in the garden. Here the sprightly staccato 6/8 accompaniment becomes halting and minor; the major seconds in its chords become minor seconds as the frustrated boy exclaims, "Who wants spring, anyhow?" In Fergus's "Father's Way" (1915), a father's yelling at *Jim* is all in good fun—until he refers to his son as *James*, the sign that the boy has angered him. The smooth, arpeggiated flourishes when the father is unruffled give way to chromatically descending chords when his mood changes. The music that accompanies the speaker of Fergus's "Mistaken Kindness" (1921) also changes according to the poem's activities; after a gentle introduction, the piano introduces a surprising modulation and ascending triplets to paint the child's suggestion that his cow should "run about and play." The center of the piece depicts him feeding candy to the cow with a frolicking 6/8 piano accompaniment, then chasing the animal to two-octave arpeggios. As the father finds out what his child has done, the accompaniment returns to its original subdued texture, now intensified by chromatic harmonies. The dramatic incident of being caught, as presented in this work, is frequently at the center of children's tales. When the child in

Peycke's setting of Fannie D. Steman's "The Tattle Tale Bird" (1928) steals an apple, the 6/8 dotted-rhythm accompaniment, with the pentatonic flavor of folk songs from the British isles, is interrupted.[74] The resulting chordal music modulates away from pastoral F major, and the piece climaxes when the bird informs the child's mother of the theft. Punishment is also a dramatic threat in Mary Wyman Williams's minor-mode "Where the Spankweed Grows" (1921), in which a nurse threatens a boy with "spankweed." However, the boy remains unrepentant.[75] In the third verse of the primarily strophic setting, he threatens to cut down the so-called weed with a sickle, and the simple melody that accompanied the previous verses is now heard ominously in the bass.

Some texts set by female composers stress an honesty in children that comes to reveal adult hypocrisy, a characteristic that children exhibited in nineteenth-century literature as well.[76] Peycke's "Woes of a Boy" (1920) is similar to a classic example, "Miss Edith Helps Things Along" by Bret Harte, frequently reprinted in elocution anthologies.[77] In Harte's poem, a young girl causes consternation in her sister's suitor when she is honest about his flaws and compares him to a previous beau. Peycke's loquacious boy provides a similar series of humorous anecdotes; his mother instructs him to tell the truth, which leads him to engage in offensive comments. He acknowledges, honestly, that he *isn't* happy to see Uncle John, and when his sister's boyfriend gives her twenty pearls, one for each of her years, he announces that she actually needs thirty. Ultimately, the problem in the boy's eyes is not truthful boys but the problematic expectations of grownups. A similarly naughty boy in Fergus's "An Ideal" (1915) recognizes that his mother can't believe that he would "mix up with anything ugly, mean or bad," and acknowledges "how grand 'twould be—Gee Whiz—if a feller could be the feller his mudder tinks he is."[78] The music's humor is created through exaggerated gestures: its mournful C minor mode and lament-like descending minor tetrachord in the piano's left hand, brightened only by G major chords strategically accompanying the mother's naively positive thoughts.

Peycke produced several compositions that feature conflicts between children and mothers, pieces that express both child rebellion and adult authority. In "The Annual Protest" (1921), the boy feigns illness and complains of the loss of his outdoor freedoms, the weight of his books, and the cleanliness required of schoolchildren, recalling McGowan's "Gee Whiz: When Mother Washes Me" and Fergus's "Soap, the Oppressor" (in chapter 6).[79] In Peycke's recording of "The Annual Protest," the music is preceded by a dramatic dialogue between mother and son, both voiced by the composer. Although the mother's voice features correct pronunciation, her son's utilizes some characteristic slurred pronunciations, even though the published text of

Peycke's piece contains almost no child dialect. The work's frequently changing meters, keys, and motivic content reflect the boy's swirling emotions, marked with many expressive indications in the score, and the constantly transformed accompaniment is often more like one designed for recitative than for song. The frustrated boy's refrain, "Aw Pshaw, Ma! I don't want to go to school!," is punctuated by large chords. Peycke apparently did not like her recording of "The Annual Protest," the only recording she released, because of the faintness of the musical accompaniment. It is nonetheless an example of the vocal imitations of boys that she performed throughout her career. One unpublished composition, "Lost Illusions" (1932), based on a text by Angela Crispin, is not obviously in the voice of a boy; however, Peycke's two recorded performances of it from 1948 have the inflections of her typical "boy" voice. The piece's two verses contrast a man's recollections of his younger self, complaining of his mother's insistence that "it's time to go to bed," with his adult attitude:

> I thought, if only some fine day I grow to be a man
> I'll sit up every single night, and now you know I can.
> Well, the greatest treat in life I find, when all is done and said
> Is to steal away from everyone at eight and go to bed.

The adult's desire to turn in early implicitly acknowledges that, despite his previous attitude, his mother's prescriptions were correct. The phrase, "and now you know I can," is surrounded by the piano's interjection of fleeting arpeggios, emphasizing the speaker's current adult freedom, and the pause before "and go to bed" highlights the punch line in typical fashion.

In addition to their rebellious attitudes, the boys in Fergus's and Peycke's compositions also possess a goodness and spiritual sensitivity that both links them to their nineteenth-century predecessors and insures that musical recitations retained morally acceptable content (also necessary to Chautauqua performers' success). Peycke's "Chums" (1919) is a tale that would not have been out of place in an earlier parlor anthology. The speaker is a boy who has befriended a younger, disabled, and impoverished child; he studies schoolwork with him and brings him extra clothes and food "because me and him are 'chums.'" Peycke's accompaniment to this extended narrative, which also describes the grateful mother of the adopted friend, features a melodic line that rhythmically mirrors the text, as in many simpler works. However, it is harmonically complex, modulating from A-flat to B major for the center of its ternary form. The text is a slightly less sentimental version of a common type of Victorian poem, best represented by David Proudfit's frequently anthologized "Poor Little Joe," but in earlier versions, the younger child sometimes meets a tragic death.

# Jus' Keep On Keepin' On:
# Moral and Religious Recitations

The potential for power and rebellion expressed through women's musical settings of humorous recitations about domestic life or in boys' voices was tempered by their treatment of texts that stressed a positive outlook and religious faith. These works extended ideals presented by Progressive-Era elocutionists into the mid-twentieth century and would have been appropriate for school and church programs, as well as being suitable for mixed audiences. Some pieces expressed the ideals of community and civic cooperation that motivated towns to host Chautauquas and the social activism of the women's clubs at which many performers appeared. Others, such as Fergus's settings of Psalm 23 (with violin obbligato), Psalm 91, and Psalm 121, published between 1925 and 1927, were overtly religious. Fergus's "And Ruth Said" (1927) was a setting of Ruth 1:16 for speaking voice and organ, so that it could be played in churches, perhaps for weddings.[80] Fergus advertised her biblical text settings separately from her lighter, humorous story poems, but she occasionally programmed them in her concerts.

Although boys were portrayed as free to engage in unruly behavior, both Fergus and Peycke authored pieces that emphasized children's underlying spiritual nature through their musings on the existence and character of God. In such works, boys' freedom to be truthful rather than hemmed in by societal expectations is a moral advantage. These works' association of childhood innocence with the divine is not unlike that cultivated in the persona of Kitty Cheatham more than a decade earlier. In Fergus's "Lie Awake Song" (1922), a child compares God, who "stays awake for kindness," faithful through the night, to the furnace man who arrives in the early-morning hours to warm homes. The atmospheric work has a higher degree of chromaticism than many of Fergus's pieces, and open-fifth pedal tones on the flat second scale degree in the bass support its nocturnal mood. The introduction's dissonant church bells return midway through the piece, as the child recalls candles burning all night in a church, "because God never goes to sleep" (example 10.9). Instead of a humorous punch line, the final phrase emphasizes the spiritual communion possible during the hours in which all are asleep except "God, the furnace man, and me."

In Peycke's "A Boy and God" (ca. 1939–40), which she recorded but did not publish, the boy describes how he experiences God in nature; here boys' association with the outdoors is elevated above mere escape from the domestic sphere and becomes imbued with spiritual purpose.[81] The musical accompaniment is made up entirely of ascending arpeggios, with the exception of four chords that emphasize the boyish exclamations "That ain't like God!" and

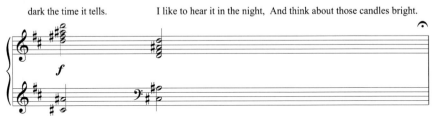

Example 10.9. Phyllis Fergus, "Lie Awake Song" (Chicago: Clayton F. Summy, 1922), mm. 12–14.

"That's how I feel." Instead of expressing rebellion against the limitations on boys' behavior, the speaker stresses his belief in a kindly God who allows children to play as children, without the threat of punishment. This sort of depiction of boys' personal relationship with God is not unlike nineteenth-century hymns, used for accompanied recitations and Delsarte poses, that domesticated the divine. The God of Peycke's "A Boy and God," in particular, is envisioned as allowing the speaker to be who he truly is; yet it was seemingly necessary to express such a sentiment through the voice of a male, albeit it a male child, not a girl or an adult woman.

Peycke and others penned numerous compositions conveying an experience of God in the natural world, as well as a fundamental optimism in the face of life's difficulties; Peycke's correspondence reveals that this sense of optimism was a part of the composer's personality, and it clearly appealed to her audiences as well. Peycke's "Watch the Corners of Your Mouth" (1926), in which the listener is exhorted to continue to smile, is characteristic of these works' moralistic tone.[82] The piece's minimal accompaniment makes it playable by pianists far less accomplished than the composer. The music paints the turned-down mouth through bass tones and chords accented with grace notes; Peycke's recording of this piece exaggerates the musical "frown" even further with growling grace notes added to the two pitches that leap into the piano's low register, notes that are also penciled into a copy of the piece owned by her student, Coral Olsen.[83] In contrast, the smile is evoked through jaunty dotted rhythms; the piece concludes with ascending chords to accompany the words "turn up!" Similar in musical style, Peycke's "Jus' Keep On Keepin' On" (1927) calls for fortitude in the face of adversity: "Jus' keep on smiling cheerfully / If hope is nearly gone, / And bristle up, grit your teeth, keep *on* keepin' on."[84] Lilting dotted rhythms give way to firm chords to accompany the reading's moral. Floy Little Bartlett (1883–1955) produced a simple 6/8 setting of Edgar A. Guest's "It Can Be Done" (1922), which takes a similar attitude in asserting that obstacles can be overcome, in spite of naysayers:

> There are thousands to tell you it cannot be done,
> There are thousands to prophesy failure;
> There are thousands to point out to you, one by one,
> The dangers that wait to assail you.
> But just buckle in with a bit of a grin,
> Just take off your coat and go to it;
> Just start to sing as you tackle the thing
> That "cannot be done," and you'll do it.[85]

Like Peycke's "Jus' Keep On Keepin' On," the simple chordal accompaniment with eighth-note figures has few technical impediments, so "it can be done" by an amateur performer. The audience for the speaker of Peycke's "If You Want to Live" (1925) is also admonished into self-awareness and responsibility; if they want to live in the kind of town that is "what you want it to be," it is up to them to engage in cooperation to improve their community, rather than focusing merely on their own needs. The major-mode chordal accompaniment is "Brisk and lively," and its occasional triplet figures reflect the text's rhythms.

Fergus composed two pieces that employ weather as an analogy for life's experiences. The dialect text "Rain or Sun!" (1919), set to A-flat major accompaniment with parallel fourths and a pentatonic flavor, encourages a "heart full o' fun" regardless of bad weather. The center of the piece, in which listeners are exhorted to "Take off frettin,'" modulates to *grazioso* C major. The line "De sun's arisin' when it's a-settin'" is heard to a dramatic ascending glissando. In one of Fergus's most lyrical works, "Ain't It Fine Today" (1920), the speaker acknowledges that life is full of dark clouds, but instead of dwelling on past tribulations recognizes the goodness of the present moment. The three verses align with the piece's ABA formal structure: the A sections, in a sorrowful D minor, have chromatically descending bass chords, and the D-flat center of the work is in a thinner two-voice texture, with an arpeggiated bass line. At the close of verses 1 and 3, a fermata sets off the speaker's refrain, "ain't it fine today," over dominant seventh sonorities with an added ninth that then cadence on an uplifting major tonic chord. The close of the B section is similar, but with a striking deceptive cadence at "But today is fine"; the seventh chord

Example 10.10. Phyllis Fergus, "Ain't It Fine Today" (Chicago: Clayton F. Summy, 1920), mm. 15–17.

on A-natural sounds like an augmented sixth sonority, but serves as a pivot chord to return to D minor. As if to emphasize the moral of the piece, the speaker seems to linger in this moment; a 5/4 measure causes a slight delay before the return of the minor mode of the A material (example 10.10).

Both Fergus and Peycke produced compositions that extol the beauties of nature. The text of Fergus's "Radiance" (1920), a short, *grazioso* piece in 6/8, describes a divine vision of sunlight shining on a tree with feminine imagery: as "falling with the grace of exquisite and rare old lace." The piano accompaniment features open fifth pedal sonorities in the bass and delicate pentatonic chords, which fall in triplet figures over three octaves in the right hand, reflecting the poetic content. Peycke composed two works about finding spiritual consolation in nature that she recorded but that remained unpublished—"Things" (before 1928) and "God's Bonfires" (ca. 1935)—as well as a published piece, "Comfort" (1922). All three feature slow tempos and quiet arpeggios, without much sense of a distinct, overriding melody, in order to create a meditative mood. The narrator of Peycke's "Things" longs for material possessions she doesn't have; but when she watches the sun set, she finds that she ultimately prefers God's natural world to the creations of human beings. The speaker's unsettling longings occur to contrasting music in the subdominant minor in the center of the work's ternary form. The final rhetorical question, "What is wishing and what are things?," serves as the composer's typical closing gesture. The accompaniment for "God's Bonfires" is set in 9/8 with triplet arpeggios running from the bass to the treble; a single repeated note in the right hand is to be struck "like a bell," marking the passage of time. The speaker describes how at the end of the "used up day" God burns up human beings' mistakes, "futile cares," and "petty wars" in a sunset. The work is one of the rare instances in which Peycke's accompaniment features word painting, heard in the piano tremolo in the upper range of the keyboard at the final words "all tangled up with stars." In "Comfort," as in Fergus's pieces, the beauties of the natural world are presented as consolation for "hard luck." The basic chordal texture typical of Peycke's accompaniments is suddenly transformed into thirty-second-note arpeggios in the upper ranges of the keyboard for descriptions of sky, earth, sun, and birds. The central arpeggios, which serve to portray the natural world and divine transcendence in all of these works, return pianissimo to close the work after the text states, "You've got God, and God is love."

The musical style of Peycke's unpublished "Proof?" (1931) is in the same vein, but its text, from *Nautilus* magazine, makes it a musically illustrated reading more characteristic of its age. The text differs in its emphasis on technological wonders, describing how radio waves communicate over long distances. However, the modern world does not contradict traditional religious beliefs; the text's final twist stresses that with such marvels, "is it any wonder, that God hears prayer?" The last three words of the question are emphasized with chords in the composer's typical fashion. In Peycke's works, in particular, women are capable of having their own spiritual connections and do not always have to express their religious feelings through the voices of boys.

Frieda Peycke described the desired aesthetic goals for musical recitation as "sincerity, naturalness, and life," and she believed that its aim was communication with her audiences, writing, "Musical readings make a dramatic, romantic, and humorous appeal to the imaginations of all."[86] For Peycke, Fergus, and the other women who took up the genre, the subjects that they depicted were viewed from a woman's perspective and communicated to the women who dominated their audiences. Their occasional quotations of well-known music resembled the accompanied recitations of an earlier era. Yet unlike nineteenth-century elocutionists, they no longer desired to embody the high art of great literature by male geniuses but instead underscored the dramas, big and small, in women's worlds: the struggles of domestic life, finding and living with a life partner, motherhood, children, aging, becoming a grandmother, and finding spiritual consolation. Some of their compositions express nostalgia for a simpler, pastoral time and continue nineteenth-century religious expression and sentimentality in a gentler form. The settings by Fergus and Peycke, in particular, demonstrated a musical sophistication at the same time that their chosen texts had a wide accessibility unrelated to literary aspirations. Ultimately, women composers feminized melodrama, creating a genre to speak for and to women. The strongly comedic approach of the texts that female composers chose to set, and the ways in which their musical settings consistently underlined their climactic humor, allowed women to assert themselves in a new way. Although musical recitation never became a widely recognized genre, it held an important historical place in American women's culture and became a means by which some twentieth-century female composers found their voice.

# Afterword

## Echoes of Elocutionary Arts

I am a curious girl who likes books.
—Lauren Hancock

Read the poem to the rhythm of the music.
(Use a big voice!)
(Read with feeling!) . . .
Entertain and amaze your friends with this new way to read.
—Nancy Polette, "How to Do Concert Reading"

In the 1940s, when Maureen Howard's brother began to stutter, their mother located Mrs. Holton, who had graduated from the Emerson School sometime in the 1890s. George, finding himself to be a "sissy" taking lessons amid little girls, quickly abandoned them, but his sister began to study etiquette and elocution. In the elderly teacher's "lifeless house," she found a world "so far removed from mine that I never believed in it." Yet Howard's mother insisted because Mrs. Holton "*was* Boston and culture" and could teach her "the clear rich speech and poise of a lady." For her mother's generation, elocution, culture, and femininity continued to be closely entwined. In her 1978 memoir, *Facts of Life*, the author recalled how in the "phantom world" of Mrs. Holton she learned vocal production and Delsartean "attitudes."[1] She acknowledged that "the notion was farfetched, that I would ever nestle into the curve of a grand piano at some church social or stand in a drawing room flanked by potted palms, clear my throat, take the position of Welcome, left then right, balanced just slightly over the ball of the foot." Yet she performed at school assemblies and birthday parties and for holiday visitors until she found herself "humiliated by my past performances" and convinced her mother to let her give up the lessons. The training that had given women the freedom to express themselves in the nineteenth century seemed artificial and restrictive in the twentieth.

After college, when Howard was "learning to hold my liquor and trying to enchant the world," she used to perform Delsarte poses at parties. "Most anyone could sing old songs, but my skill in pantomime was acknowledged as special and antic. . . . I like to think I am the only living person who can perform this lost art form. All the gestures of life boiled down, jelled to routine." Eventually Mrs. Holton's parting gift to Howard, a carton of elocution materials, was destroyed in a flooded basement. The writer felt only "good riddance to the bloated eloquence of perfectly enunciated poetry, the techniques of good behavior which had not implemented my salvation," concluding, "I am not the lady I was meant to be." Nonetheless, she became defensive when her family rejected her readings in a musical, elocutionary style:

> Today I can't read a poem out loud that my family doesn't ridicule me. They groan and titter. They intone a line after me with false resonance. No one ever, ever reads like that, they say, deep from the chest like a Barrymore. They claim it's not *me*. La-dee-dah they make my reading sound and I'll be damned if it is—for it's perfectly natural. It *is* me—the tone held up at the end of a line, the elisions and glides, the glottal softening, the hitch of caesura in my voice. Funny, of course, if you've heard nothing but the flat crackle of television voices, thin as cheap beer, clinging to the microphone for dear life.

The elocutionary education to which Howard had been subjected in her childhood had enriched her life; it was still part of her.

The recollections in Howard's memoir, described alongside the pain in her personal life, are about far more than Mrs. Holton's lessons, but they provide the opinion of elocution of later generations, well after the reaction against it in the early twentieth century, and the modern lens through which they viewed what they considered to be a dead art form. The process by which spoken-word performance fell from prominence is difficult to trace. At the same time that elocution faded farther from cultural memory, bits of its practices continued to be influential. Delsarte's effects on the arts were wide ranging, from acting styles in early silent films, to modern dance, to pageantry, even as its actual poses and drills were forgotten. Early sound recordings captured the end of the era of recitation, and a few concert companies and their readers made radio appearances. Modern poetic forms replaced Victorian ones, and radio and movies hastened the demise of homegrown entertainments and Chautauqua.

Many cultural changes, including educational reforms that rejected oral repetition, precipitated the decline in poetic recitation. Some modernist poets made sound recordings, seemingly eliminating the need for women to interpret their intentions audibly; Derek Furr has found that their recordings were considered "a kind of curiosity, a sideline to serious print material."[2] Perhaps the strongest factor in the decline of elocution was the increasing social acceptance of theatrical performance. College yearbooks document the shift from elocution to full-fledged dramatic productions; when Rose E. Barker, elocution instructor at Cornell College, died in 1928, the speech arts club there of thirty young women disbanded and was replaced the following year by a new women's debate team and a theatrical group, the Purple Masqueraders. A few performers who began in spoken-word performance went on to become theatrical professionals; in 1922, late in her career, elocutionist Nellie Peck Saunders appeared in three films. Although primarily an actress, Zara Cully Brown was advertised in the 1950s as a dramatic reader; she played in the CBS sitcom *The Jeffersons* in the 1970s in her old age.[3] Women were important in the rise of the Little Theater movement in America, where, according to Dorothy Chansky, as both artists and audiences, they became the "fall girls of modernism," subject to similar sorts of criticism as female elocutionists because of the perceived feminization of theater.[4] A few actresses, such as Ruth Draper, became known for their solo performances, but by the mid-twentieth century they were considered to be somehow unique, not part of a continuing tradition of oral performance.

Some institutions that began as elocution schools continued to reflect their heritages even as they began to diversify their offerings to include storytelling, pageantry, dance, acting, and radio production. Many schools closed, although some were transformed; by the 1940s the Bard-Avon School of Expression in Baltimore, Maryland, had become a business and secretarial school, presumably retaining a predominately female student body.[5] Other elocution schools evolved into full-fledged institutions of higher education, such as Emerson College, Curry College, and Columbia College. As they changed, schools sometimes deliberately attempted to shed their associations with women. For example, at Northwestern Ralph Dennis worked to eliminate the School of Oratory's reputation as a women's finishing school and to increase offerings that appealed to men, which caused the number of male students to double between 1928 and 1941.[6] David Gold and Catherine Hobbs have documented the influence of female graduates of elocution schools, especially Emerson and Curry, on the curriculum of women's colleges in the South, although in several cases women faculty trained in spoken literature lost their positions as curricula were transformed from expression to public speaking. At the Florida State College for Women, coeducation brought a new chairman to the speech department, who rid it of all female instructors except Elizabeth Thompson, who was tenured.[7]

Spoken poetry has continued to be heard in various musical incarnations throughout the twentieth century, though many of the best-known performers, from beat poets to rap artists, have been male. Only occasional references to art forms from an earlier era have been retained in popular culture: elocution in *Anne of Green Gables*, Delsarte in *The Music Man,* or the "diction coach" urging "round tones" on a squeaky silent-film star learning to speak correctly in *Singing in the Rain* (1952). Nonetheless, aspects of elocution's practices, most often reformulated under the term *oral interpretation*, remain, sometimes with echoes of ideals from a previous era. In a YouTube video titled "Oral Interpretation Poetry Examples 0001," one reciter describes oral interpretation as a skill that "will help us later on when we're trying to read to our children,"[8] recalling similar nineteenth-century justifications. She then performs Christina Rossetti's "No, Thank You, John," a woman's rejection of a male suitor, a poem similar to texts previously set by female composers in that it humorously depicts a woman's agency: "I'd rather answer 'No' to fifty Johns / Than answer 'Yes' to you." No longer heard in concerts, poetic interpretation is now often centered in sports-style competitions, sponsored by forensic organizations for high school and college students. Students reciting poetry for the National Forensics Association are required to hold a notebook containing their text; although they undoubtedly memorize their selections, points are deducted if their renditions depart too obviously from "reading." It seems some of the reluctance surrounding performance that shaped women's activities a century ago remains.

Even less a part of American collective memory than elocution, choral speaking peaked in the 1930s and 1940s, but verse-speaking choirs existed in the 1950s and beyond. Emerson College had such a choir until the early 1970s, and the City College of New York sponsors choral speaking by schoolchildren in conjunction with its Langston Hughes Festival. With some stylistic differences, the practice also continues to flourish in festivals and competitions for children held in Southeast Asia and other regions culturally influenced by British colonialism. In 2012 the Verse-Speaking Choir of the Witherspoon Street Presbyterian Church in Princeton, New Jersey, celebrated its twenty-sixth year. The group was formally established by Cecelia B. Hodges, a graduate of Northwestern's oral-interpretation program, after a successful Woman's Day church performance.[9] The anniversary appearance of the ten women, mostly African Americans, included texts celebrating women that individual members had chosen: choral settings of Proverbs 31:10–31, describing how a good woman is "far more precious than jewels," and "Things My Mother Taught Me," a text typical of women's humorous portrayals of delinquent children shaped by their mother's power:

> Choir: My mother taught me time travel.
> Solo: If you don't straighten up, I'm gonna knock you into the middle of next week.
> Choir: My mother taught me irony.
> Solo: Keep crying, and I'll give you something to cry about.

After the performance, Hodges told the delighted audience, "It's God's spirit that drives us, but it's also a real belief that there is a power in the spoken word."[10]

In the same way that choral speaking served as a tool to teach children, music is still sometimes part of language pedagogy. In the late 1980s, Nancy Polette of Lindenwood University published two volumes of "concert readings" accompanied with cassette tapes of music for children to recite to.[11] Her idea of reading to music was to be "a means to impress language on the brain," motivated by educational research that suggests children learn language through extensive repetition, which could be achieved with musical rhythms.[12] Polette used marches and waltzes with young children and allowed older children to pick "mood music"—"happy, sad, peaceful, scary"[13]—to accompany reading prose out loud, finding that it helped them to read with more expression. Her tapes featured songlike melodies that resembled popular Americana such as "Turkey in the Straw" or "Skip to My Lou," and compositions for piano in a classical style, played with a steady beat for rhythmic recitation; this stylistic dichotomy is somewhat reminiscent of the sorts of musical works used for accompaniment by female performers at the turn of the twentieth century. Polette's workshops for educators on using music have been popular, but she was personally unaware of the history of accompanied recitation or of choral speaking.

"I Am," a poem by Lauren Hancock that Polette provided for children to perform to quiet music, features the refrain "I am a curious girl who likes books." Yet other than imagining what it would be like to be Mark Twain's Becky Thatcher, the girl who "hopes for an educated America" dreams of men's adventures penned by male authors: Captain Ahab, Captain Nemo, and Robinson Crusoe. Accompanied by drawings of men, the poem offers a young girl masculine masterpieces without any recognition of the possibility of women's literary creativity. The little poem nonetheless expresses the deep relationship of women with literature that motivated their entry into elocution and inspired the performances described in this book, from the accompanied recitations of Jane Manner to the choral poetic arrangements of Cécile de Banke to the comedic interpretations of Frieda Peycke.

Speech is heard in conjunction with music so frequently—on radio and in television and movies—that audiences find nothing remarkable about the combination. Yet a literary motivation is no longer the principal force behind these word-music combinations. In YouTube videos, many people speak poetry as background music plays quietly, or occasionally mix poetry and song in highly informal practices, yet the addition of music from an outside source (other than their own vocal production) is not permitted in students' forensics performances. The rules for the National Poetry Slam, in which poets compete in oral performances of their own texts, specifically forbid music.[14] In the twenty-first century, literature combined with music is still hailed as new and experimental; in 2014, when author Neil Gaiman read his story *The Truth Is a Cave in the Black Mountains* with music by the FourPlay String Quartet, he stated they were "doing something nobody's ever done before."[15]

Women performing to music can now recite their own poetry rather than that of male authors; they can speak for themselves. British poet Kate Tempest, who began her career as a rap artist, performs her own poems to a musical background. Her *Brand New Ancients*, a "self-performed epic poem to a live score" won the Ted Hughes prize in 2013.[16] Of Tempest's performance style, one critic has written, "You get the sense that she wants to create something tangible and real through language, that she's giving birth to her words."[17] Like the fictional Marjorie in Ruth Suckow's *The Odyssey of a Nice Girl,* Tempest performs something "real," the "clear soprano note" that is her own, but she has not found her voice without a struggle. When she was a teenager, rappers would refuse to let her perform because she didn't fit the stereotypical mold: she had a male friend pretend he wanted to rap so that he could hand her the microphone: "I'd start talking and people would be like: 'What? You can actually spit rhymes?'" Tempest uses a musical background because solo recitation seems too self-indulgent, and she worries that either the music or the poetry will not appeal to her fans. American poet Hedwig Gorski, who performs in a highly pitched recitation style with jazz accompaniment, describes herself as "the first performance poet to designate her voice as performance poetry" and, along with the East of Eden band, claims to have "named and defined the genre."[18] Despite the large number of women who recited to music, modern performers can still face both the rejection of musico-poetic combinations, and the need, more than a century later, to define the genre yet again.

The combinations of music and speech by female composers did not become established in a lasting performance tradition, and many women's compositions advertised by publishers appear to be no longer extant. In spite of the Progressive-Era roots of accompanied recitation in the aspiration to literary high culture, texts set by women drew on popular poems, bound to their times, and thus were likely to be quickly forgotten. The best of these compositions, those by Phyllis Fergus and Frieda Peycke, were perhaps too closely associated with the performances of their individual creators. Despite Peycke's private instruction in her performing style and her initial foray into sound recording, her efforts to gain a broader audience for musical readings came long after the height of popularity of accompanied recitation. The clubs in which Fergus was deeply involved and that served as the venues for women's performances declined in membership or ceased to exist in the late twentieth century as societal changes and second-wave feminism helped make more professional opportunities for women available.

It would be easy to assume that the spoken-word pieces of women composers disappeared along with the demise of elocution teachers like Mrs. Holton and women's literary societies. Nonetheless, musical readings performed by students of female instructors continued to appear sporadically in newspaper accounts of children's musical and dramatic recitals into the middle of the twentieth century. More frequently, notices of women's civic or church organizations reported their members' occasional performances of musical readings into the 1950s and beyond. One work, Phyllis Fergus's "The Usual Way," became a regular feature of entertainments arranged for bridal showers; in addition to refreshments and games, many brides were honored with programs that featured songs, piano solos, readings, or instrumental solos, a continuation of the musical and literary entertainment in which women had engaged since the nineteenth century.[19] "The Usual Way" was heard at numerous such events, from a shower for Miss Lorene Haynie in Ardmore, Oklahoma, in 1924, to another as late as 1976, held in Milford, Iowa, at the Excelsior United Methodist Church. More than sixty years after it was composed, two already married women performed Fergus's musical reading to celebrate the wedding of Gerlane Godrey.[20] The piece retained remnants of accompanied recitation in its quotation of Mendelssohn's famous Wedding March, and its comic mockery of ideals of domestic bliss, through the subversive humor of dissonant tone clusters depicting marriage's "usual way," were heard by a female audience. Fergus's story poem, an art form combining recitation and music, still had the power to speak to women of their lives.

# Appendix

*Accompanied Recitations
of Jane Manner*

Found in *Readings with Music*, Jennie Mannheimer [Jane Manner] Papers, Ms. Collection no. 259, box 1, folder 3, American Jewish Archives, Hebrew Union College, Cincinnati, and *The Silver Treasury* (New York: Samuel French, 1934). Works included in Manner's handwritten volume *Readings with Music* that are not songs and for which she gave no indication of music have been omitted. The volume also contains several brief, sketchy lists of additional accompanied recitations, which have not been included here.

| Author | Poem/Text | Composer | Musical Accompaniment |
| --- | --- | --- | --- |
| Karle Wilson Baker | "Growing Old"* | [Irish air, T. Moore] | "Last Rose of Summer" |
| Bible | Psalm 23* | G. F. Handel | Largo [*Xerxes*, act I, "Ombra mai fù"] |
| | | | |
| Anna Hempstead Branch | "Her Words" | Antonín Dvořák | *Songs My Mother Taught Me* |
| George Croly | "Belshazzar"* | | improvisation |
| John Dryden | "A Song for St. Cecilia's Day" | [G. B.] Draghi | |
| Rose Fyleman | "There Are Fairies at the Bottom of Our Garden" | Liza Lehmann | [song] |
| | | | |
| Crosbie Garstin | "A Fantasy" | Felix Mendelssohn | *Spring Song* [op. 62, no. 6] |
| Johann Wolfgang von Goethe | "The Erlking"*/"Der Erlkönig"* | Franz Schubert | [song] |
| Heinrich Heine | "Auf Flügeln des Gesanges"/ "On Song's Bright Pinions"* | Felix Mendelssohn | [song, op. 34, no. 2] |
| | | | |
| Henrik Ibsen | Ase's Death from *Peer Gynt** | Edvard Grieg | [incidental music] |
| Vachel Lindsay | "The Lame Boy and the Fairy" | Frédéric Chopin | Berceuse [op. 57] |
| Henry Wadsworth Longfellow | "The Bridge"* | Camille Saint-Saëns | *The Swan* |
| Henry Wadsworth Longfellow | "The Day Is Done" | Wilhelm Schäffer | [published reading with music] |
| Henry Wadsworth Longfellow | "The Fiftieth Birthday of Agassiz"* | Schutte | "In a Garden" |
| Henry Wadsworth Longfellow | "Sandalphon"* | Harvey W. Loomis | [published melodrama] |
| Henry Wadsworth Longfellow | "Hiawatha's Wooing"* | Rosetter G. Cole | [published melodrama] |
| Louise Mannheimer | "Segen Wirkend"* | Antonín Dvořák | *Songs My Mother Taught Me* |
| John Masefield | "Sea Fever" | John H. Densmore | [song] |

| Author | Poem/Text | Composer | Musical Accompaniment |
|---|---|---|---|
| Owen Meredith | "Aux Italiens"* | Giuseppe Verdi | "Non ti scordar di me" from Il Trovatore |
| A. A. Milne | "A Bear with a [Very] Little Brain" | H. Fraser-Simson | [song] |
| German folk song | "Spin, Spin, My Little Daughter" ["Spinnerliedchen"]* | arr. Heinrich Reimann | [song] |
| John Howard Payne | "Home, Sweet Home" | Henry Bishop | [song] |
| Edgar Allan Poe | "The Raven"* | Arthur Bergh | [published melodrama] |
| James Whitcomb Riley | "An Old Sweetheart of Mine"[1] | Robert Schumann | Träumerei, op. 15, no. 7 |
| Lee Shippey | "Mother" ("Candlelight") | Charles Cadman | [song] |
| Frank L. Stanton | "Just A-Wearyin' for You" | Carrie Jacobs-Bond | [song] |
| Elinor C. Stewart | "The Day"* | Johannes Brahms | Valse in A-flat [op. 39, no. 15] |
| Ivan S. Turgenev | "How Beautiful Were Once the Roses"* | Anton Arensky | [published declamation, op. 68] |

* Included in The Silver Treasury.

1. Not included in either volume, but regularly performed by Manner.

# Notes

*Preface*

1. Marian Wilson Kimber, "Reading Shakespeare, Seeing Mendelssohn: Concert Readings of *A Midsummer Night's Dream*, ca. 1850–1920," *Musical Quarterly* 89 (2006): 199–236.

2. *Daily Evening Transcript* (Boston), January 27, 1849, quoted in Gerald Kahan, "Fanny Kemble Reads Shakespeare: Her First American Tour, 1849–1850," *Theatre Survey* 24 (May/November 1983): 85.

3. Michael V. Pisani, *Music for the Melodramatic Theatre in Nineteenth-Century London and New York* (Iowa City: University of Iowa Press, 2014), xx–xxi.

4. For example, William Weber's *The Great Transformation of Musical Taste: Concert Programming from Haydn to Brahms* (Cambridge: Cambridge University Press, 2008).

5. Joan Shelley Rubin, *Songs of Ourselves: The Uses of Poetry in America* (Cambridge, MA: Belknap Press, 2007).

6. Nan Johnson, *Gender and Rhetorical Space in American Life, 1866–1910* (Carbondale: Southern Illinois University Press, 2002); "Parlor Rhetoric and the Performance of Gender in Postbellum America," in *Rhetorical Education in America*, ed. Cheryl Glenn, Margaret Lyday, and Wendy B. Sharer (Tuscaloosa: University of Alabama Press, 2004), 107–28.

7. One exception is John S. Gentile's *Cast of One: One-Person Shows from the Chautauqua Platform to the Broadway Stage* (Urbana: University of Illinois Press, 1989).

8. Jane Donawerth, *Conversational Rhetorics: The Rise and Fall of a Woman's Tradition, 1600–1900* (Carbondale: Southern Illinois University Press, 2012), 105–25.

9. Nancy Lee Chalfa Ruyter, *The Cultivation of Body and Mind in Nineteenth-Century American Delsartism* (Westport, CT: Greenwood Press, 1999); Nancy Lee Chalfa Ruyter and Thomas Leabhart, eds., *Essays on François Delsarte, Mime Journal* (2004–5) (Claremont, CA: Pomona College Theatre Department for the Claremont Colleges, 2005).

10. Sarah Hibberd, ed., *Melodramatic Voices: Understanding Music Drama* (Aldershot, UK: Ashgate Press, 2011).

11. Jacqueline Waeber, *En musique dans le text: Le mélodrame, de Rousseau à Schoenberg* (n.p.: Van Dieren, 2005).

12. *Portraits of Freedom: Music of Aaron Copland and Roy Harris*, Seattle Symphony Orchestra, cond. Gerard Schwartz (Delos DE 3140, 1993).

13. See male performers in Marian Wilson Kimber, "Mr. Riddle's Readings: Music and Elocution in Nineteenth-Century Concert Life," *Nineteenth Century Studies* 21 (2007): 163–81.

14. For example, Catherine Robson, *Heartbeats: Everyday Life and the Memorized Poem* (Princeton, NJ: Princeton University Press, 2012).

15. The remainder of the female composers of melodrama was British.

16. *Music News* 24, no. 37 (September 9, 1932): 1.

17. Judith Tick, "Passed Away Is the Piano Girl: Changes in American Musical Life: 1870–1900," in *Women Making Music: The Western Art Tradition, 1150–1950*, ed. Jane Bowers and Judith Tick (Urbana: University of Illinois Press, 1986), 325–48; Catherine Parsons Smith, "'A Distinguishing Virility': Feminism and Modernism in American Art Music," in *Cecilia Reclaimed: Feminist Perspectives on Gender and Music*, ed. Susan Cook and Judy S. Tsou (Urbana: University of Illinois Press, 1994), 90–106.

## Chapter 1. The Odyssey of a Nice Girl

1. Karen Neubauer, "The Interrupted Adventures of the Female Experience in Ruth Suckow's *Odyssey of a Nice Girl*" (June 3, 2007), http://www.ruthsuckow.org/home /resources-on-ruth-suckow, accessed March 30, 2016.

2. Ruth Suckow, *The Odyssey of a Nice Girl* (New York: Alfred A. Knopf, 1925), 57.

3. Ibid., 72.

4. Ibid., 109.

5. Ibid., 140.

6. Ibid., 71.

7. Ibid., 191–92.

8. Ibid., 140.

9. Ibid., 122.

10. Ibid., 345–46.

11. Ibid., 230.

12. Ibid., 140–41.

13. Ibid., 268.

14. Ibid., 268–69.

15. Ibid., 348.

16. "The Social Union," *Algona (IA) Courier*, January 6, 1899.

17. Ruth Suckow, *Some Others and Myself: Seven Stories and a Memoir* (New York: Rinehart, 1952), 190, 196–97.

18. Papers of Ruth Suckow, MsC 706, series 1, box 11, folder 1, University of Iowa Libraries, Special Collections, Iowa City (hereafter cited as Suckow Papers).

19. Ruth Suckow, "From an Iowa Notebook . . . a Little Girl's World," *Midwest Literary Review* 3, no. 2 (1960): 4.

20. Ruth Suckow, "Iowa," *American Mercury* (September 1926): 44–45.

21. Suckow, *Some Others*, 233.

22. Leedice McAnelly Kissane, "Ruth Suckow: Interpreter of the Mind of Mid-America (1900–1933)" (PhD diss., University of Minnesota, 1967), 105.

23. *Curry School of Expression, Boston, Mass., a Few Positions Held by Our Graduates*, Curry College Archives, Milton, Massachusetts, lists Belhaven, Whitworth, and Mississippi Women's Colleges.

24. *Miss Ruth Suckow, Teacher of Expression*, flyer [Manchester, IA, 1915], Suckow Papers, series I, subseries 5, box 9.

25. Lindal Buchanan, *Regendering Delivery: The Fifth Canon and Antebellum Women Rhetors* (Carbondale: Southern Illinois University Press, 2005), 12.

26. Angela Sorby, *Schoolroom Poets: Childhood, Performance, and the Place of American Poetry, 1865–1917* (Durham: University of New Hampshire Press, 2005), xxix.

27. See Jean Ferguson Carr, Stephen L. Carr, and Lucille M. Schultz, *Archives of Instruction: Nineteenth-Century Rhetorics, Readers, and Composition Books in the United States* (Carbondale: Southern Illinois University Press, 2005), 25–27, 111–16.

28. Margaret Nash, *Women's Education in the United States, 1780–1840* (New York: Palgrave Macmillan, 2005), 88–89.

29. Sorby, *Schoolroom Poets*, xiv.

30. Buchanan, *Regendering Delivery*, 14.

31. "Life Work Opens for Southern Woman," *Boston Traveler*, January 25, 1904, quoted in Carole Merritt, *The Herndons: An Atlanta Family* (Athens: University of Georgia Press, 2002), 27.

32. L[ouisa] C[aroline] Tuthill, ed., *The Young Lady's Reader* (New Haven, CT: S. Babcock, 1839), iii.

33. *The American Lady's Preceptor: A Compilation of Observations, Essays and Poetical Effusions, Designed to Direct the Female Mind in a Course of Pleasing and Instructive Reading*, 10th ed. (Baltimore: Edward J. Coale, 1821), xi.

34. Anna U. Russell, *The Young Ladies' Elocutionary Reader* (Boston: James Munroe, 1846), 9.

35. L. H. Sigourney, *The Girl's Reading-Book, in Prose and Poetry: For Schools*, 12th ed. (New York: Clement and Packard, 1841), preface.

36. *Gems of Deportment*, 392, quoted in Clifton Joseph Furness, ed., *The Genteel Female: An Anthology* (New York: Alfred A. Knopf, 1931), 170.

37. Russell, *Young Ladies' Elocutionary Reader*, 13–14.

38. Buchanan, *Regendering Delivery*, 31, 37.

39. Mr. [E. M.] Booth, "Discussion," *Proceedings of the National Association of Elocutionists* 9 (1900): 73.

40. Carolyn Eastman, *A Nation of Speechifiers: Making an American Public after the Revolution* (Chicago: University of Chicago Press, 2009), 78.

41. Buchanan, *Regendering Delivery*, 54.

42. Ibid., 42.

43. Janet Carey Elred and Peter Mortensen, *Imagining Rhetoric: Composing Women of the Early United States* (Pittsburgh: University of Pittsburgh Press, 2002), 8. The authors are referring to celebrations at a Kentucky school.

44. A. R. Phippen, ed., "How the Boys Become Good Speakers," *Schoolmate Monthly Reader for School and Home Instruction of Youth* 4, no. 12 (October [ca. 1855]): 365.

45. Programs for Rhetorical Exercises, Albany High School (1881); Barre Academy Rhetorical Exercises of the Senior and Middle Classes (1879); Craftsbury Academy, North Craftsbury, Vermont (1883); Ohio Valley Academy, Decatur, Ohio (1864), Warren School (1880); all from the Jerry Tarver Elocution, Rhetoric, and Oratory Collection, Ohio State University Libraries, Rare Books and Manuscripts Library, Columbus, Ohio (hereafter cited as Tarver Collection), box 1, folder 9.

46. Carl Arthur Dallinger, "History of Speech Training at William Jewell College and Park College, 1850–1940" (PhD diss., University of Iowa, 1952), 587–606.

47. Christie Farnham, *The Education of the Southern Belle: Higher Education and Student Socialization in the Antebellum South* (New York: New York University Press, 1994), 91.

48. Mrs. St. Julian Ravenel, *Charleston, the Place and the People* (New York: Macmillan, 1912), 475.

49. On ornamental education, see Nash, *Women's Education*, 72–75. Despite the designation of music as "ornamental," many women achieved a high level of proficiency, and a similar situation undoubtedly existed for those studying elocution.

50. Mabel Newcomer, *A Century of Higher Education for American Women* (New York: Harper, 1959), 49, cited in Lynn D. Gordon, *Gender and Higher Education in the Progressive Era* (New Haven, CT: Yale University Press, 1990), 7.

51. Judith Tick, "Passed Away Is the Piano Girl: Changes in American Musical Life: 1870–1900," in *Women Making Music: The Western Art Tradition, 1150–1950*, ed. Jane Bowers and Judith Tick (Urbana: University of Illinois Press, 1986), 325–48; cited on pp. 326–27.

52. Earl Barnes, "The Feminizing of Culture," *Atlantic Monthly* 109, no. 6 (June 1912): 770.

53. See Theodora Penny Martin, *The Sound of Our Own Voices: Women's Study Clubs, 1860–1910* (Boston: Beacon Press, 1987), and Anne Ruggles Gere, *Intimate Practices: Literacy and Cultural Work in U.S. Women's Clubs, 1880–1920* (Urbana: University of Illinois Press, 1997).

54. Martin, *Sound of Our Own Voices*, 79–80.

55. Quoted in Mrs. J. C. Croly, *The History of the Woman's Club Movement in America* (New York: Henry G. Allen, 1898), 59.

56. Anna Morgan, "The Art of Elocution," in *The Congress of Women: Held in the Woman's Building, World's Columbian Exposition, Chicago, U.S.A., 1893*, ed. Mary Kavanaugh Oldham Eagle (Chicago: Monarch, 1894), 597.

57. See Linda Whitesett, "'The most potent force' in American Music: The Role of Women's Music Clubs in American Concert Life," in *The Musical Woman*, vol. 3, ed. Judith Lang Zaimont et al. (Westport, CT: Greenwood Press, 1991), 663–81;

Ralph Locke and Cyrilla Barr, eds., *Cultivating Music in America: Women Patrons and Activists since 1860* (Berkeley: University of California Press, 1997).

58. Karen J. Blair, *The Torchbearers: Women and Their Amateur Arts Associations in America, 1890–1930* (Bloomington: Indiana University Press, 1994), 4.

59. Thomas Edie Hill, *Hill's Manual—Never Give a Lady a Restive Horse: A 19th Century Handbook of Etiquette*, ed. David MacKenzie and W. B. Blankenburg (Berkeley, CA: Diablo Press, 1967), 102.

60. E. B. Warman, *The Voice: How to Train It—How to Care for It* (Boston: Lee and Shepard, 1889), 18–25.

61. Henry Davenport Northrop, *The Ideal Speaker and Entertainer* (n.p., 1910).

62. See Nan Johnson, *Gender and Rhetorical Space in American Life, 1866–1910* (Carbondale: Southern Illinois University Press, 2002), 19–47.

63. Anna Lætitia Barbauld, *The Female Speaker; or, Miscellaneous Pieces in Prose and Verse: Selected from the Best Writers, and Adapted to the Use of Young Women* (Boston: Wells and Lilly, 1824), vi.

64. For example, Ebenezer Bailey, *The Young Ladies' Class Book: A Selection of Lessons for Reading, in Prose and Verse*, 21st ed. (Boston: Gould, Kendall, and Lincoln, 1839).

65. For example, Anna Randall Diehl, *Exercises in Elocution* (1868); Caroline B. Le Row, *A Practical Reader: With Exercises in Vocal Culture* (1883); Mary Ferris Bishop, *A Brief Outline of Elocution: Combined with a Few Choice Dramatic and Other Selections, Taken from the Best Authors* (1887); Eleanor O'Grady, *Aids to Correct and Effective Elocution: With Selected Readings and Recitations for Practice* (1890); Ermine Owen, *Readings, Recitations, and Impersonations* (1891); and Eloise A. Hafford, *Drill-Book of Elocution* (1894).

66. Laura Yerkes, Maude Jackson, Mathilda Blair, and Marie Irish authored multiple works for children.

67. For example, Mrs. [Harriet] Scott Saxton, *The Newest Elocution Text-Book: The Syllabic Law of Expression* (1893); Bessie Bryant Bosworth, *Mrs. Bosworth's Elocutionary Studies for Amateurs* (1889); and Julia Anna Orum, *The Orum System for Voice Education* (1895).

68. Pogle can be seen in an 1894 scrapbook photo, Records of Zeta Phi Eta, 1893–1992, series 31/6/79, box 4, Northwestern University Archives, Evanston, Illinois. See Frances Putnam Pogle and George M. Vickers, *Speaker and Entertainer: Recitations, Readings, Plays, Drills, Tableaux, etc., etc.* (Philadelphia: John C. Winston, 1900).

69. See William R. Rickert, "Commercializing Elocution: 'Parlor Books' for Home Entertainments," *Southern Speech Communication Journal* 43 (Summer 1978): 384–94.

70. "Public Reader's Convention: Delegates Present from Every Part of the Country," *New York Times*, June 28, 1892.

71. Elsie M. Wilbor, ed., *Werner's Directory of Elocutionists, Readers, Lecturers and Other Public Instructors and Entertainers* (New York: E. S. Werner, 1887), 273.

72. Quoted in Merrill Whitburn et al., "Elocution and Feminine Power in the First Quarter of the Twentieth Century: The Career of Carolyn Winkler (Paterson) as Performer and Teacher," *Rhetoric Review* 30 (2011): 397.

73. First verse: "I'm the most oratic girl at old N.U., I just love to orate honest yes I do." Lynn Miller Rein, *Northwestern University School of Speech: A History* (Evanston, IL: Northwestern University, 1981), 32.

74. For other women's schools, see Judy Baker Goss, "'Expression' in the Popular Culture of Dallas in the Early 1900s," in *Performance of Literature in Historical Perspectives*, ed. David W. Thompson (Lanham, MD: University Press of America, 1983), 259–81.

75. Mary Joanna Rizzo, "Lily C. Whitaker: Founder of the New Orleans College of Oratory and Elocution" (PhD diss., University of Wisconsin, 1954), 2 vols.

76. Edythe Ashmore, ed., *Lest We Forget* (Detroit: Eby and Stubbs, 1904), 35–204.

77. Ibid., 159.

78. Ethel Robinson (1890?–1975?) Papers 1909–1914, scrapbook, p. 38, Northwestern University Archives, Evanston, Illinois.

79. Elaine Carol Main, "'Miss Paul' Hits the Glittering Chautauqua Trail," *Palimpsest* 66, no. 4 (July/August 1985): 131–33, 140.

80. Nena Couch, "Pauline Sherwood Townsend: Expression and Pageantry," in *Women in the Arts in the Belle Epoque: Essays on Influential Artists, Writers and Performers*, ed. Paul Fryer (Jefferson, NC: McFarland, 2012), 28–47.

81. *Miss Mannheimer: Monologues*, Redpath Chautauqua Collection, University of Iowa Libraries, Special Collections, http://digital.lib.uiowa.edu/cdm/ref/collection /tc/id/38355, accessed March 1, 2016.

82. Jacob W. Shoemaker and Rachel H. Shoemaker Ephemeral Papers, 1862–1877, McNairy Library and Learning Forum, Special Collections and Archives, Millersville University, Millersville, Pennsylvania.

83. Jessie Alexander, *Encore! New Book of Platform Sketches* (Toronto: McClelland and Stewart, 1922), 129.

84. *Shaftesbury Magazine of Oratory* 1, no. 1 (September 1895): 1.

85. Olive Logan, *Before the Footlights and behind the Scenes: A Book about "the Show Business" in All Its Branches* (Philadelphia: Parmelee, 1870), 46.

86. October 8, 1880, Katherine Alvord (1861–1963) Papers, 1880–1969, folder 4, Northwestern University Archives, Evanston, Illinois.

87. Cora Urquhart Potter, *My Recitations* (Philadelphia: J. B. Lippincott, 1887).

88. Craig Clinton, *Cora Urquhart Potter: The Victorian Actress as Provocateur* (Jefferson, NC: McFarland, 2010), 17–23.

89. Charles L. Wagner, *Seeing Stars* (New York: G. Putnam's Sons, 1940), 34.

90. Florence C. Peck, February 22, 1901, diaries, 1898–1903, quoted in Jane H. Hunter, *How Young Girls Become Ladies: The Victorian Origins of American Girlhood* (New Haven, CT: Yale University Press, 2002), 375.

91. Ashmore, *Lest We Forget*, 35–204.

92. Whitburn et al., "Elocution and Feminine Power," 399.

93. H. L. Mencken, "Fiction Good and Bad," *American Mercury* 7 (April 1926): 506.

94. *Chautauqua Assembly Herald* (July 29, 1898), quoted in Dorothy Siedenburg, "Oral Interpretation at the Chautauqua Institution and the Chautauqua School of Expression, 1874–1900" (PhD diss., Northwestern University, 1956), 80.

95. S. R. Kelley, catalog of *New England Conservatory School of Elocution and College of Oratory* (Boston, 1890), 9.

96. See Joyce Lorranie Chalcraft Sozen, "Anna Morgan: Reader, Teacher, and Director" (PhD diss., University of Illinois, 1961), 159–92.

97. Scrapbook, September 1913–May 1918, Curry College Archives, Milton, Massachusetts.

98. *Morse School of Expression Catalog*, ca. 1925–31 [photocopy], 10, Tarver Collection, box 4, folder 43.

99. Sorby, *Schoolroom Poets*, xxxiii.

100. Mrs. Arthur Ransom, "The Open Door," *Proceedings of the National Association of Elocutionists* 9 (1900): 46.

101. Nan Johnson, "The Popularization of Nineteenth-Century Rhetoric: Elocution and the Private Learner," in *Oratorical Culture in Nineteenth-Century America: Transformations in the Theory and Practice of Rhetoric*, ed. Gregory Clark and S. Michael Halloran (Carbondale: Southern Illinois University Press, 1993), 148.

102. Anna Morgan, *The Art of Speech and Deportment* (Chicago: A. C. McClurg, 1909), 146.

103. Jessie Eldridge Southwick, "Unity of Spirit," *Emerson College Magazine* 7, no. 3 (January 1899): 75.

104. Helen Potter program, Kennedy Hall, January 11, 1882, Tarver Collection, box 2, folder 20.

105. Lawrence Levine, *Highbrow/Lowbrow: The Emergence of Cultural Hierarchy in America* (Cambridge, MA: Harvard University Press, 1988), 155.

106. William Chamberlain, "The President's Opening Address," *Proceedings of the National Association of Elocutionists* 5 (1896): 20; "Should Public Readers Follow or Lead Public Taste in the Choice of Selections?," *Proceedings of the National Association of Elocutionists* 4 (1896): 92.

107. Eleanor O'Grady, *Elocution Class: A Simplification of the Laws and Principles of Expression* (New York: Benziger Brothers, 1895), 20.

108. Brochure for Mrs. Helen E. Carpenter, Teacher of Vocal Culture, Oneonta, New York, Tarver Collection, box 7, folder 53.

109. George E. Hunt, letter to Ethelwyn Anderson, April 4, 1912, John Beecher Papers, Perkins Library, Duke University, Durham, North Carolina.

110. Christoph Irmscher, *Longfellow Redux* (Urbana: University of Illinois Press, 2006), 17–23.

111. Edward Amherst Ott, "Enemies inside the Elocution Profession," *Werner's Magazine* 26 (1901): 203.

112. "Should a Young Man Take Up Elocution?," *Werner's Magazine* 22–23 (1899): 468–73, 73–79, 190–95.

113. Quoted in "Readers and Singers," *Werner's Magazine* 26 (November 1900): 277.

114. *Bulletin of General Information* (Chicago: Columbia College of Expression, 1911), 13.

115. Eleanor Gates, *Miss Mannheimer, Reader: An Appreciation* [1917], American Jewish Archives, Hebrew Union College, Cincinnati, Ohio.

116. "Elocutionary Girls," *Voice* 8 (December 1886): 199.

117. James E. Murdoch and Lily Hollingshead, "Vocal Culture," *Proceedings of the National Association of Elocutionists* 1 (1892): 12–13.

118. Mr. [Henry Gaines] Hawn, "Discussion," *Proceedings of the National Association of Elocutionists* 9 (1900): 37–38.

119. Giles Wilkeson Gray, "What Was Elocution?," *Quarterly Journal of Speech* 46 (February 1960): 1.

120. John S. Gentile, *Cast of One: One-Person Shows from the Chautauqua Platform to the Broadway Stage* (Urbana: University of Illinois Press, 1989), 71.

121. Alyene Porter, *Consider Miss Lily* (New York: Abingdon Press, 1962), 13–14.

122. Agnes Curren Hamm, August 8, 1953, quoted in Rizzo, "Lily C. Whitaker," 2:416, and see also 2:397–430.

123. Paul Edwards, "Unstoried: Teaching Literature in the Age of Performance Studies," *Theatre Annual* 52 (Fall 1999): 42–43.

124. Elizabeth Bell, "Performance Studies as Women's Work: Historical Sights/Sites/Citations from the Margin," *Text and Performance Quarterly* 13 (1993): 362.

125. Johnson, *Gender and Rhetorical Space*, 38–39.

126. "Musically-Accompanied Recitations, Bird Notes, and Statue Posing and Their Relation to the Art of Elocution," *Proceedings of the Annual Meeting of the National Association of Elocutionists* 4 (1896): 120–27.

127. Maude May Babcock, "Interpretative Presentation vs. Impersonative Presentation," *Quarterly Journal of Public Speaking* 2 (1916): 23, 20–21.

128. Ibid., 25.

129. Gray, "What Was Elocution?," 7.

130. Mencken, "Fiction Good and Bad," 506.

131. Mary Jean DeMarr, "Ruth Suckow's Iowa 'Nice Girls,'" *Midamerica: The Yearbook for the Society for the Study of Midwestern Literature* 13 (1986): 72.

132. December 1925, letter to Mr. Chrischilles [copy], Suckow Papers, MsC 706, series I, subseries III, box 2.

133. Leedice McAnelly Kissane, *Ruth Suckow* (New York: Twayne, 1969), 61.

134. Kissane, "Ruth Suckow: Interpreter of the Mind of Mid-America," 116.

135. Mencken, "Fiction Good and Bad," 507.

136. "Study in Girlhood," *New York Times*, November 8, 1925.

137. "Books and Their Writers," *Davenport (IA) Democrat and Leader*, November 22, 1925; Edmund Morrison, quoted in Kissane, "Ruth Suckow: Interpreter of the Mind of Mid-America," 124.

138. John T. Frederick, "Ruth Suckow and the Middle Western Literary Movement," *English Journal* 20 (January 1931): 6.

139. Ibid., 7.

140. Mildred Cook, May 17, 1931, Suckow Papers, MsC 706, series I, subseries III, box 2.

141. For conflicts at the Elocutionists' Association 1897 meeting, see Edwards, "Unstoried," 63–75.

142. Frank M. Rarig and Halbert S. Greaves, "National Speech Organizations and

Speech Education," in *A History of Speech Education in America: Background Studies*, ed. Karl R. Wallace (New York: Appleton-Century-Crofts, 1954), 501–2, 505. Women did come to participate in debate.

## Chapter 2. Making Elocution Musical

1. "New Profession for Ladies," *Home Journal* 20, no. 170 (May 12, 1849): 2.

2. Michael V. Pisani, *Music for the Melodramatic Theatre in Nineteenth-Century London and New York* (Iowa City: University of Iowa Press, 2014), 9, 321.

3. Henry Davenport Northrop, *The Peerless Reciter; or, Popular Program Containing the Choicest Recitations and Readings from the Best Authors* (Atlanta: D. E. Luther, 1894), iv.

4. British composer Frederic Corder listed melodramas, including incidental music, in Robert D. Blackman, ed., *Voice, Speech, and Gesture: A Practical Handbook to the Elocutionary Art*, new ed. (Edinburgh: John Grant, 1912), 194–95, as did David Bispham, in "Melodrama, or Recitation with Music," *Harper's Bazaar* 43 (January 1909): 23–24.

5. Emma Griffith Lumm, *The Twentieth-Century Speaker* (Chicago: Dominion, 1898), 425.

6. Letters of Nellie Peck Saunders to Harry P. Harrison [September 1910], and September 25, 1910, Redpath Chautauqua Collection, MsC150, series 1, box 295, University of Iowa Libraries, Special Collections.

7. Letter of Saunders to Harrison, December 15, 1909, Redpath Chautauqua Collection, MsC150, series 1, box 295, University of Iowa Libraries, Special Collections.

8. L. M. Montgomery, *Anne of Green Gables* (London, 1908; repr. New York: Putnam, 2008), 186–87.

9. "How to Arrange a Program," *Werner's Magazine* 17 (July 1895): 537.

10. [*Peoria Star*, May 28, 1905] in scrapbook, Jennie Mannheimer [Jane Manner] Papers, Ms. Collection no. 259, box 2, folder 5, American Jewish Archives, Hebrew Union College, Cincinnati, Ohio (hereafter cited as Mannheimer Papers).

11. Ethel Robinson (1890?–1975?) Papers 1909–1914, scrapbook, Northwestern University Archives, Evanston, Illinois.

12. Programs listed in Klio Association (Chicago, Illinois) records, 1887–1901, vol. 1, Chicago History Museum.

13. "Chaminade Club Observes 60th Anniversary," clipping in scrapbook, box 4, Icey Lenora Teel Harling Papers, Iowa Women's Archives, University of Iowa Libraries.

14. "Questions of Good Form," *Harper's Bazaar* 34, no. 14 (April 6, 1901): A943.

15. Anna Wentworth Sears, "Midwinter Entertainments," *Harper's Bazaar* 38, no. 1 (January 1904): 88.

16. The only full melodramas published were Schumann's op. 122, no. 2, setting Shelley's *The Fugitives*, and Guenther Kiesewetter's *The Fable of the Rainbow*, op. 73, no. 2.

17. Stanley Schell, ed., *Werner's Readings and Recitations, No. 48: Musical Effects* (New York: Edgar S. Werner, 1911). Many selections were reprinted from *Werner's Magazine*.

18. Caroline B. Le Row, "Recitations with Music," *Werner's Voice Magazine* 13 (November 1891): 300.

19. See Grace Vaughan Bail, "Musically Accompanied Recitations," *Werner's Magazine* 19 (March 1897): 226.

20. Lumm, *Twentieth-Century Speaker*, 408.

21. Gustave Becker, "Recitation with Music," in Jane Manner, *The Silver Treasury: Prose and Verse for Every Mood* (New York: Samuel French, 1934), 122, 151.

22. Lucia W. Raines, "Musical Recitations: Suggestions Wanted as to Their Rendering," *Werner's Voice Magazine* 11 (July 1889): 147.

23. "Musically Accompanied Recitations," *Werner's Magazine* 19 (February–May 1897): 122–37, 225–30, 313–16, and 413–19.

24. Henry Davenport Northrop, *The Delsarte Speaker; or, Modern Elocution Designed Especially for Young Folks and Amateurs* (n.p.: J. R. Jones, 1895), 341–42.

25. Northrop, *Peerless Reciter*, 43–45.

26. Emma Dunning Banks, *Original Recitations with Lesson Talks*, enlarged ed. (New York: Edgar S. Werner, 1908), 142–44.

27. Werner published texts by Mrs. Frederick W. Pender, but she was foremost an elocutionist, teaching in New York City.

28. Longfellow's *The Song of Hiawatha* was set melodramatically by Robert Stoepel (ca. 1859), Rossetter G. Cole (1904), and Sadie Knowland Coe (1905). See Michael V. Pisani, *Imagining Native America in Music* (New Haven, CT: Yale University Press, 2005), 126–57. Poe's "The Raven" was set by Max Heinrich (1905) and Arthur Bergh (1910).

29. Melodramatic settings of "King Robert of Sicily" also include those by John Ebenezer West (ca. 1896) and John J. Wootton (1888).

30. *Fünf Dichtungen frei nach Kornell Ujejski über Kompositionen von Friedrich Chopin übersetzt von Emilya Bett und für melodramatischen Vortrag eingerichtet von Richard Burmeister* (Leipzig: Rob. Forberg, 1908); Suzanne d'Olivera Jackowska, *Tristesse Eternelle* [based on Chopin's Étude op. 10] (New York: Edward B. Marks, 1930).

31. "Readers and Singers," *Voice* 8 (March 1886): 48; Gustav Kobbé, "Reciting to Music: A Home Entertainment," *Good Housekeeping* 44 (1907): 222.

32. Kelley's correspondence, Western College Archives, Oxford, Ohio, reveals no reason for the arrangement. Kelley lectured before the "Werner Society" ["Concerning Incidental Music for the Drama"], *Werner's Magazine* 19 (February 1897): 125–35, immediately after which King performed the scene with Beethoven's music.

33. "Musically Accompanied Recitations," advertisement, *Werner's Voice Magazine* 26 (1901): 548.

34. Elsie M. Wilbor, ed., *Werner's Directory of Elocutionists, Readers, Lecturers and Other Public Instructors and Entertainers* (New York: E. S. Werner, 1887), 386.

35. [C. P.] Bronson, *Abstract of Elocution and Music, in Accordance with the Principles of Physiology and the Laws of Life, for the Development of Body and Mind* (Auburn, NY: Henry Oliphant, 1842), 9.

36. Frank H. Fenno, *The Science and Art of Elocution* (New York: Hinds, Noble and Eldredge, 1878), 25–42, described by Nan Johnson in "The Popularization of

Nineteenth-Century Rhetoric: Elocution and the Private Learner," in *Oratorical Culture in Nineteenth-Century America: Transformations in the Theory and Practice of Rhetoric,* ed. Gregory Clark and S. Michael Halloran (Carbondale: Southern Illinois University Press, 1993), 154. James Rush's book, *Philosophy of the Human Voice* (1827) went through more than six editions.

37. Henry N. Day, *The Art of Elocution Exemplified in a Systematic Course of Exercises,* rev. ed. (Cincinnati: Moore, Wilsyach, Keys, 1863), 58.

38. Charles W. Sanders, *The New School Reader, Fourth Book* (New York: Ivison and Phinney; Chicago: S. C. Griggs, 1854), 35; *McGuffey's New Juvenile Speaker* (Cincinnati and New York: Van Antwerp, Bragg, 1860), 19. See also George Raymond, *The Speaker* (New York: Silver Burdett, 1893), 47.

39. Robert E. Fulton and Thomas C. Trueblood, *Practical Elements of Elocution,* 3rd ed. (Boston: Ginn, 1893), 278.

40. According to John Hullah, the pitched style helped speakers be heard in large halls. Quoted in Charles John Plumptre, *King's College Lectures on Elocution,* 5th ed. (London: Kegan Paul, Trench, Trübner, 1895), 98.

41. Rush, in William Russell, *The Introductory Discourse and the Lectures Delivered before the American Institute of Instruction at Worcester, (Mass.), August 1837* (Boston: James Munroe, 1838), 246.

42. William B. Chamberlain, *Principles of Vocal Expression* (Chicago: Scott, Foresman, 1899), 142.

43. C. P. Bronson, *Manual of Elocution: Embracing the Philosophy of Vocalization,* ed. Laura M. Bronson (Louisville, KY: John P. Morton, 1873), 35.

44. Henry N. Day, cited in Mary Margaret Robb, *Oral Interpretation of Literature in American Colleges and Universities: A Historical Study of Teaching Methods* (New York: H. W. Wilson, 1941), 117.

45. Bronson, *Abstract of Elocution and Music,* 45; E. A. Ott, *How to Use the Voice in Reading and Speaking* (New York: Hinds, Noble, and Eldredge, 1901), 121.

46. Robert McLean Cumnock, *Choice Readings for Public and Private Entertainments and for the Use of Schools, Colleges, and Public Readers, with Elocutionary Advice* (Chicago: A. C. McClurg, 1914), 89–93.

47. Ibid., 97–98.

48. Mark Bailey, *An Introductory Treatise on Elocution* (New York: Taintor Brothers, Merill, 1880), 33.

49. For example, Bronson, *Manual of Elocution,* 97–98.

50. An earlier speech notation is described in Paul K. Alkon, "Joshua Steele and the Melody of Speech," *Language and Speech* 2 (1959): 154–74.

51. Alexander Melville Bell, *Elocutionary Manual: The Principles of Articulation and Orthoepy, the Art of Reading and Gesture* (Edinburgh: W. P. Kennedy, 1852), 57–59.

52. Bronson, *Abstract of Elocution and Music,* 43–44.

53. R. F. Brewer, "Speech," in Blackman, *Voice, Speech, and Gesture,* 84.

54. Poet-flutist Sidney Lanier divided the step into nine audible divisions. John R. Scott, *The Technic of the Speaking Voice* (Columbia, MO: E. W. Stephens, 1915), 316–17.

55. Fulton and Trueblood, *Practical Elements of Elocution*, 275.

56. Katherine Jewell Everts, *The Speaking Voice: Principles of Training Simplified and Condensed* (New York: Harper and Brothers, 1908), 50–51.

57. Scott, *Technic of the Speaking Voice*, 380–81. Scott describes *radical stress* as "Explosion + Effusion" produced through intense breath pressure and sudden release. *Vanish* is the conclusion of a vocal sound.

58. Ibid., 381.

59. Chamberlain, *Principles of Vocal Expression*, 128.

60. Ott, *How to Use the Voice*, 142.

61. Anna U. Russell, *The Young Ladies' Elocutionary Reader* (Boston: James Munroe, 1846), 17.

62. *The Art of Improving the Voice and Ear; and of Increasing Their Musical Powers, on Philosophical Principles* (London: Printed by S. and R. Bentley, for Septimus Prowell, 1825), 76.

63. Banks, *Original Recitations*, 76; Kelley, "Mr. Kelley's Address," *Werner's Magazine* 19 (March 1897): 132–33.

64. "Musically Accompanied Recitations," *Werner's Magazine* 19 (March 1897): 230.

65. William Smith Rockstro, "Melodrama," in George Grove, *Grove's Dictionary of Music and Musicians*, 2nd ed., 5 vols., ed. J. A. Fuller-Maitland (New York: Macmillan 1904–10), 3:107.

66. "Bispham's Milwaukee Success," *Musical Courier* (February 24, 1909), *Robinson Locke Collection of Dramatic Scrapbooks*, 502 vols. (New York: New York Public Library, 1977), 72:82.

67. "Musically Accompanied Recitations," *Werner's Magazine* 19 (April 1897): 313.

68. "Musically Accompanied Recitations," *Werner's Magazine* 19 (March 1897): 225–26.

69. For changes in theatrical training, see Francis Hodge, "The Private Theatre Schools in the Late Nineteenth Century," in *History of Speech Education in America: Background Studies*, ed. Karl R. Wallace (New York: Appleton-Century-Crofts, 1954), 552–71.

70. Edgar Allan Poe, *The Raven, Incidental Music by Max Heinrich*, Percy Hemus and Gladys Craven, pianoforte (Victor 35316, 1913).

71. Heinrich notated a repeated pitch for "Nevermore"; however, Hemus performed different pitches than indicated.

72. Edward Kravitt, "The Joining of Words and Music in Late Romantic Melodrama," *Musical Quarterly* 62 (October 1976): 583; Max von Schillings, *Das Hexenlied und andere Kompositionen* (Preiserrecords MONO 90294 b, 1996).

73. See Richard Bebb on the assertions that each succeeding generation of actors had a more "natural" style. "The Actor Then and Now," *Recorded Sound* 47 (July 1972): 85–86.

74. John Seaman Garns, "Reading to Music," *Journal of Expression* 1 (December 1922): 156.

75. Eleanor Gates, *Miss Mannheimer, Reader: An Appreciation* [1917], in Mannheimer Papers.

76. "Maiden's Song" was published by John Church in German and English ca. 1895.

77. For example, an entry on March 15, 1907, Mannheimer Papers, diary, box 1, folder 1.

78. Manner's Cincinnati DAR performance was in 1908; her Evansville, Ohio, Temple Sisterhood performance was in 1913. She seems to have presented Zangwill's novel rather than the later play version.

79. Clara Eleanore Babst advertised performances of *Peer Gynt* with Victrola in 1917, Redpath Chautauqua Collection, University of Iowa Libraries, Special Collections, http://digital.lib.uiowa.edu/cdm/ref/collection/tc/id/54055. Manner's Smith and Nixon player piano is noted in her diary entry for June 6, 1907, Mannheimer Papers.

80. Goethe's translated poem appears in Henry Llewellyn Williams, ed., *The Ellen Terry Ladies' Reciter* (New York: Hurst, 1884), and Anna Randall Diehl, ed., *Elocutionary Studies and New Recitations* (New York: Edgar S. Werner, 1898), 189–95, here arranged by Mabelle B. Biggart with a Schubert lecture.

81. *Erlkönig. Lied von Fr. Schubert für das Piano übertragen von Franz Liszt* (Wien, Austria: A. Diabelli, [1838]).

82. Riley settings are by A. J. Goodrich (1906), Leslie Harris (1909), Walter Howe Jones (1912), Fritz (Frederic) Krull (1913), and Paul Theodor Miersch (1921).

83. Mannheimer Papers, box 1, folder 3.

84. Manner's other lists in the volume (pp. 4, 33–34, and elsewhere) include pieces to accompany poems, songs (presumably to be recited), and published melodramas, perhaps under consideration for her anthology. An additional list contains works with timings and three more texts with music indicated.

85. "Segen Wirkend" was published in Louise and Sigmund Mannheimer, *Poems* (New York: n.p., 1921).

86. Arthur Bergh, *The Raven* (Boston: Oliver Ditson, 1910); Harvey Worthington Loomis, *Sandalphon* (New York: Edgar S. Werner, 1896).

87. "Music Notes," *New York Times*, February 9, 1935.

88. "Jane Manner Speech and Drama Studio, "Favorite Scenes and Poems from *The Silver Treasury*," Saturday, April 21, and Sunday, April 29, 1934, Mannheimer Papers, box 2.

89. Wilhelm Schäffer, *Day Is Done: A Reading with Music* (New York: M. Witmark and Sons, 1932).

90. Henry Wadsworth Longfellow, "The Day Is Done," lines 25, 31–32.

91. The song by this name quoted "Old One Hundredth": William B. Gray and G. L. S. Spaulding, *The Volunteer Organist. Descriptive Song* (New York: W. B. Gray, 1893), in *Lester S. Levy Collection of Sheet Music*, http://levysheetmusic.mse.jhu .edu/catalog/levy:144.099, accessed March 30, 2016.

92. March 3, 1918, Victor 18599, Frances J. Lapitino, harp, Library of Congress National Jukebox, http://www.loc.gov/jukebox/recordings/detail/id/6550 and http://www.loc.gov/jukebox/recordings/detail/id/6557.

93. Graduation program from 1894, Cleveland School of Elocution and Oratory, Jerry Tarver Elocution, Rhetoric, and Oratory Collection, Ohio State University Libraries, Rare Books and Manuscripts Library, Columbus, Ohio.

94. One postgraduate recital featured Robert Browning's "Saul" with music arranged for string quartet.

95. Ellen Decker Hall, in "Musically Accompanied Recitations," *Werner's Magazine* 19 (April 1897): 315.

96. Quoted in Garns, "Reading to Music," 156.

97. "Musically Accompanied Recitations," *Werner's Magazine* 19 (February 1897): 122.

98. Garns, "Reading to Music," 157–58.

99. Margaret E. Brooks, in "Musically Accompanied Recitations," *Werner's Magazine* 19 (February 1897): 123.

100. "Mr. Josephs's Address," *Werner's Magazine* 19 (February 1897): 134. This description is similar to the performance of Rose Coghlan (Victor 31728, 1909), with trumpet calls, timpani rolls, and a funeral march in the final verse.

101. Cora Worrell-Alford, in "Musically Accompanied Recitations," *Werner's Magazine* 19 (March 1897): 225.

102. Garns, "Reading to Music," 157.

103. Ibid., 160.

104. Laura E. Aldrich, in "Musically Accompanied Recitations," *Werner's Magazine* 19 (March 1897): 225.

105. David Bispham, *A Quaker Singer's Recollections* (New York: Macmillan, 1920), 282.

106. Leonora Oberndorfer, in "Musically Accompanied Recitations," *Werner's Magazine* 19 (February 1897): 136.

107. Becker, "Recitation with Music," in Manner, *Silver Treasury*, 121.

108. Stanley Hawley, "Recitation-Music," in Blackman, *Voice, Speech, and Gesture*, 1106.

109. See Michael Talbot, "The Work-Concept and Composer-Centeredness," in *The Musical Work: Reality or Invention?*, ed. Michael Talbot (Liverpool, UK: Liverpool University Press, 2000), 168–86.

## Chapter 3. Reading the Fairies

1. See Nan Johnson, "Shakespeare in American Rhetorical Education, 1870–1920," in *Shakespeare Educations: Power, Citizenship, and Performance*, ed. Coppélia Kahn, Heather S. Nathans, and Mimi Godfrey (Newark: University of Delaware Press, 2011), 112–27.

2. Marian Wilson Kimber, "Victorian Fairies and Felix Mendelssohn's *A Midsummer Night's Dream* in England," *Nineteenth-Century Music Review* 4 (2007): 56–58.

3. Gary Jay Williams, *Our Moonlight Revels: "A Midsummer Night's Dream" in the Theatre* (Iowa City: University of Iowa Press, 1997), 110.

4. Henry C. Lunn, "Fairy Music," *Musical Times* 23 (March 1882): 135.

5. "Some of Canada's Leading Elocutionists," *Ladies' Journal* 14, no. 2 (February 1894): 6.

6. Ben Arnold, "Music in Lancaster, Kentucky, 1885–1910: Local Talent, Touring Artists, and the Opera House," in *Music and Culture in America, 1861–1918*, ed. Michael Saffle (New York: Garland, 1998), 205–6.

7. Scrapbook of Addie G. Fowle, Curry College Archives, Milton, Massachusetts.

8. Michael V. Pisani, *Music for the Melodramatic Theatre in Nineteenth-Century London and New York* (Iowa City: University of Iowa Press, 2014), 247–51.

9. George Riddle performed *Macbeth* with music by Friedrich August Dressler, and selections from *Faust* with music by Schumann, Boito, Berlioz, Gounod, and Mendelssohn. Marian Wilson Kimber, "Mr. Riddle's Readings: Music and Elocution in Nineteenth-Century Concert Life," *Nineteenth Century Studies* 21 (2007): 163–81.

10. Marian Wilson Kimber, "Performing *Athalia*: Mendelssohn's Op. 74 in the Nineteenth-Century Choral World," *Choral Journal* 49 (April 2009): 18–33.

11. Robert Schumann's *Manfred* often appears in reciters' repertoire, but performances were not frequent. Delsarte performer Genevieve Stebbins recited M. Beer's tragedy *Struensee* to Giacomo Meyerbeer's 1846 music in 1880. *New York Times*, February 20, 1880.

12. "Mrs. Fanny Kemble at Exeter Hall," *Musical World* 33, no. 6 (February 10, 1855): 90.

13. William Hazlitt, "The Midsummer Night's Dream," *London Examiner* (January 21, 1816), in *The Selected Writings of William Hazlitt*, 9 vols., ed. Duncan Wu (London: Pickering and Chatto, 1998), 3:108.

14. *New York Herald*, August 31, 1841, quoted in George Clinton Densmore Odell, "'A Midsummer Night's Dream' on the New York Stage," in *Shaksperian [sic] Studies*, ed. Brander Matthews and Ashley Horace Thorndike (New York: Russell and Russell, 1962), 127.

15. See Trevor R. Griffiths, introduction to *A Midsummer Night's Dream*, Shakespeare in Production (Cambridge: Cambridge University Press, 1996), 17–21. See also Jonas Barish, *The Antitheatrical Prejudice* (Berkeley: University of California Press, 1981), 326–32.

16. On the visual in period theater, see Michael R. Booth, *Victorian Spectacular Theatre, 1850–1910* (London: Routledge and Kegan Paul, 1981).

17. Williams, *Our Moonlight Revels*, 123, 127.

18. "Astor Theatre Opens with Lovely Spectacle," *New York Times*, September 22, 1906.

19. Hazlitt, "Midsummer Night's Dream," 3:108.

20. Quoted in Odell, "'A Midsummer Night's Dream' on the New York Stage," 135.

21. *New York Evening Post*, November 10, 1826, quoted in Odell, "'A Midsummer Night's Dream' on the New York Stage," 123.

22. Desmond MacCarthy, "*A Midsummer Night's Dream*: The Production of Poetic Drama (1914)," in *Theatre* (New York: Oxford University Press, 1955), 159.

23. "The Status of Public Reading: An Interview with Mrs. Harriet Webb," *Werner's Magazine* 22 (January 1899): 334.

24. Kathy Fletcher, "Planché, Vestris, and the Transvestite Role: Sexuality and Gender in Victorian Popular Theatre," *Nineteenth Century Theatre* 15 (Summer 1987): 22.

25. Cuts retained the lovers and fairies; evidence suggests that Kemble removed the rustics' play for concert readings.

26. "Mr. George Riddle," *New York Times*, March 28, 1886.

27. See Douglass Seaton, "Mendelssohn's Dramatic Music," 204–22, and Thomas Grey, "The Orchestral Music," 460–65 and 493–98, both in *The Mendelssohn Companion*, ed. Douglass Seaton (Westport, CT: Greenwood Press, 2001).

28. George Grove, *Beethoven, Schubert, Mendelssohn* (London: Macmillan, 1951), 382.

29. Percy Fitzgerald, *Shakespearean Representations: Its Laws and Limits* (London: Elliot Stock, 1908), 62.

30. "St. James's Theatre, 'A Midsummer Night's Dream,'" *Athenæum* 1267 (February 7, 1852): 178. Kemble omitted the melodramatic sections, but included the music associated with the fairies.

31. Dutton Cook, "*A Midsummer Night's Dream*," in *Nights at the Play: A View of the English Stage* (London: Chatto and Windus, 1883), 274.

32. Tracy Davis, *Actresses as Working Women: Their Social Identity in Victorian Culture* (London: Routledge, 1991), 109.

33. Ibid., 110.

34. Lunn, "Fairy Music," 136.

35. Marian Wilson Kimber, "The Composer as Other: Gender and Race in the Biography of Felix Mendelssohn," in *The Mendelssohns: Their Music in History*, ed. John Michael Cooper and Julie Prandi (Oxford: Oxford University Press, 2003), 335–39.

36. Dorothy Marshall, *Fanny Kemble* (New York: St. Martin's Press, 1977), 244.

37. Fanny Kemble, *The Journal of Frances Anne Butler*, 2 vols. (London: John Murray, 1835; repr. New York: Benjamin Blom, 1970), 2:26–27.

38. Frances Anne Kemble, *Records of Later Life* (New York: Henry Holt, 1882), 639.

39. W. D. King, "'Shadow of a Mesmerizer': The Female Body on the Dark Stage," *Theatre Journal* 49 (1997): 189.

40. See Gerald Kahan, "Fanny Kemble Reads Shakespeare: Her First American Tour, 1849–50," *Theatre Survey* 24 (May/November 1983): 77–98.

41. Michael R. Booth, *Theatre in the Victorian Age* (Cambridge: Cambridge University Press, 1991), 114–17.

42. Leota S. Driver, *Fanny Kemble* (Chapel Hill: University of North Carolina Press, 1933), 183.

43. Entry from March 13, 1849, *The Diary of Philip Hone, 1828–1851*, 2 vols., ed. Allan Nevins (New York: Dodd, Mead, 1927), 2:863.

44. *Letters and Journals of Thomas Wentworth Higginson*, ed. Mary Thacher Higginson (Boston: Houghton Mifflin, 1921), 35.

45. *Boston Herald*, January 17, 1849, quoted in Kahan, "Fanny Kemble Reads Shakespeare," 85.

46. See Kemble's markings in Marian Wilson Kimber, "Reading Shakespeare, Seeing Mendelssohn: Concert Readings of *A Midsummer Night's Dream*, ca. 1850–1920," *Musical Quarterly* 89 (2006): 211.

47. Kemble, *Records of Later Life*, 210.

48. Ibid., 613.

49. "Music and the Drama," *Athenæum* 1265 (January 24, 1852): 122.

50. "St. James's Theatre, 'A Midsummer Night's Dream,'" 178.

51. Higginson, *Letters and Journals*, 37.

52. "Mrs. Frances Anne Kemble," *Galaxy* 6 (December 1868): 801.

53. "St. James's Theatre, 'A Midsummer Night's Dream,'" 178.

54. See Kemble's so-called masculine attributes considered by her contemporaries, in Faye E. Dudden, *Women in the American Theatre: Actresses and Audiences, 1790–1870* (New Haven, CT: Yale University Press, 1994), 52–58.

55. "Mrs. Fanny Kemble at Exeter Hall," *Musical World* 33, no. 6 (February 10, 1855): 90.

56. "Musical Correspondence," *Dwight's Journal of Music* 29, no. 19 (December 4, 1869): 149.

57. "The Editor's Easy Chair," *Harper's New Monthly Magazine* 56 (April 1878): 782; "Mrs. Fanny Kemble's Reading of the 'Midsummer Night's Dream,' with Mendelssohn's Incidental Music," *Leeds (UK) Mercury*, February 12, 1853.

58. "First Philharmonic Concert," *New York Herald*, November 28, 1869.

59. "'Hiawatha' at Chautauqua," *Musical America* 10, no. 15 (August 21, 1909): 26.

60. Dudden, *Women in the American Theatre*, 50.

61. Ibid., 27.

62. Ibid., 55.

63. Manner also gave a performance in Oxford, Ohio, in 1902 and performed the play with Mendelssohn's music on piano in 1913.

64. Jane Manner, "Longfellow on Reading Aloud," *New York Times*, June 15, 1932, responding to "Reading Aloud," *New York Times*, June 6, 1932.

65. McCormick (1873–1957) was a poet, editor, and literary critic. The poem is in Manner's "Readings with Music" book, discussed in chapter 2.

66. "A Midsummer Night's Dream," undated clipping [ca. 1911], scrapbooks, Curry College Archives, Milton, Massachusetts.

67. *William Shakespeare's "A Midsummer Night's Dream," Arranged for Public Reading, with the Performance of Mendelssohn's Music*, by Eben Francis Thompson (Boston: Houghton Mifflin, 1887); *The Episode of the Quarrel between Titania and Oberon, from Shakespeare's "A Midsummer Night's Dream,"* arr. for representation with Mendelssohn's music by F. A. [Frederick Augustus] Dixon (Ottawa: J. Durie, 1898); and *Verbindener Text zu Felix Mendelssohn Bartholdy's Sommersnachtstraum-Musik*, ed. Gustav Gurski, trans. August Wilhelm Schlegel (Leipzig: Breitkopf and Härtel, 1875).

68. "The Music Composed for Shakspeare's [*sic*] 'Midsummer Night's Dream.' By F. Mendelssohn Bartholdy," *Musical Times* 16, no. 384 (February 1, 1875): 778; italics added.

69. William Shakespeare, *Midsummer Night's Dream*, 2nd ed., condensed by Kate Weaver Dallas (New York: Edgar S. Werner, 1911).

70. March 5, 1910, program in scrapbooks, Curry College Archives, Milton, Massachusetts.

71. "Commencement Elocution Recital, June 4, 1894," in *Fifty-First Annual Register and Announcement of Hollins Institute* (Roanoke, VA: Hollins Institute, 1894), 90–91.

72. The speakers were George Riddle and David Bispham. See David Bispham, *A Quaker Singer's Recollections* (New York: Macmillan, 1920), 310–11.

73. "Young People's Concerts," *New York Times*, February 7, 1915.

## Chapter 4. Sentimentality and Gender in Musically Accompanied Recitations

1. Joanne Dobson, "Reclaiming Sentimental Literature," *American Literature* 69, no. 2 (1997): 285.

2. Ibid., 287, 269.

3. Ibid., 286.

4. Ibid., 272.

5. Ibid., 273.

6. Ibid., 279.

7. Anna Randall Diehl, ed., *Elocutionary Studies and New Recitations* (New York: Edgar S. Werner, 1898), x, described baby imitations. Harriet Saxton's *The Newest Elocution Text-Book: The Syllabic Law of Expression* (1893), 176–77, provided bell exercises and selections for wind practice.

8. Mary Thompson, *Rhythmical Gymnastics: Vocal and Physical* (New York: Edgar S. Werner, 1892), 87–106.

9. Diehl, *Elocutionary Studies and New Recitations*, x.

10. Henry M. Soper, *Soper's Select Speaker* ([Chicago]: Soper School of Oratory, 1901), 376–77.

11. "Discussion," *Proceedings of the National Association of Elocutionists* 10 (1901): 58.

12. Marian Wilson Kimber, "Ringing Bells in Accompanied Recitation and Musical Melodrama," *Journal of Musicological Research* 34 (2015): 252–54.

13. Margaret Walker Price, "Subscriber's Exchange," *Werner's Magazine* 29 (April 1902): 282. Price identified "Vision" as being by Sternberg; Constantine von Sternberg published some Schumann selections in 1915, so perhaps she confused the composer with the editor of an earlier edition.

14. Some vocal sound effects appear in early recordings. Raymond Wile, "Record Makers in 1891," *ARSC Journal* 3 (1971): 10–12, quoted in Jason Camlot, "Early Talking Books: Spoken Recordings and Recitation Anthologies, 1880–1920," *Book History* 6 (2003): 166.

15. "How Grandma Danced," *Theatre* 6 (1890): 414–15, states that the text was recited and danced to by Laura Sedgwick Collins.

16. Louise Preece, *A System of Physical Culture Prepared Expressly for Public School Work* (Syracuse, NY: C. W. Bardeen, 1894), 123, 192; Elsie M. Wilbor, *Delsarte Recitation Book and Directory* (New York: Edgar S. Werner, 1890), 35. The minuet by Hummel was *Six pièces très faciles*, op. 42, no. 3 (listed in *Grove Music Online* as op. 52).

17. Laura Augusta Yerkes, *Young Americans' Speaker* (Philadelphia: John Winston, 1902), 122.

18. Edith S. Tupper, "Grandmamma's Fan," in *Werner's Readings and Recitations No. 26* (New York: Edgar S. Werner, 1902), 139.

19. Soper, *Soper's Select Speaker*, 380. *Daughters of America* is presumably J. B. Lampe's march, even though it has an inappropriate meter.

20. Cora Vandemark, "Grandma at the Masquerade," in *The Modern Elocutionist or Popular Speaker*, ed. Guy Steeley (Chicago: Thompson and Thomas, 1900), 180–82.

21. Emma Dunning Banks, "Lesson-Talk," *Werner's Voice Magazine* 13 (December 1891): 320.

22. In Wilcox's anthology *How Salvator Won and Other Recitations* (New York: E. S. Werner, 1891), the title of "A Waltz-Quadrille" includes "With Musical Accompaniment."

23. John Harris Gutterson, "Musically Accompanied Recitations," *Werner's Voice Magazine* 20 (December 1897): 80; italics in original.

24. Stanley Schell, ed., *Werner's Readings and Recitations, No. 48: Musical Effects* (New York: Edgar S. Werner, 1911), 48, 23–26.

25. Anselm Bayly (1719–94) wrote the song.

26. John Wesley Hanson Jr. and Lillian Woodward Gunckel, eds., *The Ideal Orator and Manual of Elocution* (n.p.: Wabash, 1895), 328–30; Belle Bryant Bosworth, *Mrs. Bosworth's Elocutionary Studies for Amateurs* (Chicago: Belford, Clarke, 1889), 327–30; and Thomas W. Handford, *Fireside Pleasures for Young and Old* (Chicago: Mammoth, 1894), 84.

27. Lyrics by W. B. Glenroy [William Gray], music by Henry Lamb [Henry Spaulding], sung by Derek B. Scott, *The Victorian Web: Literature, History, and Culture in the Age of Victoria*, http://www.victorianweb.org/mt/parlorsongs/9.html, accessed March 1, 2016.

28. Frances Maude Wood notebook, Alton School of Oratory, Jerry Tarver Elocution, Rhetoric, and Oratory Collection, Ohio State University Libraries, Rare Books and Manuscripts Library, Columbus, Ohio (hereafter cited as Tarver Collection). Frances also copied Wilcox's "Waltz-Quadrille" into her notebook.

29. Thanks to Chris Goertzen for this insight.

30. Emma Dunning Banks, *Original Recitations with Lesson-Talks*, enlarged ed. (New York: Edgar S. Werner, 1908), 72–74.

31. Ibid., 74.

32. Ibid., 111.

33. The poem may have inspired Myrtle Reed's 1912 short story, in which a performance of Schumann's *Träumerei*, excerpts of which are published in the text, helps to reunite lovers. Ivan Raykoff, "Schumann's Melodramatic Afterlife," in *Rethinking Schumann*, ed. Roe-Min Kok and Laura Tunbridge (Oxford: Oxford University Press, 2011), 168–70.

34. Owen Meredith, *Aux Italiens: Musical Recitation with Lesson Talk*, music by Giuseppe Verdi, arr. Charles Roberts (New York: Edgar S. Werner, 1907).

35. Hanson and Gunckel, *Ideal Orator*, 321–25.

36. Alfred, Lord Tennyson, *Enoch Arden*, lines 738–53, in *The Poems of Tennyson*, 2nd ed., 3 vols., ed. Christopher Ricks (Harlow, UK: Longman, 1987), 2:645.

37. Thomas J. Assad, "On the Major Poems of Tennyson's *Enoch Arden* Volume," *Tulane Studies in English* 14 (1965): 51.

38. Donald S. Hair, *Domestic and Heroic in Tennyson's Poetry* (Toronto: University of Toronto Press, 1981), 95–96.

39. See Edward F. Kravitt, *The Lied: Mirror of Late Romanticism* (New Haven, CT: Yale University Press, 1996), 100–103; Tania Elizabeth Fleischer, "Richard Strauss' *Enoch Arden*: Rediscovering a Gem in a Lost Art Form" (DMA diss., University of California Los Angeles, 2000), 55–76; Jacqueline Waeber, *En musique dans le text: Le mélodrame, de Rousseau à Schoenberg* (n.p.: Van Dieren, 2005), 299–308.

40. Kravitt, *Lied*, 103.

41. E. Esther Owen, "Pantomime of 'The Story of a Faithful Soul,'" *Werner's Magazine* 23 (March 1899): 45–46.

42. Stanley Hawley, *The Story of the Faithful Soul: Founded on an Old French Legend* (Leipzig, Germany: Bosworth, 1899).

43. "Readers and Singers," *Werner's Voice Magazine* 13 (April 1891): 117, and "Readers and Singers," *Werner's Voice Magazine* 14 (June 1892): 186.

44. Bosworth, *Mrs. Bosworth's Elocutionary Studies*, 263.

45. William B. Chamberlain, *Principles of Vocal Expression* (Chicago: Scott, Foresman, 1897), 341.

46. Richard Lewis, *Lewis's Readings and Recitations: Adapted for Public and Private Entertainments* (Toronto: Belford, 1876), 57.

47. Hanson and Gunckel, *Ideal Orator*, 313.

48. Soper, *Soper's Select Speaker*, 369. Léandre Arthur DuMouchel was the organist of the Cathedral of the Immaculate Conception in Albany, New York, 1876–1919.

49. Handford, *Fireside Pleasures*, 74.

50. Harvey Worthington Loomis, *Sandalphon* (New York: E. S. Werner, 1896).

51. Ithaca Conservatory Concert Company program, Tarver Collection, box 7, folder 49.

52. James Murdoch, *Analytic Elocution* (Cincinnati, OH: Van Antwerp, Bragg, 1884), 497–98; Jacob Shoemaker, *Practical Elocution: For Use in Colleges and Schools and by Private Students* (Philadelphia: National School of Elocution and Oratory, 1886), 295–96.

53. Mrs. J. W. Shoemaker, *Advanced Elocution* (Philadelphia: Penn, 1896), 390–99.

54. E. B. Warman, *How to Read, Recite and Impersonate* (Chicago: M. A. Donohue, [1889]), 16–76.

55. June Hadden Hobbs, *"I Sing for I Cannot Be Silent": The Feminization of American Hymnody, 1870–1920* (Pittsburgh: University of Pittsburgh Press, 1997), 102–3.

56. Ibid., 102.

57. For example, Henry Davenport Northrop, *The Peerless Reciter; or, Popular Program Containing the Choicest Recitations and Readings from the Best Authors* (Atlanta: D. E. Luther, 1894), 43–45.

58. Soper, *Soper's Select Speaker*, 375.

59. Elizabeth Ingram Hubbard, "The Catholic Psalm," arr. Charles Carlise, in Emma Griffith Lumm, *The Twentieth-Century Speaker* (Chicago: Dominion, 1898), 398, 401.

60. Neffie Palmer Lindsey, *The Young Speaker's Library* (Chicago: Imperial, 1893), 212–14.

61. Hanson and Gunckel, *Ideal Orator*, 281–82; Schell, *Musical Effects*, 57–60.

62. Hallie Quinn Brown's anthology includes "Rock of Ages," to be performed with musical accompaniment by "Mr. L. N. D. P." Hallie Quinn Brown, *Bits and Odds: A Choice Selection of Recitations for School, Lyceum and Parlor Entertainments* (Xenia, OH: Chew Press, n.d.), 71.

63. Frank H. Fenno, *The Science and Art of Elocution* (Philadelphia: John H. Potter, 1878), 264.

64. "A Very Pleasant Entertainment," *Waterford Advertiser,* September 22, 1882, scrapbook, Tarver Collection, box 12.

65. Lumm, *Twentieth-Century Speaker*, 407–8.

66. Mrs. J. F. Kinsey, *Juvenile Speaker and Songster: For Use in Sunday-School Entertainments* (Lafayette, IN: Echo Music, 1893), 70–71.

67. Marie Irish, *Tableaux and Scenic Readings* (Chicago: T. S. Denison, 1906), 76–78.

68. James Henry Brownlee, *Martial Recitations, Heroic, Pathetic, and Humorous* (Chicago: Werner, 1896); George M. Baker, *The Grand Army Speaker: A Collection of the Best Patriotic Pieces in Prose and Verse for Reading and Recitation* (Boston: Lee and Shepard; New York: Charles T. Dillingham, 1888).

69. Joan Shelley Rubin, *Songs of Ourselves: The Uses of Poetry in America* (Cambridge, MA: Belknap Press, 2007), 169–77.

70. Scott McConnell, *Glorious Contentment: The Grand Army of the Republic, 1865–1900* (Chapel Hill: University of North Carolina Press, 1992), 180; Kate Brownlee Sherwood, *Camp-Fire, Memorial-Day, and Other Poems* (Chicago: Jansen, McClurg, 1885).

71. Helen Gray Cone, "The Ballad of Cassandra Brown," in Kate Sanborn, *The Wit of Women* (New York: Funk and Wagnalls, 1885), 181.

72. Christian McWhirter, *Battle Hymns: The Power and Popularity of Music in the Civil War* (Chapel Hill: University of North Carolina Press, 2012), 129–30; see sources of the story in n. 41, p. 243.

73. Captain George E. Pingree, "Reminiscences," in Leander Winslow Cogswell, *A History of the Eleventh New Hampshire, Regiment Volunteer Infantry, in the Rebellion War, 1861–1865* (Concord, NH: Republican Press, 1891), 64.

74. The poems included Charles L. Ford's "Between the Lines" (1883); "Home, Sweet Home," published in the *Southern Bivouac* (1883); and T. T. Kenower's "The Challenge," in the *Toledo Blade* (before 1892).

75. H. M. Soper, *The Speaker's Friend* (Chicago: A. B. Kuhlman, 1901), 366, 369.

76. "Jim the Penman," *Brooklyn Eagle*, April 10, 1891.

77. McConnell, *Glorious Contentment*, 181. Richmond writer John Reuben Thompson edited the *Southern Literary Messenger* and served as a Confederate correspondent, so perhaps Southern reciters used "Music in Camp."

78. Jessie Alexander, *Encore! New Book of Platform Sketches* (Toronto: McClelland and Stewart, 1922), 244–47.

79. Hanson and Gunckel, *Ideal Orator*, 326.

80. Jessie Alexander, *Jessie Alexander's Platform Sketches: Original and Adapted* (Toronto: McClelland, Goodchild and Stewart, 1916), 83.

81. James Clarence Harvey, *Recitations for the Social Circle* (New York: Bible House, 1896), 199.

82. Kinsey, *Juvenile Speaker and Songster*, 145.

83. The settings of "Curfew Must Not Ring Tonight" composed by David W. Levett and Stanley Hawley do not seem to have been popular in America.

84. Brown, *Bits and Odds*, 75.

85. Ibid., 49–51.

86. Dobson, "Reclaiming Sentimental Literature," 273.

## Chapter 5. Grecian Urns in Iowa Towns

1. Women's clubs' programs, State Historical Society of Iowa, Iowa City.

2. See Linda A. Robinson, "Far from Simple: Nostalgia for America's Turn-of-the-Century Small Town in Film and Television, 1940–1963" (PhD diss., Northwestern University, 2007), 263–342; and Cara Leanne Wood, "Representing the Midwest in American Stage and Film Musicals, 1943–1962" (PhD diss., Princeton University, 2010), 156–261. Scott Miller notes the show "takes wicked potshots at most of what Americans hold dear—small-town generosity, family values, representative government, education, the Fourth of July. . . . Why is it we consider this show just another sappy, old-fashioned musical? It's really not." *Deconstructing Harold Hill: An Insider's Guide to Musical Theatre* (Portsmouth, NH: Heinemann, 2000), 73.

3. The final script for *The Music Man* refers to "Del Sarte," as if neither Hill nor Mrs. Shinn (nor perhaps Willson) understand what it is. Meredith Willson Papers, University of Iowa Libraries, Special Collections.

4. See Nancy Lee Chalfa Ruyter, *Reformers and Visionaries: The Americanization of the Art of Dance* (New York: Dance Horizons, 1979), 17–30. Delsarte influenced Ruth St. Denis and Ted Shawn.

5. Gilbert Austin, *Chironomia* (London: Printed for T. Cadell and W. Davies; by W. Bulmer, 1806), plates.

6. For example, Henry M. Soper, *Soper's Select Speaker* ([Chicago]: Soper School of Oratory, 1901), 369–74.

7. Quoted in Ted Shawn, *Every Little Movement: A Book about François Delsarte*, 2nd ed. (1963; repr. New York: Dance Horizons, 1974), 20.

8. See Nancy Lee Chalfa Ruyter, *The Cultivation of Body and Mind in Nineteenth-Century American Delsartism* (Westport, CT: Greenwood Press, 1999), 31–56.

9. Ibid., 12–13.

10. Taylor Susan Lake, "American Delsartism and the Bodily Discourse of Respectable Womanliness" (PhD diss., University of Iowa, 2002), 99.

11. Genevieve Stebbins, *Delsarte System of Expression*, 6th ed. (New York: E. S. Werner, 1902), 415–16.

12. Lake, "American Delsartism," 98.

13. Ibid., 108–9.

14. Ruyter, *Cultivation of Body and Mind*, 125.

15. For example, Lenox Browne and Emil Behnke, "Voice, Song, and Speech: Sixth Paper," *Werner's Magazine* 17 (1895): 485–88.

16. "Which Is the Better?," *Voice* 5 (November 1883): 168. The picture came from *Dio Lewis's Monthly*; Lewis was a women's exercise advocate.

17. See Lisa Suter, "The Arguments They Wore: The Role of the Neoclassical Toga in American Delsartism," in *Rhetoric, History, and Women's Oratorical Education: American Women Learn to Speak*, ed. David Gold and Catherine L. Hobbs (New York: Routledge, 2013), 134–53.

18. Emily M. Bishop, *Americanized Delsarte Culture* (Meadville, PA: Hood and Vincent, 1892), 29–30, quoted in Judy Burns, "The Culture of Nobility/The Nobility of Self-Cultivation," in *Moving Words: Rewriting Dance*, ed. Gay Morris (London: Routledge, 1996), 216.

19. Henry Davenport Northrop, *The Delsarte Speaker; or, Modern Elocution Designed Especially for Young Folks and Amateurs* (n.p.: J. R. Jones, 1895), 55.

20. Lake, "American Delsartism," 191.

21. Clara Power Edgerly, *Tableaux Mouvants and Poses Plastiques, No. 1* (New York: Edgar S. Werner, 1891), [13].

22. Paige V. Banaji, "Womanly Eloquence and Physical Bodies: Regendering the Public Speaker through Physical Culture," in *Rhetoric, History, and Women's Oratorical Education: American Women Learn to Speak*, ed. David Gold and Catherine L. Hobbs (New York: Routledge, 2013), 160.

23. Lake, "American Delsartism," 70 and 121.

24. Ibid., 153.

25. "Review of *The Art of Pantomime: Gesture and Pantomimic Action*," *New York Times*, December 13, 1891.

26. Some women also objected to Delsarte. See Anna Baright Curry, "Discussion," *Proceedings of the National Association of Elocutionists* 6 (1898): 55–61.

27. F. Townsend Southwick, "Delsarte Definitions," *Werner's Voice Magazine* 12 (April 1890): 106.

28. Anna Morgan, *An Hour with Delsarte: A Study in Expression* (Boston: Lee and Shepard, 1889).

29. George M. Baker, *Forty Minutes with a Crank; or, The Seldarte Craze* (Boston: Walter H. Baker, 1889).

30. Philip Thomson, "A Delsarte Tragedy," *Werner's Voice Magazine* 19 (March 1897): 214.

31. See Joseph Fahey, "Quiet Victory: The Professional Identity American Women Forged through Delsarte," in *Essays on François Delsarte*, ed. Nancy Lee Chalfa Ruyter and Thomas Leabhart, *Mime Journal* (2004–5) (Claremont, CA: Pomona College Theatre Department for the Claremont Colleges, 2005), 43–83; see also Lisa Suter, "Living Pictures, Living Memory: Women's Rhetorical Silence within the Delsarte Movement," in *Silence and Listening as Rhetorical Arts*, ed. Cheryl Glenn and Krista Ratcliffe (Carbondale: Southern Illinois University Press, 2011), 99–106.

32. I. H. J., "Cupid vs. Delsarte," *Werner's Voice Magazine* 12 (December 1890): 322.

33. "Latest Thing in Delsarte," *New York Sun*, reprinted in *Emmetsburg (IA) Democrat*, September 13, 1893.

34. Howard Rann, "This and That," *Moulton (IA) Weekly Tribune*, May 16, 1913.

35. "Nymphs, Naiads, Graces," clipping, scrapbook [March 1891], Des Moines Women's Club Archives, Hoyt Sherman Place, Des Moines, Iowa (hereafter cited as Des Moines Women's Club Archives). Four of the tableaux may have come from Edgerly, *Tableaux Mouvants and Poses Plastiques, No. 1*: "Toilet of the Bride," "The Death of Virginia," "The Niobe Group," and "Dance of the Muses."

36. *Des Moines Mail and Times*, March 21, 1891, press clippings books, vol. 1, Women's Club Archives.

37. "Nymphs, Naiads, Graces," clipping, scrapbook [March 1891], Des Moines Women's Club Archives.

38. "Reviving Grecian Art," *Cedar Rapids Gazette*, February 5, 1894. Several tableaux were not related to Greek art.

39. "Oratory Recital Given Friday Night," *Collegian* 35 (January 17, 1919): 1.

40. Mary Joanna Rizzo, "Lily C. Whitaker: Founder of the New Orleans College of Oratory and Elocution" (PhD diss., University of Wisconsin, 1954), 2 vols., 1:87, 2:349.

41. "Social Festivities," *Carroll (IA) Sentinel*, June 23, 1892.

42. "Mt. Pleasant Matters," *Burlington (IA) Hawk Eye*, January 29, 1892. Saunders' Opera House seated 1,100 people.

43. *Atlantic (IA) Daily Telegraph*, December 1, 1892.

44. "Personal and General," *Cedar Rapids Evening Gazette*, February 6, 1894.

45. "Miss Detwiler Beaten," *Waterloo (IA) Courier*, June 17, 189.

46. *Waterloo (IA) Evening Courier*, June 18, 1914; "Commencement Recital," *Waterloo (IA) Evening Courier*, June 23, 1915.

47. *Pelican*, yearbook (Pella, IA: Central College, 1914).

48. "An Evening with America's Best Loved Poet," *Cornellian* 29 (February 1, 1908): 183. The pantomime may have drawn on Florence A. Fowle Adams, *Gesture and Pantomimic Action*, 4th ed. (New York: Edgar S. Werner, 1897), 155–81.

49. "The Juveniles: Kindergarten Commencement Exercises This Morning," *Cedar Rapids Evening Gazette*, June 15, 1894.

50. "The Gym Program," *Cedar Rapids Evening Gazette*, May 16, 1896.

51. *Waterloo (IA) Daily Courier*, September 19, 1901.

52. R. Anna Morris, *Physical Culture in the Public Schools* (Des Moines, IA: G. A. Miller, 1888).

53. "The Gym Program," *Cedar Rapids Evening Gazette*, May 16, 1896.

54. "Girls Were Good," *Daily Iowa Capital*, March 24, 1899.

55. "The Declamatory Contest," *Monticello (IA) Express*, April 12, 1894; *Algona Upper Des Moines*, May 16, 1894, p. 4; "Algona's Big Celebration," *Algona (IA) Courier*, June 28, 1895.

56. *Malvern (IA) Leader*, January 14, 1892.

57. *Algona (IA) Republican*, March 15, 1893.

58. The *Times* of Bowling Green, Kentucky, quoted in "Tableaux D'Art Company Tomorrow Night," *Waterloo (IA) Daily Courier*, November 22, 1901. See Jack W.

McCullough, *Living Pictures on the New York Stage* (Ann Arbor, MI: UMI Research Press, 1983).

59. *Algona (IA) Advance*, November 22, 1901.

60. *Semi-Weekly Cedar Falls Gazette*, May 7, 1901, and *Waverly (IA) Democrat*, April 4, 1901.

61. As late as 1940, Griswold's Tuesday Music Club offered a Guest Day program featuring poses in costume representing stages of a woman's life, performed mostly to popular songs.

62. Florence A. Fowle Adams, "Studies in Posing," *Werner's Magazine* 15 (December 1893): 416–17; Eleanor H. Denig, "Statue Posing with Musical Accompaniment," in Soper, *Soper's Select Speaker*, 14.

63. Ruyter, *Cultivation of Body and Mind*, 106.

64. Mrs. J. W. Shoemaker, *Delsartean Pantomimes with Recital and Musical Accompaniment* (Philadelphia: Penn, 1902), 176–79.

65. Anna Morris, *Physical Education in the Public Schools* (New York: American Book Company, 1892), 161–92; Grace Chamberlin, *Emerson College Chansonettes* (Boston: Emerson College, 1898).

66. Genevieve Stebbins, *Society Gymnastics and Voice-Culture. Adapted from the Delsarte System*, 6th ed. (New York: E. S. Werner, 1888), 97–106.

67. "Living Pictures," *Humboldt County (IA) Republican*, May 22, 1902.

68. Mary Tucker Magill, *Pantomimes; or, Wordless Poems* (New York: Edgar S. Werner, 1882, 1894), 75–86.

69. Ibid., 16.

70. The third example (p. 32), accompanied by quiet agitato music, is labeled "Remorse" in previous editions of Lumm's book.

71. "Nellie Peck Saunders," *Elyria (OH) Reporter*, October 15, 1903.

72. "Miss Thomas' Reading," *Northern Vindicator* (Estherville, IA), March 12, 1891.

73. Margaret Virginia Jenkins, "A Study in Attitude," *Werner's Voice Magazine* 12 (December 1890): 298–99. Jenkins desired the girls' sense of the meaning of accompaniments to the "Exercise in Harmonic Poise" because its physical motions were considerably less referential to extramusical meanings than the combined music and motions of the attitudes and tableaux.

74. Elizabeth Akers Allen, *Rock Me to Sleep, Mother: Illustrated Pantomimed Song*, poses by Lucy Harris, directed by E. V. Sheridan, pantomime by Anna D. Cooper (New York: Edgar S. Werner, 1907).

75. Found in Grace Faxon, *Popular Recitations and How to Recite Them* (Dansville, NY: F. A. Owen, 1909), published well after many Iowan performances.

76. See reprinted photos in "Speaking of Pictures . . . These Are Song-Pantomimes," *Life* (September 27, 1937): 18–21.

77. "New Musical in Manhattan," *Time* (December 30, 1957), quoted in Carol J. Oja, "*West Side Story* and *The Music Man*: Whiteness, Immigration, and Race during the U.S. in the Late 1950s," *Studies in Musical Theatre* 3 (2009): 15. For similarities between *The Music Man* plot and Mason City, see Bill Oates, *Meredith Willson, America's Music Man* (Bloomington, IN: Author House, 2005), 115–17, 123–24.

78. Including Mrs. Stilson, who died in 1901, and Midlands Normal School's May Long.

79. "German Club," *Mason City (IA) Globe-Gazette*, May 2, 1916.

80. "Kindergarten Work," *Cerro Gordo (IA) Republican*, March 10, 1898.

81. *Poses Plastiques for the Little Ones*, words by George Cooper, music by Charles E. Pratt (New York: Edgar S. Werner, 1899).

82. Women's Clubs' Programs, box 9 and box W, State Historical Society of Iowa, Iowa City. The Wa-Tan-Ye girls in *The Music Man* were named after a women's service organization founded in Mason City in 1921.

83. For example, Grace Faxon's *Favorite Pantomimed Songs and Poses* (Danville, NY: F. A. Owen, 1917), 85.

84. History of the Columbian Club (1958), Brooklyn, Iowa, State Historical Society of Iowa, Iowa City.

85. History of Clio Club (November 1938), Carroll, Iowa, State Historical Society of Iowa, Iowa City.

86. Women's Clubs' Programs, box 20, State Historical Society of Iowa, Iowa City; N. N. Club (Iowa City, Iowa) Records, 1886–2004, Ms. R25, State Historical Society of Iowa, Iowa City.

87. Kimberly Fairbrother Canton, "Who's Selling Here? Sounds Like *The Music Man* Is Selling and We're Buying," *Modern Drama* 51 (Spring 2008): 44. Canton sees the tension as highbrow versus lowbrow culture, with Hill's musical choices representing a conformist, commercial middlebrow.

88. In the original musical, Marian pumps the player piano for the Delsarte rehearsal.

89. Raymond Knapp, *The American Musical and the Formation of National Identity* (Princeton, NJ: Princeton University Press, 2005), 145–46.

90. Roberta Freund Schwartz, "Iowa Stubborn: Meredith Willson's Musical Characterization of His Fellow Iowans," *Studies in Musical Theatre* 3 (2007): 33–40.

91. Knapp, *American Musical*, 149–51.

92. Canton, "Who's Selling Here?," 53, identifies Beethoven as highbrow culture, but does not differentiate the simple Minuet in G from large-scale masterworks.

93. Knapp, *American Musical*, 146.

## Chapter 6. In Another Voice

1. On dialect literature, see Gavin Roger Jones, *Strange Talk: The Politics of Dialect Literature in Gilded Age America* (Berkeley: University of California Press, 1999), 1–36; and Lisa Cohen Minnick, *Dialect and Dichotomy: Literary Representations of African American Speech* (Tuscaloosa: University of Alabama Press, 2004), 1–27.

2. Willis Fletcher Johnson, "Dialect in Literature and Expression," *Werner's Magazine* 21 (1898): 51.

3. African American elocutionist Frances E. Preston taught "Negro dialect" at the Detroit Training School in the mid-1880s.

4. "Chicago Schools of Expression," *Lyceumite and Talent* (May 1903): 115.

5. Jason Camlot, "Early Talking Books: Spoken Recordings and Recitation Anthologies, 1880–1920," *Book History* 6 (2003): 159–66.

6. Walter Blair and Raven I. MacDonald Jr., eds., *The Mirth of a Nation: America's Great Dialect Humor* (Minneapolis: University of Minnesota Press, 1983), x, xii.

7. Johnson, "Dialect in Literature and Expression," 61.

8. Gertrude E. Johnson, *Dialects for Oral Interpretation, Selections and Discussion* (New York: Century, 1922), 31.

9. Jerry Tarver Elocution, Rhetoric, and Oratory Collection, Ohio State University Libraries, Rare Books and Manuscripts Library, Columbus, Ohio (hereafter cited as Tarver Collection), box 1, folder 13.

10. Evelyne Hilliard, "The Study of Dramatics a Help in Earning a Living," in *Amateur and Educational Dramatics* (New York: Macmillan, 1917), 161.

11. Johnson, "Dialect in Literature and Expression," 53.

12. See Camlot, "Early Talking Books," 165.

13. Hallie Quinn Brown, *Bits and Odds: A Choice Selection of Recitations for School, Lyceum and Parlor Entertainments* (Xenia, OH: Chew Press, n.d.), 37–40.

14. See the program in Grace Lillian Hunter, *Twenty-Five New and Unique Entertainments* (Des Moines, IA: Ladies Aid Society, 1899), 51–53.

15. Frank H. Fenno, *The Science and Art of Elocution* (Philadelphia: John H. Potter, 1878), 403–7.

16. "How Ruby Played" was so popular that on Rubinstein's death, Willa Cather called for elocutionists to banish it from their repertoires. "As You Like It," *Nebraska State Journal*, November 25, 1894, in *The Willa Cather Archive*, http://cather.unl.edu /j00094.html.

17. "Aunt Deborah Hears 'The Messiah,'" in *Werner's Readings and Recitations No. 25*, ed. Rachel Baumann (New York: Edgar S. Werner, 1900), 31–35.

18. Lucius Perry Hills, *Echoes* (Atlanta: printed by author, 1892), 80–85. "Aunt Deborah Hears 'The Messiah'" and "The Opera Encore" were copied together into the notebook of Frances Maude Wood, Tarver Collection.

19. *Werner's Readings and Recitations No. 21*, ed. Pauline Phelps (New York: Edgar S. Werner, 1899), 183.

20. "Aunt Sophronia Tabor at the Opera," in *Choice Dialect and Other Characterizations*, ed. Charles Shoemaker (Philadelphia: Penn, 1915), 77–81.

21. Jean Wagner, *Black Poets of the United States, from Paul Laurence Dunbar to Langston Hughes* (Urbana: University of Illinois Press, 1973), 49.

22. Yuval Taylor and Jake Austen, *Darkest America: Black Minstrelsy from Slavery to Hip-Hop* (New York: W. W. Norton, 2012), 64–68.

23. Annemarie Bean, "Black Minstrelsy and Double Inversion, ca. 1890," in *African American Performance and Theater History: A Critical Reader*, ed. Harry J. Elam Jr. and David Krasner (New York: Oxford University Press, 2001), 171.

24. Two photos, folder 10; clipping, "Women in Black Face: West Chicago Songs and Wit," in Cornelia Neltnor Anthony scrapbook, Lake Forest College Archives and Special Collections, Lake Forest, Illinois.

25. Stanley Schell, "Ten Little Nigger Boys," *Werner's Magazine* 28 (December 1901): 622.

26. W. Gordon McCabe, Mary Bell pamphlet, quoted in Micki McElya, *Clinging to Mammy: The Faithful Slave in Twentieth-Century America* (Cambridge, MA: Harvard University Press, 2007), 62.

27. Harry Stillwell Edwards, "Black-Ankle Break Down," adapted by Kate Weaver Dallas, music by Minnie Schoeller, in Stanley Schell, ed., *Werner's Readings and Recitations, no. 48: Musical Effects* (New York: Edgar S. Werner, 1911), 26–30.

28. James Edwin Campbell, "De 'Sprise Pa'ty," in *Echoes—From the Cabin and Elsewhere* (Chicago: Donohue and Henneberry, 1895), 20, lines 25–32.

29. On the Mammy stereotype, see McElya, *Clinging to Mammy*, cited in n. 27; Patricia Morton, *Disfigured Images: The Historical Assault on Afro-American Women* (New York: Greenwood Press, 1991); Cheryl Thurber, "The Development of the Mammy Image and Mythology," in *Southern Women: Histories and Identities*, ed. Virginia Bernhard et al. (Columbia: University of Missouri Press, 1992), 87–108; Kimberly Wallace-Sanders, *Mammy: A Century of Race, Gender, and Southern Memory* (Ann Arbor: University of Michigan Press, 2008); Phil Patton, "Mammy: Her Life and Times," *American Heritage* 44, no. 5 (1993): 78–85; and Susan C. Cook, "'In imitation of my negro mammy': Alma Gluck and the American Prima Donna," in *The Arts of the Prima Donna in the Long Nineteenth Century*, ed. Rachel Cowgill and Hilary Poriss (New York: Oxford University Press, 2011), 290–307.

30. Harry Stillwell Edwards, "Mammy's Li'l' Boy," *Century* 37, no. 1 (November 1888): 128–29, http://www.unz.org/Pub/Century-1888nov-00128, lines 5–9.

31. Elsie M. Wilbor, *Delsarte Recitation Book and Directory* (New York: Edgar S. Werner, 1905), 262.

32. Donald Graham French, ed., *Standard Canadian Reciter: A Book of the Best Readings and Recitations from Canadian Literature* (Toronto: McClelland and Stewart, 1918), 14–15.

33. Lucy C. Jenkins, "Mammy's Pickanin,'" *Werner's Magazine* 27 (July 1901): 360.

34. Emma Griffith Lumm, *The Twentieth-Century Speaker* (Chicago: Dominion, 1898), 397–98.

35. "M' Li'l' Black Baby," monologue by Stanley Schell, song by Josephine Merwin Cook, in Schell, *Musical Effects*, 89–93.

36. "Readers and Singers," *Werner's Magazine* 27 (June 1901): 301. The text was also set as a song; see the 1899 sheet music cover in Jo-Ann Morgan, "Mammy the Huckster: Selling the South for the New Century," *American Art* 9 (Spring 1995): 98.

37. Lisa M. Anderson, *Mammies No More: The Changing Image of Black Women on Stage and Screen* (Lanham, MD: Rowman and Littlefield, 1997), 11.

38. Brown, *Bits and Odds*, 64–65.

39. Brown toured with the Stewart Concert Company in the early 1880s to raise money for Wilberforce University. See "Elocution and African American Culture: The Pedagogy of Hallie Quinn Brown," in Susan Kates, *Activist Rhetorics and American Higher Education, 1885–1937* (Carbondale: Southern Illinois University Press, 2001), 53–74.

40. Catherine Clinton, *The Plantation Mistress: Woman's World in the Old South* (New York: Pantheon Books, 1983), 202.

41. Henry Gaines Hawn, Lesson Talk for Dorothy Dix, "Higher Culture in Dixie," in *Werner's Selections with Elocution Lessons No. 1* (New York: Edgar S. Werner, 1902), 153.

42. "Arche Club Members Have Rag-Time Afternoon Way Down South," *Chicago Tribune*, November 20, 1901.

43. For a sampling of this literature, see Jones, *Strange Talk*, 182–207; Jay Martin, ed., *A Singer in the Dawn: Reinterpretations of Paul Laurence Dunbar* (New York: Dodd, Mead, 1975), 94–134; Ralph Story, "Paul Laurence Dunbar: Master Player in a Fixed Game," *College Language Association Journal* 27, no. 1 (September 1983): 30–55; Caroline Gebhard, "Inventing a 'Negro Literature': Race, Dialect, and Gender in the Early Work of Paul Laurence Dunbar, James Weldon Johnson, and Alice Dunbar-Nelson," in *Post-Bellum, Pre-Harlem: African American Literature and Culture, 1877–1919*, ed. Barbara McCaskill and Caroline Gebhard (New York: New York University Press, 2006), 162–68; Nadia Nurhussein, "'On Flow'ry Beds of Ease': Paul Laurence Dunbar and the Cultivation of Dialect Poetry in the *Century*," *American Periodicals* 20 (2010): 46–67; Willie J. Harrell Jr., ed., *We Wear the Mask: Paul Laurence Dunbar and the Politics of Representative Reality* (Kent, OH: Kent State University Press, 2010), 49–70; and the Dunbar issues of *Midwestern Miscellany* 36 (2006) and *African American Review* 41 (Summer 2007).

44. Henry Louis Gates Jr., *The Signifying Monkey: A Theory of African-American Literary Criticism* (New York: Oxford University Press, 1988), 176.

45. Program from 1891, Paul Laurence Dunbar Papers, box 16, Ohio Historical Society, Columbus, Ohio (hereafter cited as Dunbar Papers).

46. "Readers and Singers," *Werner's Magazine* 18 (October 1896): 963.

47. For example, "Lager Beer," published in the Dayton, Ohio, *Tattler* in 1890 under the pseudonym "Pffenberger Deutzelheim," or the Irish "Circumstances Alter Cases."

48. "Negro Poet Reads Well," *New York Sun*, September 9, 1896.

49. Alice Moore Dunbar-Nelson, *The Dunbar Speaker and Entertainer* (Naperville, IL: J. L. Nichols, 1920).

50. "The Dunbar Concert," August 16, 1898, Dunbar Papers, http://goo.gl/3bXV2.

51. "Dunbar & Douglass," July 9, 1901, Dunbar Papers, box 9, http://goo.gl/q0 RFI.

52. Lida Keck Wiggins, *The Life and Works of Paul Laurence Dunbar* (Naperville, IL: J. L. Nichols, 1907; repr. New York: Kraus, 1971), 65.

53. "Colored Poet Reads," [*Terre Haute Examiner*, May 25, 1901], Dunbar Papers, box 19.

54. "Dunbar Heard Again: Recital of Clever Lyrics," Dunbar Papers, box 16.

55. *Toledo Commercial*, Dunbar Papers, box 15.

56. "Like Return of a Hero," *Dayton Evening News*, January 7, 1904, Dayton [Ohio] History.

57. "Expressional Power of the Colored Race," *Werner's Magazine* 26 (February 1901): 478.

58. Ibid., 476.

59. "Suggested Evening with Paul Laurence Dunbar," *Werner's Magazine* 26 (February 1901): 512. "The Old Apple-Tree" is more related to the Hoosier-style dialect of James Whitcomb Riley than to African American dialect and is somewhat similar in content to Riley's "Old Sweetheart of Mine."

60. "Educators and Entertainers," *Werner's Magazine* 28 (December 1901): 659.

61. Elizabeth McHenry, *Forgotten Readers: Recovering the Lost History of African American Literary Societies* (Durham, NC: Duke University Press, 2002), 370–71; Anne Ruggles Gere, *Intimate Practices: Literacy and Cultural Work in U.S. Women's Clubs, 1880–1920* (Urbana: University of Illinois Press, 1997), 223.

62. Brochure for Emily Farrow Gregory in *Tales and Songs of the Old Plantation*, Redpath Chautauqua Collection, University of Iowa Libraries, Special Collections, http://digital.lib.uiowa.edu/cdm/ref/collection/tc/id/16237.

63. "Southern in Sentiment," *Werner's Magazine* 28 (December 1901): 813–14. Kemble illustrated three of Dunbar's books, Twain's *Huckleberry Finn*, and writings by Joel Chandler Harris.

64. Edward W. Kemble, *Kemble's Coons: A Collection of Southern Sketches* (New York: R. H. Russell, 1896). See Adam Sonstegard, "Kemble's Figures and Dunbar's Folks: Picturing the Work of Graphic Illustration in Dunbar's Short Fiction," in Harrell, *We Wear the Mask*, 116–37.

65. James Weldon Johnson, *Along This Way: The Autobiography of James Weldon Johnson* (New York: Viking Press, 1933), 159.

66. Grace Lucas-Thompson, "What Our Women Are Doing!," *Freeman*, July 10, 1915.

67. Monroe A. Majors, *Noted Negro Women: Their Triumphs and Activities* (Chicago: Donohue and Henneberry, 1893), 239–40.

68. Errol Hill, *Shakespeare in Sable: A History of Black Shakespearean Actors* (Amherst: University of Massachusetts Press, 1984), 64–76. Hill sometimes mistakes elocutionary standards Davis customarily performed solo for dramatic roles.

69. "Educators and Entertainers," *Werner's Magazine* 29 (1902): 883.

70. *The Marcus Garvey and Universal Negro Improvement Association Papers*, vol. 1 (Berkeley: University of California Press, 1983), 419–20 and 437. Davis gave "Li'l Brown Baby" in 1919 to praise a company that made black dolls.

71. Dunbar Papers, box 9.

72. Sylvestre Watkins, "Dunbar Life Story Reads like a Novel," *Chicago Tribune*, September 7, 1947.

73. Nancy D. Tolson, "Besides Nursery Rhymes, I Learned Paul," and Sandra Seaton, "'The Great Big Pahty': My Grandmother and Paul Laurence Dunbar," both in *Midwestern Miscellany* 34 (Spring/Fall 2006): 78 and 85.

74. Hamlin Garland, *Roadside Meetings* (New York: Macmillan, 1930), 182–83, quoted in Nurhussein, "'On Flow'ry Beds of Ease,'" 60.

75. Discussion after Miriam Nelke, "How to Teach Children Elocution," June 30, 1897, *Proceedings of the Sixth Annual Meeting of the National Association of Elocutionists* (New York, 1898), 210.

76. Nurhussein, "'On Flow'ry Beds of Ease,'" 56.

77. "The Poet Dunbar a Chicagoan," *Chicago Daily Tribune*, September 13, 1902.

78. "First Lenten Musicale," [*Cleveland News Herald*, March 1901], Dunbar Papers, box 19.

79. "Some Special Programs," *Werner's Magazine* 29, no. 6 (August 1902): 865.

80. Henry Louis Gates Jr. has called "The Ol' Tunes" and "Ol' Banjo" revisions of James Whitcomb Riley's poetry in *Signifying Monkey*, 122.

81. Joanne M. Braxton, ed., *The Collected Poetry of Paul Laurence Dunbar* (Charlottesville: University Press of Virginia, 1993), 156–58.

82. Two possibilities for this unidentified melody are the fiddle tune "Pompey Ran Away," also known as "Negroe Jig," and Thomas Moore's "Oft, in the Stilly Night," although neither is similar enough to clearly be its source.

83. Nathaniel Dett, ed., *Religious Folk Songs of the Negro as Sung at Hampton Institute* (Hampton, VA: Hampton Institute Press, 1927; repr. New York: AMS Press, 1972), 131.

84. Paul Laurence Dunbar, "Corn-Stalk Fiddle," in Schell, *Music Effects*, 162–66.

85. Lines 17–24, 48–55, in Braxton, *Collected Poetry of Paul Laurence Dunbar*, 82–83.

86. "When Malindy Sings, Negro Dialect Recitation," J. A. Myers, Victor 35097 Matrix Number/Take Number C-8456/1, recorded December 9, 1909, National Jukebox, Library of Congress, http://www.loc.gov/jukebox/recordings/detail/id/1816.

87. "Voluntary Recitals for Criticism," *Proceedings of the National Association of Elocutionists* 12 (1903): 57–60.

88. On coon songs, see John Graziano, "The Use of Dialect in African-American Spirituals, Popular Songs, and Folk Songs," *Black Music Research Journal* 24 (Autumn 2004): 261–86.

89. "Colonia Club Reception," *Brooklyn Eagle*, February 22, 1901, Dunbar Papers, box 18.

90. For example, "Itching Heels" by Arthur Koerner and "Li'l Brown Baby" by Ward Stephens and Jean Elizabeth Van Dyke.

91. Phyllis Fergus, *When Mistah Sun am Blazin'* (Chicago: Clayton F. Summy, 1919).

92. Natalie Whitted Price, *A Group of Songs or Cantillations* (Chicago: Clayton F. Summy, 1912).

93. Aileen H. Tye, *Mammy's Philosophy* (Chicago: Gamble Hinged Music, 1929).

94. Frieda Peycke, *Angelina* (Chicago: T. S. Denison, 1928).

95. Jean Elizabeth Van Dyke, *B'neath the Willers, Little Brown Baby* (Lebanon, OH: March Bros., 1915).

96. Matt Sandler, "The Glamour of Paul Laurence Dunbar: Racial Uplift, Masculinity and Bohemia in the Nadir," in Harrell, *We Wear the Mask*, 109–10.

97. Mary Jordan Lea, *Boogah Man* (Franklin, OH: Eldridge Entertainment House, 1910).

98. Personal communication with Brooke; Dale B. J. Randall, "Dialect in the Verse of 'The Hoosier Poet,'" *American Speech* 35 (February 1960): 41.

99. Harriet Saxton, *The Newest Elocution Text-Book: The Syllabic Law of Expression* (1893), 137.

100. Mrs. Frederick W. Pender, *I'se dood: Illustrated Pantomimed Poem with Lesson-Talk*, poses by Marie Schiffer (New York: Edgar S. Werner, 1903), 7.

101. On women's stereotypical humorlessness, see Linda Martin and Kerry Segrave,

*Women in Comedy* (Secaucus, NJ: Citadel Press, 1986), 13–25; and June Sochen, ed. *Women's Comic Visions* (Detroit: Wayne State University Press, 1991), 9–16.

102. Tarver Collection, box 1, folder 13.

103. Nancy A. Walker, *A Very Serious Thing: Women's Humor and American Culture* (Minneapolis: University of Minnesota Press, 1988), 28.

104. Joanne R. Gilbert, *Performing Marginality: Humor, Gender, and Cultural Critique* (Detroit: Wayne State University Press, 2004), 131.

105. "Readers and Singers," *Werner's Magazine* 24 ([December] 1899): 447.

106. Gilbert, *Performing Marginality*, 97.

107. Jessie Alexander, *Encore! New Book of Platform Sketches* (Toronto: McClelland and Stewart, 1922), 129–30.

108. Ora Jenkins, Child Impersonator and Entertainer, Redpath Chautauqua Collection, University of Iowa Libraries, Special Collections, digital.lib.uiowa.edu/cdm/compoundobject/collection/tc/id/35889/rec/1.

109. Maude M. Jackson, *New Speaker for the Little Folks; or, Songs and Rhymes for Jolly Times* ([Chicago], 1902).

110. Grace Townsend, *The Speaker's Companion; or, Popular Reciter* (Chicago: Monarch, 1895), 159–60.

111. Frances Putnam Pogle and George M. Vickers, *Speaker and Entertainer: Recitations, Readings, Plays, Drills, Tableaux, etc., etc.* (Philadelphia: John C. Winston, 1900), 314.

112. Henry Davenport Northrop, ed., *Recitations for Young Speakers; or, Popular Program* (n.p., 1899), 249.

113. Stanley Schell, *Goodnight Drill and Songs*, 2nd rev. ed. (New York: Edgar S. Werner, 1905).

114. Northrop, *Recitations for Young Speakers*, 64–66.

115. Miriam Formanek-Brunell, *Made to Play House: Dolls and the Commercialization of American Girlhood, 1830–1930* (New Haven, CT: Yale University Press, 1993), 31–32. Robin Bernstein has examined violent play with black dolls by white children in *Racial Innocence: Performing American Childhood from Slavery to Civil Rights* (New York: New York University Press, 2011), 69–71, 201–26.

116. *The Capitol Speaker for Boys and Girls* (United States: [D. Z. Howell?], n.d.).

117. Herman A. Wade and Henry E. Warner, *I've Got a Pain in My Sawdust* (New York: Edward B. Marks, 1920), IN Harmony Sheet Music from Indiana, http://purl.dlib.indiana.edu/iudl/lilly/devincent/LL-SDV-164059. Cheatham recorded the song for Columbia A, 1910; http://radiovickers.blogspot.com/2011/12/music-project-tough-to-find-songs-14.html.

118. "A Busted Dolly," monologue by Stanley Schell, song by Josephine Merwin Cook, in Schell, *Musical Effects*, 132–36.

119. E. J. Biedermann, *The Broken Doll*, words, directions, and illustrations by Mrs. Frederick W. Pender (New York: Edgar S. Werner, 1915).

120. E. J. Biedermann, *Folks Think We Are Related*, op. 48, no. 4; words by Mrs. Frederick Pender (New York: Edgar S. Werner, 1915). It seems likely that Biedermann was hired by Werner to create musical recitations made to order.

121. G. Stanley Hall, *Adolescence*, 2 vols. (New York: D. Appleton, 1904), 2:625. Tom Riis, in personal communication with the author, has pointed out that the play *Peter Pan* by J. M. Barrie, in which the boy who wouldn't grow up was portrayed by an adult female, debuted in 1904, the same year that Hall's book was published.

122. Joseph Dana Miller, "Some Women Elocutionists," *Puritan* 3 (April 1898): 29.

123. Anna Morgan, *The Art of Speech and Deportment* (Chicago: A. C. McClurg, 1909), 149.

124. Saxton, *Newest Elocution Text-Book*, 138–52.

125. Anne Trensky, "The Bad Boy in Nineteenth-Century American Fiction," *Georgia Review* 27 (1973): 508–9.

126. Gilbert, *Performing Marginality*, 98–99, 128. These included Lotta Crabtree, Irene Franklin, and Fanny Brice.

127. Mary V. McGowan, *Gee Whiz: When Mother Washes Me*, text by Retta Jacobs (Franklin, OH: Eldridge Entertainment House, 1928).

128. Phyllis Fergus, *Soap, the Oppressor*, text by Burges Johnson (Chicago: Clayton F. Summy, 1915).

129. W. R. Vansant, *The Progressive Speaker* (Oakland, CA: Occidental, 1897), 83.

130. Mary Wyman Williams, *The New Brother* (Chicago: Clayton F. Summy; London: Weekes, 1920).

131. "Wanted—A New Title for Kitty Cheatham," [*Musical America* (May 17, 1913)], in *Robinson Locke Collection of Dramatic Scrapbooks*, vol. 114, New York Public Library (hereafter cited as RL), 88.

132. Cheatham's biography is well covered in Brian Moon, "The Inimitable Miss Cheatham," *Bulletin of the Society for American Music* 32 (Spring 2006): 25–27.

133. "Kitty Cheatham's Matinee," *New York Times*, January 4, 1913.

134. A. W. Kramer, "Kitty Cheatham's Summer Abroad," *Musical America*, May 11, 1912, cited in Moon, "Inimitable Miss Cheatham," 26.

135. Archie Bell, "Kitty Cheatham Is Popular," [*Cleveland Plain Dealer*, November 1912], RL, 79.

136. For example, see these *New York Times* articles: "Kitty Cheatham's Matinee," January 4, 1913; "Mrs. Cheatham-Thompson," March 27, 1903; "Society at Home and Abroad," March 13, 1904; and "Summer Concerts for London Society," July 5, 1908.

137. "Dainty Kitty Cheatham Resumes Career," *Sunday Telegram* (n.p.), March 27, 1904, RL, 3.

138. These included Amy Beach's op. 75 songs and works by Henry Hadley, Harvey Worthington Loomis, John Alden Carpenter, and others.

139. Nordica attended a 1911 concert.

140. "Chicago's $30,000 Opera House Where the Stars Had to Walk," [*New York Sun*, April 21, 1908], RL, 28.

141. Including Frederick Norton, Minnie Cochrane (in London), and Harvey Worthington Loomis.

142. Reger's Lieder may be his op. 76. "Catch Us If You Can" with words by Waldo, is no. 20 from book 2 of Bartók's *For Children*, BB 53 (1908–10). It is published in Kitty Cheatham, *A Nursery Garland* (New York: G. Schirmer, 1917), 75.

143. "Miss Cheatham's Easter Matinee," [*Musical America*, April 13, 1912], RL, 74.

144. "Charming Kitty Cheatham Delights a Large Audience," [November 18, 1909], RL, 40.

145. H. T. P., "The Variegated Pleasures of Miss Cheatham," [*Boston Transcript*, March 28, 1913], RL, 87.

146. "Miss Cheatham's Juvenility," *New York Times*, August 7, 1910.

147. "Miss Cheatham Holds Audience Spellbound," [*Musical America*, January 27, 1912], RL, 67.

148. Lantern Slides, box 3, no. 94, Kitty Cheatham Papers, Tennessee State Library and Archives, Nashville, Tennessee (hereafter cited as Cheatham Papers).

149. Archibald Sullivan, "Kitty Cheatham a Great Impersonator," *Musical America*, RL, 15.

150. *Kitty Cheatham: Her Book* (New York: G. Schirmer, 1915).

151. Bell, "Kitty Cheatham Is Popular," RL, 79.

152. "Miss Cheatham's Juvenility," *New York Times*, August 7, 1910.

153. "An Entertainer of Small People," [*New York Mail,* May 3, 1906], RL, 14.

154. "Recital by Miss Cheatham," [*New York Sun,* April 2, 1907], RL, 21.

155. "Miss Cheatham's Recital," *New York Times*, January 4, 1911.

156. "The Art of Kitty Cheatham," advertisement, *Musician* (1913): 224.

157. "Truth and Simplicity the Keynote of All Great Arts, Says Kitty Cheatham," *Musical America* [December 12, 1908], RL 34.

158. "Portrayer of Child Life Tells of Quest for Good Material," [*Cincinnati Times Star*, October 26, 1911], RL, 63.

159. Ibid.

160. Evelyn Nichols Kerr, *Kitty Cheatham: An Appreciation*, Redpath Chautauqua Collection, University of Iowa Libraries, Special Collections, http://digital.lib.uiowa.edu /cdm/compoundobject/collection/tc/id/33555/rec/1.

161. "Miss Cheatham's Recital," *New York Times*, December 29, 1908.

162. W. Graham Robertson, "Let's Pretend, a Christmas Fantasy," in *Kitty Cheatham: Her Book*, ix–x.

163. "Kitty Cheatham's Triumph," [*Nashville Banner,* ca. 1911], RL, 65.

164. "Kitty Cheatham Again Delights with Her Interesting Songs of Childhood," *Musical America* [April 24, 1909], RL, 37.

165. "Miss Cheatham Holds Audience Spellbound," [*Musical America*, January 27, 1912], RL, 67.

166. *Börsen-Courier*, quoted in "Kitty Cheatham," advertisement, [*Musical America*, November 13, 1913], RL, 94; italics in original.

167. "A Singer of Nursery Rhymes" *Leslie's Weekly*, January 26, 1911, RL, 55; "Songs for Children at Hudson Theatre" [*New York Telegraph*, April 2, 1907], RL, 21.

168. Rogers's song appeared in the 1905 Boston production of the African American musical *In Dahomey*. See Thomas L. Riis, ed., *The Music and Scripts of "In Dahomey,"* Recent Researches in American Music, 25/Music of the United States of America, vol. 5 (Madison, WI: A-R Editions, 1996), 178–80.

169. Neither setting appears to be extant. Cheatham published Cochrane's melodramatic "Slumberland" in her first book.

170. George Chadwick Stock, "Tone Talks," [reprinted from *New Haven (CT) Register*], RL, 5.

171. Jessie L. Gaynor, *My Dear Jerushy*, text by Alice Riley (Chicago: Clayton F. Summy, 1896).

172. Ewan Dale, *Dolly's Holiday*, words by St. John Hamund (London: Edwin Ashdown, n.d.), Cheatham Papers, oversized box 2.

173. "Miss Cheatham at the Lyceum," *New York Times*, April 21, 1908.

174. John Alden Carpenter, *Improving Songs for Anxious Children*, words and pictures by Rue Carpenter (1907; repr. Boca Raton, FL: Masters Music, 1992). Some songs had been published in *When Little Boys Sing* (Chicago: A. C. McClurg, 1904).

175. "Kitty Cheatham's Recital," *Brooklyn Daily Eagle*, December 2, 1917.

176. Cheatham Papers, oversized box 4, contains three copies of the "Waltz of the Flowers" and manuscripts of Cheatham's handwritten working out of her lyrics.

177. "Varied Fare Is Spread Before Music-Lovers in Coming Week," *New York Times*, January 18, 1914.

178. Minuet in F, K. 2, with words by Graham Robertson and Fullerton Waldo, and Allegro in B[-flat], K. 3.

179. Cheatham, *Nursery Garland*, 34 and 157. Milton's text is the hymn "Let us all with gladsome mind," and Tennyson's is "Flower in the Crannied Wall."

180. Cheatham, *Nursery Garland*, 111. Recorded but not released, Victor Matrix B-19868 and B-21177. These recordings also included a Bach minuet, with added text by Fullerton Waldo, found in *Nursery Garland*, 4–5. See http://victor.library.ucsb.edu.

181. "Little Theatre," [1912], RL, 77.

182. "Miss Kitty Cheatham's Matinee," RL, 11; Theodore D. Rousseau, [March 15, 1907], RL, 20.

183. "I Like to Sing 'Swing Low, Sweet Chariot,'" [*Bohemian*, November 1909], RL, 39–40.

184. "Mrs. Cheatham-Thompson," *New York Times*, December 25, 1904.

185. "I Like to Sing 'Swing Low, Sweet Chariot,'" [*Bohemian*, November 1909], RL, 39–40.

186. This appears to be the first verse of the arrangement by Harry Burleigh or very much like it. *The Spirituals of Harry T. Burleigh* (Melville, NY: Belwin Mills, 1984), 129–30.

187. "Kitty Cheatham's Recital," *New York Times*, April 18, 1911; "Easter Matinee with Miss Cheatham," [*New York Herald*, April 18, 1911], RL, 57.

188. See Karen Orr Vered, "White and Black in Black and White: Management of Race and Sexuality in the Coupling of Child-Star Shirley Temple and Bill Robinson," *Velvet Light Trap* 39 (Spring 1997): 52–65.

189. Paul Lawrence [*sic*] Dunbar, "When Malindy Sings," performed by Kitty Cheatham (A5224 Columbia, 1910), Beinecke Rare Book and Manuscript Library, Yale University.

190. "Kitty Cheatham Gives Her Easter Recital," [ca. 1906], RL, 14.

191. "Negro Folk Songs, How They Came to Be Composed," [*Pall Mall (London) Gazette*, ca. 1905], RL, 11.

192. John Wesley Work, *Folk Song of the American Negro* (Nashville, TN: Fisk University Press, 1915), 98; "Music and Art," *Crisis* 12, no. 3 (July 1916): 114.

193. "Kitty Cheatham Recital" [program], Woolsey Hall, Yale University, Monday, May 4, RL, 101.

194. "Miss Cheatham's Matinee," *Musical America*, [ca. 1910], RL, 52.

195. "Negro Folk Music Declines as Race Shuns Slave Memory Says Interpreter of Melody," [*Detroit News Tribune*, November 16, 1912], RL, 79.

196. "Diseuse Charms Audience," [*Dallas News*, April 14, 1913], RL, 87. Emphasis added.

197. "Kitty Cheatham Urges Fisk University Students to Preserve Old Spirituals," *Musical America*, May 30, 1914, RL, 102.

198. "Settlement Children Play," *New York Times*, January 22, 1911. On this Young People's Concert, Cheatham was accompanied by both an adult and a settlement orchestra, which may have consisted of African American children.

199. [*New York Sun*, March 29, 1910], RL 45.

200. "Miss Cheatham Charms Club with Readings," [*Indianapolis News*, March 22, 1910], RL, 43.

201. Silvio Hein, "Don't Be What You Ain't," words by George V. Hobart and Edwin Milton Royle (New York: Edward B. Marks, 1920), in *The E. Azalia Hackley Collection, Nineteenth- and Twentieth-Century Sheet Music of Negro Themes*, Detroit Public Library, http://www.thehackley.org.

202. "Negro Folk-Songs," [*London Times*, June 25, 1912], RL, 77.

203. "Portrayer of Child Life Tells of Quest for Good Material," [*Cincinnati Times Star*, October 26, 1911], RL, 63.

204. "Playtime with Kitty Cheatham," *Delineator* (June 1912), RL, 76.

205. *Benjamin Franklin Gazette* (May 1936), [p. 5], in box 4, Cheatham Papers.

206. "Playtime with Kitty Cheatham," *Delineator* (June 1912), RL, 76; italics in original.

## Chapter 7. Womanly Women and Moral Uplift

1. Harry P. Harrison, as told to Karl Detzer, *Culture under Canvas: The Story of Tent Chautauqua* (New York: Hastings House, 1958), 97.

2. See Charlotte Canning, "Under the Brown Tent: Chautauqua in the Community Landscape," in *Land/Scape/Theater*, ed. Elinor Fuchs and Una Chaudhuri (Ann Arbor: University of Michigan Press, 2002), 209–27.

3. For the transition of Chautauquas from locally run assemblies to a commercial business, see Andrew C. Rieser, *The Chautauqua Movement: Protestants, Progressives, and the Culture of Modern Liberalism* (New York: Columbia University Press, 2003), 254–59, 269–74.

4. See John E. Tapia, *Circuit Chautauqua: From Rural Education to Popular Entertainment in Early Twentieth-Century America* (Jefferson, NC: MacFarland, 1997); and Charlotte Canning, *The Most American Thing in America: Circuit Chautauqua as Performance* (Iowa City: University of Iowa Press, 2005).

5. Canning, *Most American Thing*, 10.

6. Ibid., 9. Charles F. Horner cites ninety-three circuits in *Strike the Tents* (Philadelphia: Dorrance, 1954), 95–97.

7. Donald Linton Graham, "Circuit Chautauqua, a Middle Western Institution" (PhD diss., University of Iowa, 1953), 104; Canning, *Most American Thing*, 11. Graham gives the lower figure, Canning the higher.

8. Victoria Case and Robert Ormond Case, *We Called It Culture: The Story of Chautauqua* (Garden City, NY: Doubleday, 1948; repr. Freeport, NY: Books for Libraries Press, 1970), 148.

9. See "The Power behind Eagle Grove" and "Women Win Auburn," *Lyceumite and Talent* (May 1911): 18 and (November 1911): 19.

10. Canning, *Most American Thing*, 14.

11. All of the brochures quoted are held in the Redpath Chautauqua Collection, University of Iowa Libraries, Special Collections, and are available at http://digital.lib.uiowa.edu/tc/index.php (hereafter cited as Redpath Chautauqua Collection).

12. Marian Scott, *Chautauqua Caravan* (New York: D. Appleton-Century, 1939), 37.

13. Nydia Joan Reynolds, "A Historical Study of the Oral Interpretation Activities of the Circuit Chautauqua, 1904–1932" (PhD diss., University of Southern California, 1961), 185.

14. Edward Amherst Ott, "Some Interviews with Committee Men," *Lyceumite and Talent* (May 1910): 7.

15. Elias Day, "The Art of Entertaining," *Lyceum Magazine* (November 1918): 14.

16. *Lyceumite* (September 1913): 85.

17. Charles L. Wagner, "The Evolution of a Reader," *Lyceumite* (March 1903): 67.

18. Harry P. Harrison to Isabel Garghill Beecher, September 21, 1910, Redpath Chautauqua Collection, MsC150, series 1, box 28.

19. D. W. Meldrum, "Great Readers of the Platform," flyer of Nanah Rense, Redpath Chautauqua Collection.

20. Clark also programmed Edward Eggleston's *The Hoosier Schoolmaster* and Alice Hegan Rice's *Mrs. Wiggs of the Cabbage Patch*, prose selections popular with women; Rossetter G. Cole's melodrama *Hiawatha's Wooing* is also listed on the group's flyer.

21. Gay MacLaren, *Morally We Roll Along* (Boston: Little, Brown, 1938), 49.

22. "Unkapupa the Critic," *Lyceumite* (July 1904): 230–31.

23. MacLaren, *Morally We Roll Along*, 133.

24. Mike Chasar, *Everyday Reading: Poetry and Popular Culture in Modern America* (New York: Columbia University Press, 2012), 58.

25. Harrison, *Culture under Canvas*, 26.

26. "Plagiarism on the Pacific Slope," *Lyceumite and Talent* (April 1909): 46.

27. Harrison, *Culture under Canvas*, 190.

28. *Franklin (MA) Sentinel*, quoted in the flyer of Ethel Batting.

29. Reynolds surveyed former Chautauquans and received mixed responses, but concluded that most performers were not elocutionists. "Oral Interpretation Activities of the Circuit Chautauqua," 173. Reynolds describes (on p. 123) the demonstration of Coyla May Spring in 1959 of a typical child-dialect performance that had little motion

or gesture, was conversational in tone, contained laughter, and had projection suitable for a large space, but no exaggerated emotion or posing.

30. Canning, *Most American Thing*, 174.

31. Paige Lush, *Music in the Chautauqua Movement, from 1874 to the 1930s* (Jefferson, NC: MacFarland, 2013), 25.

32. Horner, *Strike the Tents*, 175.

33. The only female African American concert company with a reader that I have identified in the Redpath Bureau files is the Olympia Ladies Quartette, although mixed-gender vocal ensembles sometimes had a reader.

34. MacLaren, *Morally We Roll Along*, 135.

35. Clay Smith, "How to Get a Start in Chautauqua," *Etude* 40, no. 9 (September 1922): 591.

36. Frances Perry-Cowan, *Chautauqua to Opera: An Autobiography of a Voice Teacher and Daughter of a Chautauqua Pioneer* (Hicksville, NY: Exposition Press, 1987), 25.

37. Harrison to Katharine Ridgeway, February 22, 1911, Redpath Chautauqua Collection, series 1, box 283.

38. MacLaren, *Morally We Roll Along*, 168.

39. Horner, *Strike the Tents*, 168. The separation of dramatic or poetic reading from political oratory, even though both would involve vocal training, affected their critical reception. Canning's *Most American Thing* divides theater and oratory into separate chapters, although both constitute "performance."

40. "Making Companies to Your Measure," *Lyceum* (December 1917): 31.

41. Letter to L. B. Crotty, October 24, 1916, Redpath Chautauqua Collection, series 1, box 306; italics in original.

42. Paul M. Pearson, Reader's Round Table, International Lyceum and Chautauqua Association, September 17, 1924, and Jeannette Kling, "If the Managers Permit, What Can We Do about It?," in *Lyceum* 34 (November 1924): 12–13, quoted in Reynolds, "Oral Interpretation Activities of the Circuit Chautauqua," 65.

43. On Chautauqua's women, see Canning, *Most American Thing*, 88–97.

44. Flyer of Hazel Neen Johnson, Redpath Chautauqua Collection.

45. Such letters were included for potential audiences, as experienced performer Clay Smith stated they meant "exactly nothing whatsoever" to hiring agents. Smith, "How to Get a Start in Chautauqua," 592.

46. Paul M. Pearson, "Isabel Garghill Beecher: An Appreciation," *Lyceumite and Talent* (December 1907): 11–12; emphasis added.

47. A. W. Van Hoose, president, Brenau Conservatory, Gainesville, GA, in flyer of Evelyn Lewis, Redpath Chautauqua Collection.

48. Pearson, "Isabel Garghill Beecher," 11–12.

49. *Methodist Advocate Journal*, quoted in flyer of Irene Bewley, Redpath Chautauqua Collection.

50. Letters of Nellie Peck Saunders to Harry P. Harrison, [September 1910], and 25 September 1910, Redpath Chautauqua Collection, series 1, box 295.

51. Not all of these ensembles are included in the list of performers who toured the circuits in Lush, *Music in the Chautauqua Movement*, 196–207.

52. These included the Horner Institute of Fine Arts founded in Kansas City in

1914 and the Ellison-White circuit's music conservatory in Portland. Louis Runner, Ralph Dunbar, and Elias Day produced Chautauqua ensembles.

53. Harrison, *Culture under Canvas*, 107.

54. Horner, *Strike the Tents*, 182.

55. Beulah Buck to Harrison, October 6, 1914, Redpath Chautauqua Collection, series 1, box 49.

56. Clay Smith, "Are You Booking Pictures or People?," *Lyceum* (1920): 38.

57. Scott, *Chautauqua Caravan*, 22–23.

58. Horner, *Strike the Tents*, 182–83. Performers often did not meet the standards of dress and demeanor required. Canning, *Most American Thing*, 164–65, and fn. 50 on 252–53.

59. Interview with Coyla May Spring (Mitchner), March 16, 1959, quoted in Reynolds, "Oral Interpretation Activities of the Circuit Chautauqua," 77–78.

60. Harrison, *Culture under Canvas*, 28.

61. Pearson, "Isabel Garghill Beecher," 15.

62. Jean Handley Adams, *Second Fiddle to Chautauqua* ([Springfield, MO]: J. H. Adams, 1983), 42. The latter number may actually be Fritz Kreisler's "Tambourin Chinois."

63. Scott, *Chautauqua Caravan*, 141.

64. Harrison, *Culture under Canvas*, 109.

65. Ibid., 87.

66. Scott, *Chautauqua Caravan*, 178.

67. Smith, "How to Get a Start in Chautauqua," 591.

68. Adams, *Second Fiddle to Chautauqua*, 44.

69. "Unkapupa the Critic," *Lyceumite* (March 1903): 78. Given that the work lasted almost an hour, it is possible that it was cut or given mainly to lyceum audiences.

70. Harrison, *Culture under Canvas*, 112.

71. Jones worked for Ralph Dunbar, who managed multiple Chautauqua companies. "A Lyceum Acquisition," *Lyceumite and Talent* (July 1912): 53.

72. Harrison, *Culture under Canvas*, 26–27.

73. Pearson, "Isabel Garghill Beecher," 121.

74. "They Win Return Dates at Chautauqua, N.Y.," *Lyceumite* (January 1912): 16.

75. Interview with Coyla May Spring (Mitchener), March 16, 1959, cited in Reynolds, "Oral Interpretation Activities of the Circuit Chautauqua," 74.

76. Scott, *Chautauqua Caravan*, 113.

77. "Two Men and a Harp," *Lyceum* (December 1909): 14.

78. Kansas poet Eugene Ware is listed as the author, but his poem is titled "The Washerwoman's Song." "The Washerwoman's Friend" was a response by Thomas M. Nichol. See James C. Malin, "Ironquill's 'The Washerwoman's Song,'" *Kansas Historical Quarterly* 25 (Autumn 1959): 257–82.

79. Mary Alice Ross, August 20, 1917, Redpath Chautauqua Collection, series 1, box 288.

80. Mary Louise Cassidy-Woelber, October 17, [1916], Redpath Chautauqua Collection, series 1, box 344.

81. Smith's melodramatic works appeared in *Favorite Musical Readings and Piano-*

*logues of Coyla May Spring* (1924) and *Popular Pianologues: From the Repertoire of Coyla May Spring* (1925), as well as *Twelve Tuneful Talking Songs: Musical Readings for All Occasions* (1931), which also features works by other composers.

82. Clay Smith, "Foreword," in *Popular Pianologues: From the Repertoire of Coyla May Spring* (Philadelphia: Theodore Presser, 1925), 3.

83. Spring later broadcast pianologues in Chicago. Reynolds, "Oral Interpretation Activities of the Circuit Chautauqua," 123.

84. Reynolds, "Oral Interpretation Activities of the Circuit Chautauqua," 164–65, 296–99.

85. Adrian M. Newens, "The Coach and the Ensemble," *Lyceum* (April 1918): 24.

86. A more contextualized reading of this change is Charlotte Canning, "The Platform versus the State: The Circuit Chautauqua's Antitheatrical Theatre," *Theatre Journal* 50 (1998): 303–18.

87. Harrison, *Culture under Canvas*, 190, 272.

88. Reynolds, "Oral Interpretation Activities of the Circuit Chautauqua," 164–85.

89. Frederick J. Antcazk and Edith Siemers, "The Divergence of Purpose and Practice on the Chautauqua: Keith Vawter's Self-Defense," in *Oratorical Culture in Nineteenth-Century America: Transformations in the Theory and Practice of Rhetoric,* ed. Gregory Clark and S. Michael Halloran (Carbondale: Southern Illinois University Press, 1993), 213. M. Sandra Manderson notes that there was actually considerably less demand for traditional lectures in the 1920s in "The Redpath Lyceum Bureau, an American Critic: Decision-Making and Programming Methods for Circuit Chautauqua, circa 1912 to 1930" (PhD diss., University of Iowa, 1981), 182–87.

90. Harrison, *Culture under Canvas*, 272.

91. Hugh A. Orchard, *Fifty Years of Chautauqua* (Cedar Rapids, IA: Torch Press, 1923), 286.

92. Case and Case, *We Called It Culture*, 47–48.

93. "Good Music a Character Builder," *Lyceumite* (July 1906): 34.

94. "Unkapupa the Critic," *Lyceumite* (November 1904): 22.

95. Charles H. Dixon, "Can Music Win On Its Own Merit?," *Lyceumite and Talent* (April 1913): 17.

96. "World's Greatest Musicians Taking to the Platform," *Lyceum* 24 (June 1914): cover.

97. Ibid., 24.

98. B. C. Boer, "Keep Unpopular Music Off Programs," *Lyceum* (April 1917): 21–22.

99. See Lush, *Music in the Chautauqua Movement*, 83–87.

100. Ernest Gamble, "How to Improve Lyceum Music," *Lyceum* (May 1915): 20.

101. Typed program description, Redpath Chautauqua Collection, MsC150, series 1, box 306.

102. Lush, *Music in the Chautauqua Movement*, 66.

103. "We Must Walk before We Can Fly," *Lyceum* (October 1913): 22.

104. Clay Smith, "What the Modern Chautauqua Is Doing for Music of All Kinds Everywhere in Our Country," *Etude* 40, no. 8 (August 1922): 514. Smith lists only

songs, not instrumental music, as typical repertoire: "Toreador Song" (presumably from *Carmen*), "On the Road to Mandalay," "Rolling Down to Rio," "Gypsy Love Song," Nevin's "Rosary," and ballads such as "I Hear a Thrush at Eve," "Sunshine of Your Smile," "Somewhere a Voice Is Calling," "A Perfect Day," "Ol' Car'lina," and his own "Sorter Miss You."

105. Smith, "How to Get Started in Chautauqua," 592.

106. H. O. Rounds, "Building Programs for All in the Audience," *Lyceum* (December 1918): 26.

107. MacLaren, *Morally We Roll Along*, 141.

108. Harrison, *Culture under Canvas*, 97–98. See also Lush, *Music in the Chautauqua Movement*, 107.

109. Reynolds, "Oral Interpretation Activities of the Circuit Chautauqua," 56, responding to the critiques of John Samuel Noffsinger, *Correspondence Schools, Lyceums, Chautauquas* (New York: Macmillan, 1926), 117.

110. Lush, *Music in the Chautauqua Movement*, 91.

111. Keith Vawter in a 1921 Iowa newspaper, quoted in James R. Schultz, *The Romance of Small-Town Chautauquas* (Columbia: University of Missouri Press, 2002), 28.

112. Sheilagh S. Jameson, *Chautauqua in Canada* (Calgary: Glenbow-Alberta Institute, 1979), 1.

113. Canning, *Most American Thing*, 18. Canning discusses criticism of Chautauqua on pp. 15–19.

114. Clay Smith and Stickland Gillian, "The Listener's Faces," in *Favorite Musical Readings and Pianologues of Coyla May Spring*, 18–23.

115. Horner, *Strike the Tents*, 23.

116. Redpath Chautauqua Collection, series 1, box 328.

117. Many female performers left the circuit when they married. Irene Briggs DaBoll and Raymond R. DaBoll, *Recollections of the Lyceum and Chautauqua Circuits* (Freeport, ME: Bond Wheelwright, 1969), 6, 8–9.

118. Brochure of Elizabeth de Barrie Gill, Redpath Chautauqua Collection.

## Chapter 8. Multiplying Voices

1. Rose Walsh, "Whither the Verse-Speaking Choir," *Quarterly Journal of Speech* 21 (1935): 461–62.

2. Ibid., 463.

3. Ibid.

4. Even such a popular spoken work as Ernst Toch's *Geographical Fugue* is considered a novelty.

5. Joan Shelley Rubin, *Songs of Ourselves: The Uses of Poetry in America* (Cambridge, MA: Belknap Press, 2007), 136–37.

6. Jerry Tarver Elocution, Rhetoric, and Oratory Collection, Ohio State University Libraries, Rare Books and Manuscripts Library, Columbus, Ohio (hereafter cited as Tarver Collection), box 1, folder 9.

7. Rubin, *Songs of Ourselves*, 140.

8. Dorothy Kaucher, "The Verse-Speaking Choir," in *Practical Methods in Choral Speaking*, ed. M. E. DeWitt (Boston: Expression, 1936), 127–28.

9. Clare Quirk Riedl, "Milwaukee Leads in Art of Choir Verse Speaking," *Milwaukee Journal*, January 17, 1942.

10. Cecilia F. Gordon, "An Approach to Group-Speaking with Five-Year-Old Children," in *Choral Speaking and Speech Improvement*, ed. Edith Irene Hemphill (Darien, CT: Educational, 1945), 5.

11. Cécile de Banke, "Notes on the Verse-Speaking Choir," in DeWitt, *Practical Methods in Choral Speaking*, 71. See also Rubin, *Songs of Ourselves*, 139–40.

12. Marjorie Gullan, *The Speech Choir: With American Poetry and English Ballads for Choral Reading* (New York: Harper and Brothers, 1937).

13. See Lindsey Canting, "The Music-Poetry of Vachel Lindsay" (MM thesis, Florida State University, 2011).

14. Cécile de Banke, *The Art of Choral Speaking* (Boston: Baker's Plays, 1937), 122.

15. Agnes Curren Hamm, *Choral Speaking Technique* (Milwaukee: Tower Press, 1941), 2.

16. M. E. DeWitt, "Shall We Recite in Groups?," in DeWitt, *Practical Methods in Choral Speaking*, 3.

17. Carrie Rassmussen, *Choral Speaking for Speech Improvement (Elementary School)* (Boston: Expression, 1939; repr. 1946), 17.

18. A few directors advocated an SATB-like (soprano, alto, tenor, bass) division.

19. Harriet Marcelia Lucas, ed., *Prose and Poetry of Today: Regional America* (Syracuse, NY: L. W. Singer, 1941), 766.

20. De Banke, *Art of Choral Speaking*, 145.

21. Emma Grant Meader, "Choral Speaking and Its Values," in DeWitt, *Practical Methods in Choral Speaking*, 109.

22. Marion Parsons Robinson and Rozetta Lura Thurston, eds., *Poetry for Men to Speak Chorally* (Boston: Expression, 1939), and *Poetry for Women to Speak Chorally* (Boston: Expression, 1940). The two anthologies contain similar sections ("Religious Life," "Philosophy of Life," "Holidays"), but the poems in them differ.

23. Robinson and Thurston, *Poetry for Men*, 10.

24. Elizabeth E. Keppie, *Choral Verse Speaking: An Avenue to Speech Improvement and Appreciation of Poetry, for Use in Senior High Schools and Colleges* (Boston: Expression, 1939), 20.

25. Dorothy Kaucher, "Et Tu Brute! A Discussion of Choral Reading as Means of Teaching Oral Interpretation," in DeWitt, *Practical Methods in Choral Speaking*, 141. Merryman's poetry was also utilized for spoken-word settings by female composers (see chapter 10).

26. Grace Loar, "A Verse-Speaking Choir in High School," in DeWitt, *Practical Methods in Choral Speaking*, 198.

27. Kaucher, "Et Tu Brute!," 147.

28. "Miss De Banke Dedicates Book of Shakes[peare] Society," *Wellesley College News*, February 26, 1953.

29. Cécile de Banke, *Hand over Hand* (London: Hutchinson, 1957), 215.

30. "The 'Art' of Recitation. Elocutionary Methods," *Johannesburg Star*, September 23, 1918, in scrapbooks, vol. 2, p. 6, in Papers of Cécile de Banke, 1913–1964, Harvard Theatre Collection, Harvard University, Cambridge, Massachusetts (hereafter cited as de Banke Papers, Harvard).

31. "Out of the Capetown Studio," *Stage, Cinema* [n.d.], in scrapbooks, vol. 2, p. 9, de Banke Papers, Harvard.

32. "Verse-Speaking Choir: Success of Novelty in Elocution: Saturday Popular Concert." *Cape Times*, May 6, 1929; "Popularising Poetry: Miss De Banke's Verse-Speaking Choir," and W. A. Sewell, "Verse-Speaking in Chorus" [clippings], in scrapbooks, vol. 2, pp. 59–60, de Banke Papers, Harvard.

33. "Popularising Poetry: Miss De Banke's Verse-Speaking Choir," and "A Human 'Talkie'" [clippings], scrapbooks, vol. 2, p. 59, de Banke Papers, Harvard.

34. Cécile de Banke, *American Plaid* (London: Hutchinson, 1961), 252–53.

35. Edith M. Smaill, "Malvina Bennett (1857–1934)," *Wellesley Magazine* [clipping, ca. 1934], 134, Malvina Bennett file, Wellesley College Archives, Wellesley, Massachusetts.

36. It is not clear if individual students listed were solo speakers or arrangers, or provided commentary on the poems.

37. See http://www.pilgrimhallmuseum.org/thanksgiving_proclamations.htm.

38. De Banke, *American Plaid*, 259.

39. Ibid.

40. Ibid., 258.

41. De Banke, letter to Phyllis Gauntlett, March 22, 1955, de Banke Papers, Harvard.

42. Ibid.

43. Cécile de Banke, "Speech Education and the Future Citizen," *Wellesley Magazine* 28 (June 1944): 265.

44. Ibid.

45. *Unity, Chicago*, [March 7, 1938], quoted in *Bridgeport (CT) Post*, January 4, 1942, Cécile de Banke Papers, Wellesley College Archives, Wellesley, Massachusetts (hereafter cited as de Banke Papers, Wellesley).

46. No festival was held in 1945.

47. The poets included Leonard Bacon, William Rose Benét, Morris Bishop, Florence Converse, Roberta Grahame, John Holmes, Virginia Huntington, Archibald MacLeish, David McCord, David Morton, Muriel Rukeyser, May Sarton, Winfield Townley Scott, and Theodore Spencer.

48. Cécile de Banke, rough draft of letter to Robert Hillyer, December 1943, de Banke Papers, Wellesley.

49. John Holmes, letter to Cécile de Banke, June 7, 1943, de Banke Papers, Wellesley.

50. Copy of rough draft of letter to John Holmes [ca. December 1942]; John Holmes, letter to de Banke, December 31, 1942, de Banke Papers, Wellesley.

51. De Banke, rough draft of letter to Archibald MacLeish, de Banke Papers, Wellesley. An archivist has dated this letter as perhaps January 1948, but the reference to the war suggests an earlier origin.

52. William Rose Benét, undated letter to de Banke, de Banke Papers, Wellesley.

53. Winfield Townley Scott, letter to de Banke, March 27, 1944, de Banke Papers, Wellesley.

54. Leonard Bacon, letter to de Banke, April 2, 1944, de Banke Papers, Wellesley. Emphasis mine.

55. Copy of rough draft of letter to John Holmes [ca. December 1942], de Banke Papers, Wellesley.

56. De Banke, *American Plaid*, 259–60.

57. De Banke, copy of rough draft of letter to Archibald MacLeish [early May 1948], de Banke Papers, Wellesley.

58. Archibald MacLeish, letter to de Banke, May 17, [1948], de Banke Papers, Wellesley.

59. One exception was the inclusion of instructions for pronunciation of vowels and consonants, common in pedagogical texts.

60. Florence E. Pidge, "Verse Speaking in the Classroom," in Hemphill, *Choral Speaking and Speech Improvement*, 1.

61. Walsh, "Whither the Verse-Speaking Choir," 466; italics in original.

62. Helen Gertrude Hicks, ed., *The Reading Chorus; with Selections Especially Arranged for Choral Reading* (New York: Noble and Noble, 1939), 15.

63. Agnes Curren Hamm, *Selections for Choral Speaking; "Hiawatha" Arranged as a Choric Drama together with Tested Problems in Prose and Poetry* (Boston: Expression, 1935).

64. Loar, "Verse-Speaking Choir in High School," in DeWitt, *Practical Methods in Choral Speaking*, 199. See "The National Flag Drill," in Emma Griffith Lumm, *The Twentieth-Century Speaker* (Chicago: Dominion, 1898), 391–92.

65. Louise Abney, *Choral Speaking Arrangements for the Upper Grades* (Boston: Expression, 1937), 9.

66. Mona Swann, *An Approach to Choral Speech* (Boston: Expression, 1935; repr. 1936), 18.

67. Hamm, *"Hiawatha,"* 8.

68. L. M. Simpkins, "Choral Speaking for the Primary Grades," in Hemphill, *Choral Speaking and Speech Improvement*, 7.

69. Elizabeth E. Keppie, *The Teaching of Choric Speech* (Boston: Expression, 1932; repr. [1950]), 16–17, 25.

70. De Banke, "Notes on the Verse-Speaking Choir," in DeWitt, *Practical Methods in Choral Speaking*, 70.

71. Keppie, *Teaching of Choric Speech*, 22.

72. [Gordon] Bottomley, quoted in Marjorie E. Burdsall, "Choral Speech in the English Class," in DeWitt, *Practical Methods in Choral Speaking*, 177–78.

73. De Banke, *Art of Choral Speaking*, 25; italics in original.

74. Louise Abney, *Choral Speaking Arrangements for the Junior High* (Boston: Expression, 1939), 28.

75. De Banke, *Art of Choral Speaking*, 40–41.

76. Ibid., 74.

77. Ibid., 79–89.

78. Swann, *Approach to Choral Speech*, 22.

79. Hicks, *Reading Chorus*, 1.

80. Meader, "Choral Speaking and Its Values," in DeWitt, *Practical Methods in Choral Speaking*, 110–11.

81. Gullan, *Speech Choir*, 18.

82. Ibid., 12–13.

83. Swann, *Approach to Choral Speech*, 68.

84. Alice W. Mills, "Choral Speaking at Mount Holyoke," in DeWitt, *Practical Methods in Choral Speaking*, 66.

85. DeWitt, "Shall We Recite in Groups?," in DeWitt, *Practical Methods in Choral Speaking*, 25–26.

86. Cécile de Banke, *Choral Speaking in the English Course, Pamphlet 1: Forms of Presentation* (Boston: Baker's Plays, 1942), 9.

87. De Banke, *Art of Choral Speaking*, 166.

88. 78 rpm recording labeled "Verse Speaking. Xmas Verses. C. de Banke," Audio Disk 1211, Wellesley. A lost recording by the choir included "We Have Seen the Wind" by May Sarton, as well as two unidentified poems, "Sea Wind" and "The Fountain."

89. The solo voices on the two recordings are different speakers.

90. Keppie, *Choral Verse Speaking*, 80.

91. Virginia Sanderson, "Choirs That Speak," in DeWitt, *Practical Methods in Choral Speaking*, 123.

92. Mildred Jones Keefe, ed., *Choric Interludes, Poetry Arranged for Times and Seasons* (Boston: Expression Co., 1942), xvii.

93. De Banke, *Art of Choral Speaking*, 182–83.

94. DeWitt, "Shall We Recite in Groups?," in DeWitt, *Practical Methods in Choral Speaking*, 26.

95. Mona Swann, *Many Voices: A Collection of Poems Suitable for Choral Speech*, 3 vols. (London: Macmillan, 1948–49), 3:viii.

96. Marion Parsons Robinson and Rozetta Lura Thurston, "Literature for Choral Speaking," in DeWitt, *Practical Methods in Choral Speaking*, 236.

97. Swann, *Approach to Choral Speech*, 68.

98. De Banke, *Choral Speaking in the English Course, Pamphlet 1*, 9.

99. Gullan also complained about old-fashioned vocal word-painting. Marjorie Gullan, *Spoken Poetry in the Schools*, 6th ed. (London: Methuen, 1935), 66.

100. Marjorie Gullan, "Spoken Verse," in DeWitt, *Practical Methods in Choral Speaking*, 205.

101. Here my view differs from that of Joan Shelley Rubin's description of a contemporary psychoanalytic approach to the individual reader. Rubin, *Songs of Ourselves*, 138–39.

102. Gullan, "Spoken Verse," in DeWitt, *Practical Methods in Choral Speaking*, 205.

103. Marjorie Gullan, "A Recital of Choral Speaking," in DeWitt, *Practical Methods in Choral Speaking*, 220.

104. De Banke, *Art of Choral Speaking*, 152.

105. Agnes Curren Hamm, "Why the Professional Cold Shoulder?," *Quarterly Journal of Speech* 46 (February 1960): 80–81.

106. Clive Samson, "Choral Speaking," *Quarterly Journal of Speech* 46 (October 1960): 306.

107. Samson also identified the use of music and sound effects, but I have found these practices primarily described by DeWitt, who was markedly more experimental than her colleagues (DeWitt, "Shall We Recite in Groups?," in DeWitt, *Practical Methods in Choral Speaking*, 27–29). Three 1931 photos of the San Jose State College Choir in exaggerated poses designed to visually depict specific passages suggest a theatrical performance style. Dorothy Kaucher, "The Verse Speaking Choir of San Jose State College," *Journal of Expression* 5, no. 2 (June 1931): 97–99.

108. Samson, "Choral Speaking," 306.

109. Ibid., 307.

## Chapter 9. Words and Music Ladies

1. "Edward Clarke Stresses Art of Musical Reading," *Lyceum* (March 1924): 37, in Phyllis Fergus's scrapbook [hereafter cited as PF] 3, 28r, collection of Reynolds Clifford. Peycke had arranged for Fergus to perform at Hollywood's Community Sing in 1923, and Fergus invited her to Chicago in return. "Noted Composer on Sing Program," *Hollywood Daily Citizen*, February 12, 1923, p. 2, PF3, 20r.

2. Quoted in "Edward Clarke Stresses Art of Musical Reading."

3. It appeared in the *Musical Leader*, the *Music News*, the *Lyceum* magazine, *Music and Musician*, and *Pacific Coast Musician*. Slightly different articles appeared in *Musical America* and again in the *Music News*.

4. "Musical Readings No Passing Fad, New Art Form Asserts Publisher," *Musical America* (March 8, 1924), PF3, 23r.

5. "The Development of the Musical Reading," in Chicago Woman's Musical Club scrapbook, 1921–30, Chicago History Museum.

6. Ibid.

7. Clayton Summy, quoted in "Musical Readings No Passing Fad, New Art Form Asserts Publisher."

8. "Unique Musical Program Given by Phyllis Fergus and Frieda Peycke," *Music News* (February 22, 1924): 23, PF3, 27r.

9. Ibid.

10. "The Development of the Musical Reading," in Chicago Woman's Musical Club scrapbook, 1921–30, Chicago History Museum.

11. Evangeline Person, "Music in the Home," *Farmer's Wife* (April 1924): 482.

12. *Who Was Who among North American Authors, 1921–1939*, 2 vols. (Detroit: Gale Research, 1976), 2:1143.

13. Quoted in Bertha Fenberg, "The Country Is Best for Children. Composer of Story Poems in Mother Role," *Chicago Daily News*, July 23, 1931, 14, PF1, insert after 14v.

14. Barbara Miller Solomon, *In the Company of Educated Women: A History of Women and Higher Education in America* (New Haven, CT: Yale University Press, 1985), 70. Fergus's brother Robert probably assisted with tuition.

15. Summy's role as Fergus's publisher was noted on a 1915 program of Weidig's students.

16. Kathryn Loring, "Chicago's Past Lives On in Famed House; It's 80-Year-Old Hoyt Home," *Chicago Daily Tribune*, March 22, 1957.

17. Fenberg, "The Country Is Best for Children."

18. Program, After-Dinner Musicale, Women's League of Chicago, PF3, 7v.

19. Karen J. Blair, *The Torchbearers: Women and Their Amateur Arts Associations in America, 1890–1930* (Bloomington: Indiana University Press, 1994), 4–5.

20. Lake View Musical Society, 1929–30 program booklet, Chicago History Museum.

21. Ruth Klauber, *History of the Musicians Club of Women, Formerly Amateur Musical Club, Chicago, Illinois* (Chicago: Musicians Club, 1975), 30.

22. Margaret Williams, "The Cordon Story," June 24, 1977, Cordon Club Papers, box 1, Chicago History Museum.

23. After 1941–42, club booklets stopped indexing members as readers, but several women listed under the heading continued as members.

24. For example, the couple performed at a Cordon "Dinner-Musicale," in December 1929. Mrs. Cole was the sixteenth president of the Musicians Club of Women around 1913.

25. Clarke also performed Rossetter G. Cole's *King Robert of Sicily* in 1914.

26. PF1, insert after 4v. Because these notes also mention Psalm 23, Fergus may have been writing to its publisher, Theodore Presser.

27. [E. P. Borden], "Penn Points: Phyllis Fergus, Composer, Says Those Who Can't Sing, Shouldn't," *Pennsylvania Register*, [New York: Hotel Pennsylvania, n.d.], PF1, 3r.

28. Ibid.

29. Amy Leslie, "Good Entertainment at the Majestic," [*Chicago Daily News*], July 23, 1918, PF2, 20r.

30. Phyllis Fergus, Story Poems, flyer, PF5, 29r.

31. The Lyon and Healy Recitals, program booklet, PF3, 15r.

32. "Lyon and Healey present Phyllis Fergus, Chicago Composer, in a program of her own compositions," program, in Hoyt, Phyllis (Fergus), 1887–1964, file, Chicago History Museum.

33. The invitation card for the event is in PF1, insert after 14v.

34. "Phyllis Fergus," *Music News* (September 9, 1932), 2.

35. *Kenosha (WI) Evening Herald*, November 20, 1919, PF1, taped to 3r.

36. "Luncheon and Recital Were Delightful," *Daily Republican-Register* (Galesburg, IL), December 12, 1921, PF1, 8r.

37. "Miss Fergus Commended," *Daily Republican-Register* (Galesburg, IL), December 6, 1921, PF1, 7v.

38. "Galesburg Woman's Club Bulletin," *Daily Republican-Register* (Galesburg, IL), December 8, 1921, PF1, 11r, article 2.

39. N. W. P., "Mr. and Mrs. Clarke Entertain for Phyllis Fergus," *Music News* (December 3, 1920), PF1, 7r.

40. "Luncheon and Recital Were Delightful."

41. "Delightful Program Given," *Evening Mail* (Galesburg, IL), December 12, 1921, PF1, 8r.

42. "Pleasing Feature at Sing, Presenting Own Compositions Phyllis Fergus Makes Popular Success," *Hollywood News* [ca. 1923], PF3, 18r.

43. Bertha Fenberg, "[title missing] Accorded Honors in Music Competition Contest," *Chicago Daily News*, February [18, 1927], PF1, insert after 14v.

44. "Pleasing Feature at Sing."

45. "Luncheon and Recital Were Delightful."

46. Wesley La Violette, "Solo Artistes Score Success," *Kenosha (WI) Evening News*, November 20, 1919, PF1, 5r.

47. "Some Reflections on the New Music," [*Musical Leader*, April 3, 1919], PF1, 11r.

48. *The Triangle of Mu Phi Epsilon* (February 1933): 85.

49. Some published story poems did not regularly appear on Fergus's programs. Perhaps they were less popular with audiences or she saved them for encores.

50. See Laurine Elkins-Marlow, "'Music at Every Meeting': Music in the National League of American Pen Women and the General Federation of Women's Clubs, 1920–1940," in *Politics, Gender, and the Arts: Women, the Arts, and Society*, ed. Ronald Dotterer and Susan Bowers (London: Associated University Presses, 1992), 185–99.

51. Suzanne Martin, "Counterpoint," *Seattle Post-Intelligencer*, September 24, 1944; Frederick Gamble, Frieda Peycke Papers, 1914–1952, John Hay Library, Brown University, Providence, Rhode Island (hereafter cited as Peycke Papers), A 84.142, box 1, folder 73. Unless noted, all archival documents, including letters, programs, and article reprints related to Peycke, come from this collection. All letters are to Frederick Gamble.

52. Program, March 25, 1907, and clipping [*Los Angeles Examiner*, August 23, 1908], Frieda Peycke scrapbook, Los Angeles Public Library (hereafter cited as LAPL).

53. "Peycke to Show Here" [undated], Peycke Papers, box 2, folder 67.

54. [Fred Gamble], typed obituary, Peycke Papers, document 334, A 86–47, folder 13.

55. Dorothy Brant Brazier, "About People," *Seattle Times*, August 13, 1948.

56. Letter, [1946], Peycke Papers, A 86–47, folder 8.

57. Frederick Gamble's corrected blurb, Peycke Papers, A 86–47, folder 1.

58. "Peycke to Show Here" [undated], Peycke Papers, box 2, folder 67.

59. "Catholic Club Entertainer," *Press-Courier* (Oxnard, CA), October 6, 1928.

60. "Miss Peycke's Activities," [*Pacific Coast Musician*, March 1912], scrapbook, LAPL.

61. George La Mont Cole, "How the Lyceum Helps a Railroad System," *Lyceumite and Talent* (December 1910): 18–19.

62. "Santa Fe Reading Room Concert Is Enjoyed by Many," in Mrs. Henry Hadley scrapbook, William B. Cairns Collection of American Women Writers, 1650–1920, Memorial Library, University of Wisconsin–Madison. There are also press reports of the Frieda Peycke Entertainment Company or Concert Company.

63. "Frieda Peycke's Song Preachment of Love and Philosophy," reprint from *Long Beach Telegram*, October 29, 1914, Peycke Papers.

64. *Long Beach (CA) Daily Telegram*, May 24, 1910, and "Gamut Club Holds A

Merry Reunion," October 5, [1910], in scrapbook, LAPL. Peycke's first known program consisting of her own compositions took place in 1911.

65. "Frieda Peycke, Composer-Entertainer," reprint from *Western Woman* 9, no. 6, Peycke Papers, A 82–147, box 2, folder 67.

66. Letter, May 29, 1936, Peycke Papers, A 86–47, folder 3.

67. Letter 80, [May] 16, 1944, Peycke Papers, A 86–47, folder 6.

68. Frieda E. Peycke, Composer-Entertainer, Musically Illustrated Poems, flyer, Peycke Papers, A 86–47, folder 5. The flyer appears to date from the 1920s.

69. Letter, April 5, 1936, Peycke Papers, A 86–47, folder 3.

70. Letter 294, Peycke Papers, A 86–47, folder 13; "What Women Are Doing," *Los Angeles Times,* March 21, 1926.

71. For example, letter 188, [1948?], Peycke Papers, A 86–47, folder 9, documents a Dominant Club performance.

72. Letter 207, December 16, 1950, Peycke Papers, A 86–47, folder 10; letter 288, Peycke Papers, A86–47, folder 13.

73. Letter 46, ca. 1943, Peycke Papers, A 86–47, folder 5.

74. Letter 48, November 18, 1943, Peycke Papers, A 86–47, folder 5.

75. Letter 83, July 6, 1944, Peycke Papers, A 86–47, folder 6.

76. Letter 113, May 22, 1945, Peycke Papers, A 86–47, folder 7.

77. Letter 203, November 10, 1947, Peycke Papers, A 86–47, folder 10.

78. Ibid.

79. Letter 67, ca. 1944, Peycke Papers, A 86–47, folder 6.

80. Letter, October 31, 1953, Peycke Papers, box 1, folder 79.

81. Letter 34, ca. 1942, Peycke Papers, A 86–47, folder 5.

82. Four hundred works is Peycke's own estimation of her entire oeuvre (letter 291, Peycke Papers, A 86–47, folder 13). Peycke stated that 172 of her pieces, which included songs and pedagogical piano pieces, were published. Many cannot be located, so it is possible that they were issued in small runs.

83. Program, Women's Century Club Theater, Seattle, August 17, 1948, Peycke Papers, A 84–142, folder 7.

84. Many undated manuscripts in the John Hay Library may have originated from later in Peycke's life.

85. Letter 177, February 19, 1947, Peycke Papers, A 86–47, folder 8.

86. "How to Read to Music: From a Conference with Frieda Peycke, Well Known Composer, Pianist, and Diseuse," *Etude* (March 1947): 127–28; Frieda Peycke, "Phases of the Creative Instinct," *Etude* (July 1949): 412.

87. Letter 83, [1947?], Peycke Papers, A 86–47, folder 9.

88. Letter [160, October 1946], Peycke Papers, A 86–47, folder 8.

89. Letters, October 1946, Peycke Papers, A 86–47, folder 8, and November 13, 1946, A 86–47, folder 3.

90. See Marian Wilson Kimber, "'Music that speaks—Poems that sing': The Performance Style of Frieda Peycke," in *Festschrift for Jeffrey T. Kite-Powell,* ed. Allen Scott (Ann Arbor, MI: Steglein Press, 2012), 384–402.

91. Letter 152, October 16, 1946, Peycke Papers, A 86–47, folder 8.

92. Gamble, Frieda Peycke Records.

93. At a banquet of vocal teachers, Biltmore Hotel, Los Angeles. Letter 222, 20 June 1959, Peycke Papers, box 2, folder 63.

94. Frederick Gamble, "Frieda Peycke: a Biographical Sketch," Peycke Papers, A 82–147, box 1, folder 73, p. 2; Marguerite Thompson Schmidt, *And This Was Home* (Lynwood, CA: Three Arts, 1980), 177.

95. Peycke Papers, A 84.142, folder 1, written on the program and in Peycke's description for Marguerite Thompson Schmidt on the verso.

96. *Lakewood Log*, Tacoma, Washington, October 4, 1946, Peycke Papers, A 84–142, folder 12.

## Chapter 10. Women's Work, Women's Humor

1. "To Ride to Claremont," *New York Times*, April 26, 1896.

2. "The Red Fan Recital," *Musical Courier* (New York) 32, no. 19 (May 6, 1896): 27. The concert also featured Delsarte poses, a soprano, a harpist, the Swedish Ladies' Quartet, a boy pianist who performed an excerpt from *A Midsummer Night's Dream*, and a "Lady Orchestra" playing two selections by Brown.

3. *Woman's Who's Who of America, 1914–15* (New York: American Commonwealth, 1914), 853.

4. "Readers and Singers," *Werner's Magazine* 18 (September 1896): 890.

5. "Nettie Arthur Brown," *Werner's Magazine* 18 (December 1896): 1179.

6. "The Red Fan" can be heard performed by members of the Vocal Arts Ensemble on *Goodbye My Lady Love* (Turnabout TV-S 34630, 1975). My description is based on this recording, which has some subtle textual differences from the published poem.

7. In addition to the recitation, the Carnegie Hall recital also featured an arrangement of "The Red Fan" sung by a soprano with the ladies' quartet wielding red fans.

8. See Susan Loraine Porter, "Knowing She Has Wings: Laura Sedgwick Collins," *Sonneck Society Bulletin* 18 (Summer 1992): 54–55; Clare Thornley, "Talented Composer or Merely Dvořák's Student?" *Pan Pipes* 99 (Spring 2007): 23–27.

9. *Werner's Directory*, 384.

10. The poem was anthologized anonymously; Hammond is the identified author in J. T. Trowbridge and Lucy Larcom, eds., *Our Young Folks: An Illustrated Magazine for Boys and Girls* 8 (April 1872): 202.

11. Jennie Mannheimer [Jane Manner] Papers, diary, box 1, folder 1, American Jewish Archives, Hebrew Union College, Cincinnati, Ohio. George Albert Coe, *Sadie Knowland Coe: A Chapter in a Life: October 9, 1864–August 24, 1905* (1906), 63–69; Saidee [*sic*] Knowland Coe, *The Melodrama of Hiawatha* (Chicago: Clayton F. Summy, 1905).

12. Phyllis Fergus's scrapbook [hereafter cited as PF] 3, 10r, collection of Reynolds Clifford. Two composers were identified by initials only.

13. Nan Johnson, *Gender and Rhetorical Space in American Life, 1866–1910* (Carbondale: Southern Illinois University Press, 2002), 31.

14. Clay Smith pointed out that Chautauquans had been giving Edmund Vance Cooke's "The Moo-Moo Cow" for ten years when Mary Wyman Williams set it. "Music Reviews," *Lyceumite* (July 1920): 15.

15. Guy d'Hardelot (1858–1936) set Ella Wheeler Wilcox's *The Birth of the Opal* (London: Chappell, 1916).

16. Mana-Zucca composed *The First Concert*, op. 121; *The Mumps*, op. 124, *J'ever-Hm? I did!*, op. 117; and *Teach Me*, all from 1934, and *Supposing*, op. 153 (1939).

17. Tina B. Cornic, *Jilted* (Ann Arbor: photo-lithoprinted by Edwards Brothers, 1932), Rita Benton Music Library, University of Iowa Libraries.

18. Christopher Reynolds, "Documenting the Zenith of Women Song Composers: A Database of Songs Published in the United States and the British Commonwealth, ca. 1890–1930," *Notes* 69 (June 2013): 675.

19. The other settings are of Browning's Song from "A Blot on the 'Scutcheon" and "Prospice," Kingsley's "O That We Two Were Maying," Hillyer's "April Morning" (1953), and Coates's "Supplicant." Because of the manuscript's messiness, Bauer scholar Susan Pickett believes that *The Forsaken Merman* remained unfinished.

20. Marion Bauer, *The Relief of Lucknow: An Incident of the Sepoy Mutiny*, holograph in ink, Library of Congress.

21. Ruth Crawford Seeger, *The Adventures of Tom Thumb for Piano and Narrator*, additional lyrics by Peggy Seeger, ed. Amy Beal et al. (Lebanon, NH: Frog Peak Music, 2004).

22. Reynolds, "Documenting the Zenith of Women Song Composers," 671–74.

23. Evangeline Person, "Music in the Home," *Farmer's Wife* 28 (February 1925): 74.

24. These songs may have been Chautauqua encores.

25. Stanley Schell, ed., *Werner's Readings and Recitations, No. 48: Musical Effects* (New York: Edgar S. Werner, 1911), 171–74. The poem appeared in *The Speaker* 6 (1911): 112, with the indication that it was performed by Edna Wallace Hopper to accompaniment in the last act of *Jumping Jupiter*, which ran for twenty-four performances in March 1911. The accompaniment in *Musical Effects* differs from M. Witmark's published sheet music featuring the same lyrics, by Gus Kahn, but music by Grace LeBoy: http://contentdm.baylor.edu/cdm/ref/collection/fa-spnc/id/50248.

26. Phyllis Fergus, *The Highwayman: A Dramatic Reading for Speaking Voice and Orchestra*, op. 26 (Chicago: Clayton F. Summy, 1926). Fergus's and Peycke's works were published by Summy unless otherwise noted.

27. Letter 177, 19 February 1947, A 86–47, folder 8, Frieda Peycke Papers, 1914–1952, John Hay Library, Brown University, Providence, Rhode Island (hereafter cited as Peycke Papers).

28. In Peycke's recordings, introductions can vary in length from those of the score.

29. Marian Wilson Kimber, "'Music that speaks—Poems that sing': The Performance Style of Frieda Peycke," in *Festschrift for Jeffrey T. Kite-Powell*, ed. Allen Scott (Ann Arbor, MI: Steglein Press, 2012), 391–96.

30. "How to Read to Music: From a Conference with Frieda Peycke, Well Known Composer, Pianist, and Diseuse," *Etude* (March 1947): 127.

31. Ibid.

32. The piece was dedicated to Leanore O'Brien.

33. Harry L. Aleford and Zoe Hartman, *The Old Family Album* (Chicago: T. S. Denison, 1926).

34. Ann Douglas, *The Feminization of American Culture* (New York: Knopf, 1977), 12.

35. Joanne R. Gilbert, *Performing Marginality: Humor, Gender, and Cultural Critique* (Detroit: Wayne State University Press, 2004), xv.

36. Gina Barreca, *They Used to Call Me Snow White but I Drifted: Women's Strategic Use of Humor* (New York: Viking, 1991; repr. Lebanon, NH: University Press of New England, 2013), 86.

37. Nancy A. Walker, *A Very Serious Thing: Women's Humor and American Culture* (Minneapolis: University of Minnesota Press, 1988), 26.

38. Gilbert, *Performing Marginality*, 172, 177.

39. Walker, *Very Serious Thing*, x.

40. Gilbert, *Performing Marginality*, 138.

41. Walker, *Very Serious Thing*, 11.

42. Umberto Eco, "Frames of Comic Freedom," in *Carnival!*, ed. Thomas Sebeok (Berlin: Mouton, 1984), 8. Discussed in Walker, *Very Serious Thing*, 150.

43. Walker, *Very Serious Thing*, 36.

44. Emily Toth, "A Laughter of Their Own: Women's Humor in the United States," in *American Women Humorists: Critical Essays*, ed. Linda A. Morris (New York: Garland, 1994), 85.

45. Walker, *Very Serious Thing*, 13.

46. Toth, "Laughter of Their Own," 95.

47. Zita A. Dresner, "Domestic Comic Writers," in *Women's Comic Visions*, ed. June Sochen (Detroit: Wayne State University Press, 1991), 98.

48. Frieda Peycke, "Telephone Order of a Young Bride" (text by Helen Welshimer), ms., book 17. All unpublished Peycke manuscripts are in Peycke Papers, John Hay Library, Brown University, Providence, Rhode Island.

49. The accompaniment was composed in 1927 for a humorous text called "Summer Love" about a woman's hesitation to engage in a vacation romance. The second text was added in 1932.

50. Frieda Peycke, "Red Slippers," Peycke Papers, ms., book 17.

51. Henry S. Sawyer and Lytton Cox, *The Ladies' Aid* (Chicago: T. S. Denison, 1923).

52. Italics added.

53. Adele Weber gave "On the Rappahannock" with accompaniment and "The Usual Way" before New York's Chautauqua Union, although it is unknown whether she used music with the latter text. "Readers and Singers," *Werner's Voice Magazine* 12 (April 1891): 109.

54. Lalla Ryckoff, *To Marry—or Not to Marry* (Chicago: Clayton F. Summy, 1916).

55. Lalla Ryckoff, *"I Doubt It!"* (Chicago: Clayton F. Summy, 1923).

56. DeLoss Smith, *Retribution* (Philadelphia: Theodore Presser, 1923).

57. Guy d'Hardelot, *A Lesson with a Fan* (London: Chappell, 1898).

58. Ms., personal collection of Reynolds Clifford.

59. Frieda Peycke, "Wishful Waiting," Peycke Papers, A 82.149, box 2; disc recorded March 19, 1948, John Hay Library, Brown University, Providence, Rhode Island.

60. Frieda Peycke, *The Family Album* (New York: G. Schirmer, 1931).

61. Helen Wing, *Family Static: Four Musical Recitations* (Philadelphia: Theodore Presser, 1929).

62. Aileen Howell Tye, *Mismated Pairs* (Chicago: Gamble Hinged Music, 1930).

63. Mary Wyman Williams, *If (After Kipling—About Two Miles)* (Chicago: Clayton F. Summy, 1922).

64. Clay Smith, "Music Reviews," *Lyceum* (November 1922): 20.

65. Letter, July 23, 1945, Peycke Papers, A 86–47, folder 3.

66. This text is similar to Riley's "Old Sweetheart of Mine," although told from the woman's perspective.

67. Mary Wyman Williams, *An Old Fashioned Garden* (Chicago: Clayton F. Summy, 1920).

68. Natalie Whitted Price, *The Patchwork Quilt* (Chicago: Clayton F. Summy, 1913). The work was performed by Chicago reciter Jessie Armager Power.

69. Frieda Peycke, "Age," Peycke Papers, A 82.149, box 2; audio disc, Recording Bank; recorded New York, New York; March 19, 1948; Peycke Papers, John Hay Library, Brown University, Providence, Rhode Island.

70. Wilson Kimber, "'Music that speaks—Poems that sing,'" 395–96.

71. Victor B-19182, https://archive.org/details/SallyHamlin. Hamlin was fifteen years old at the time.

72. Frieda Peycke, *What the Boy Said* (New York: Harold Flammer, 1921). Tribit was also the cartoonist of *Gretchen Gratz* (*Philadelphia Inquirer,* 1904–5) and *Snooks and Snicks* (*Philadelphia North American,* 1913–15), both of which featured Dutch children.

73. Anne Trensky, "The Bad Boy in Nineteenth-Century American Fiction," *Georgia Review* 27 (1973): 511, 513.

74. Frieda Peycke, *The Tattle Tale Bird* (Cincinnati, OH: Willis, 1928).

75. Mary Wyman Williams, *Where the Spankweed Grows* (Chicago: Clayton F. Summy, 1921).

76. Trensky, "Bad Boy," 509.

77. Frieda Peycke, *Woes of a Boy: Musical Monologue* (Philadelphia: Theodore Presser, 1920).

78. "An Ideal" appeared with "Father's Way" as "Two Sketches," contrasting men's and women's parenting styles, similar to Fergus's paired pieces "The Dark."

79. Frieda Peycke, *The Annual Protest* (New York: Harold Flammer, 1921).

80. Fergus's religious works were published by Theodore Presser.

81. Frieda Peycke, "A Boy and God," Peycke Papers, ms., book 19; National Radio Shop, Los Angeles, California, March 2, 1948, side A.

82. Frieda Peycke, *Watch the Corners of Your Mouth* (New York: Harold Flammer, 1926).

83. Author's personal copy.

84. Frieda Peycke, *Jus' Keep On Keepin' On* (Philadelphia: Theodore Presser, 1927).

85. Floy Little Bartlett, *It Can Be Done* (Boston: Arthur P. Schmidt, 1922).

86. "How to Read to Music," 127.

## Afterword

1. Maureen Howard, "The Attitudes," in *Facts of Life* (Boston: Little, Brown, 1978), 17–33.

2. Derek Furr, *Recorded Poetry and Poetic Reception from Edna Millay to the Circle of Robert Lowell* (Basingstoke, UK: Palgrave Macmillan, 2010), 12.

3. "Neighborhood Guild Presents Musical Treat," *Los Angeles Sentinel*, May 28, 1953.

4. Dorothy Chansky, *Composing Ourselves: The Little Theatre Movement and the American Audience* (Carbondale: Southern Illinois University Press, 2004), 107–8.

5. According to the Maryland Historical Society, the last time the school appears in city directories as the Bard-Avon School of Expression is 1933, when it was directed by Kathryn Howard Lowes (1892–1959).

6. Lynn Miller Rein, *Northwestern University School of Speech: A History* (Evanston, IL: Northwestern University, 1981), 52.

7. David Gold and Catherine L. Hobbs, *Educating the New Southern Woman: Speech, Writing, and Race at the Public Women's Colleges, 1884–1945* (Carbondale: Southern Illinois University Press, 2014), 79, 81.

8. See jmalldr, "Oral Interpretation Poetry Examples 0001," http://www.youtube.com/watch?v=3Gd61wfWvGI, accessed March 3, 2016.

9. Jean Stratton, "Princeton Personality," *Town Topics* (April 1, 2009), http://www.towntopics.com/apr0109/stratton.php, accessed March 3, 2016.

10. "Witherspoon People's Verse Speaking Choir—26th Year" (parts 1, 5, and 6), https://www.youtube.com/watch?v=5EGwbC9-q-A, https://www.youtube.com/watch?v=RRohV-hELm4, and https://www.youtube.com/watch?v=7fyhseg-08c, accessed March 3, 2016.

11. Nancy Polette, *Concert Reading: Poems and Stories to Read with Music* (O'Fallon, MO: Book Lures, 1988). *Concert Reading* was issued in a second edition in 1999.

12. Personal correspondence, May 26 and June 1, 2011.

13. Polette, *Concert Reading*, 2.

14. "The Rules of the National Poetry Slam: I. Poems and Performance," http://my.poetryslam.com/i-poems-performance, accessed March 3, 2016.

15. Listing for June 27, 2014, http://www.neilgaiman.com/where/, and "Neil Gaiman: The Truth Is a Cave in the Black Mountains," http://www.youtube.com/watch?v=Hyqt9ZfsacY, accessed June 26, 2014. Recorded on Harper Audio UACD 7014(1), 2010. The performances also included color paintings by Eddie Campbell.

16. "About" page, Kate Tempest website, http://katetempest.co.uk/about, accessed March 3, 2016.

17. Megan Clark, "A Life of Rhyme: Kate Tempest's Poetry-Music Fusion," *Independent* (London, UK), March 10, 2010.

18. See https://sites.google.com/site/hedwiggorskisite/ and http://www.cdbaby.com/cd/hedwiggorski. Gorski has performed to compositions by D'Jalma Garnier.

19. It was also sometimes heard on programs celebrating wedding anniversaries.

20. "Miss Haynie Honored Monday," *Ardmore (OK) Ardmoreite*, May 6, 1924; "Shower," *Milford (IA) Mail*, October 7, 1976.

# Index

for women and girls, 148–49; in criticisms of Delsarte movement, 91–92; depictions of boys' character, 134, 142, 234–35; elocution and culture associated with femininity, 245; in evaluation of women's performance, 49–51; fairies', 55–56; feminized values, 122, 141; in *The Music Man*, 105–7; poetry and, 176–77; stereotypes of, 212, 214–15, 219–23, 226, 234; women trying not to appear threatening, 131, 134
gender differences, 8, 11, 157; in choral speaking repertoires, 176–77; in Delsarte poses, 88–90; in dialect recitations, 110–12, 114, 116, 133, 234–35; in elocution field, 12–13, 21–23, 81; in humor, 130–31; in marketing of Chautauqua performers, 155, 161–62; in recitations with music, 49–51, 63; in speech, 34, 134
gender norms: Chautauqua programs maintaining, 152–55, 167; Cheatham and, 141, 148; women limited by, 7–9, 148, 234–35
gender relations, in spoken-word compositions, 214–15, 219–31
gender roles, 9–10; in choral speaking, 176–77; discomfort with, 132, 134–36, 142, 230; elocutionists accommodating, 16, 26; in poetry, 131–33; in spoken-word compositions, 220–23; women limited by, xii, 4, 7–8, 25–26, 229; women maintaining, 1, 16
Gentile, John, 22
Gibert, Henry, 143
Gielow, Martha, 155
Gilbert, Joanne, 131, 134, 219
Gilley, Charles T., 164–65
"The Girl I Left Behind Me," 123
"Git on Board, Little Children," 123
Godard, Benjamin, 123
"God's Bonfires" (Peycke), 242
Gold, David, 247
Gordon, Cecilia, 175
Gordon, Elizabeth, 135
Gorski, Hedwig, 250
Goss, Aletta Waterbury, 60
Gottschalk, Louis Moreau, 99
Gounod, Charles, 99, 133
Grand Army of the Republic, 81
"Grandma at the Masquerade" (Vandemark), 67, 231
"Grandmamma's Fan" (Tupper), 67
grandmothers, 231; as topic of recitations, 67; as topic of spoken-word compositions, 231–34

Gray, Giles Wilkeson, 22
Gregory, Emily Farrow, 120
Grieg, Edvard, 44–45, 53
Grilley, Charles T., 164–65
Grove, George, 56
Guest, Edgar, 163, 230, *231*, 241
Gullan, Marjorie, 173–74, 186–87, 189–90

"Hail, Columbia," 83
Hair, Donald, 72
Hall, Ellen Decker, 48
Hall, G. Stanley, 133
Hamlin, Sally, 47, 235
Hamm, Agnes Curren, 175, 184, 190
Hancock, Lauren, 245, 249
Handel, Georg Frideric, 44, 113, 170–71
Handley, Enola Calvin, 162
*The Happy Prince* (Lehmann), 141
Harling, Icey Teel, 30
Harris, Joel Chandler, 146
Harrison, Harry P., 150, 154–55, 161, 163, 166, 168
Hart, Ione Leonore, *158*
Harte, Bret, 237
Hartman, Zoe, 218
Harvey, James Clarence, 84
*Haste to the Wedding*, 69
Hawley, Stanley, 50, 74, 142
Hawn, Henry Gaines, 22, 118
Haydn, Franz Joseph, 143–44
Hazlitt, William, 54, 57
Hein, Silvio, 141, 148
Heinrich, Max, 41
Hemans, Felicia, 96
Hemus, Percy, 41
Hensel, Fanny Mendelssohn, 143
Herndon, Adrienne, 7
heroines, 84–85, 90
*Das Hexenlied* (Schillings), 28, 41, 163
*Hiawatha* (Longfellow), 4, 9, 30, 32, 90, 95, 96, 163, 184, 211
*Hiawatha's Wooing* (Cole), 44–45
Hicks, Helen, 184, 188
Higginson, Thomas Wentworth, 58–59
*The Highwayman* (Fergus), 192, 200, 215
Hill, R., *23*
Hilliard, Evelyne, 111
Hobbs, Catherine, 247
Hodges, Cecelia B., 248
Hollingshead, Lily, 22
Hollins Institute, 13, 61
Holmes, John, 182–83
Holton, Mrs., 245–46

MARIAN WILSON KIMBER is an associate professor of music at the University of Iowa.

## Music in American Life

The Golden Age of Gospel   *Text by Horace Clarence Boyer;*
  *photography by Lloyd Yearwood*
Aaron Copland: The Life and Work of an Uncommon Man   *Howard Pollack*
Louis Moreau Gottschalk   *S. Frederick Starr*
Race, Rock, and Elvis   *Michael T. Bertrand*
Theremin: Ether Music and Espionage   *Albert Glinsky*
Poetry and Violence: The Ballad Tradition of Mexico's Costa Chica
  *John H. McDowell*
The Bill Monroe Reader   *Edited by Tom Ewing*
Music in Lubavitcher Life   *Ellen Koskoff*
Zarzuela: Spanish Operetta, American Stage   *Janet L. Sturman*
Bluegrass Odyssey: A Documentary in Pictures and Words, 1966–86
  *Carl Fleischhauer and Neil V. Rosenberg*
That Old-Time Rock & Roll: A Chronicle of an Era, 1954–63   *Richard Aquila*
Labor's Troubadour   *Joe Glazer*
American Opera   *Elise K. Kirk*
Don't Get above Your Raisin': Country Music and the Southern Working Class
  *Bill C. Malone*
John Alden Carpenter: A Chicago Composer   *Howard Pollack*
Heartbeat of the People: Music and Dance of the Northern Pow-wow
  *Tara Browner*
My Lord, What a Morning: An Autobiography   *Marian Anderson*
Marian Anderson: A Singer's Journey   *Allan Keiler*
Charles Ives Remembered: An Oral History   *Vivian Perlis*
Henry Cowell, Bohemian   *Michael Hicks*
Rap Music and Street Consciousness   *Cheryl L. Keyes*
Louis Prima   *Garry Boulard*
Marian McPartland's Jazz World: All in Good Time   *Marian McPartland*
Robert Johnson: Lost and Found   *Barry Lee Pearson and Bill McCulloch*
Bound for America: Three British Composers   *Nicholas Temperley*
Lost Sounds: Blacks and the Birth of the Recording Industry, 1890–1919
  *Tim Brooks*
Burn, Baby! BURN! The Autobiography of Magnificent Montague
  *Magnificent Montague with Bob Baker*
Way Up North in Dixie: A Black Family's Claim to the Confederate Anthem
  *Howard L. Sacks and Judith Rose Sacks*
The Bluegrass Reader   *Edited by Thomas Goldsmith*
Colin McPhee: Composer in Two Worlds   *Carol J. Oja*
Robert Johnson, Mythmaking, and Contemporary American Culture
  *Patricia R. Schroeder*
Composing a World: Lou Harrison, Musical Wayfarer   *Leta E. Miller*
  *and Fredric Lieberman*
Fritz Reiner, Maestro and Martinet   *Kenneth Morgan*
That Toddlin' Town: Chicago's White Dance Bands and Orchestras, 1900–1950
  *Charles A. Sengstock Jr.*

The University of Illinois Press
is a founding member of the
Association of American University Presses.

——————————————————————

University of Illinois Press
1325 South Oak Street
Champaign, IL 61820-6903
www.press.uillinois.edu


Cover images from *The Twentieth-Century Speaker*
(Chicago: K. T. Boland, 1899); music of "The
Sheep's Sermon" from *The Technic of the Speaking
Voice* (Columbia, MO: E. W. Stephens, 1915).